Volume 25

Marianne Sieker

The Role of the German Political Foundations in International Relations

Transnational Actors in Public Diplomacy

Nomos

The Deutsche Nationalbibliothek lists this publication in the Deutsche Nationalbibliografie; detailed bibliographic data are available on the Internet at http://dnb.d-nb.de

a.t.: Nottingham, University of Nottingham, Diss., 2016

ISBN 978-3-8487-4537-1 (Print)
978-3-8452-8790-4 (ePDF)

British Library Cataloguing-in-Publication Data
A catalogue record for this book is available from the British Library.

ISBN 978-3-8487-4537-1 (Print)
978-3-8452-8790-4 (ePDF)

Library of Congress Cataloging-in-Publication Data
Sieker, Marianne
The Role of the German Political Foundations in International Relations
Transnational Actors in Public Diplomacy
Marianne Sieker
332 pp.
Includes bibliographic references.

ISBN 978-3-8487-4537-1 (Print)
978-3-8452-8790-4 (ePDF)

1st Edition 2019

"Penser ne suffit pas, il faut penser à quelque chose."

(Jules Renard)

"So steht es denn da, unser Werk, so steinern und fremd, so eigenmächtig, so ein für allemal. Es sieht dich an, ohne zu nicken, ohne zu lächeln, so, als hätte man sich nie gekannt; ohne zu danken und ohne zu verzeihen. Nachdem man es lange betrachtet und auch die ersten Schrecken überwunden hat, sagt man sogar: Es ist nicht schlecht, man kann nicht sagen, es ist schlecht! Es erinnert an dieses und jenes, was uns im Entwerfen, da es noch ein Einfall war, erfreut und beglückt hat."

(Max Frisch, Bin oder Die Reise nach Peking)

Abstract

The six German political foundations, backed by substantial public funds, have several hundreds of foreign offices around the globe and more than 2000 staff members. As specific manifestations of the German political landscape, the *Stiftungen* are affiliated to the German political parties at the German *Bundestag*.

This study researches the international activity of the German political foundations and their position within international relations theory. It juxtaposes the rationalist and constructivist approaches on the state and non-state relationship and the possible impact of transnational actors. After having identified the German political foundations as transnational actors, a model of public diplomacy is used to systematically study the foundations' transnational interaction processes. The model integrates different public diplomacy approaches and is based on the assumption of public diplomacy as a diplomatic process in a network environment, where transnational actors and states are equally important and where values and ideas are emphasised. At the same time, it considers propaganda activity, a criticism sometimes voiced by foreign governments with regard to the foundations' undertakings. The foundations' democracy assistance as well as their conflict management ambitions are explored, as collaborative or catalytic public diplomacy forms. In two case studies, one on the Rule of law program of the Konrad-Adenauer-Stiftung in Southeast Europe and another on the activities of the Friedrich-Ebert-Stiftung in Southern Thailand, the strategies of ideational diffusion processes and networking, the soft power resources and social relationship building of the political foundations are investigated.

This theoretically informed empirical study aims at first contributing to the object of the German political foundations' international undertakings which has been subject to little research so far. Second, it connects IR theory on transnational actors as well as the literature on public diplomacy to these activities. Finally, the study identifies the *Stiftungen* as reproducers of the German civilian power identity by implementing abroad major parts of German policy.

This study was submitted as thesis to the University of Nottingham for the degree of Doctor of Philosophy in September 2015. The degree was awarded without conditions in February 2016.

Acknowledgements

This study would not have been possible without the support of a number of people. I would like to thank the research participants from the German political foundations and the other interview partners for their willingness to talk to me and for the amount of time and effort to answer my questions. Thanks also to those who suggested potential interview partners to me or helped establish the necessary contacts. I cannot thank enough my PhD supervisors Dr. Andrew Denham and Prof. Dr. Neville Wylie for sharing their wide knowledge of IR theory, public policy, think tanks and political parties with me, for their enthusiasm, their sympathetic ear for all my questions and their confidence. Furthermore, I would like to thank the examiners of this thesis, Dr. habil. Martin Thunert and Prof. Dr. Andreas Bieler for their very helpful advises and for making the Viva a very positive experience to me. I owe particular thanks to Sybille Koch, Head of Protocol of the German Bundestag, for her support and her help to make contact to the foundations' management level while I was working as a junior lawyer and research assistance at the Bundestag. Rick Ginns and Alison Ginns, I would like to thank for their friendship, their continuous proofreading late at night and for driving through the country to pick me up in Nottingham even under extreme weather conditions. Many thanks to my colleague Fraser Bowen who was so kind to read parts of this study during his Christmas holidays. As this research project was carried out long distance, I am particularly grateful to Dr. Sara de Jong, Dr. Bernhard Weicht, Dr. Sirisha Hesketh and Dr. Christopher Hesketh for being my link to the Nottingham Post-graduate community and for their warm hospitality whenever I came to Nottingham. During the field work in Thailand, Kerstin Winkler und Wolfgang Heinze were important anchors. I strongly appreciate their help in establishing contacts to members of the international community on site. Dr. Julia Hutchinson and Mike Hutchinson I would like to thank very much for hosting me during the days of the Viva and for celebrating with me afterwards. For their proof-reading, last minute help and important remarks but most importantly for their friendship over many years and long talks about life in general, I am very thankful to Alexandra Huber, PD Dr. Robert Frau, Kristine Franzen, Daniel Iranyi, Deb Ain and Sebastian Kunz. I am also grateful to Gudrun Lohmüller for her cooking and reminding me to eat regularly in summer 2015. I would like to thank Dr. Sabine Wagner for being my older sister and for all which goes along. That I accepted the challenge of this intellectual project, I owe also Dr. Cordula Jaletzke. I still keep the post card she gave to me almost 30 years ago suggesting to "lead a wild and dangerous life". To outline all noteworthy things my parents have done for me would go beyond the scope of these acknowledgements. I am grateful to them for having supported my willpower and for having made me aware of the value of education throughout my life. I am very thankful to my mother that she never forgot to express her pride and for encouraging the thought that my father would have been proud of me too. Finally, I would like to express my deep gratitude to my husband Sebastian Lohmüller for the initial idea of this research project, his continuous support and encouragement, the undertaking of the daily tasks especially in the (very long) last phase of this project and for everything else.

Contents

List of figures

List of tables

List of abbreviations

AA	Federal Foreign Office
AAPA	Federal Foreign Office, Political Archive
AFTA	ASEAN Free Trade Area
AKBP	German foreign culture and education policy
APEC	Asian Pacific Economic Cooperation
ASEAN	Association of Southeast Asian Nations
BINGO	Business-oriented non-governmental organisation
BMF	Federal Ministry of Finance
BMJV	Federal Ministry of Justice and Consumer Protection
BMU	Federal Ministry for the Environment, Nature Conversation, Building and Nuclear Safety
BMVg	Federal Ministry of Defence
BMWi	Federal Ministry for Economic Affairs and Energy
BMZ	Federal Ministry for Economic Cooperation and Development
BT	Deutscher Bundestag
BVerfG	Federal Constitutional Court
BVerwG	Federal Administrative Court
B90/DIE GRÜNEN	Alliance 90/The Greens
CDU	Christian Democratic Union
CIMIC	Civil-military co-operation
CSFP	EU's Common and Foreign Security Policy
CSU	Christian Social Union
DDR	Disarmament, demobilisation and reintegration
DIE LINKE	The Left
EC	European Commission
EU	European Union
F.D.P.	Free Democratic Party
FES	Friedrich-Ebert-Stiftung
FNS	Friedrich-Naumann-Stiftung
FZ	Financial assistance in German development policy
GDR	German Democratic Republic
GIZ	German Society for International Cooperation
GONGO	Governmental-non-governmental organisation
GPPN	Global public policy network
HBS	Heinrich-Böll-Stiftung
HSS	Hans-Seidel-Stiftung
ICC	International Criminal Court
IGO	Intergovernmental organisation

IMF	International Monetary Fund
INGO	International non-governmental organisation
IO	International organisation
IR	International relations
KAS	Konrad-Adenauer-Stiftung
KNET	Knowledge network
MNC	Multinational companies
NGO	Non-governmental organisation
OECD	Organisation for Economic Co-operation and Development
PCIA	Peace and Conflict Impact Assessment
PDS	Party of Democratic Socialism
PINGO	Public-interest-oriented non-governmental organisation
PR	Public relations
QUANGO	Quasi-non-governmental organisation
RLP	Rule of law Program of the Konrad-Adenauer-Stiftung
RLS	Rosa-Luxemburg-Stiftung
R2P	Responsibility to protect
SEECP	Southeast European Cooperation Process
SPD	Social Democratic Party of Germany
SSR	Security sector reforms
TAN	Transnational advocacy network
TNC	Transnational company
TZ	Technical assistance in German development policy

Chapter 1 – Introduction

In 2012, German political foundations received state subsidies totalling of 434 million Euros, a web of 340 foreign offices spanned around the globe and they had around 2000 staff members. Affiliated to the political parties at the German *Bundestag* they offered considerable educational, advisory and exchange programs in Germany and abroad. They were provided with substantial public funds and situated in a grey area between public and private, offering freedom and room for manoeuvre. Abroad they were assumed to accompany and relieve German foreign policy.[1] Their distinctive political and legal organisation had even been imitated by other countries, such as France, India and Turkey as well as on European level.[2] However, research on German political foundations has been astonishingly limited.

1.1. Research object

The research project aims at analysing the German political foundations' role in international relations. In investigating the practice of their international activity, the foundations' uniqueness as players of global presence and their influential character can be understood. The term "German political foundations" (*Politische Stiftungen* or *Parteistiftungen*) is drawn up of six German organisations:

- Friedrich-Ebert-Stiftung (FES);
- Konrad-Adenauer-Stiftung (KAS);
- Friedrich-Naumann-Stiftung (FNS);
- Hanns-Seidel-Stiftung (HSS);
- Heinrich-Böll-Stiftung (HBS) and
- Rosa-Luxemburg-Stiftung (RLS).[3]

The choice of name indicates their political party affiliation at a Federal level. The FES is closely linked to the Social Democratic Party (SPD) but also affiliated with the German trade union confederation *(Deutscher Ge-*

1 *Pogorelskaja* (2009a) p. 7.

2 *Woyke* (2011) p. 431; *Baddenhausen/Grey* (2007).

3 For their internet representation (in English, if available) see:
FES at: http://www.fes.de/de/; KAS at: http://www.kas.de/wf/en/; FNS at: https://www.freiheit.org/content/stiftung; HSS at: http://www.hss.de/english.html; HBS at: https://www.boell.de/en; RLS at: http://www.rosalux.de/english/foundation.html.

werkschaftsbund).[4] The KAS was formed as a close associate of the conservative Christian Democratic Union (CDU). The smaller FNS is close to the liberal Free Democratic Party (F.D.P.). The Bavarian HSS is linked to the right-wing Christian Social Union (CSU). The HBS is affiliated to the Green Party (*Bündnis90/Die Grünen*), while the RLS is connected to the left-wing *DieLinke*, formerly the Party of Democratic Socialism (PDS) which succeeded the German Democratic Republic (GDR).[5]

In 2015, the political aims and objectives of the German political foundations circled around the strengthening of democracy, the support of civil political commitment, dialogue and cooperation among different sociopolitical stakeholders as well as research and knowledge transfer.[6] Despite the democratic consensus, each foundation was committed to a certain normative background that determined activities in Germany and abroad. The FES was engaged in social democracy, freedom, justice and solidarity. It promoted political participation, social cohesion and a fair social and economic order and furthered political dialogue with trade unions.[7] The KAS took as a basis a Christian conception of human being created by God in its equality, diversity and imperfection. It promoted liberal democracy, social market economics and strengthening of the value consensus. It commited itself to liberty, justice and solidarity.[8] The FNS was committed to liberalism and wanted to encourage the principle of freedom in human dignity in all aspects of society.[9] The HBS felt bound to ecology, sustainability, democracy, human rights, self-determination and justice. It had a special focus on gender equality, minority rights and active peace policy.[10] The RLS considered itself as part of democratic socialism focused on critical thinking and political alternatives.[11] The HSS more broadly felt bound to democracy, peace and development emphasising Christianity and historical roots.[12]

In 2015, the scope of the foundations' domestic and international activities was enormous. Originally, the German political foundations' activities

4 *Mair* (2000) p. 129 fn. 5.
5 Party affilated political foundations existed also in the *Land* level.
6 Cf. FES/KAS/FNS/HSS/HBS (1998).
7 FES at: https://www.fes.de/de/?id=232.
8 KAS at: http://www.kas.de/wf/de/71.4972/.
9 FNS at: https://www.freiheit.org/content/50-jahre-stiftung.
10 HBS at: https://www.boell.de/de/navigation/ueber-uns-519.html.
11 RLS at: http://www.rosalux.de/stiftung.html.
12 HSS at: http://www.hss.de/stiftung.html.

concerned political or civic education in Germany.[13] In the first study of the German political foundations in 1976 *Watson* gave a short introduction to the German political foundations in a report published by the Anglo-American Foundation. He described the original intention of the establishment of the *Stiftungen* to encourage democratic structures in post-war Germany against the background of the National Socialist era.[14] In 2015, political education was still the core of the *Stiftungens'* domestic activity. It included the maintenance of educational institutions offering seminars, workshops and discussions. The KAS, for instance, had an educational institution (*Bildungsforum*) in every Federal country.[15] Its activities addressed citizens interested in politics, and subjects range from fundamental issues concerning democracy, to international-relations and day-to-day politics.[16] Other domestic activities concerned the award of prizes, mainly dedicated to writers and journalists, the organisation of exhibitions to further art and culture, as well as dialogue forums on emerging policy issues between political and economic stakeholders and those from civil society.[17] Moreover, the foundations gave educational grants to gifted German and foreign students. Graduate and post-graduate programs supported all fields of studies. They contained financial support but also regular seminars and advice services.[18] The KAS, for example, annually gave around 3500 grants to students.[19] In 2014, the FES supported around 2.800 young people with scholarships (of which 320 abroad).[20] Scholars were not necessarily political adherents of the donor body.[21] However, the list was long of prominent German politicians having been supported by a political foundation in former times.[22] Moreover, every political foundation did research in the fields of

13 For studies on the foundations' civic education see *Hellwig* (1998); *Langguth* (1993) and *Vieregge* (1977b). *Leuthold* (2000) dealt with the civic education of the HBS. *Pechtl* (1996) analysed the foundations' educational opportunities in the *Länder* of Brandenburg and Bavaria.

14 The report also considered the establishment of British political foundations according to the German model (*Watson* [1976] p. 18).

15 KAS annual report 2013 p. 99.

16 FES/KAS/FNS/HSS/HBS (1998).

17 FES/KAS/FNS/HSS/HBS (1998); KAS annual report 2014 p. 85.

18 Interview 18.

19 KAS annual report 2014 p. 87.

20 FES annual report 2014 p. 62.

21 Interview 18; differently *Pinto-Duschnisky* (1991a) p. 204.

22 KAS former scholarship holders are, for instance, *Uwe Barschel* (Prime Minister for Hesse, 1982-1987), *Thomas de Maizière* (Federal Interior Minister) and *Christian Wulff* (Federal President, 2010-2012).

politics and social science. The research activity was often carried out in collaboration with external research institutes. In addition, the foundations organised specialists' conferences and discussion groups as well as lectures, and constantly published books, articles and reports. Historical research was done with the help of the foundations' own archives, libraries and documentation facilities.[23] The FES, for example, maintained a specialised library with 1.000.000 volumes on labour movement.[24]

In 2014, nearly three quarters of the expenditure of the German political foundations was devoted to projects in foreign countries.[25] The international activities started in the 1960s. They have continuously adapted to the international political developments and geo-political focal points. The two major cornerstones of the foundations' international activities were the work in the development and transition countries and their dialogue-based undertakings in the EU countries and in North America. The first activities aimed at "implementing humanitarian projects and programs and assisting the establishment of free democratic and constitutional-based structures in being committed to human and civil rights".[26] They were mainly part of the German bilateral development policy. According to the Ministry of Development and Cooperation (BMZ), it "involves strengthening the key institutions in a democratic social order, such as parliaments, political parties and an independent judiciary, as well as promoting good governance and opportunities for civil society participation".[27] Projects and activities were generally implemented together with partner organisations on site. In Europe the foundations focused specifically on "the European unification process and international understanding through information and international meetings".[28] In the industrialised countries, the *Stiftungen* were mainly active with the interlinking of transatlantic and European elites.[29] In 2013, the *Stiftungen* had offices all over the world. The KAS maintained 69 offices abroad, the FES had 107 offices, the FNS 33, the HBS 30, the HSS 57 and the RLS had 16 international offices.[30] Recent works on the *Stiftungen* assumed that their activities circled around pro-

---

23 FES/KAS/FNS/HSS/HBS (1998).

24 FES annual report 2014 p. 64.

25 See Ch. 1.7.3.

26 FES/KAS/FNS/HSS/HBS (1998).

27 BMZ at: http://www.bmz.de/en/what_we_do/approaches/bilateral_development_cooperation/players/political_foundations/index.html.

28 FES/KAS/FNS/HSS/HBS (1998).

29 *Bartsch* (2007) p. 280; see *Renvert* (2014) on the transatlantic activities.

30 See fn. 915 on the sources.

moting approximation ambition in the Southeast European countries to the EU, the management of crises, and dealing with the danger of states' fragility and terrorism.[31] Systematic analysis of most of these aspects is missing, however. Moreover, considerations which take into account the respective foreign and development political concepts of the German government are almost non-existent.[32] This is necessary, however, in order to understand the relationship between the foundations and the state as well as their extensive public funding.

The research project concentrates on the activities of the German political foundations in developing and transition countries where the major part of their international activity takes place. It will connect transnational and constructivist-inspired international relations' (IR) theory to these undertakings by looking at the process of public diplomacy which includes democracy assistance and the newer conflict management. This will help to position the *Stiftungen* in international relations as either independent political actors or instruments of state power. It will also offer some explanation on what the foundations change and why they are supported by massive funds. Finally, this research project is neither financially supported by one of the German political foundations nor has it been suggested by them.

1.2. Theory

The research is informed by several theoretical assumptions which will be outlined and systematised in detail in the following chapters.

International relations can no longer be defined as only covering relations between states. The dominant rationalist approaches of neorealism and neoliberalism discuss, whether transnational actors matter. Both see the state at the centre of their analysis, though. Constructivist theory, however, best explains the importance of transnational actors in international relations, as it concentrates on transnational interaction processes among different actors. Rather than debating whether transnational actors matter, constructivism does not assume that one type of actor is more important than the other.[33] In looking at social interaction, ideational diffusion processes and perceptions, constructivist thinking can help uncover important

31 *Bartsch* (2007) p. 289.
32 Exceptionally see *Pogorelskaja* (1997).
33 *Chandler* (2005) p. 154; *Hartmann* (2001) p. 68; *Risse* (2002) p. 259.

issue neglected by neorealism and neoliberalism. It focuses more directly on the question of the international role of political foundations maintaining links with the German government, the political party landscape as well as politicians and civil societies abroad. However, the German political foundations cannot be easily identified among the transnational actors, since due to their public funding the organisational characteristics of private and public are blurred. There have also been attempts to describe the activity of German political foundations as "movement on the threshold between governments and civil society".[34] Although we expect that the German political foundations can operate as transnational actors, it will finally depend on whether the foundations are state-controlled or active on behalf of the German government.

With the help of an integrated model on public diplomacy, transnational activities can be studied systematically. The model includes constructivist-led considerations on transnational interactions in the international sphere which are not guided by state-centrism. The diplomatic process can be conceived without bias as taking place in a network environment, comprising various actors and different resources. In this way, we regard public diplomacy as an important - if not as the main - transnational interaction process. We do not assume that diplomacy is a formalised negation process only. Rather, transnational interactions take place in a less structured environment. The foundations' international activities are incidentally perceived as diplomatic undertakings. Systematic analysis is missing, however. We expect that most of what the *Stiftungen* do internationally can in fact be understood as public diplomacy. We also expect that the German political foundations as important parts of the domestic political culture in Germany[35] mainly diffuse those values which correspond to the narratives of official policy. This correspondence, still, might not keep the *Stiftungen* from being transnational actors with independent power resources, including access to foreign figures, information channels and knowledge resources.

Democracy assistance and conflict management have been identified as different modes of how public diplomacy can be practiced. Increasingly, there are fields where transnational actors find their niche. Although some literature on the German political foundations considers their support of democracy, it has never been connected to a diplomatic activity nor to the literature on transnational actors. As regards conflict management, the lite-

---

34 *Bartsch* (1998); *Czempiel* (1993).

35 *Bartsch* (2007) p. 280.

rature has almost completely ignored the undertakings of the German political foundations. We assume that the *Stiftungen* are predominantly active as transnational actors in democracy assistance as well as in conflict management.

1.3. Research questions

I am mainly interested in the following central questions:

What role do the German political foundations have in international relations? Are rationalists correct in saying that states are the key international actors, or can it be demonstrated, as constructivists argue, that through the interaction with many different actors, the German political foundations as transnational actors have a significant impact? If the latter is the case, what is the reason for their substantial public funding?

Several sub-questions are necessary to address the central questions. They can be grouped into three areas:

(1) Public diplomats?

To what extent can German political foundations be considered as public diplomats? Are they independent generators of public diplomacy or do they work on behalf of the German government? Does their work substitute, supplement or conflict with traditional diplomacy? Who benefits and who loses from these activities? Do the foundations have advantages (e.g. resources) in comparison to other diplomatic actors? Are transnational networks established? If yes, who controls them?

(2) Democracy assistants?

What makes the German political foundations democracy assistants? Do they follow a developmental or a political conception of democracy assistance? What ideas are diffused and are they different from those of official German policy? What do the foundations change? Are prerequisites established by the foundations for German companies?

(3) Conflict management?

Is conflict management implemented by the *Stiftungen*? If yes, what ideas are diffused and are they different from those of official German policy? What do the foundations change? Are prerequisites established by the foundations for German companies?

This study does not include recommendations for action for the German political foundations. Their activities were analysed and assessed to the established systematisations.

1.4. State of research

The academic focal points of the few existing pieces of literature on the German political foundations changed over the decades and adjusted to political realities. While in the first publications 40 years ago, academic authors concentrated more on the organisation of the *Stiftungen* in itself, subsequentially researchers and also the *Stiftungen* in their publications gave further attention to the foundations' activities and their effects abroad. The literary process can therefore be described as from the inside out. Literature published from the 1970s to the 1980s discussed organisational matters of the *Stiftungen* concerning the foundations' party affiliation and financial matters, while the foundations' international activity remained in the background.[36] The literature written in the 1980s and 1990s showed increased interest in the foundations' international activities. Authors agreed that the German foundations were highly political organisations.[37] From the 1990s onwards, literature became more complex and less descriptive. We can identify four major themes treated in the literature: Firstly, the publications considered development policy governed by the literature on democracy assistance. Case studies happened to be carried out in the transforming countries of the Eastern bloc whereas before they had focused more on Latin America and Africa.[38] Secondly, literature treated foreign policy on a national and European level.[39] A third body of literature con-

36 See *Vieregge* (1977a), (1977c), (1980); *Papst* (1982).

37 See *Werner* (1982); *Krieger* (1983); *Forrester* (1985); *Kress* (1985); *Schürmann* (1989); *Pinto-Duschinsky* (1991a); *Wagner* (1994).

38 *Mehler* (1996); *Mair* (1997), (2000); *Philipps* (1999); *Hearn/Robinson* (2000); *Pinto-Duschinsky* (2002); *Erdmann* (2006a), (2006b); *Egger* (2007); *Mohr* (2010).

39 See *Nuscheler* (1993); *Progorelskaja* (1997); *Eyinla* (1999); *Weilemann* (2000); *Dakowska* (2002), (2005a), (2005b), (2005c); *Thunert* (2004); *Pratsch-Hucko* (2004);

sidered the foundations' adaptations to globalisation processes.[40] Finally, scholars looked at domestic themes, such as legal and financial conditions as well as civic education.[41] The foundations' descriptions of themselves published over the decades represent a literature type of their own. Despite advertising character, they show improved self-reflection in recent times offering an additional source for researchers.[42] Present day academics, however, face the problem of sparse literature. Despite an increase in publications in the last years the number of monographs is limited. Recent works often tend to throw in keywords like "diplomacy" of the foundations or their "conflict prevention" without taking the time or having the possibility for a thorough analysis. As far as the research questions are concerned, the respective chapters review the literature in more detail.

1.5. Organisation of the chapters and specific interest in knowledge

The study consists of ten chapters. After having defined the study's overall theoretical frame and methodology of this study, I specify some characteristics of the German political foundations. They are important for general understanding and analysis.

In chapter 2 and chapter 3 we consider the theoretical background of this study. Chapter 2 offers definitions and concepts of transnational actors, their activities and impact by referring to IR theory. Chapter 3 focuses on the concepts of public diplomacy which can be understood as a transnational interaction process in a network environment. It is particularly apt to integrate the main thoughts on transnational relations, as outlined before. It connects the different approaches into an integrated model of public diplomacy which serves as a framework to study the activities of

Renvert (2005), (2014); *Schneider-Deters* (2005); *Pogorelskaja* (2006), (2002a), (2009a).

40 See *Bartsch*, (1998), (2007); *Ronge/Pascher* (1999); *Optenhögel* (2002); *Pascher* (2002); *Mohr/Weßels/Beyers/Kerremans* (2005); *Burnell* (2006); *Grävingholt/Hofmann/Klingebiel* (2007).

41 See *Pinto-Duschinsky* (1991b); *Langguth* (1993); *Prechtl* (1995); *Hellwig* (1998); *Leuthold* (2000); *Pogorelskaja* (2002b); *Beyer* (2002). See Ch. 1.7.4. on legal literature.

42 See *Deussen* (1981); *Krieger* (1983); *Thesing* (1987), (1997); Die Grünen (1987a), (1987b); *Fülle* (1992); *Kahane* (1998); *Hennig* (1998); *Beaugrand* (2003); *Meier-Walser* (2004); *Wahlers* (2005); KAS (2005), (2006), (2007d); *Fischer-Bollin* (2006); *Vinnai* (2007); *Von zur Mühlen* (2007).

the German political foundations in the chapters that follow. Chapter 3 also introduces briefly public diplomacy as practiced by the Federal Foreign Office in order to make some claims on the possible involvement of the German political foundations later on.

In chapter 4 we link the theoretical consideration of chapters 2 and 3 to the research methods which I applied in this study.

Chapter 5 applies the integrated public diplomacy model to the international activities of the German political foundations. It estimates whether the German political foundations are transnational actors and puts a special focus on the network environment in which transnational activity takes place while focusing on parts of the research sub-questions (1).

In chapter 6 and 7 the study looks at democracy assistance and conflict management of the German political foundations. Both are forms which have been identified as how public diplomacy can be practically conducted by transnational actors. Since the public diplomacy literature remains rather vague on both concepts, the chapters start with systematisations of the concepts. They then briefly introduce the German official ambitions in the fields, before reviewing the existing literature on the German political foundations and subsume their activities more generally under the systematisation. Finally, differences and commonalities as regards the official ambitions in the fields are indentified. These chapters concentrate on the research sub-questions (2) and (3) respectively.

Chapter 8 and chapter 9 consider the two cases of the KAS's democracy assistance in Southeast Europe as well as the FES's conflict management in Southern Thailand and connect them to the integrated model of diplomacy. German official ideas and narratives are also considered. Specifically, we look at what values are diffused within the established network environment. Both chapters finally try to make some claims on the political impact of the foundations addressing all sub-questions.

The final chapter links the main findings to the central research question on the role of the German political foundations in international relations. It discusses whether state-centric assumptions of rationalists are right in that the German political foundations are sheer instruments of state power or whether constructivists are correct in assuming that the *Stiftungen* as transnational actors have their independent position and "reason for being" in the international environment. It also tries to explain the tremendous public funding of the *Stiftungen*.

Overall, the research provides a much-needed analysis of the international activity of the German political foundation and its uniqueness. The literature relating to the phenomenon of political foundations - especially published over the last 10 years – is sparse. There is little German literature and even less foreign literature available. The literature published recently, consists of articles and very few monographs.

1.6. Use of language

The notion of the "developing country" is used in this study by referring collectively to those countries whose economic-technical and social standard of living is low in comparison to industrialised countries. However, I am aware that the notion as well as the synonymous term of "third world" is problematic due to the historical connotation. The definition dates back to the 1950s and, from the perspective of industrialised countries, refers predominantly to post-colonial regions. Development was linked here with the understanding of a capitalist economic model akin to that of the USA and contrasted to socialism.[43] Despite the doubtfulness of the term we use the notion of developing countries as many other academics have done before. An in-depth and critical discussion on this matter would lead away from the original research question. Furthermore, we use the term "international" not as referring to state-to-state interactions between sovereign states only but from its original understanding of *inter* (between) *national* (nations). This can include interactions beyond the national border of public, societal and economic actors among others. By "global" we refer to trans-border interactions which can take place in the entire world system.[44] To other notions and their definitions I refer in the respective chapters.

1.7. Characteristics of the German political foundations

The following section introduces some characteristics of the *Stiftungen* which are important for the overall understanding of the research object and the following chapters.

---

43 *Randall* (2008) pp. 16f.; *Nohlen* (2005) p. 174.
44 *Hale/Held* (2011) p. 5.

1.7.1. Origins

The beginnings of the German political foundations' activities, domestic activities then only, date back to 1925.[45] Founded by members of the social democratic parties the oldest of the political foundations is the Friedrich-Ebert-Stiftung. *Friedrich Ebert* (1871-1925) a saddler from Heidelberg became member of the German Reichstag for the Social Democratic Party in 1912. After the revolution of 1918 he was one of the new government's chairmen and became the first German head of state democratically elected in 1919. *Ebert* himself had proposed the establishment of a foundation aiming at political education and international understanding. The foundation's funds came from funereal donations following his death.[46] Before the FES was banned by the Nazis in 1933, it had provided almost 300 bursaries for talented young people. The creation of political foundations after World War Two happened mainly for historical reasons and aimed at strengthening the German democracy, since the experience of the Weimar Republic's democratic destructiveness finally led to the criminal dictatorship of National Socialism.[47] In 1947, the FES was re-established and later compensated for the confiscation of its assets by the Nazi regime. The FES served as a model for the Friedrich-Naumann-Stiftung which was founded in 1957. *Friedrich Naumann* (1860-1919) a protestant theologian was elected member of the German Reichstag in 1907. Re-elected in 1919, he became chairman of the German Democratic Party (DDP) which he co-founded. *Naumann* elaborated the part on fundamental rights and duties of the constitution of Weimar Republic. He is considered as the founder of modern liberalism.[48] The creation of the FNS was instigated by the then Federal President *Theodor Heuss*. He considered the establishment of the FNS as a support for the F.D.P in crisis at that time.[49] Supporters of the ruling Christian Democratic Party (CDU) soon set up a counterpart to the FES.[50] The KAS, initially a society for Christian democratic education established in 1956, evolved out of a political association of the *Politische Akademie Eichholz e.V.* and the "Institute for international solidarity". It changed its name to Konrad-Adenauer-Stiftung in 1964.[51] The lawyer *Konrad Adenauer*

45 On the history of the foundations' international activities see Ch. 6.3.1.

46 FES at: https://www.fes.de/de/?id=233.

47 *Langguth* (1993) p. 39; *Pinto-Duschinsky* (1991a) p. 181.

48 FNS at: https://www.freiheit.org/content/geschichte.

49 *Vieregge* (1977) pp. 137f.; *Papst* (1982).

50 *Pinto-Duschinsky* (1991a) p. 183.

51 *Deussen* (1981) pp. 23ff.; *Beaugrand* (2005) pp. 71ff.

(1876-1967) was elected Lord Mayer of Cologne in 1917. When the Nazis came to power in 1933, he was replaced. In connection with the assassination attempt on Hitler in 1944 he was held prisoner by the Gestapo. After being Chairman of the Rhineland CDU, Chairman of the British Zone's CDU (1946) and President of the Parliamentary Council (1948), *Adenauer* was elected Federal Chancellor (1949-1963). He assumed, in addition, the office of the foreign minister (1951-1955).[52] The Bavarian Hans-Seidel-Stiftung was created in 1967. *Hanns Seidel* (1901-1961) studied law and economics. One of the founding fathers of the Bavarian Christian Social Union, he became Minister of state for Economics in Bavaria (1947-1954), Party Chairman of the CSU (1955-1961) and Bavarian Prime Minister (1957-1960).[53] In 1988, the *Stiftungsverband Regenbogen*, an association of several foundations (*Buntstift e.V., FrauenAnstiftung e.V.* and *Heinrich-Böll-Stiftung e.V.*) affiliated to the Greens, was set up. Each foundation had its own field of activity until they fused to become the new Heinrich-Böll-Stiftung in 1997.[54] *Heinrich Böll* (1917-1985) published novels, short stories, radio dramas and (television) plays and worked as a translator from 1947 onwards. He was awarded the Nobel Prize for Literature in 1972.[55] The youngest of the German poltical foundations is the Rosa-Luxemburg-Stiftung. Founded as *Verein Gesellschaftsanalyse und Politische Bildung e.V.* in 1990, it became the RLS in 1999. *Rosa Luxemburg* (1871-1919), a Polish Jew and participant in the Russian Revolution of 1905, was one of the founders of the Social Democratic Party in the joint kingdom of Poland and Lithuania, one of the most important representatives of the German Social Democratic Party's (SPD) left wing next to *Karl Liebknecht*, and later co-founder of the German Communist Party (KPD). In 1919, *Luxemburg* and *Liebknecht* were murdered possibly by extremists of the *Freikorps*.[56]

The attempt to create a political foundation affiliated to the right-wing poltical party *"Die Republikaner"* was abolished in 1995. The German administrative court mainly substantiated its decision against the set-up of the Franz-Schönhuber-Stiftung by declaring it a "danger for public welfare".[57] However, in 1996, the Gottlieb-Fichte-Stiftung was created. Still, it is different from the other political foundations since it is not close to a po-

52 KAS at: http://www.kas.de/wf/de/71.3717/.
53 HSS at: http://www.hss.de/stiftung/hanns-seidel.html.
54 HBS at: https://www.boell.de/de/geschichte-der-stiftung.
55 *Fülle* (1992) p. 11.
56 RLS at: http://www.rosalux.de/geschichte/thema/rosa-luxemburg/2369/283.html.
57 BVerwG of 12/02/1998 (3 C 55/96); *Merten* (1997).

litical party of a "permanent and significant political mainstream". Given that it does not receive public funding, it could only develop activities on a small scale.[58] According to press reports, in 2005 also the National Democratic Party (NPD) failed to establish a party-affiliated foundation on the *Land* level in memory of *Walter Bachmann*, a former volunteer at the *Waffen SS.*[59] Until 2015, the organisation operated in Saxony under the name "*Bildungswerk für Heimat und Nationale Indentität e.V.*" observed by the Saxon office for protection of the constitution.[60]

1.7.2. Legal classification and organisational structure

The German political foundations carry the term "foundation" (*Stiftung*). In most cases, however, this is legally incorrect as the *Stiftungen* hold the form of a registered society (*eingetragener Verein: e.V.*). Only the FNS is indeed a "foundation under private law" (§ 1 charter of the FNS) making applicable §§ 80ff. *BGB*[61] and the corresponding law. Foundations are institutions that are set up by the founder himself.[62] They are supposed to constantly serve the specific and fixed foundation goal with the help of the trust fund. Since 2002, foundations need to be recognised officially.[63] In compliance with §§ 54ff. *BGB* the other five political foundations are nonprofit registered societies. When legally registered (§ 21 *BGB*) the freedom of association (Article 9 German Basic Law) is applicable to them. For these political foundations the term "foundation" is misleading. Although the law still allows to them to carry the term as part of the society's name, the name affix *e.V.* has to be borne permanently (i.e. Konrad-Adenauer-Stiftung e.V.).[64] Some authors assume that the *Stiftungen* decided to become a registered society as it is less bureaucratic compared to being an actual foundation.[65] We will return to other explanations later on. After the movement of the German *Bundestag* from Bonn to Berlin in 1999 the German political foundations set up headquarters in Berlin. Additionally, the

58 *Born* (2007) p. 109.
59 N24 at: http://dokmz01.blogspot.de/2005/02/n24de-npd-will-parteinahe-stiftung-in.html; Taz Online, 1/09/2009.
60 LfV Sachsen (2005) p. 33.
61 *Bürgerliches Gesetzbuch* (German Civil Code).
62 *Rawert* (2011) Vorbm. 3 zu § 80ff.
63 *Seifart* (1987) § 1 RZ. 6.
64 *Born* (2007) pp. 63ff.; differently, *Sikora* (1997) pp. 52ff. seeing a law abuse.
65 *Vieregge* (1977a) pp. 31ff.

FES, the KAS and the HSS kept their respective offices in Bonn, St. Augustin and Munich. Furthermore, all political foundations maintain offices abroad. The five political foundations organised as registered societies have a similar administrative structure consisting of a board of members (*Mitgliederversammlung*) and an executive board (*Vorstand*) elected by its members. The FNS, in contrast to the *Mitgliederversammlung*, has a board of trustees (*Kuratorium*). The FES and the KAS both have a *Kuratorium* as well, including stakeholders from society, politics and culture to advise the *Vorstand* in important matters. Compared to the *Kuratorium* of the FNS, however, it is legally insignificant.[66] Within the political foundations' different boards, the composition of members is very much affected by the foundations' party affiliation. Members of the foundations are parliamentarians of the German *Bundestag*, the German federal countries' parliaments or the European parliament as well as former members of the government and functionaries of political parties.[67] The executive board of the KAS, for instance, has prominent members like the Federal Chancellor *Angela Merkel*, the former President of the German *Bundestag Norbert Lammert* and the former President of the European Parliament *Hans-Gert Pöttering*.[68] The foundations generally have divisions of political education, research, international cooperation and administration including finances and human resources subsections. Other sections, such as archives, libraries, and political consultancy as well as the communication and press offices are either integrated into these divisions or independent divisions. In 2014, the *Stiftungen* had around 2200 staff members in total of which 15% worked abroad.[69]

1.7.3. Sources of finance

In 2015 (and earlier), the German political foundations obtained significant public funds which came mainly from the *Bund* (around 95%) but

---

66 *Kress* (1985) p. 25.
67 *Pinto-Duschinsky* (1991a) p. 196.
68 KAS at: http://www.kas.de/wf/de/71.4892/.
69 In detail: FES: 612 (of which 99 abroad); KAS: 579 (of which 94 abroad); FNS: 203 (of which 35 abroad); HBS: 249 (of which 28 abroad); HSS: 283 (of which 34 abroad); RLS: 256 (of which 45 abroad) (c.f. foundations' annual reports of 2014: FES [p. 73], KAS [p. 93], HBS [p. 85], HSS [p. 69], RLS [p. 69]. For FNS data was only available at annual report 2013 [p. 67]). For data on 2012 see Bundesrechnungshof (2014) p. 162.

also from the *Länder* and international organisations.[70] The federal funds could be divided into three types: *Projektmittel* (project funds) the foundations received for special projects for which they needed to apply. Other organisations, such as NGOs active with projects in developing countries, obtained such funds as well. Project funds came from the Foreign Office (AA), the ministry for development and cooperation (BMZ) and other ministries. The AA funded social policy measures in North America, Europe[71] and other industrial countries as well as the provision of scholarships to foreign students[72] while the BMZ financed measures important to development.[73] The means of the BMZ were higher than those of the AA. In 2014, the ratio between AA funding was 6% (AA) to 94% (BMZ).[74] The second type of funding, so called *Globalmittel* (budget funds), the *Stiftungen* received from the interior ministry for their statutory aims, such as educational measures, research projects, archival activities as well as personnel and administration expenses.[75] Approximately a quarter of their funding was given to the foundations via *Globalmittel.* A third minor group of funds from the ministry of interior, the *Bauglobalmittel*, was received by the foundations for investments.[76] The distribution of funds among the foundations followed a quota. It was politically negotiated, defined by the Budget Committee and fixed by the statuary budget law following the proportion of the political parties in the parliament.[77] In 2015, the following quota existed: the FES received 30,29%, the Konrad-Adenauer-Stiftung 29,57%, the Friedrich-Naumann-Stiftung 10,21%, the Heinrich-Böll-Stiftung 10,51%, and the Hanns-Seidel-Stiftung 9,71%. The Rosa-Luxemburg-Stiftung received 9,71%. Apart from public funding, the foundations had some limited income from donations, attendance fees, fund raising, fixed assets and inheritances.[78]

---

70 C.f. foundations annual reports; extensively on the foundations' funding see *Geerlings* (2003); *Meertens/Wolf* (1996); *Günter/Vesper* (1994); *Von Arnim* (1992), (1993); *Pinto-Duschinsky* (2002), (1991b); *Barth* (1986); *Vieregge* (1977b), (1990).

71 Since 2015 this concerns EU member states and candidates.

72 Federal budget, Kapitel 0502 Titel 68727.

73 Federal budget, Kapitel 2302 Titel 68704.

74 Cf. comparison with the data from federal budget of 2014 without foreign scholarship funding.

75 Federal budget of 2012: Kapitel 0602 Titel 68502, Kapitel 0504 Titel 68111.

76 Bundesrechnungshof (2014) p. 162.

77 KAS at: http://www.kas.de/wf/de/71.3712/.

78 C.f. foundations annual reports.

In the 1990s, the German political foundations endured significant budget cuts.[79] However, in the last years funding was considerably increased.[80] In 2012, the *Stiftungen* received around 328.4 Mio. Euro of *Projektmittel*, 98 Mio. Euro of *Globalmittel* and 7.7 Mio. Euro of *Bauglobalmittel*. This was an increase of public funding by 35% compared to 2003.[81]

1.7.4. The political party links

In 2015, a pivotal point in the discussion on German political foundations remained their party affiliation and independence from their "parent" party. The legal literature added to the debate. The conceptual diversity of whether the German organisations should be called "political foundations" (*politische Stiftungen*), "party-affiliated foundations" (*parteinahe Stiftungen*) or "party foundations" (*Parteistiftungen*) already shows the complexity of the subject and the positioning of the author. Overseen by the Federal Constitutional Court, the issue is passionately debated to this day. The political parties act (*Gesetz über die politischen Parteien*) of 1994 (last amended 2018) governs the relationship between the *Stiftung* and the political party as follows: the chairman and the treasurer of a party are not allowed to exercise comparable functions in the political foundation (§ 11) and political parties are not allowed to receive donations from political foundations (§ 25). Still, the crux of the discussion was the public funding of the foundations via budget funds (*Globalmittel*). Historically, the public financial support of the *Stiftungen* results from a ruling of the German constitutional court in 1966.[82] The court concluded that public subsidies for political parties for "civic education" were unlawful. By 1967, the federal budget had already assigned the amount of 9 million *Deutsche Mark* of *Globalmittel* to the political foundations, thus bypassing the limitations on state aid to parties resulting from the ruling.[83] The HSS was established specially for the purpose of receiving these subsidies.[84] In 1986, the constitutional court finally had to decide about the legitimacy of the founda-

79 *Thunert* (2004) p. 81. On funding of the foundations in the 1990s see BT (2000) pp. 10ff., (1995).
80 *Nolke*, Deutschlandfunk, 29/03/2015.
81 Bundesrechnungshof (2014) p. 162.
82 BVerfGE 20, 134 (143) of 19/07/1966 (Decision of the Federal Constitutional Court).
83 *Pinto-Duschinsky* (1991b) p. 186.
84 *Von Arnim* (1993) p. 282.

tions' public financing.[85] The process was initiated by the Green Party at that point still without a foundation counterpart. The party considered the *Stiftungens'* public funding via *Globalmittel* as hidden party financing. However, the court upheld the constitutionality of the funding on the grounds that the political foundations were "independent enough from their affiliated party in matters of organisation and personnel".[86] The judgement became henceforth the "Magna Carta" for the political foundations' financing.[87] In 1992, the discussion resumed when the constitutional court overruled its previous decision on political party financing. Political parties were again allowed to receive public funding for the whole scope of their duties, even for "civic education".[88] Since that time, critics agreed that the foundations' funding should be integrated into the funding of political parties. They campaign for transparently standardising and regulating the amount and kind of foundations' public funding. Initiatives and draft laws had, however, not yet been successful.[89] The question in dispute remained how to define the relation of the political foundations to their parent parties. In 1996, the political foundations (except for the RLS) made a joint declaration on their public funding outlining their public benefit, and the fact that they publicise their use of funds (in the form of annual reports). They were not obliged to do this.[90]

Lawyers discussed whether the political foundations were (part of) political parties. Some authors assumed that the political foundations were parties and Article 21 GG (German Constitution) was applicable to them.[91] Article 21 GG defines that that "(1) political parties shall participate in the formation of the political will of the people. They may be freely established. Their internal organisation must conform to democratic principles. They must publicly account for their assets and for the sources and use of their funds". Others claimed that the *Stiftungen* had rights and duties of Article 21 GG but they did not count as parties.[92] A third group saw only the foundations' funds as equivalent to party funds but did not consider the foundations as parties or parts of them.[93] According to *Born,* Article 21 GG

85 BVerfGE 73, 1 of 14/07/1986 (Decision of the Federal Constitutional Court).
86 BVerfGE 73, 1 (31) of 14/07/1986 (Decision of the Federal Constitutional Court).
87 *Günther/Vesper* (1994) p. 290.
88 BVerfGE 85, 264 of 9/04/1992 (Decision of the Federal Constitutional Court).
89 *Born* (2007) p. 49; *Pogorelskaja* (2009a) p. 21; BT (1993).
90 FES/KAS/FNS/HSS/HBS (1998).
91 E.g. *Sikora* (1997) p. 75.
92 E.g. *Merten* (1999) p. 159.
93 E.g. *Kißlinger* (1998) pp. 114f.

was not applicable to the *Stiftungen.*[94] However, the discussion did not clarify the actual relationship between both organisations. From the perspective of activities, it is wrong to qualify the main activities of the political foundations as exclusively party activities. According to *Pinto-Duschinsky*, the "foundations and parties are distinguished by the fact that much of their work is different, though often complementary".[95] However, it was the effect of the foundations' party links that the parent party can benefit from the activities.[96] In 2015, the foundations were central carriers of the political education for political parties but were autonomous concerning the planning and the carrying out of the events.[97] The consulting the foundations offered to the parent party, showed a strong connection between both organisations and the foundations were often considered as a testing ground for new ideas. However, their recommendations were often ignored by politicians.[98] The foundations' research and the maintaining of archives were of public as well as party interest.[99] Furthermore, strong personnel links existed between the political parties and the *Stiftungen*, as already outlined.[100] The constitutional court's ruling in 1986 did not change this. *Thunert* estimated that important posts at the foundations were often given to "deserving but retired or even failed politicians."[101] Although the foundation was "headed by senior party figures" it exchanged relatively few staff with the party.[102] Party aims and those fixed in the foundations' charters often varied.[103] Moreover, the ruling of the constitutional court in 1986 inhibited financial contributions from the foundations to the parties.[104] Both financing operations were strictly separated. Nonetheless, an indirect influence of the party on the financing of the *Stiftungen* existed through the members of parliament as the parliamentarians decided on the amount of the foundations' budget funds.

---

94 BVerwGE 106, 177 of 12/02/1998 (Decision of the Federal Administrative Court); *Born* (2007) pp. 132ff., for the summary of the opinions see p. 48.

95 *Pinto-Duschinsky* (1991b) p. 217.

96 *Von Arnim* (1993) p. 293.

97 *Langguth* (1993) pp. 40f.; *Prechtl* (1996) p. 181.

98 *Thunert* (2004) p. 80; *Born* (2007) p. 127.

99 *Nuscheler* (1993) pp. 228f.; *Born* (2007) p. 129.

100 *Vieregge* (1977a) p. 35.

101 *Thunert* (2004) p. 80.

102 *Pinto-Duschinsky* (1991b) pp. 217ff.

103 *Born* (2007) p. 114.

104 BVerfGE 73, 1 of 14/07/1986 (Decision of the Federal Constitutional Court).

In summary, the *Stiftungen* had a dilemma: On the one hand, they had to be legally independent from the parent parties in order to receive public funding, according to the constitutional court. On the other hand, the foundations had to be close to a political party to secure their public funding.[105] In consequence, the foundations could be considered a governmental and party "hybrid" of "relative autonomy".[106] Some assume that the foundations were active in the "pre-political" sphere not involved in political competition and winning elections.[107] However, the funding of the *Stiftungen* depended indirectly on the success of the political party owing to the distribution quota. Whether they were indeed only active in pre-politics will be analysed in detail in the following chapters. Certainly, the *Stiftungen* had long ago acquired a right to exist which is not based on the efforts of the affiliated party.[108]

105 *Günther/Vesper* (1994).
106 *Pascher* (2002) p. 91; *Pinto-Duschinsky* (1991b) p. 221; *Glagow/Schimanck* (1983) p. 162; *Vieregge* (1977a) pp. 29, 282.
107 *Langguth* (1993) p. 41.
108 *Nuschler* (1993) p. 239.

Part I: Theoretical framework and research methods

Chapter 2 – Transnational actors in IR theory

The following chapter will offer a theoretical framework for explaining the role of the German political foundations in international relations (IR). For this purpose, transnational actors will be conceptualised first. Furthermore, the theory of constructivism and the rationalist theoretical approaches of neorealism and neoliberalism will be juxtaposed. Their views on the significance of transnational actors in IR will be outlined. It will be shown how they explain the occurrence and importance of transnational actors in the international system, whereby the explanatory strength of the constructivist will be considered. In order to understand what these actors characterise and what they actually do, it will be referred to constructivist inspired existing analysis on the role of transnational actors in the last section. Since constructivism highlights transnational interaction and communication processes while taking network environments into consideration, it can help explaining comprehensively the position in IR of transnational actors and the German political foundations alike. However, borrowing thoughts from transnationalism and rationalism can be beneficial. In liberalism they share with constructivism a common ground.

2.1. Defining transnational actors

Defining transnational relations is relatively easy. Still, defining transnational actors presents us with a challenge. Numerous types of actors are included whose definitions partly overlap. This study follows *Risse-Kappen* in defining transnational relations as "regular interactions across national boundaries when at least one actor is a non-state agent or does not operate on behalf of a national government or an intergovernmental organisation".[109] The definition builds upon but slightly modifies the definitions of *Kaiser* and *Keohane/Nye*. *Kaiser* stresses the existence of transnational societies as a condition for transnational politics which he defines as those po-

109 *Risse-Kappen* (1995a) p. 3.

litical processes between national governments and/or between transnational societies and governments, which result from interactions within transnational societies. Transnational societies develop through interaction between different societies in specific areas.[110] According to *Keohane* and *Nye*, transnational relations are "contacts, coalitions, and interactions across state boundaries that are not controlled by the central foreign policy organs of government".[111] Transnational interactions are "the movement of tangible and intangible items across state boundaries when at least one actor is not an agent of a government or an intergovernmental organisation". These items can be, for instance, money, information or people[112] but also political ideas and policy proposals.[113] Transnational interactions are distinguished from interstate interactions, or in other words, traditional diplomacy, which are started off and maintained by governments including interaction in intergovernmental organisations (IGOs). Transnational interaction, by contrast, "may involve governments but it may not involve only governments". It is therefore necessary that a non-state actor is involved in this process and plays an important role. In their work, *Nye* and *Keohane* concentrate on the activities of transnational organisations, such as non-governmental organisations (NGOs), transnational companies and international trade unions.[114] Transnational relations also include "the activities of transnational organisations, except within their home states, even when some of their activities may not directly involve movements across state boundaries and my not therefore, be transnational interactions as defined above".[115] Proceeding from the transnational actors' standpoint, transnational interaction can arise with foreign governments, foreign societies and intergovernmental organisations whereas vis-à-vis its home state the actor is connected by domestic politics.[116] *Risse-Kappen's* definition leaves out the extension of *Keohane* and *Nye* to include indirect movements across state boundaries. Although it is possible that foreign actors can operate abroad from their home base and not necessarily cross state boundaries, it is still beneficial to think of transnational actors to directly engage over their own national border and to narrow the definition in favour of precision. Otherwise the definition embraces virtually even those interactions

110 *Kaiser* (1969) p. 95.
111 *Keohane/Nye* (1971) p. 331.
112 *Keohane/Nye* (1971) p. 332.
113 *Willetts* (2011b) p. 338.
114 *Keohane/Nye* (1971) p. 332.
115 *Keohane/Nye* (1971) p. 335.
116 Cf. *Keohane/Nye* (1971) p. 334 figure 2.

with marginal international contexts. *Risse-Kappen* also restricts transnational relations to "regular interaction".[117] This can include coalition building and contacts, if subsumable under the term of interaction, but simple encounters alone are not sufficient. Since we look at relations, it is important to consider more frequent interaction.

There is not much unity in the definition of non-state actors and how it relates to the definition of transnational actors. Both terms are often used alternatively or transnational to avoid implying that states are more important than other actors.[118] Others bring into play "transnational non-state actors".[119] According to *Risse-Kappen*, transnational actors are either "non-state agents" or actors which do "not operate on behalf of a national government or an intergovernmental organisation".[120] Consequently, the notion excludes IGOs and governments whereas it covers transnational companies (TNCs), multinational companies (MNCs), non-legitimate groups and liberation movements as well as (international) NGOs. *Risse-Kappen's* definition also comprises transgovernmental actors as long as they are independent enough from the national government's policy.[121] *Reinalda* further unravels the distinction and differentiates between transnational and international actors. The latter are INGOs, internationally active national NGOs, MNCs, governments and IGOs which do not pursue national views and try to influence processes on the international level.[122] Apart from that and the inclusion of NGO variants, *Reinalda's* definition of transnational actors is consistent with that of *Risse-Kappen*. *Reinalda* views non-state actors as the sum of transnational and international actors, excluding only governments and transgovernmental actors.[123] His differentiation between transnational actors and international actors, however, seems problematic

117 See fn. 109.

118 *Willets* (2005) p. 427.

119 E.g. *Curbach* (2009) p. 31.

120 *Risse-Kappen* (1995a) p. 3. State is understood as a construct of three elements, that is state territory, state people and state power. The latter is legitimised by the people and is the exercise of power by the state organs and institutions of the legislative, executive and judicative (*Jellinek* [1900]). Intergovernmental organisations (IGOs) are defined as organisations "in which full legal membership is officially solely open to states and decisionmaking authority lies with government representatives" (*Taylor/Curtis* [2005] p. 420).

121 *Risse-Kappen* (1995a) p. 10.

122 *Reinalda* (2001) p. 12.

123 *Reinalda* (2001) pp. 12ff.: Transgovernmental refers to "cross-border relations between representatives of (semi-)governmental institutions below governmental level" (p. 13).

since the criteria rather refer to the actor's role. In practice, it will be difficult to differentiate between the actor's national and international position which likely overlaps. The actor even might have a mixed role varying from case to case. The term transnational actor makes clear that it includes activities across national boundaries and contains an element of movement. This characteristic cannot be derived from the notion of non-state actor which instead sets the actor in reference to another actor (i.e. the state).

Similar to non-state actors, NGOs are not defined consistently. Even the United Nations (UN) providing for NGOs to be accredited for consultative reasons (Art. 71 UN Charta) does not define the term. Some requirements can be derived from UN Resolution 1996/31: NGOs are not formed by a government or an intergovernmental agreement and operate on the basis of their own constitutional arrangements.[124] The UN also accepts that various NGOs have both non-governmental and governmental members, "provided that such membership does not interfere with the free expression of views of the organisation".[125] NGOs are domestic actors. They become transnational actors when they operate across national boundaries. An INGO is established when various NGOs from three or more countries establish an international non-governmental organisation.[126] NGOs are furthermore expected to be independent societal actors originating from the private sector because they are primarily financed by donations and membership contributions.[127] Increasingly, NGOs have become heterogeneous and the premise "non-governmental" has been watered-down. *Reinalda* contradicts the above definition as he considers NGO variants that act on behalf of a government as transnational actors. For state-sponsored NGOs the term "QUANGO" was coined. It refers to a "quasi NGO" i.e. an independent actor receiving the majority of their resources from public bodies and which therefore cannot be clearly assigned to the state or the private sector.[128] Moreover, despite its formal independence it is often assumed to undertake activities on behalf of a government as it is supposed to fulfill duties which are in fact those of the government.[129] *Glagow*

---

124 UN (1996) §I.10-12; similar UIA (1986) p. 1591.

125 UN (1996) §I.12; *Reinalda* (2001) p. 14; *Gordenker/Weiß* (1995) p. 260.

126 *Reinalda* (2001) p. 12.

127 *Martens* (2002) p. 282.

128 *Reinalda* (2001) p. 14; *Nohlen* (2005) pp. 614f.; UN (1996) considers the possibility of government funded NGOs in which case the NGO must declare to the UN (see §I.13). Still, the NGO needs to be independent in its expression of views (§I.12).

129 *Schubert* (2005) p. 802.

and *Schimank* look at QUANGOs from an administrative sciences' perspective involving in their consideration the original motivation for the organisation's establishment. According to them, both NGOs and QUANGOs accomplish "public" tasks. But in contrast to the NGO's private origin, the QUANGO is an attempt of the public administration to perform public duties in a non-sovereign form.[130] State-sponsored NGOs are therefore not necessarily QUANGOs and, might the amount be little, can be relative autonomous from the funding governments.[131] Their relations with funding governments can be further defined according to the distribution of resources. The relation is stable when the resources are balanced, labile when the state's resources outweigh or formal when the resources of the organisation prevail.[132] *Glagow* and *Schimank* consider information, finances and legitimate power as resources crucial for political decisions and their implementation.[133] For formally independent NGOs which are financially dependent on state funds the term GONGOs (Governmental-non-governmental organisations) has been coined.[134] In the consequence of these considerations, QUANGOs should not be considered as transnational actors while for other forms of publicly funded organisations the dependency needs to be analysed on a case-to-case basis. The equivalent term for QUANGO in the German foreign political context is *Mittlerorganisation,*[135] which can also be translated as "mediating organisation". The German *Mittlerorganisationen* aim at deepening bilateral relations with other countries through civil activities, events and publications. They impact on relevant elites and establish contacts with similar organisations abroad. Reasons for the activity can either be the importance of the bilateral relations with the specific country for Germany, the burdened relations with countries in the past or the future importance of the country due to political or economic reasons. *Mittlerorganisationen* can complement German foreign affairs as they fulfil tasks official foreign policy is unable to.[136] Most of the

130 *Glagow/Schimank* (1983) pp. 148f.
131 *Glagow/Schimank* (1983) p. 159.
132 *Glagow/Schimank* (1983) p. 162.
133 *Glagow/Schimank* (1983) pp. 155f. with further citations.
134 *Reimann* (2007) p. 93; elsewhere GONGOs (governmentally organised NGOs) have been defined as NGOs founded on government initiative (*Reinalda* [2001] p. 14); *Naím* (2007) applies GONGOs to government-sponsored NGOs which are governmentally initiated and controlled. Both definitions are misleading as they show overlaps with QUANGOs as applied here.
135 *Witte* (1993) p. 197.
136 *Kaiser/Mildenberger* (1998) pp. 199f.

implementing agencies (*Durchführungsorganisationen*) of German development cooperation are QUANGOs.[137]

Transnational actors can furthermore be distinguished according to their dimension. The first dimension concerns the structure according to which the transnational actor is part of a formal organisation or is loosely connected to others in the form of networks. The second dimension relates to the motivation of the transnational actor, whether the actor is focused on its wellbeing or whether it promotes the common good which equates to the distinction between profit and not-for-profit actors.[138] This is similar to *Reinalda's* distinction between non-governmental public-interest-oriented "PINGOS" and non-governmental profit-oriented "BINGOS".[139]

2.2. Theoretical perspectives on transnational actors

Explicit analytical work on transnational actors and relations started in the late 1960s although neither transnational relations nor theorising about transnational actors is new.[140] The explosion in the number of NGOs over the past three decades, the end of the Cold War and globalisation processes have been catalysts for the interest in studying transnational actors.[141] However, theoretical considerations are still missing. Reasons for this are seen in political science and its traditional differentiation between a domestic and a foreign sphere. Domestic policy theories rarely consider transnational political processes and activities by transnational actors, such as political parties, which are then threatened to fall into "conceptual no-man's-land". Foreign and international political literature, in turn, hardly ever deals with transnational actors, since scholars mainly proceed from the assumption of a sovereign nation state as central actor in world politics and focus on the relations between governments. Although transnational

137 *Glagow/Schimank* (1983) pp. 150f.; see Ch. 7.2.1. on these organisations.

138 *Risse* (2002) pp. 255f.

139 *Reinalda* (2001) p. 14.

140 *Risse* names family businesses like the Medicis and Fuggers dating back to medieval times and expanding their production across Europe and campaigns to end slavery in the USA starting in the early 19th century; similar *Halliday* (2001) who regards it as possible that IR in its entire 500 years development has been shaped and driven by non-state actors (pp. 27f.).

141 *Nölke* (2010) p. 395; *Josselin/Wallace* (2001) p. 1.

activities challenge the latter assumption most of the international relations' approaches have adopted this state-centrism.[142]

In the following sections we will examine how the role of transnational actors in IR can be explained. For this purpose, the rationalist and constructivist thinking as the conventional IR traditions will be examined. This will help to understand what both theories hold with regards to interactions of transnational actors. The theories' selection is oriented towards the major debates between neorealism and neoliberal institutionalism starting in the 1970s and between rationalism and constructivism in the 1990s. Although the constructivist framework has its explanatory strength borrowing from the rationalist approaches can be fruitful. The considerations will be added by transnationalist thoughts as they put prominently to the centre cross-border relations between societies and states. Although it is not denied that other approaches, such as Marxist and critical theory could have added value for this work, the look is limited at the causal theories of the neo-neo synthesis and the constitutive constructivist approach to avoid an overload catch-all theoretical framework. While causal theories try to answer "why" questions and focus explanatorily on causal logic and the existence of laws, constitutive theories try to understand how structure forms social kinds by asking "how" questions. Constitutive theories provide explanations which are not necessarily causal[143] and refuse laws in support of generalisations.[144] Normative theories which focus on the moral dimension of IR and address the ethical nature of relations between actors,[145] are not considered. Still, some thoughts will be lent from *Gramsci* and *Bourdieu* in the following sections to establish a plausible and enriched framework.

2.2.1. Rationalist approaches

Since the beginning of IR at the end of World War One and until the end of the Cold War, the research agenda was dominated by rationalist ap-

---

142 *DeMars/Dijkzeul* (2015) p. 7; *Nölke* (2010) p. 396; *Risse-Kappen* (1995a) pp. 4f.; *Halliday* (1991) p. 197.

143 *Wendt* (1999) pp. 85f. Partly constructivism is criticised for being rather descriptive than explanatory (*Walt* [1998] p. 38). *Wendt* (1999) counters that all constitutive theories have a large descriptive dimension (p. 86).

144 *Price/Reus-Smit* (1998) p. 273.

145 *Brown* (1992) pp. 2f.

proaches.[146] They assume the nation-state to be the key actor in international relations acting rationally in the pursuit of pre-given national interests. In application of methodological individualism, pre-given means that states' interests are unaffected by interaction with others.[147] Rationalism is characterised by a number of disagreements regarding these interests' nature and whether cooperation or conflict is the predominant mean of attaining them.[148] In the third great debate dominating the academic scholarship in international relations since the 1970s, neo-realists focus on the limits of cooperation and the possibility of conflict among states whereas neoliberals concentrate on the possibilities for cooperation and the limits to conflict.[149]

Neoliberalism (or neoliberal institutionalism) connects the theories of interdependence and institutionalism. Interdependence, a concept developed by *Keohane* and *Nye*, exists when one state depends on another in order to reach its goals. To avoid costly effects, it needs to cooperate. Cooperation can be increased through and gains a permanent structure within institutions, such as international regimes and international organisations (IOs).[150] Interdependence and international regimes are believed to diminish insecurity (created by anarchy), the use of military force and power struggles.[151] Neoliberalism drops the realists' assumption of a power-seeking state and assumes that states operate self-interested. In the consequence of interdependence and cooperation, states are able to look for absolute gains i.e. mutual advantages from which everyone benefits instead of con-

---

146 The term "rationalism" was coined by *Keohane* (1988) in order to demonstrate the similarities between neorealist and neoliberal theories. They share with each other the assumption of rationality and tend to apply the rules of positivism. *Keohane* contrasts rationalism with "reflectivism" which relates to theories critical of mainstream rationalist approaches, such as constructivism, critical theory, poststructuralism, and feminism (p. 2).

147 *DeMars/Dijkzeul* (2015) p. 8.

148 *Chandler* (2005) p. 149.

149 There are four important debates (*Wæver* [1996]). While the first two great debates in the 1950 and 1960s largely discussed the construction of an IR discipline and scientific methods, the abovementioned inter-paradigm third debate treats how best to explain and understand international process. The fourth great debate emerging in the mid-1980s looks at what should be studied and how it should be studied. Sometimes the fourth debate is called the third debate (e.g. *Fearson/Wendt* [2002]) when the inter-paradigm debate is not considered as great (*Kurki/Wight* [2013] pp. 20f.).

150 *Keohane/Nye* (1989) pp. 8f.

151 *Keohane* (1984) p. 50.

centrating on the loss of power.[152] According to *Krasner's* foundational definition, international regimes are identified as "sets of implicit or explicit principles, norms, rules and decision making procedures around which actors' expectations converge in a given area of international relations".[153] *Rittberger* and *Zürn* consider necessary some minimal level of effectiveness and durability to qualify as regime.[154] Regimes allow interactions in issue-areas and facilitate for actors to pursue their interests collectively.[155] They are also assumed to foster peace and have a "civilizing effect" which improves conflict situations through confidence building.[156] Regimes, although connected to them, are different from organisations. As institutions, regimes are part of the social structure but, in contrast to organisations, they are not capable of acting. With a basis on functional institution theory, neoliberals assume that regimes perform functions useful to states helping them to maximise their gains: Depending on whether regimes are strong or weak they can implement precise rules and interpret them, collect information on the behaviour of regime members, make it available to the states and sanction violation of rules.[157] Neoliberals take microeconomic and game theory to explain regime formation which, in short, starts from the premise of two actors having the possibility either to cooperate or to compete. States fail to cooperate (in regimes) when they imagine other members of the anarchic system to adopt a competitive strategy. Neoliberals therefore concentrate on aspects that will strengthen reciprocity among actors which furthers regime establishment and maintenance.[158] Although neoliberals acknowledge that not only governments interact but also IOs, transnational actors and individuals, they see states in

152 *Dunn* (2011) p. 107; *Schimmelpfennig* (2010) p. 97. Still, asymmetrical interdependence in contrast to mutual balanced dependence can be a source of power in terms of control over resources and the ability to affect outcomes (*Keohane/Nye* [1989] pp. 10f.).

153 Principles are "believes of fact, causation, and rectitude". Norms are understood as "standards of behavior defined in terms of rights and obligations" and rules as "specific prescriptions or proscriptions for action". Decision-making procedures refer to "prevailing practices for making and implementing collective choice" (*Krasner* [1983] p. 2).

154 *Rittberger/Zürn* (1990) p. 17.

155 *Keohane* (1983) p. 170.

156 *Rittberger* (1993) p. 19.

157 *Schimmelpfennig* (2010) pp. 102ff.

158 *Little* (2011) pp. 301ff.

the centre while those other actors are mostly not treated as playing a significant role.[159]

All forms of realism which has been the dominant theory of world politics since the beginning of IR theorising, subscribe to statism as the state characterised by sovereignty is the only relevant actor in the international system.[160] Due to the anarchic structure of the international system (viz. the absence of a central authority) states are interested in gaining or preserving power in order to maintain national sovereignty. *Waltz's* neorealist theory developed in the 1970s emphasises the importance of structure of the international system as a primary determinant for states' behaviour. Insecurity of the international system makes states to seek power in order to defend themselves.[161] The power of one state is relative to the power of others, leading to competition where states try to gain more power than others.[162] Power in the neorealist view is understood as capabilities, i.e. economic and military strength, resources, size of population and territory among others.[163] Hegemonic states are those with high concentration and wide diffusion of power.[164] The distribution of power among states is the dominant explanatory factor for international cooperation.[165] Neorealists rationalise the development of regimes with the interest of most powerful states since regimes depend on the power structure. Regimes are therefore epiphenomenal[166] and internationally institutions "have mattered rather a little".[167] Neoliberals in contrast argue that regimes are able to create a stable international structure even in absence of hegemony since regimes often persisted when hegemony declined.[168] They stress that regimes enable states to collaborate whereas neorealists believe that regimes allow states to

159 E.g. *Rittberger/Zürn* (1990) p. 17; *Mayer/Rittberger/Zürn* (1993) acknowledging that transnational regimes become increasingly important (p. 404); *DeMars/Dijkzeul* (2015) pp. 9f.; *Arts* (2000) p. 516.

160 *Dunn/Schmidt* (2011) p. 93.

161 *Waltz* (1979) p. 104.

162 *Mearsheimer* (2011) p. 80.

163 *Waltz* (1979) p. 131.

164 *Lentner* (2006) p. 91. Hegemony can also be associated with leadership, dominance and control (*Gilpin* [1981] p. 29), the "preponderance of material resources" and their control (*Keohane* [1984] p. 32) or military resources (*Mearsheimer* [2001] p. 40).

165 *Lamy* (2011) pp. 116ff.

166 *Arts* (2000) p. 518.

167 *Mearsheimer* (1994) p. 49 referring to the examples of the failure of the League of Nations to stop aggression of Germany and Japan in the 1930s.

168 *Keohane* (1984) p. 50; *Little* (2011) p. 303.

coordinate.[169] Also neorealists look at game theory but highlight that actors follow a common strategy in order to avoid unwanted outcomes on both sides due to opposing strategies.[170] Similar to institutions also transnational actors are marginalised as they are not part of the structure.[171] Neorealists claim that US post-war foreign policy and US economic hegemony enabled the rise of MNCs and economic independence in the first place.[172] Others stress the limitations of IOs and NGOs through their exploitation and instrumentalisation by states.[173] While neoliberals rejected the neorealist assumption that states are the sole important actors on the international stage and added a focus on institutions they concede, even in regimes, that states are in fact the dominant actors.[174] Both neorealists and neoliberals furthermore neglected the possibility that political activities may be shifting away from the state.[175] In sum, neorealism and neoliberalism share several core assumptions about actors, values, issues, and power arrangements in the international system: (1) due to international anarchy, states have to pursue self-help strategies, limiting the nature of international cooperation and making the international sphere one of strategic interaction in which security concerns are paramount; (2) the interest of states as rational actors is to maximise their power and influence by pursuing their self-interest; (3) states are the key subjects in international relations.[176]

What these theories lack is the possibility to explain the role of transnational actors in the international environment. As will be outlined in the following section, the constructivist approach challenges the core assumptions of the rationalist theory. In doing so, it takes convincingly into account how transnational actors affect the sphere across national boundaries. The constructivist approach will be enhanced further on by transnationalist considerations. Moreover, some assumptions of the neo-neo synthesis on states and institutions will be applied to networks later. It has been a recurring idea to combine some rationalist and constructivist expla-

169 *Little* (2011) p. 306.

170 *Little* (2011) pp. 304ff.; neoliberal and neorealist game theoretical considerations on regimes are not mutually exclusive as cooperation and coordination can follow upon each other, see *Stein* (1983) p. 128.

171 *Waltz* (1979) p. 95; *Krasner* (1995) pp. 267ff.; *Risse* (2002) p. 260.

172 *Gilpin* (1971), (1975).

173 *Drezner* (2007) pp. 73, 88, 205f.; *Donini* (2012) with regards to humanitarian aid.

174 *Martin* (2007) pp. 110f.; *Strange* (1983) p. 349.

175 *Lamy* (2011) p. 125.

176 Summarized by *Chandler* (2005) p. 150.

nations as both traditions have connecting points.[177] From the 1970s on, they have been musroomed as actor- or structure-centered variants of liberalism.[178] In particular, it will be returned to the neorealist emphasis on power resources and the possibility of transnational actors being instrumentally used by states, and the neoliberal thoughts on regime functions. Chapter 3 considers, furthermore, the competitive and cooperative arrangements among different actors.

2.2.2. Constructivist assumptions

In the early 1990s constructivism developed as a reaction to the postpositivist debate in the 1980s and the failure of traditional international relations theory to predict or initially explain the end of the Cold War.[179] Constructivists challenge the assumptions of rationalism in arguing that the social world is constructed. They focus on the centrality of ideas, i.e. norms, values and knowledge, as well as discourses which form political identities and interests.[180] In his famous article "Anarchy is what states make of it: the social construction of power politics" *Wendt* refers to *Onuf* who is usually credited with coining the term "constructivism" in 1989.[181] *Wendt's* basic assumption is that politicians interpret world affairs. These interpretations (i.e. constructs) begin to falter when the conditions change in which they had demonstrated validity. Wars, for instance, end with the revaluation of the world view. Constructivist theory points out to the variety of views and images of society, to tradition, religion and established social practices which can offer solutions to some puzzles regarding the differences of politics in Europe, North America, East-Asia and the Arab world.[182] According to *Wendt*, constructivism makes the following core claims related to the deviating rationalist views: "(1) states are the principal units of analysis for international political theory; (2) the key structures in the state system are intersubjective rather than material; and (3) state identities and interests are in important part constructed by these social struc-

---

177 *Barnett* (2011) pp. 158f.; similar *Wendt* (1992) p. 394; *Rittberger* (1993) p. 22; *Noortmann/Arts/Reinalda* (2001); most recently *DeMars/Dijkzeul* (2015) applied an integrated approach to strategies and impact of NGOs in IR.

178 *Panke/Risse* (2007) pp. 89 ff.

179 *Fierke* (2013) pp. 187f.; *Risse* (2002) p. 258.

180 *Finnemore/Sikkink* (2001) pp. 392f.

181 *Wendt* (1992) p. 393; *Onuf* (1989).

182 *Hartmann* (2001) pp. 66f.

tures rather than given exogenously to the system by human nature or domestic politics".[183]

In responding to the first and second core assumption of rationalism, constructivists argue that it is not the structure of anarchy creating the conditions of possibility and structural limitations for states and state interests. Rather, states reproduce anarchy by mutually constituting themselves as self-interested and power seeking.[184] Rationalists follow rational choice theory in the focus on strategic interaction in which egoistic actors with given interests intend to maximise these interests and for this reason allow cooperation.[185] The constructivist assumption is, instead, that actors are not uniform and not rational. They have particular identities which are characterised by cultural, social, political and material circumstances they are anchored to.[186] State identities can be understood as "varying constructions of nation- and statehood" and are affected by international and domestic environments.[187] According to *Wendt*, states do not have identities and perception of self and other, apart from or prior to interaction with others. Identities are the basis of interests and shape them.[188] Interests and identities are not pre-given or "exogenously constituted" outside of the international sphere. They are constructed endogenously through the process of international interaction. Intersubjective knowledge created through interaction constitutes the interest and identity of the subject rather than the subject itself or the structure.[189] Knowledge as a causal idea shapes how social reality is interpreted and constructed.[190] Intersubjective knowledge is the result of social acts of signalling, interpreting and responding within interaction. Intersubjectivity therefore develops through social communication.[191] The continuing interaction between states builds agreement, regularity and misunderstanding and creates structure in international relations.[192] The structure manifests itself in norms which regulate states' be-

---

183 *Wendt* (1994) p. 385.
184 *Chandler* (2005) p. 150; *Wendt* (1999).
185 *Elster* (1989) p. 22; *Lamy* (2011) p. 119.
186 *Fierke* (2013) p. 191.
187 *Katzenstein* (1996) pp. 6, 22.
188 *Katzenstein* (1996) p. 30; *Wendt* (1992) pp. 398, 401 giving the fitting example: "If society forgets what a university is, the power and practices of professors and students cease to exist" (p. 397).
189 *Wendt* (1992) pp. 402, 410, 417.
190 *Barnett* (2011) pp. 159, 157.
191 *Adler* (1997) p. 327.
192 *Wendt* (1992) p. 405.

haviour[193] and in institutions which are stable sets of identities and interests.[194] Other constructivist scholars consider norms of international society as defining the identities and interests of states instead of interaction.[195] Norms are intersubjectively "shared expectations about appropriate behaviour hold by a community of actors".[196] In both strands, unlike in the rationalist view, interests are therefore not fixed but adaptable.[197] The focus on interaction processes and norms allows constructivism to explain change, which the structural fixity of neorealism and neoliberalism does not.[198] While scholars of the rationalist theories failed to predict or initially explain the end of the Cold War, constructivists emphasis the social dimensions of international relations: while the sovietisation of East and Central Europe after World War Two had established a permanent sense of threat and let to rivalry of the USA and the Soviet Union, the end of the Cold War and the collapse of the socialist state system resulted in a reconstruction of the world's image. In the Western perception the Soviet Union lost its threatening character.[199] Whereas rationalists assume strategic security and peace as "high politics" questions connected to defence and sovereignty to be on the top of states' agendas and "low" political economic and social issues as secondary,[200] constructivists counter with the concept of issue saliency. What actors regard as important depends on the importance attached to values discussed in a political debate and the extent to which the actor expects to be affected by the outcome. Priorities therefore can vary from actor to actor and over time.[201] Values are "elements of a shared symbolic system which serve as criteria or standard for selection on the alternatives of orientation which are intrinsically open in a situation".[202] Constructivists believe that it is not power which shape the behaviour of states but ideas that determine the meaning of power. Both neorealism and –liberalism subscribe to materialism believing that the structure constraining behaviour is determined by material factors such as technology, military

193 *Hartmann* (2001) p. 69.
194 *Wendt* (1992) p. 399.
195 *Finnemore* (1996).
196 *Finnemore* (1996) p. 22.
197 *Keck/Sikkink* (1998); *Risse* (2002) p. 259.
198 *Donnelly* (2000) p. 31.
199 *Fierke* (2013) p. 188; *Risse* (2002) p. 259; *Barnett* (2011) p. 155.
200 *Hoffmann* (1966) p. 874; *Willetts* (2011b) pp. 337f.
201 *Willetts* (2011a) p. 129.
202 *Parson* (1991) p. 7.

hardware and other resources which they view as power.[203] Constructivism emphasis that ideas and communicative processes determine at first which material factors states perceive as important and how they impact the interests' understanding.[204] Ideas are "mental constructs held by individuals, set distinctive beliefs, principles, and attitudes that provide broad orientations for behaviour and policy".[205] One can differentiate between causal beliefs, such as knowledge, and principled ideas, such as norms and political values.[206] Power can therefore not only be understood in material terms but also in ideational.[207] In contrast to rational actors following the logic of consequences, constructivists assume that actors behave according to the logic of appropriateness. Appropriateness in this view is seen as action that follows in a specific situation the rules, norms, social roles or the cultural values of that actor's community.[208] Ideas are therefore the key variables for constructivist to explain political behaviour.[209] Power in the constructivist view does not only aim at changing other actors' behaviour, it also exists when knowledge and the construction of identities allocate capacities.[210] With the power of social practice constructivists refer to the capacity to reproduce the intersubjective meaning constituting social structures and actors which can create predictability and diminish uncertainty among actors in a socially constructed community.[211]

The ability of constructivism to grasp change becomes also clear when looking at the impact of institutions and transnational actors in the international system. The third core assumption of the rationalist approaches shows their state-centrism as state actors are the key ontological object and point of departure making it difficult to explain the presence and role of transnational actors.[212] Neoliberals see the impact of institutions on international relations in expanding gains through cooperation. Neorealists view such impact in terms of coordination. Constructivists believe, instead, that the institutions' significance lies in the intensification of interac-

---

203 *Hurd* (2008) p. 300; *Barnett* (2011) p. 151.
204 *Risse/Sikkink* (1999) pp. 6f.
205 *Tannenwald* (2005) p. 15.
206 *Schimmelpfennig* (2010) pp. 164f.
207 *Hopf* (1998) p. 177.
208 *Olsen/March* (1989) pp. 160f.
209 *Hale/Held* (2011) p. 21.
210 *Barnett* (2011) p. 157.
211 *Hopf* (1998) p. 178.
212 *Hay* (2013) p. 289.

tion.[213] Although granting that non-state actors are participants within regimes, neoliberalism generally does not consider transnational actors as taking the lead or even establish such regimes.[214] It is only logical that regimes cannot change identities and interests when both are assumed to be pre-given.[215] Constructivists emphasise ideas, arguments, problem perceptions and social identities of the involved actors for explaining regime creation.[216] They stress that the composition of states' identity also shapes regimes as being part of interstate normative structures.[217] Regimes are believed to "embody a degree of collective identity".[218] Collective identity is understood as the "positive identification with the welfare of others, such that the other is seen as the cognitive extension of the self" leading to empathetic interdependence among actors as the foundations for collective interests.[219] They are therefore assumed to be intersubjective.[220] Regimes are social institution in which actors practice communication and argumentatively develop their interests oriented towards the principles and norms of the respective regime.[221] Some variants of constructivism can still be conceived of as state-centric.[222] For *Wendt*, for instance, the state is the subject of analysis.[223] Others extend constructivist theory to give a prominent role to transnational agents highlighted in the concept of transnational or global relations[224] as will be shown below. In *Haufler's* study on private regimes defined as "integrated complex of formal and informal institutions that is a source of governance in an economic issue area as a whole"[225], non-state actors are key, and states have a minor role in the establishment and maintenance of regimes. According to her, there is no reason for thinking that private actors are unable to establish principles, norms, rules and decision-making procedures.[226] From a functional theoretical point of view, private regimes have additional service provision function. Originally in the states'

213 *Woods* (2011) p. 258.
214 *Dijkzeul/DeMars* (2011) p. 214; *Haufler* (1993) p. 95.
215 *Kratochwil/Ruggie* (1986) p. 774; *Wendt* (1992) p. 393.
216 *Hasenclever/Mayer/Rittberger* (1997) pp 136ff.
217 *Jepperson/Wendt/Katzenstein* (1996) p. 62.
218 *Wendt* (1994) p. 392.
219 *Wendt* (1994) p. 386.
220 *Ruggie* (1998) p. 85.
221 *Wesel* (2012) p. 59.
222 E.g. *Ruggie* (1998).
223 See above fn. 183 on *Wendt's* first claim.
224 *Risse* (2002) p. 258; *Chandler* (2005) p. 154.
225 *Cutler/Haufler/Porter* (1999) p. 13.
226 *Haufler* (1993) p. 97.

responsibility the service was transferred to private organisations due to a lack of capacity or for reasons of efficiency.[227] According to *Willetts*, NGOs should be put in the centre of regime analysis as their "prime activity [...] is the mobilisation of support for values".[228] Others highlight the normative concerns when public functions are attributed to private actors due to the erosion of the public and private distinction.[229] *Haas* argues that professional knowledge communities (epistemic communities) are able to develop and form regimes.[230] An epistemic community is a "network of professionals with recognised expertise and competences in a particular domain and an authoritative claim to policy-relevant knowledge within that domain or issue-area". Experts having different academic backgrounds share "a set of normative and principled beliefs", "causal beliefs, which are derived from their analysis of practices", intersubjective "notions of validity" of knowledge and "a common policy enterprise", i.e. a common understanding of a problem and its solution.[231] Changed understanding in the epistemic community can lead to regime reform.[232] With the focus on epistemic communities *Haas* considers non-state actors as being important for learning processes in international institutions.[233] According to *Chandler*, "the international sphere is no longer seen as one in which states project their national interests, instead the process is reversed – through participation in international and transnational relations the national interests of states are constituted and reconstituted".[234] In this context, *Risse* and *Ropp* highlight Western liberal values diffused by transnational actors which partly influenced the *Gorbachev* leadership.[235] Although constructivism assumes that, for the foreseeable future, the world will remain a world of states, it accepts that the international agenda has been transformed since the end of the Cold War and that non-state actors have become increasingly involved in policy-making at the state and inter-state level.[236] Taking ideas at least as equally important as military or economic power, transna-

227 *Börzel/Risse* (2005) p. 208.
228 *Willetts* (2011a) p. 125.
229 *Cutler* (2002) pp. 33f.
230 *Haas* (1993) p. 169, (1989) pp. 377f.
231 *Haas* (1992) p. 3; others stress the necessary similarity of discipline, see *Holzner/Marx* (1979).
232 *Hopkins* (1992).
233 *Haas* (1993) pp. 188, 201.
234 *Chandler* (2005) p. 154.
235 *Risse/Ropp* (1999) p. 268.
236 *Hartmann* (2001) p. 68; *Risse* (2002) p. 259.

tional actors can be influential through their "communicative capabilities"[237] and "power of persuasion".[238] Both are connected to soft power and its key instrument of public diplomacy as will be introduced in chapter 3. Soft power is about the attraction of the way of life and the values of a society towards the rest of the world. [239] According to *Nye*, soft power is "(…) getting others to want what you want [and] might be called direct or co-optive power behavior. It is in contrast to the active command power behavior of getting others to do what you want. Co-optive power can rest on the attraction of one's ideas or on the ability to set the political agenda in a way that shapes the preferences that others express".[240] *Nye* states that "NGOs and network organisations have soft-power resources and do not hesitate to use them".[241] *Wallace* notes that "intellectual soft power" can also be found when looking at the activities of U.S. think tanks.[242]

The framework where states and non-state actors communicatively interact is often referred to as global civil society.[243] Global civil society can be termed as "the global process through which individuals debate, influence and negotiate an ongoing social contract or a set of contracts with the centres of political or economic authority"[244] and "through voluntary associations, movements, parties, unions, the individual is able to act publicly".[245] Since public and private actors play an equal part, constructivists do not concentrate on whether one is more important than the other. Rather, they highlight that it does not make sense to consider the world of transnational actors as opposed to the world of states since transnational work often conforms to the interest of states and international organisations and both actor types reciprocally influence each other.[246] As we have

---

237 *Willetts* (2011a) p. 128.

238 *Chandler* (2005) p. 153. Power of persuasion concerns communication functions of NGOs and includes the creation of international standards and mechanisms to implement norms, shaming techniques against abusers, the set-up of institutions and the provision of documentations to institutions (*Korrey* [1990] pp. 173f.).

239 *Nye* (1990) pp. 193ff., (2004).

240 *Nye* (1990) pp. 31f., (2004) p. 5; originally the concept builds on the "second face of power" of *Bachrach/Baratz* (1963) (*Nye* [2004] p. 5 fn. 5).

241 *Nye* (2004) p. 94.

242 *Wallace* (2004) pp. 286f.

243 *Chandler* (2005) p. 157. The existence of global civil society is highly contested (see *Chandler/Baker* [2005]).

244 *Kaldor* (2003b) p. 79.

245 *Kaldor* (2003a) p. 585.

246 *Haufler* (1995) p. 110.

seen above, transnational actors can depend on state funding.[247] International development and humanitarian assistance originates to a large extent from public sources. Transnational actors also often performed tasks that states and IOs could not or did not want to undertake. In foreign and humanitarian aid non-state actors often are subcontracted to help less bureaucratically and cost intensive as well as more flexibly. Transnational actors also supply monitoring and information to states.[248] Constructivism allows focusing on the question of transnational actors as instruments of state power. This resembles neorealism in its marginalisation of transnational actors. However, in contrast to neorealism, it might be true for some cases but less so for others. Constructivism therefore allows moving beyond the question of whether transnational actors matter. In the following section we will examine how constructivism can help to examine the role of transnational actors in international relations by looking at constructivist inspired models.

2.3. Transnational-constructivist explanations for the role of transnational actors in international relations

Theorising about transnational actors and their impact on world politics remains complicated. Transnational actors are rarely alike as they differ in structure, scope of activities and the issues they concentrate on.[249] As a consequence, theoretical assumptions often lack generalisability since the scientific statements relate to certain types of actors and the findings cannot be transferred to others.[250] Constructivist-inspired research, however, was able to develop some explanations on the role of transnational actors in international relations.[251]

When constructivism and non-state actors encountered after the end of the Cold War, transnationalism revived leading to an idealist-constructivist approach comprising a pluralist and a globalist strand.[252] In an early pluralist work *Risse-Kappen* focuses on the institutional conditions for the im-

247 See Ch. 2.1.
248 *Risse* (2002) p. 260.
249 *Risse* (2002) p. 255.
250 *Nölke* (2010) p. 398.
251 *Nölke* (2010) p. 389, apart from the constructivist approach there is a second body of literature pointing out normative issues in dealing with the democratic legitimacy of transnational actors.
252 *DeMars/Dijkzeul* (2015) p. 11.

pact of transnational actors on the behaviour of states. In his complex model, a combination of the domestic structure and the institutionalisation of the international environment conditions the access and possible policy impact of transnational actors. In contrast, neorealism and neoinstitutionalism separate both structures of governance.[253] *Risse-Kappen* compares cases in which transnational coalitions and actors aim at influencing state behaviour in the foreign policy arena. He argues that the impact of transnational actors and coalitions on state policies is likely to vary according to the institutional structure. He first considers the differences in domestic structure referring to the structure of the state (i.e. the political institutions, centralised vs. fragmented), the society (strong vs. weak) and the policy networks (consensual vs. polarised). The domestic structure determines the access of the transnational actors to domestic institutions and their policy impact in case of access which can vary from profound to unlikely. In state-controlled domestic structures the access is most difficult although the impact can be profound while in fragile domestic structures access is easy and impact unlikely.[254] In a second step *Risse-Kappen* looks at the degrees of international institutionalisation, i.e. the extent to which the specific issue-area is regulated by bilateral agreements, multilateral regimes, and/or international organisations. Highly regulated and cooperative structures of international governance tend to legitimize transnational activities and to increase transnational actors' access to the national polities as well as their ability to form "winning coalitions" for policy change.[255] In sum, domestic and international governance structures interact in conditioning the access to institutions and policy impact of transnational actors.[256] Differences in domestic structures affect state autonomy "from below"; variations in international institutions can equally influence state capacities "from above".[257] While *Risse-Kappen's* model is able to explain the structural conditions under which transnational actors can have a policy impact, it cannot explain how transnational actors work, i.e. how micro-mechanisms of persuasion and communication strategies influence outcomes or how ideas are diffused transnationally. In his summary and in later works *Risse-Kappen* highlights that domestic and international structure determines not only the transnational actors' impact on policies but also

253 *Risse-Kappen* (1995b) p. 283.
254 *Risse-Kappen* (1995a) p. 28.
255 *Risse-Kappen* (1995a) pp. 22-32.
256 *Risse-Kappen* (1995a) p. 33, (1995b) p. 288.
257 *Risse-Kappen* (1995a) p. 29.

their characteristics, their strategies and tactics.[258] However, his work does not systematically scrutinize transnational actors' properties in terms of strategies or power resources.[259] Furthermore, the model itself is not able to explain why different transnational actors in one country are not equally successful.[260] It is also not the case that transnational activity only takes place in a more or less institutionalised international environment. Finally, what transnational actors actually do, remains nebulously. Notwithstanding these drawbacks, *Risse-Kappen's* work renewed the interest in transnational actors and led to increased theorising on transnational actors' impact.[261]

For future research *Risse-Kappen* proposes network analysis to study the different interactions between transnational and state actors within international institutions.[262] Drawing from his work in assuming that political contexts as "opportunity structures" need to be taken into account for the emergence and success of transnational advocacy networks, *Keck* and *Sikkink* focus on the impact of transnational actors through the so-called "boomerang effect" model analysing from an actor-centred view the ideational situation of domestic groups and how they influence the interests of political decision makers.[263] A boomerang pattern of influence exists when domestic groups in a repressive state bypass their government and directly search out international contacts. These contacts pressure their states or international organisations which again pressure the blocking state from outside to achieve the desired policy goal. The involved transnational actors are members in transnational advocacy networks (TAN)[264] which can be defined as "actors working internationally on an issue, who are bound together by shared values, a common discourse, and a dense ex-

258 *Risse-Kappen* (1995b) p. 283.
259 *Risse-Kappen* (1995b) p. 308.
260 *Risse* (2002) p. 266; *Keck/Sikkink* (1998) p. 202.
261 *Hale/Held* (2011) p. 8.
262 *Risse-Kappen* (1995b) p. 286.
263 *Keck/Sikkink* (1998) p. 7; *Panke/Risse* (2007) pp. 92, 95. *Keck* and *Sikkink* inhabit a hybrid liberal and constructivist perspective (*Dijkzeul/DeMars* [2011] p. 215). Liberal theories assume that domestic actors or structures influence foreign policy identities of states and their behaviour in the international arena (*Panke/Risse* [2007] p. 90).
264 *Keck/Sikkink* (1998) pp. 12ff.; *Willetts* (2011a) presents a revisioned version of the boomerang approach with more routes for the boomerang effect by adding transnational advocacy networks which obviously do not have to include the involved NGOs (p. 133).

change of information and services".[265] In order to describe what the network does, *Keck* and *Sikkink* use the term "persuasion" which refers to several tactics of network members. These tactics are: (1) Information politics: This is the ability to quickly and credibly generate politically usable information and move it to where it will have the most impact; (2) symbolic politics, i.e. the ability to call upon symbols, actions, or stories that make sense of a situation for an audience that is frequently far away; (3) leverage politics refers to the strategic use of information in order to make more powerful states and IOs cut off military and financial assistance for the pressured state (material leverage) or when the activities of the pressured state are internationally scrutinised and a "mobilization of shame" takes place (moral leverage); and (4) accountability politics, i.e. to hold powerful actors to their previously stated policies and principles.[266] Within this context, *Keck* and *Sikkink* highlight the competition between various problems, ideas and interests of domestic and political actors in interactions.[267] The problem with the boomerang approach is that the process can only be successful when target states are "sensitive to leverage".[268] Dependency on economic or military assistance will not be found in the industrialised countries and moral leverage only will work when the practices of the target state vary from those asserted.[269] *Chandler* outlines that the reliance on state actors in the process could also be read as the states' centrality and that power relations are downplayed.[270] Notwithstanding, *Keck* and *Sikkink* established a sound explanation of transnational actors' undertakings stressing the idea that interactions between different actors take place aside from states' relations.[271] Furthermore, they added networks as the source of new ideas to the concept of transnational politics. Network environments are of importance for the view presented here. We will return to this aspect further on.

What is visible in the work of *Keck* and *Sikkink* can also be found in other pluralist perspectives stressing global civil society's independence from the government and picturing non-state actors as the mouthpiece of the weak on the grassroots level where power emerges from the bottom up.[272]

265 *Keck/Sikkink* (1998) p. 2.
266 *Keck/Sikkink* (1998) pp. 16ff.
267 *Panke/Risse* (2007) p. 95.
268 *Keck/Sikkink* (1998) p. 29.
269 *Keck/Sikkink* (1998) p. 29; *Chandler* (2005) p. 160.
270 *Chandler* (2005) pp. 161, 165.
271 *Reinalda* (2001) pp. 31f.
272 *DeMars/Dijkzeul* (2015) p. 11; *Dijkzeul/DeMars* (2011) p. 217.

Such positions are often characterised by optimism regarding the potential of global civil society assuming that states which were long in the centre of international relations are increasingly restricted by transnational actors and networks.[273] Often global civil society is described as an emancipation possibility for humans and citizens.[274] Others criticise that these standpoints repeat the moral claims of transnational actors rather than considering what actors actually do.[275] Transnational actors are also not per se critical and have different views on political outcomes instead.[276] The neomarxist approach of *Gramsci* makes the valid reproach that the pluralist conception on global civil society is overconfident. In *Gramsci's* hegemonic model of civil society, the state makes use of civil society, its organisations and networks to secure the states' hegemonic project by diffusing a particular way of life through norms and values. It is more than sheer manipulations as a social consensus is created. In this case, civil society becomes part of an extended state feigning openness.[277] According to *Cox*, it was US hegemony that made possible the rise of transnational relations after World War Two.[278] These considerations resemble the state-centric claims of neorealists. Since transnational actors often depend on the funding of states or IOs which even set up their own NGOs to push through certain ideas or to access additional funding, it does not make sense considering neither global civil society nor transnational actors as against the state world.[279] Private influence can at times be an "(inter)governmental political strategy" especially useful when interference should be avoided and an alternative to official political engagement is needed.[280] As already outlined, a less anticipating model is necessary where states or non-state actors are not per se considered as taking the lead or are normatively heightened.

Scholars increasingly look at communication practices of transnational actors (and others) and connect it to the constructivist emphasis on norms and values taking *Risse-Kappen's* former suggestions into account to study these micro-mechanisms. Pluralist perspectives consider, for example, the

---

273 *Baker/Chandler* (2005) p. 2.

274 E.g. *Kaldor* (2003b) p. 143; *Falk* (2005) p. 82.

275 E.g. *Finnemore/Sikkink* (1998) p. 898 on the altruism of norm entrepreneurs; critically *DeMars/Dijkzeul* (2015) p. 11; *Chandler* (2005) p. 166.

276 *Reinalda* (2001) p. 27.

277 *Gramsci* (1971) pp. 245ff.; *Katz* (2006) pp. 334f.; *Parmar* (2004) p. 31 applying this thought to institutes of international affairs.

278 *Cox* (1987) pp. 263, 266.

279 *Chandler* (2005) p. 164; *Risse* (2002) p. 260.

280 *Reinalda* (2001) p. 26.

lobbying activities of pressure groups vis-à-vis governments and propaganda in relation to the general public.[281] *Finnemore* and *Sikkink* look in detail on the policy change through norms in their "norm life cycle". They consider norm entrepreneurs supporting the development of new norms mainly through persuasion. Norm entrepreneurs are actors with an organisational platform: mainly NGOs, their networks or IOs. They pressure target states to adopt the new norm and monitor outcomes. When the norm reaches a critical mass of supporters (i.e. states) and a tipping point the norm cascades and achieves prevalent support within the population. This is when norm change happens. When the norm is no longer contested, it is internalised. At this stage professionals and bureaucracy are the most important agents which "practice" the norm.[282] On the basis of *Finnemore* and *Sikkink's* work, *Willetts* suggest that NGOs as significant norm entrepreneurs win support for values by persuasion through various linkages thereby exercising influence on global politics: (1) actor linkages i.e. linking the support to their UN status, whereby high status NGOs will receive more attention than low status NGOs;[283] (2) linking goals to a value with widespread support, such as security, freedom and justice; (3) bargaining linkages by forming alliances with others which leads to change own value preferences in favour of those of other actors; (4) and finally functional linkages where NGOs emphasis positive effects of their goals independent from the policy process. *Willetts* assumes that NGOs have the strongest impact through value and functional linkages.[284] Persuasion takes place in two steps: first, the salience of a policy issue needs to be enhanced and second, values need to be redefined.[285] *Risse* considers the processes of argumentation, deliberation and persuasion, which "constitute a distinct mode of social interaction to be differentiated from strategic bargaining and rule-guided behavior" as highlighted by rationalist scholars.[286] He draws from *Habermas's* theory of communicative action to conceptualise the logic of arguing and connects it to IR. Actors try to convince each other to change their causal or principled beliefs in order to reach a reasoned consensus about validity claiming.[287] Arguing implies that actors try to challenge the

---

281 *Reinalda* (2001) p. 18.

282 *Finnemore/Sikkink* (1998) pp. 895ff.

283 See Ch. 5.1. on the UN categorisation. High status refers to the UN general status (*Willetts* [2005] p. 436).

284 *Willetts* (2011a) pp. 139ff.

285 *Willetts* (2011a) pp. 141.

286 *Risse* (2000) p. 1.

287 *Risse* (2000) pp. 2, 9.

validity claims inherent in any causal or normative statement and seek a communicative consensus about their understanding of the situation. The logic implies that participants in a discourse are open to be persuaded by the better argument. Arguing is therefore as goal-oriented as strategic interaction but the goal is not to attain one's fixed preference but to seek a reasoned consensus.[288] Arguing increases the influence of actors with less material power and successful arguing beats material bargaining power.[289] We will return to the aspect of communicative practice in chapter 3.

The globalist strand of the idealist-constructivist approach lays emphasis on global processes taking place above the state in international organisations, most considered the UN. Obviously, mixed pluralist-globalist positions exist as *Willetts's* work shows. Globalists concentrate on global governance defined by "policy-making and -implementation in global politics systems through the collaboration of governments with actors from civil society and the private sector".[290] Transnational actors play important roles in this context. Their power results from several sources: the mobilisation of individuals to raise awareness for certain issues,[291] the ability to frame and define issues to exert pressure on political decision makers (IGOs and states), their specialist knowledge and expertise allowing them to support decision makers with accurate information and data as well as their personal commitment. Thereby, they are important for the drafting of political proposals and for the policy implementation monitored by them.[292] Others stress the activity of transnational actors as executing agents for the UN and the performance of public relations' tasks on behalf of the UN.[293] Transnational actors are assumed to have decision-making authority in hybrid international organisations and transnational regimes.[294] Hybrid organisations are joint organisations of governments or their agencies on the one hand and transnational actors on the other hand. Both groups are formally equal, have full rights in the policy making process and have usually the obligation to jointly fund activities.[295] Global governance characterises different forms of political activity in diverse policy fields, whose needs stem from global issues which can only be targeted through the coopera-

288 *Risse* (2000) p. 7.
289 *Risse* (2000) pp. 9, 33.
290 *Willetts* (2011a) p. 148.
291 *Nuscheler* (2006) p. 558.
292 *Koch* (2011) pp. 203f.; similar *Rucht* (1996) p. 37; *Willetts* (1982) pp. 185f.
293 *Williams* (1990) p. 265.
294 *Willetts* (2011a) pp. 123ff.
295 *Willetts* (2011a) p. 337, (2011a) p. 73.

tion of different actors (state and non-state) as a global authority is missing. There are three types of global problems: first, transboundary or cross-border problems concerning for instance drug trafficking or pollution; second, common property problems referring, for example, to the oceans or Antarctica; and finally, simultaneous problems of states regarding the areas of education, health, welfare and other.[296] Global governance perspectives in contrast to state-centric assumptions have the benefit of considering many different actors. However, they do not look at their internal functioning.[297] Moreover, non-state actors are often viewed as sheer executive bodies of the UN implementing and enforcing global norms developed by the UN or in multilateral negotiations. Finally, as power affects states from above by norms or institutions,[298] the considered processes take place exclusively above the national state which reflects only some part of the activities of transnational actors.

Both pluralists' and globalists' perspectives are focused on private actors' participating in the international policy process and/or cooperation and steering performances that is political influence.[299] This is problematic. Many transnational actors and networks aim at consciousness-raising instead of shaping policies directly. [300] In this context, *Stone* points out that "influence is a word that is itself open to a variety of interpretations". She describes the tendency of some think tanks to also claim (non-existing) influence over policy in order to convince their decision-making targets, members or financial backer.[301] Moreover, direct political impact of think tanks could not be found as one-to-one policy implementations of think tank policy ideas barely exist. [302] Also *Chandler* notes that it is rather difficult to first establish criteria for the policy-success measurement and trace back achievements to a particular factor (i.e. the transnational actors' activities) alone.[303] As for constructivist explanations in general, they are frequently criticised to concentrate far too often on the success stories of certain transnational actors' activity by studying retrospectively specific policy adoption in order to demonstrate that transnational actors matter. Moreover, the problem of measuring the influence of transnational actors in cer-

---

296 *Stone* (2008) p. 25.
297 *Dijkzeul/DeMars* (2011) p. 211.
298 *DeMars/Dijkzeul* (2015) p. 11; *Dijkzeul/DeMars* (2011) p. 217.
299 *Reinalda* (2001) pp. 24ff.
300 *Risse* (2002) p. 268.
301 *Stone* (2004) p. 10.
302 *Stone* (2004) p. 11.
303 *Chandler* (2005) p. 162.

tain cases is held to reveal that only their ideas are crucial for the result.[304] Evaluating effectiveness is methodological difficult because it needs to be imagined how the case might have differed under varying conditions.[305] From this point of view it makes sense to study transnational actors simply because they exist. Whether they matter is irrelevant as it depends on the research question and how the assessment criterion of "importance" is defined.[306]

Most transnational actors do not constantly operate as parts of formal international organisations or institutions. Rather they interact with others transnationally in policy networks.[307] This refers to the dimension of transnational activity as introduced above.[308] Similar to their considerations on institutions, constructivists highlight the development of intersubjective knowledge in terms of common understanding and shared identities in order to explain change through networks being part of global civil society.[309] Rather than seeing transnational actors as rule enforcers, their activities can be spontaneous and without planning them beforehand which makes it difficult to study single organisations at a time. Often, they are not clearly bound entities.[310] Still, there are several forms of networks which can be distinguished. Afterwards, we will look at their practice.

2.3.1. Forms of networks

Various international networks can be summarised under the umbrella term of transnational policy network.[311] The already presented transnational advocacy networks (TAN) mainly contain different NGOs central in providing information and other actors, like media, churches and politicians.[312] Transnational actors are active in both fields, they can try to impact domestic policies, and internationally they are active with ideas.[313] A

304 *Wapner* (1995) p. 320; *Chandler* (2005) pp. 164f.; *Risse* (2002) p. 268.
305 *Hale/Held* (2011) p. 25 with regards to global governance institutions.
306 *Weenink* (2001) pp. 86, 89, 90.
307 *Risse* (2002) p. 269.
308 See Ch. 2.1. at the end.
309 *Stone* (2004) p. 13, (2005) p. 102; *Risse-Kappen* (1995a) p. 10.
310 Similar *Dijkzeul/DeMars* (2011) pp. 219f.
311 *Stone* (2008) pp. 31f.; (2005) pp. 94ff.; *Maxwell/Stone* (2005) p. 11.
312 *Keck/Sikkink* (1998) p. 10.
313 *Reinalda* (2001) pp. 33f.

particular problem is that *Keck* and *Sikkink* focus on campaigns[314] when studying networks. They assume that bonding with members of the network must be visible as each actor has a certain role within the campaign. However, networking occurs often among actors that do not have anything to do with each other. Partners might be hidden, manipulative or have contradictory strategies, opinions and values.[315] Moreover, information is not the only possible resource that network members can exchange. A second type of transnational policy network is the transnational executive network.[316] Sometimes termed as transgovernmental network, it contains government officials with a dual domestic and international function trying to tackle global issues through networking governments.[317] They are of minor interest for this study since they cannot be subsumed under the definition of transnational interaction as applied here as these officials are active on behalf of a government. A third form of transnational policy network is the global knowledge network (KNET). It may "incorporate professional bodies, academic research groups and scientific communities that organise around a special subject matter or issue". Also think tanks can operate in KNETs.[318] Think tanks are "non-profit private and public organisations devoted to examining and analysing policy-relevant issues and producing research outputs in terms of publications, reports, lectures and workshops, in most cases targeted to identifiable audiences with the hope of influencing decision-making and public opinion".[319] Inclusion in KNETs rests upon professional and officially recognised expertise. The network intends to create, advance and share knowledge and at times to inform policy about this knowledge.[320] In contrast to the other networks described above, networking itself is an essential goal and the proceeding is assumed to be disinterested. It takes place in the forms of research, study, publications, intellectual exchanges and international financing among others. Often KNETs

---

314 *Keck/Sikkink* (1998) define campaigns as "a set of strategically linked activities in which members of a diffuse principled network (…) develop explicit, visible ties and mutually recognised roles in pursuit of a common goal (and generally against a common target)" (p. 6). Campaigns are also temporarily and thematically finite which differentiate them from other forms of communication (*Jarren/Donges* [2011] p. 218).

315 *Reinalda* (2001) p. 27; *Dijkzeul/DeMars* (2011) pp. 215f.; *DeMars/Dijkzeul* (2015) pp. 15, 18; *DeMars* (2015) p. 243.

316 *Stone* (2008) p. 32.

317 *Keohane/Nye* (1974); *Slaughter* (2004) p. 14; *Hale/Held* (2011) p. 16.

318 *Stone* (2004) p. 12.

319 *Thunert* (2004) p. 71.

320 *Maxwell/Stone* (2005) p. 11.

can overlap with other network forms.[321] KNETs can be analysed as epistemic communities, as outlines above, or discourse coalitions and communities. Experts i.e. consultants, NGO executives, scientists, members of research institutes and think tanks are expected to give advice in the policy-making process. Some authors stress that their power stems from neutrality and impartiality based on their expertise.[322] However, conceptualising experts as "neutral" is difficult as scientific knowledge is never free of value and may be even used instrumentally to convince others and legitimise certain actions.[323] According to *Haas*, networks of scientists can produce usable knowledge contributing to social learning. The greater their autonomy from the political environment the more scientists are able to influence the respective policy.[324] Usable knowledge encompasses "a substantive core that makes it useable for policy-makers" and an element that enables the transmission from the scientific community to the policy world.[325] Sometimes experts are termed as transnational policy professionals being part of a transnational policy community whose status of being public or private is unclear as the experts or their networks can be contracted and funded by public bodies. The professional's power is then assumed to stem from his or her semi-official position, information resources and international experience.[326] KNETs can also take the form of discourse coalition and communities "created by professionals through a boundary drawing discourse that defines who and what is to be considered inside and outside the community, establishing a distinction between professionals and non-professionals, and between good and bad professionals".[327] Symbols, language and policy narrative serve here as a source of power. Transnational identities, in contrast to national identities and views, are enhanced by international interactions.[328] In the tradition of *Foucault*, discursive practices are used to maintain and establish power relationships.[329] In sum, TANs limit the look on advocacy actors provided with information resources while KNETs in-

---

321 *Stone* (2008) p. 32; (2005) pp. 91f.
322 *Koch* (2011) pp. 204f.
323 *Wigger* (2011) pp. 89f.; *Stone* (2008) p. 30.
324 *Haas* (2004) p. 576.
325 *Haas* (2004) p. 573.
326 *Stone* (2008) p. 31.
327 *Krause Hansen/Salskov-Iversen/Bislev* (2002) p. 111.
328 *Stone* (2005) p. 95.
329 *Risse* (2007a) pp. 131f., an example for a neoliberal discourse is the Thatcher Slogan TINA ("there is no alternative!") to rationalise her policies of neoliberal economic reforms and cuts in social services in the mid-1990s (p. 132).

corporate professionals having mainly knowledge resources. However, we expect that connecting links can be established between different types of actors bringing various resources to the networking process. It is therefore useful not to narrow the network concept too much since linked actors and their resources cannot be identified otherwise. Rather, it should be looked at "all those actors that share a common partner" which includes normatively deviating and hidden partners.[330] The forth form of a transnational policy network, the Global public policy networks (GPPNs), is a quasi-public or semi-private mixed meta-network which can include other forms of networks[331] and various public and private actors whose mix is determined by the specific policy issue.[332] Generally it is trisectoral as it incorporates members of three types of transnational policy community: the "internationalised public sector official" such as judges, legislators or regulators, the "international civil servant" who is an employee of an international organisation as well as the "transnational policy professional" who can be, for instance, a consultant, a business leader, a scientific or think tank expert or a NGO executive. Actors cooperate due to a problem existing over cross-boarders enabling forms of "soft authority" in these networks. Being dependent on resources and bargaining is what characterise their interactions.[333] GPPNs resemble tripartite global governance networks including state actors, firms and advocacy groups.[334] Still, in the GPPN profit and not-for-profit actors belong to the same sector. The core feature of the GPPN is a public-private partnership[335] which in its transnational form can be defined as "institutionalized cooperative relationships between public actors and private actors beyond the nation state for governance purposes" i.e. "the making and implementation of norms and rules for the provision of goods and services".[336] For such joint activity also the term multi-stakeholder initiative was coined.[337] In sum, GPPN and its vari-

330 *DeMars/Dijkzeul* (2015) p. 18.

331 *Schimmelpfennig* (2010) p. 123.

332 *Reinicke* (2000) p. xi; *Reinicke* (1998) p. 220; *Stone* (2008) p. 28.

333 *Stone* (2008) pp. 30f.; (2005) pp. 90f.

334 *Risse* (2007a) p. 139; *Risse* (2002) p. 269.

335 *Reinicke* (1998) p. 229.

336 *Börzel/Risse* (2005) p. 198.

337 *Hale/Held* (2011) pp. 16f. There have been identified other forms of supranational networks, but they include NGOs only: Information networks make possible the communication among different actors without being politically active together; issue caucuses temporarily focus on single UN or IGO fora where NGOs

ants have the advantage to incorporate public and private actors without assuming that one is more important.

In order to avoid a premature anticipation of a certain network character, it is suggested to start from the lowest common denominator of a policy network definition: "a set of relatively stable relationships which are of non-hierarchical and interdependent nature linking a variety of actors, who share common interests with regard to a policy and who exchange resources to pursue these shared interests acknowledging that co-operation is the best way to achieve common goals".[338] As will be shown in the following chapter, this definition needs some adaptations with regards to homogeneity of interests, the assumed cooperation among network members and the relationships' stability.[339]

2.3.2. Towards the practice of transnational actors in networks

The significance of networks is evaluated differently. Some scholars highlight that they help developing regimes and the effectiveness and efficiency of international cooperation: Costs are cut when NGOs participate in international conferences for countries which cannot afford to take part. Furthermore, the monitoring of international negotiations and rule compliance through network members. Moreover, networks are assumed to help decreasing the deficit of democracy in international cooperation through the creation of transparency of international processes and through the increased participation of actors other than state delegates.[340] However, although networks open policy-making to some stakeholders, they also exclude those not getting access to the network for multiple reasons. Networks like TNAs are permeable to social partaking while epistemic communities and GPPNs are more exclusive and restricted. Helping the democratic deficit in the global sphere therefore depends on the above inclu-

---

hold strategic meetings; and governance networks which are not engaged in advocacy and have a supportive or organisational function (*Willetts* [2011] pp. 120ff.).

338 *Börzel* (1998) p. 254.

339 See Ch. 3.1.1.

340 *Raustiala* (1997) pp. 724ff.; e.g. *Reinicke/Deng* (2000) assume that GPPNs can close the participatory gap in international decision-making due to the facilitation "of social interaction among people and organisations" (p. 62); *Reinicke* (1999) p. 51; *Risse* (2007a) pp. 139f.

sion.[341] Transnationalists believe that density and symmetry of transnational networks increase the possibility for peace and cooperation.[342] Through their configuration, networks have an independent impact on the power of network members and international policy results.[343] As already outlined, focusing on political outcomes is problematic rather the "building of international networks by NGOs themselves is an outcome and example of mattering."[344] In this way, it is the establishment and fostering of networks among a variety of actors which is an essential function of transnational actors.[345] Although networking neither boosts political influence nor should it be confused with it,[346] *Stone* points out that "the network [itself] is a site and form of power".[347] As already outlined, concentrating on policy results does not produce knowledge on the internal functioning of networks or networks' parts. Hence, "organisational agency" needs to be considered.[348] Moreover, possible informality of such interactions needs to be looked at which governance scholars barely analyse. In order to describe best the "intuitional reality" of transnational actors and their relevance to IR, a more constructivist perspective needs to be taken which focuses on interaction processes in broad networks.[349]

DeMars and *Dijkzeul* assume that NGOs engage in two simultaneous anchoring practices: first they claim to pursue a public purpose which generates bridging effects, namely between the division of the state and society as they are private actors with a public purpose.[350] This anchoring practice leads to power dynamics which can have many different forms. It is not restricted to power from below or above and it considers that states may use the power resources of NGOs. Second, NGOs link with social and political partners in several countries. This generates again bridging effects. NGOs, for instance, cannot only mobilize the movement of information and norms but also those of material resources. Also, this anchoring practice

---

341 *Stone* (2005) pp. 99ff.
342 *Schimmelpfennig* (2010) p. 137.
343 *Schimmelpfennig* (2010) p. 134.
344 *Noortmann/Arts/Reinalda* (2001) p. 302.
345 Similar *Nuscheler* (2006) pp. 558f.
346 *Stone* (2004) p. 14.
347 *Stone* (2005) p. 100.
348 *Dijkzeul/DeMars* (2011) p. 211.
349 Similar *Dijkzeul/DeMars* (2011) pp. 219f.
350 There are seven divisions which NGOs bridge: between state/public and society/private, family and market, normative and material, relegious and secular, agency and structure, conflict and cooperation and national and international (*DeMars/Dijkzeul* [2015] p. 5).

can generate complex power relationships. In sum, *DeMars* and *Dijkzeul* suggest paying more attention to the partner relationships and studying NGOs in practice. Practice is viewed as a process which they term as "NGOing".[351] On the basis of these considerations, it is suggested to concentrate on the networks' operating which might have different forms and which can include various actors, especially public and private actors interacting transnationally through communication and the exchange of ideational but also material resources. This resource exchange can be traced back to the originally outlined movement of items which constitutes transnational interactions.

Conclusion

For neorealism the state theoretically remains most important. Neoliberalism accepts this view although considering the role of international institutions. Constructivist theory attaches importance to transnational actors in international relations as it concentrates on interaction process among different actors. It does not assume that one actor is more important than the other and focuses on ideational and other resources of these actors. In looking at networks and communication processes, constructivism is creating the opportunity to uncover important issues, neglected by neorealism and neoliberalism. It focuses more directly on the question of the role of the German political foundations in international relations maintaining links with the German government and political party landscape, as well as governments and civil societies abroad.

So as to tackle the criticism that constructivists are too focused on success stories detailed process tracing can help. Instead of concentrating on policy implementation results, this study will focus on the process of communication and on how transnational interaction among actors takes place. The concept of public diplomacy will allow looking at these processes in a systematic manner. Diplomacy refers to a process of communication and negotiation between states and other international actors. Public diplomacy, in a constructivist manner, is about ideas and values and can involve transnational actors.[352] Introduced in the following chapter the concept will combine a network approach with communication practices and interactions among different actors. By this, it will be possible to study

351 *DeMars/Dijkzeul* (2015) pp. 22f., 4.

352 *Melissen* (2007a) p. xxi.

thoroughly the German foundations' "power of persuasion" and to consider the multiple communication tracks between them, their partners abroad as well as the German state.

Chapter 3 – Interactions in a networked environment: Public diplomacy

In the last chapter the role of transnational actors in IR theory has been illuminated. The increasing conceptualising of these actors' undertakings can also be recognised when looking at the literature on diplomacy. The recent transformation of diplomacy has led to a shift away from state-centred forms. Diplomacy has become a complex space incorporating different relationships and various actors. From a constructivist starting point which emphasises these interactions, public diplomacy can be understood as networked process focusing on values and perceptions. It constitutes a framework for systematically analysing the German political foundations' power and their position in the international political arena. Chapter 2 discussed different network images and the transnational actors' political impact which is not necessarily a policy impact. Public diplomacy can be combined with these considerations and allows operationalising the described interaction process.

The chapter starts with several diplomatic forms which might be relevant in the context of the German political foundations' undertakings. The literature on public diplomacy will then be investigated by presenting the main approaches in detail. Subsequently, a closer look will be taken at the different concepts related to public diplomacy. The considerations will be summarised and integrated in a model which will serve as a framework for the analysis of the diplomatic activities of the *Stiftungen* in the next chapters. Finally, German public diplomacy as practised by the Federal Foreign Office will be outlined.

3.1. Non-traditional diplomacy

Traditional diplomacy has been increasingly challenged by recent developments in the international arena. Due to increasing direct contacts between political leaders on the international level, the original role of diplomats has been reduced. Through modern forms of media and information technology, former diplomatic channels are circumvented. With regards to the changing matters of war, intra-state rather than inter-state conflicts grew after the end of the Cold War delimiting traditional diplomacy. The future of the sovereign state is often called into question. Consequentially, this also concerns the workspace of traditional diplomacy as a state instrument. For this work, the subject of a changing international order due to the increasing number of different actors is most relevant.[353] Several forms of non-traditional diplomacy can involve transnational actors such as unofficial or informal, private, citizen, track two and public diplomacy. All these forms are distinct from track one or traditional diplomacy in which the main actors are always states or international organisations. *Montville* was first to define track two diplomacy as "unofficial informal interaction of members of adversary groups or nations that aims to develop strategies, influence public opinion and organise human and material resources in ways that might help resolve their conflicts".[354] Track two, second track and citizen diplomacy are often used interchangeably but the term citizen diplomacy is older. The combination of track one and track two diplomacy is called twin-track or two-track-diplomacy.[355] Multi-track-diplomacy is characterised by several different negation tracks involving transnational actors and private individuals.[356] Multi-track-diplomacy was applied at the end of the Kosovo war in 1999.[357] As track two is mainly limited to the aim of conflict resolution or confidence-building in conflict situations, a wider approach will be necessary to analyse the whole spectrum of possible interactions. Informal or unofficial diplomacy is mostly used in differentiation to traditional diplomacy and involves a non-governmental actor. *Parmar* describes this type of diplomacy as a method of institutes of foreign affairs which "unofficially" discuss matters of their own governments with their overseas counterparts.[358] *Stone* summarises by the term, track two ambitions and its variants.[359] Although secrecy is an interesting aspect in this context, the informality of this process does not help understanding the interaction. In returning to the consideration of chapter 2, the relationship

353 *Jönsson* (2002) pp. 216f.

354 *Montville* (1990) p. 162.

355 *Davies/Kaufman* (2002); partly citizen diplomacy is assumed to be a component of public diplomacy referring to exchange programs and social relationship building which later becomes important in official negotiations (*Mueller* [2009] p. 102).

356 *McDonald* (2002) defines seven additional tracks which exist next to track one and track two, i.e. media, citizen exchange programs, private-sector business, education and training, peace activism, religion and funding (p. 55).

357 *Berridge/James* (2003) p. 177.

358 *Parmar* (2004) p. 19; *Wallace* (2004) p. 287.

359 *Stone* (2011) pp. 243f.

between state actors and transnational actors is particularly important and whether the latter can be considered as independent diplomatic actors.

Theoretical perspectives on diplomacy are connected to the increased conceptualising of transnational actors. While earlier works were state-focused concentrating on interstate diplomacy and not conceding much importance to transnational actors in this process,[360] globalist perspectives, upcoming in the 1980s, stress the growth of non-state diplomacy marginalising the state in the process. Post-globalist approaches look at the relationships between states and transnational actors and the specific roles and functions performed by both actors emphasising public diplomacy as a concept which is able to grasp these interactions.[361] Public diplomacy is often associated with global civil society since public diplomacy aims at "building a public sphere in which diverse voices can be heard in spite of their various origins, distinct values, and often contradictory interests".[362] As already outlined in chapter 2, global civil society concepts often problematically present transnational actors as opposed to state actors. They also focus on global issues managed by new forms of governance and international processes. *Betsill* and *Corell* in their study on NGO diplomacy, for example, concentrate on international (environmental) negotiations. They highlight the similarities of diplomatic functions of non-state diplomats and state delegates and determine conditions under which NGOs influence the process and outcome of these negotiations.[363] As already outlined, interactions can unlikely be limited to those negotiations which are conducted above the nation state. Rather, public diplomacy will mostly take place in a less formalised process.

Values are key elements in public diplomacy and the primary currency of soft power.[364] Some authors predict that diplomacy as a whole will increasingly be about ideas in the future.[365] Others differentiate public diplomacy from traditional diplomacy in such a way that public diplomacy is about the building of relationships and dialogue with foreign audiences by concentrating on values while traditional diplomacy treats issues.[366] Although IR theories consider diplomacy as important, they rarely study the social process of relationship building. Constructivism, however, high-

360 *Tuch* (1990).
361 *Hocking* (2011) pp. 226ff.
362 *Castells* (2008) p. 91.
363 *Betsill/Corell* (2008).
364 *Nye* (2004) p. 31.
365 *Riordan* (2007) p. 188.
366 *Van Ham* (2008) p. 135.

lights norm and value diffusion through dialogue and persuasion, social interaction and perceptions.[367] Public diplomacy therefore fits well with it. As we have seen, constructivism as a point of departure offers insights on how images are constructed and reproduced.[368] Public diplomacy is "the projection in the international arena of the values and ideas of the public".[369] The concept can be combined with transnational networks allowing transnational actors to become vital but not necessarily on states' expenses. It offers a comprehensive analysis of transnational interactions.

3.1.1. Public diplomacy: Different approaches and definitions

Public diplomacy is often associated with many different activities, such as image cultivation, nation branding and propaganda. Although the interest on public diplomacy increased immensely after 9/11, it is not a new phenomenon and almost as old as diplomacy itself. The scientific discussion around the concept is very heterogeneous. Still, the basic distinction between conventional and public diplomacy is that the former concentrates on the official relationships between the representatives of states whereas the latter aims at foreign societies, such as non-official organisations and individuals.

The different approaches and definitions to public diplomacy have various roots. Although they all stem from social sciences, contributions come from IR theory, communications and public relations. Often the approaches vary according to process and actor level. Especially earlier concepts did not include transnational actors and considered states as the only actors pursuing public diplomacy. According to *Tuch*, for example, "public diplomacy is a government's process of communicating with foreign publics in an attempt to bring about understanding for its nation's ideas and ideals, its institutions and cultures, as well as its national goals and current policies".[370] Even recent works, still, stick to state-centrism. In analysing the public diplomacy of the German embassies *Ostrowski* argues that public diplomacy can merely be generated by states, and diplomats are per definition officials of the foreign ministry.[371] *Nye*, in contrast, differentiates be-

367 *Cross* (2013) pp. 3f.; *Scott-Smith* (2008) p. 186.

368 On IR theory and public diplomacy see *Van Ham* (2008), *Scott-Smith* (2008).

369 *Castells* (2008) p. 91.

370 *Tuch* (1990) p. 3.

371 *Ostrowski* (2010) p. 31.

tween three dimensions of public diplomacy whereby picking up *Leonard* and *Smewing's* categorisation of "news management", "strategic communication" and "relationship building".[372] Firstly, daily communication explains the context of domestic and foreign policy decisions to the foreign press. Secondly, strategic communication conveys a set of simple themes over a year involving political and advertising campaigns. Finally, long-lasting relationships with key individuals abroad are developed through scholarships, exchanges, training, conferences and access to media channels.[373] As generators of public diplomacy *Nye* assumes that non-state actors are at times involved in what he calls "indirect" public diplomacy as publics often view authority with scepticism. Governments therefore often efface and turn to widely trusted, even if hardly controllable private actors which are important communication channels.[374] Also *Manheim* considers several forms of diplomacy. Traditional diplomacy would take place between governments and personal diplomacy between diplomats defined as officials of the foreign ministry. Public diplomacy either involves communication between governments and people of other countries or is conducted in the form of "people-to-people" communication where it is necessary that the state initiated the activity of the semi-official transnational actor.[375] Similarly, *Signitzer* differentiates between hard public diplomacy conducted in the short-term by foreign ministries focusing on political information and influencing foreign target groups via persuasion by daily or weekly newspapers, radio and television as well as soft public diplomacy carried out by culture departments and ministerial foreign sections sometimes outsourced to semi-autonomous organisations (e.g. British Council, German *Goethe Institut*). It concentrates on long-term cultural communication and aims at mutual understanding and a presentation of the population on a whole by films, exchanges and art exhibitions among others.[376] *Scott-Smith* also treats this contracting out of activities by governments to the private sector when dealing with exchange programs. He points out that the communication channels are generally used to achieve some foreign political objective; hence, their establishment has a political intent which is either the promotion of mutual understanding or has a propagandistic and psychological warfare purpose. Mutual understanding aims at awareness and

372 *Leonard/Smewing* (2003) pp. 49ff.
373 *Nye* (2004) pp. 107ff.
374 *Nye* (2004) p. 113.
375 *Manheim* (1994).
376 *Signitzer* (1995) p. 74.

tolerance of other points of view leading to less conflict and contributing to the exchange of ideas and goods. Propaganda and political warfare refer to cultural-psychological characteristics and use the communication system of a target audience to reach an ideological, political or military goal. *Scott-Smith* regards the mutual understanding as "the public face" despite the continuous presence of propaganda and warfare which non-state actors help to make appear politically neutral.[377] *Simon* observed that experts of epistemic communities are utilised by governments to deal with overly sensitive political issues in the context of track two.[378] All these approaches include actors other than governments. However, they proceed from the assumption that actors are appointed by governments and used to conduct a "state's" public diplomacy rather than pursuing their own independent strategy. This is similar to the rationalists' belief assuming that states are the main driving forces in international processes using transnational actors for their purposes. Manipulation of transnational actors by states and utilizing them as a cloak for their own activities furthermore fits with the outlined *Neo-Gramscian* approach.[379]

Melissen deviates from the assumption of the governments' supremacy and introduces the term "new public diplomacy" referring to *Sharp's* definition of public diplomacy as "the process by which direct relations with people in a country are pursued to advance the interests and extend the values of those being represented".[380] This wider definition of public diplomacy considers governmental activities but also those of transnational actors.[381] Since diplomatic processes have changed, *Melissen* suggests a collaborative course of action in which various actors are necessary and which are essential for a "democratisation of diplomacy".[382] New public diplomacy is therefore not a one or two way information flow but a process of engagement in which learning takes place. Concerning good practices *Melissen* advocates a model where public diplomacy is not too closely tied to the foreign policy of a country since it works best when it builds trust and is unbound to the short-term moods of foreign policy.[383] Critics stress that the theoretical aspects of new public diplomacy, such as networks and narratives, rather have translated into the official arguments to justify public

377 *Scott-Smith* (2008) pp. 175ff.
378 *Simon* (2002) p. 168.
379 See Ch. 2.
380 *Sharp* (2007) p. 106; *Melissen* (2007b) p. 11.
381 *Melissen* (2007b) p. 12.
382 *Melissen* (2013) pp. 463f., (2007b) p. 5.
383 *Melissen* (2007b) pp. 14f.

diplomacy as practice of statecraft instead of transforming public diplomacy practice.[384] Similar to *Melissen*, *Gilboa* takes a wider approach towards public diplomacy and the involved actors. He developed three conceptual models.[385] The *Basic Cold War model* was originally applied by the two superpowers during the bloc confrontation to influence the other societies in the long run by international broadcasting. Today, it is applied in cases of autocratic regimes. In the *Domestic Public Relations model*, a government makes use of external professionals in the target country, such as PR firms or lobbyists, in order to support its cause. This model also bases on scientific knowledge and methods of public opinion research for which *Manheim* has coined the term "strategic diplomacy".[386] The Kuwaiti monarchs in exile, for example, hired a US PR firm during the second gulf war to receive support from the American public for the removal of Saddam Hussein from Kuwait. The *Non-state Transnational model* looks at NGOs and other actors, like individuals pursuing public diplomacy, using global news channels or media events to receive assistance for their matters. An opposition group in China, for instance, used this strategy to cultivate support for a pro-democratic campaign aiming at reforms of the Chinese government.[387] This model has similarities with *Keck* and *Sikkink's* transnational advocacy model as presented before.[388] Non-state actors are not necessarily viewed as instruments for the state to conduct public diplomacy. Like *Melissen's* model, it thus differs from the way *Signitzer*, *Nye* and *Manheim* see transnational actors in the process of public diplomacy. As *Nye* and *Leonard*, *Gilboa* picks up the dimensions of public diplomacy in terms of news management, strategic communication and relationship building. He links these elements to the involved actors. While news management is mainly led by governments, strategic communication is most effective when governments and non-governmental agencies work together. Relationship building is best carried out by NGOs only as these actors are well suited to conduct long-term tasks.[389]

For the implementation process of public diplomacy *McClellan* established a 5-phase-model starting with creating awareness in the target country for the interest of the advocate country via hard or soft public diploma-

384 *Hayden* (2013) p. 197.

385 *Gilboa* (2008), (2001), (2000).

386 *Manheim* (1994).

387 *Gilboa* (2008) pp. 59f.

388 See Ch. 2.3.

389 *Gilboa* (2008) pp. 72f.

cy. Secondly, a part of the population will gain interest in the subject and will build up knowledge through research and information events. Learning the language of the advocate country can be an essential element at this stage. Fourthly, these people can serve as disseminators in case the generated knowledge reflects their own interest or the interest of their country. Finally, the target country might take the actions desired by the advocate country if the position is sufficiently popular in the target country. Public diplomacy is hence a "strategy of communications that is goal-oriented, focused on results both short-term and long-term, and aimed at building a positive image of a country that will resonate in foreign public opinion".[390] These considerations resemble the norm diffusion model of *Finnemore* and *Sikkink*.[391]

Cowan and *Arsenault* describe three layers of public diplomacy: monologue, dialogue and collaboration. Each mode has specific advantages for a situation. Monologues in terms of one-way communication flows are often used for mass audiences in other countries. Although often treated with suspicion, monologues are important at critical moments and for daily communicating about policy. The Berlin speech of *John F. Kennedy* in connection with the construction of the Berlin Wall ending with the words "*Ich bin ein Berliner!*" is an example for this layer. Dialogue defined as "myriad situations in which ideas and information are exchanged and communication is reciprocal and multidirectional" is at times more productive and helps improve relationships across social boundaries. Germany's international broadcaster "*Deutsche Welle*", for example, launched an initiative which included dialogic communications. The "Dialogue of Cultures" transmitted discussions by prominent thinkers in Germany and the Arab World.[392] The third layer of public diplomacy concerns cross-national collaboration which is an "initiative ranging from short to long-term in which participants from different nations participate in a project together". It includes dialogue but also contains a structure enabling lasting relationships. While collaboration is often praised as useful in conflict resolution, it is also beneficial for democracy building, for increased social and political trust and for bridging racial, ethical and political divides.[393] Similarly, *Riordan* assumes that the new security agenda makes necessary a collaborative approach to foreign policy requiring dialogue-based public diplomacy by

390 *McClellan* (2004).

391 See Ch. 2.3.

392 *Zöllner* (2006) p. 174; *Cowan/Arsenault* (2008) pp. 11ff.

393 *Cowan/Arsenault* (2008) pp. 21f.

looking at international terrorism and nation building. Moreover, he views collaboration as relevant in other cases of global problems which cannot be resolved by single countries and require different actors operating transnationally. While public diplomacy has always been associated with selling policies, values and national images, *Riordan* assumes that public diplomacy will not just be "presentational". Rather, it will become part of the policy making process. This claim derives from the finding that Western values and norms are not unproblematic. Often associated with US hegemony they are perceived as tools by the target audience to preserve Western political and economic dominance. Involved actors therefore need to enjoy access and credibility to solve problems. *Riordan* considers non-state actors playing a key role in this process as they can be more effective when perceived as distant from a government. Furthermore, dialogue allows different ideas to be valid and engages at eye-level instead of imposing values and practices from the top-down. A building block in *Riordan's* approach to public diplomacy is networking as opposed to a hierarchical approach showing similarities to *Hocking's* network approach as presented below. In assuming that collaboration in the practical manifestations of democracy assistance and conflict management is part of dialogue-based public diplomacy, *Riordan* differs from *Cowan* and *Arsenault*, who differentiate between collaboration and dialogue. Although collaboration, in their view, includes dialogue, collaboration intends to establish long-lasting relationships. However, the definition of "long-lasting" is questionable and semantic as in most cases it will be difficult to anticipate how and if a relationship will develop. Dialogue with the one-sided intention to avoid relationship building rather appears to be monologue then. Although in the future much of the diplomatic work will be done by non-state actors, *Riordan* expects traditional diplomats and governments to contribute to coordination and to a larger strategy. Moreover, governments could possibly offer financial and technical support. The diplomat posted in the specific country could provide expert knowledge on the country. He could also identify and facilitate opportunities representing a node in the established networks.[394]

Cull's approach treats the perceived proximity of the public diplomatic activity from the government and the credibility that can stem from it. *Cull* established a taxonomy of public diplomacy distinguishing five elements. "Listening" which has always been part of traditional diplomacy and intelligence work, refers to "an actor's attempt to manage the interna-

394 *Riordan* (2007) pp. 187ff.

tional environment by collecting and collating data about publics and their opinions overseas and using the data to redirect its policy or its wider public diplomacy approach accordingly". "Advocacy" is defined as "the attempt to manage the international environment by undertaking an international communication activity to actively promote a particular policy, idea, or the actor's general interest in the minds of a foreign public". "Cultural diplomacy" is regarded as an "actors attempt to manage the international environment through making its cultural resources and achievements known overseas and/or facilitating cultural transmission abroad". *Cull* equates cultural diplomacy and cultural relations. "Exchange diplomacy" he defines as "an actor's attempt to manage the international environment by sending its citizens overseas and reciprocally accepting citizens from overseas for a period of study and/or acculturation". Finally, "international news broadcasting" is the "actor's attempt to manage the international environment by using the technologies of radio, television, and the internet to engage with foreign publics". It can overlap with the other public diplomacy elements. All types of public diplomacy have different time frames and information flows: Listing can be short- and long-term. The flow of information is inward to analysts and the policy processes. Advocacy is a short-term activity with an outward information flow. Cultural diplomacy has a long-term time frame and an outward information flow. Exchange diplomacy is practiced on a long-term basis. And the information flows inwardly and outwardly. Finally, international broadcasting has a medium-term time frame and the information flows outwardly but from a news bureaucracy. *Cull* considers listening as the most important duty of a public diplomat with the new media facilitating these efforts.[395] For the credibility of advocacy, government proximity is suggested, whereas cultural diplomacy works better when perceived as distant.[396] The state-centrism in *Cull's* approach is problematic. However, similar to *Riordan's* findings, it is interesting that perceived distance from a government can be helpful in certain cases. This implies from a governmental perspective that certain activities could be "outsourced" to transnational actors in order to create a governmental distance. In *Cross's* approach the credibility rather stems from whether the public diplomatic strategy is consistent with the identity of the sender. She defines the process of public diplomacy as "the communication of narratives that embody key norms about society". Narratives, i.e. "stories of the temporal character of human experience" become legiti-

395 *Cull* (2011) p. 5.
396 *Cull* (2008) pp. 32ff.

mate when they stem from the identity of the people involved. As already outlined, identities are social constructs. They perform the important function of telling you and others who you are (or want to be).[397] *Cross* expects a "continuous feedback loop" between the external image and the identity. Public diplomacy is perceived as credible only when it mirrors the identity of the people it represents. Narratives shape these perceptions and convey norms reflecting greater values within society. Public diplomacy therefore is a diffusion process of norms by entrepreneurs (public diplomatic actors) to a foreign audience. These constructivist-lead considerations allow making some claims about the successfulness of public diplomacy strategies: if the external audience finds the norms appealing and understands the narrative, it might act favourably with policies towards the public diplomacy generator.[398] It will be necessary to determine whether transnational actors transmit their own values when generating public diplomacy or rather repeat the values and policy ideas of their home state.

Hocking identifies several components offering a complex perspective on public diplomacy. [399] The first thread is democratic accountability in terms of believing in the necessity for direct public involvement in diplomacy. In line with this idea *Castells* assumes that states may also transfer power and resources to lower political levels and NGOs in order to further integrate civil society into the political process.[400] The second component of public diplomacy can be associated with the claim for open diplomacy referring to the spanning of global networks, the expansion of social relations including financial markets and terrorist groups as well as the compression of time and space. The state-centred view of diplomacy is thus increasingly challenged by forms of multilateral diplomacy involving state actors, international and NGOs among others.[401] Others stress that this is not a recent trend. *Melissen* points out that already in 1917-1918 *Wilson* and *Lenin* were competing on what he calls "soft power level" before both their countries did the same in military and economic fields. "The battle of values and ideas that dominated international relations in the second half of the twenties century evolved into the competition in the sphere of hard power, and not vice versa." During the Cold War, the United States, the Soviet Union and the three European major powers pursued traditional diplomacy and

397 *Van Ham* (2008) p. 145.
398 *Cross* (2013) pp. 5ff.
399 *Hocking* (2007) pp. 29ff.
400 *Castells* (2008) p. 88.
401 *Hocking* (2004) p. 94.

public diplomacy on parallel tracks. However, due to the domination of international relations' theory by realist thought in viewing international relations in terms of economic and military power, scholars have given, until recently, little attention to the systematic study of public diplomacy.[402] These considerations reflect the assumption of constructivism seeing ideas, if not as more important than certainly as equal to hard power. As per *Hocking*, a third piece in the public diplomacy debate is the growing impact of communication and information technology linked to foreign policy and diplomacy. These three threads are related and allow a redefinition of public diplomacy with respect to an "active role for publics rather than as passive objects of government foreign policy strategies".[403] The fourth thread in the public diplomacy debate is the impact of the media acting in a complex manner as agenda-setter in international politics and as gatekeeper determining and regulating flows of information to publics. The fifth thread concerns the possibility of states "rebranding" themselves in the global marketplace and the image of states in international politics. Regarding the matter of what is meant by "public" in public diplomacy, *Hocking* states that "contemporary analysis of public diplomacy rests on different perceptions of what constitutes the *public* and where it fits in diplomatic practice". The public can be viewed as a target of influence and a generator of pressure. Moreover, public diplomacy can be increasingly defined as diplomacy *by* rather than *of* publics while others see the public as a consumer of diplomacy referring to the twin forces of tourism and terrorism.[404] *Hocking* refers to *Nye's* soft power concept.[405] While hard power relates to the threat or use of military force, soft power rests on the ability to shape the preferences of others.[406] The sources of soft power are culture, values and policies. *Mead* added "sticky power" as the power of economic attraction, which can be referred to the economic well-being of the USA resulting from free trade and the Bretton Woods institutions.[407] While some equate soft power with public diplomacy, *Hocking* suggests instead that there is a public diplomacy of hard, sticky and soft power.[408] Some authors oppose this. In their view, public diplomacy in contrast to soft power intends a cultural dialogue between different social communities on the

402 *Melissen* (2007b) p. 4.
403 *Hocking* (2007) p. 30.
404 *Hocking* (2007) p. 32.
405 *Nye* (1990) pp. 193ff.; see Ch. 2.3.2.
406 *Nye* (2004) pp. 5, 11ff.
407 *Mead* (2004) p. 48; *Hocking* (2007) p. 33.
408 *Hocking* (2007) p. 34.

hope of shared meaning and understanding. Public diplomacy aims at communicating and listening while soft power convinces and declares.[409] This opinion ignores, however, that the involved actors might have differing intentions when pursuing public diplomacy. It also cannot explain for what purpose the sharing of meaning and understanding should happen and why it should always have an end in itself. These considerations can also be connected to whether public diplomacy is viewed in being in the national interest only or in the common interest.[410]

Hocking sees "two worlds" of public diplomacy referring to a state-centred, hierarchical model and a network model. Although both models rest on arguments about the significance of soft power, they imply different understandings of soft power and its relationship to public diplomacy. The first model stresses the centrality of intergovernmental relations, in which foreign ministries act as gatekeeper, monitoring interactions *between* domestic and international policy environments and funnelling information between them by using top-down information flows. Particularly after "9/11" public diplomacy arrangements referred to this model including programs of foreign exchanges, and such to improve public-private collaboration. However, this model rests on established realist considerations and "remains a technique for achieving policy objectives". The application of the network imagery in the context of public diplomacy is relatively new.[411] It overcomes the public-private distinction. Regarding both types of actors as equally important is a constructivists' thought.[412] Network perspectives recognise the usefulness of labour division between actors in specific policy settings and understand actor advantages.[413] We return to the basic network definition outlined in chapter 2 as "a set of relatively stable relationships which are of non-hierarchical and interdependent nature linking a variety of actors, who share common interests with regard to a policy and who exchange resources to pursue these shared interests acknowledging that co-operation is the best way to achieve common goals".[414] *Hocking* refers to *Reinicke's* concept of Global public policy networks (GPPN) for describing the public-private relationship. Other network forms might be included in the GPPN.[415] These "conglomerates"

409 *Castells* (2008) p. 91.
410 *Melissen* (2013) p. 442.
411 C.f. *Riordan* (2007) pp. 190ff.; *Castells* (2008) pp. 87f.
412 See Ch. 2.3.1.
413 *Hocking* (2011) p. 231.
414 *Börzel* (1998) p. 254.
415 See Ch. 2.3.1.

should be considered when analysing the network structures of public diplomacy. The outlined network definition needs some adaptation with regards to the network members' cooperation, the assumed stability and the non-hierarchy of relationships. *Hocking's* model does not per se support a "conflict stereotype" between state and non-state actors. The relationship among these actors is rather characterised by "co-opetition" describing the duality of competition and cooperation and originating from market economy.[416] According to *Esty* and *Geradin*, competition between governmental and NGOs takes place when the latter acts as intellectual competitor in the policy making process, coming up with creative solutions and "selling" them to the public via the media. Transnational actors and governments cooperate, on the contrary, when transnational actors provide certain resources to governments contributing to the decision-making process, such as information.[417] The basic policy network definition furthermore assumes a common interest among network members and relative stability. Some authors raise the possibility that networks do not need to be very constant and self-contained but rather diffuse with unplanned participations and activities.[418] Networks can be specified according to the degree of governmental presence. *Coleman* and *Perl* differentiate between multilevel governance, intergovernmental negotiations, private regimes and "loose couplings".[419] The interaction between transnational and governmental actors decreases from type to type. In the loose couplings variant "the network often resembles an 'issue network' based on mutual interest in pooling knowledge and ideas rather than a highly developed sense of shared values".[420] Networks are also not necessarily uniform in perusing a certain objective and conflicts can occur among network members.[421] *Falkner* analyses various public-private constellations

416 *Hocking* (2011) p. 231; *Esty/Geradin* (2000) p. 237 referring to *Brandenburg/Nalebuff* (1996).

417 *Esty/Geradin* (2000) p. 253.

418 *Hilhorst* (2008) pp. 297ff.

419 *Coleman/Perl* (1999) pp. 701ff.; *Hocking* (2011) p. 231. Multilevel governance *Coleman/Perl* (1999) define as "the complex patterns of relationships between supranational and national institutions (…)". Civil society actors, civil servants and politicians work here together. It emerges in the EU but also in other international surroundings (p. 701). In intergovernmental negotiations, heads of governments cooperate to find an agreement at the supranational level in the absence of autonomous supranational institutions (p. 704). See Ch. 2.2.2. on private regimes.

420 *Hocking* (2011) p. 231.

421 *Smith* (1990) pp. 279-81; *Reinicke* (2000) xvi.

and particularly the development of a corporist policy community at the European level.[422] According to her, issue networks, policy communities and corporatist policy communities vary according to the degree of formal inclusion of the private actors into the policy making process. Issue networks are characterised as open for admitting new participants and permeable involving different types of private actors with competence in certain policy relevant questions whose integration into the policy making process is not fixed. Informal consultation among network actors takes place.[423] This "permeability" and "fluidity" is what differentiates the activity environment of non-state actors from that of international organisations.[424] While all network members might want to collaborate, they might not share the reason for participating.[425] In the issue network case, it is thus less a common objective that the network actors try to achieve. Rather, actors profit from the network for different reasons. In issue networks politicians and officials are assumed to have low presence.[426] This is problematic. The domination of NGOs jars with the assumption of an equal understanding of public and private actors assumed by constructivist thought. The resources brought by actors to the networking process might be ideational or material. They can vary according to the involved actor. While public actors are regarded to have authority over the implementation and enforcement of rules as well as the ability to generate financial resources, civil society actors have neither. Their most important resources are information on the international political situations in diverse problem areas, knowledge on reasons and solutions of such problems as well as recognised professional or moral authority reflecting in the credibility of their information.[427] Post-Marxist add social and cultural resources. *Bourdieu* who coined the term "social capital" regards as resources education, being well connected with others and having a key role in a network.[428] Others mention the access to information channels and being able to es-

422 *Falkner* (1998) p. 1.

423 *Falkner* (1998) pp. 43ff.: While in corporatist policy community's actors are fully involved in the legislative and executive policy process, in policy communities consultation between private and public actors is still stable but less formal. It takes place, for instance, in committees. The term "issue network" goes back to *Heclo* (1978) p. 102.

424 *Dijkzeul/DeMars* (2011) pp. 218ff; *DeMars/Dijkzeul* (2015) p. 19.

425 *Fisher* (2013) p. 145.

426 *Coleman/Perl* (1999) p. 706.

427 *Schimmelpfennig* (2010) p. 122.

428 *Bourdieu* (1983) pp. 190f.

tablish networks and relationships.[429] Supply and demand of a resource result in different power relationships among actors.[430] Economists stress that several conditions can lead to an actor's competitive advantage or a key position in the network. The resource should be valuable, rare, and inimitable and cannot be substituted.[431] This is the case in exchange networks but not all resources are exchangeable. In influence and communication networks power can result from the high number of relationships and the power of the connected actors as well as from the centrality and the prestige of the network member. Some network members might be unable to communicate directly, and others might control communication channels giving them "bridging functions". Although networks differ from hierarchical structures, they might not be hierarchy free.[432]

For the operation in a network environment *Hocking* suggests a "multi-stakeholder" diplomacy where state and non-state actors are brought together in bilateral and multilateral diplomatic processes and where non-state actors are not viewed as *consumers*, as statist diplomatic models suggest, but as *producers* of diplomacy. In this context, the establishment of multidimensional networks are assumed to contain multitudinous forms of actors and relationships in which "audience", "collaborator" or network "participant" are rather fluid. These images can also include strong ties between governments and transnational actors.[433] "Representational" difficulties can occur when governments have to decide with whom to engage in the diplomatic process. Moreover, traditional rules such as the principle of non-interference in internal affairs of the host country (Article 41 Vienna Convention on Diplomatic Relations and Article 2[7] UN Charter) can be in the way when it comes to public diplomacy strategies demanding relationships with foreign non-state actors.[434] The process taken place within the networks *Hocking* describes as catalytic diplomacy.[435] Firstly, in cases of agenda setting, non-state-actors help states to frame the agenda and encourage their action by providing knowledge resources. Secondly, non-state actors support in international peace-building, peace maintenance and development-assistance activities as states delegate activities to them. And lastly, joint-management takes place between NGOs and governments when it

429 *Jansen* (2006) p. 29.
430 *Schimmelpfennig* (2010) pp. 121f.
431 *Barney* (1991) pp. 106ff.
432 *Hocking* (2011) pp. 231f.; *Jansen* (2006) pp. 29, 178.
433 *Fisher* (2013) pp. 140ff., 151.
434 *Hocking* (2011) pp. 232ff.
435 *Hocking* (2007) p. 38; *Reinicke/Deng* (2000) pp. 27ff.

comes to institution building in developing countries.[436] Modes two and three correspond with *Cowan* and *Arsenault's* layers of the public diplomacy and *Riordan's* model in terms of cross-national collaboration in conflict management and the development of institutions.[437]

In sum, most of the approaches to public diplomacy presented above are consistent with each other as they shed light on different characteristics. Hence, they can be integrated in a model which will serve as a framework of analysis for the German political foundations' transnational interaction in the following chapters.

3.1.2. Related concepts to public diplomacy

Often propaganda is defined in such way that public diplomacy is included.[438] According to *Manheim*, strategic public diplomacy is "the practice of propaganda in the earliest sense of the term, but enlightened by half a century of empirical research into human motivation and behaviour".[439] Propaganda is seen as a one-way information flow generating publicity and as different from two-way communication or the dissemination of information.[440] It is also viewed as the reinforcement or change of public opinion, domestic or foreign. "White propaganda" showing openly the source is distinguished from "black propaganda" concealing the source. Whether propaganda is anti-diplomatic depends on its content.[441] The political intention in public diplomacy is often assumed to be propaganda or psychological warfare. Propaganda as practiced by the USA within the context of World War Two, identified opinion leaders as targets for information campaigns and disseminators of information.[442] Others differentiate public diplomacy from propaganda as the first has a dialogue, liberal communication and listening element whereas the latter manipulates, lacks credibility and tends to close the audience's perspectives. Both try to persuade the addressee.[443] Although one might find that propaganda is different in its key features, it should be included in a model of public diplomacy. Certainly,

---

436 *Hocking* (2011) p. 230.

437 *Cowan/Arsenault* (2008) pp. 21ff.; *Riordan* (2007), similar *Fisher* (2013) pp. 143ff.

438 *Berridge/James* (2003) p. 218; *Kunczik* (1989) p. 166.

439 *Manheim* (1994) p. 7.

440 *Hunt/Grunig* (1994) p. 9.

441 *Berridge/James* (2003) p. 215.

442 *Scott-Smith* (2008) p. 177.

443 *Ohmstedt* (1993) pp. 2ff.; *Melissen* (2007b) pp. 17ff.; *Nye* (2004) p. 107.

propaganda has a manipulative connotation. It is less about informing truthfully than about the clever positioning of information. It has a pejorative character due to its monopolisation in dictatorships. Still, drawing a line between different forms of communication is problematic and a broader concept of public diplomacy is more useful. Especially neutrality as a main criterion of demarcation is difficult to handle as it depends on the intention of the actor and on the perception of the addressee. Therefore, equating public diplomacy and propaganda is just as inadequate. Like traditional diplomacy having different characteristics, propaganda can be one of several public diplomacy components.

Nation-branding and public diplomacy frequently overlap. Nation-branding mainly focuses on international marketing and is much more extensive than public diplomacy. It concentrates on the mobilisation of all a nation's forces in order to promote its image abroad and to project its identity. Thus, it is more holistic than public diplomacy which instead focuses on the promotion and maintenance of international relations.[444] Nation-branding makes use of agenda setting theory originated in communication science by proactively influencing the media agenda using concepts like framing or priming.[445] Branding and diplomacy are similar in terms of combining foreign policy goals with internal soft power strategies. Both focus on personal and institutional relationship building and dialogue with foreign audiences by concentrating on values while classic diplomacy gives attention to issues.[446] Nation-branding mainly concentrates on economic goals, such as export promotion, foreign direct investments and tourism.[447] Reputation and image of a country *Anholt* measures annually in the Nation Brands Index.[448] Branding has gained increasing significance on the national agendas.[449] German variants in this field are the marketing campaigns "*Deutschland – Land der Ideen*" ("Germany – Country of ideas") and "*Du bist Deutschland*" ("You are Germany"). Both started in the mid-2000s. The "*Deutschland – Land der Ideen*" offensive was originally initiated by the German government and the industry for the World Football Championship in Germany in 2006 and was later extended to a long-term

444 *Melissen* (2007b) pp. 20f.
445 *Ostrowski* (2010) p. 36 with citations.
446 *Van Ham* (2008) p. 135.
447 *Olins* (2007) pp. 172ff.
448 *Anholt* (2005).
449 *Olins* (2007) p. 178.

initiative in order to strengthen Germany as economic and research location.[450]

Cultural diplomacy or cultural communication is a part of the public diplomacy spectrum.[451] Cultural diplomacy is the "exchange of ideas, information, art and other aspects of culture among nations and the people to foster mutual understanding".[452] It has a long-term component and is not focused on the explanation of short-term policies.[453] Its instruments are exchanges with writers and artists, the support of literary and scientific publications as well as the dissemination of music and art. During the Cold War cultural diplomacy was intensely practiced by the USA and Germany as a weapon against communist ideology.[454]

Public diplomacy is often considered a foreign variant of public relations.[455] Although public diplomacy comprises much more aspects, public relations can be a component of it.[456] From a PR perspective, *Hunt* and *Grunig* developed the press agentry/publicity model purposing propaganda, and the public information model aiming at the dissemination of information. Both models use one-way communication. The two-way asymmetric model focuses on scientific persuasion, while the two-way symmetric model purposes mutual understanding.[457] In sum, they give impetus to the public diplomacy debate. The clear differentiation between the concepts is often difficult and it can only be estimated on a case by case basis.

3.2. The integrated model of public diplomacy

The presented approaches of public diplomacy and related concepts will now be integrated into one model of public diplomacy without repeating the single approaches in detail. The systematisation will serve as a framework for studying the international activities of the German political foundations in the following chapters.

---

450 *Körber* (2009) p. 185; *Karten* (2008) p. 172.
451 *Cull* (2008); differently *Stone* (2011) p. 244.
452 *Cummings* (2003) p. 1.
453 *Ostrowski* (2010) p. 35.
454 *Schneider* (2007) pp. 157f.
455 *Kunczik* (1989) p. 169.
456 *Gilboa* (2008).
457 *Hunt/Grunig* (1994) p. 9.

3.2.1. Generators

In order to analyse the public diplomacy of the German political foundations, a model is necessary, which includes actors other than governments. Those models can therefore be dropped where governments are the only generators of diplomacy. This is the case when underlying the public diplomacy definition of *Tuch*, the basic cold war model and the domestic PR model of *Gilboa* as well as *Hocking's* hierarchy model.[458] A constructivist starting point allows taking an unbiased look at the interaction of states and transnational actors by not assuming that one actor is more important than the other. Moreover, it acknowledges an independent policy making by transnational actors but also the exploitation of these organisations for states' purposes. In several public diplomacy models governments use transnational actors as tools for their own policies.[459] The government might even use rhetorically the contemporary narratives on the new public diplomacy to justify its strategic public diplomacy.[460] It cannot be anticipated whether transnational public diplomacy is conducted for the state or whether transnational actors pursue their independent strategy as *Melissen* and *Gilboa* assume in their transnational public diplomacy model.[461] As dependence of these actors might vary from case to case, *Hocking's* network model where the roles of actors are not fixed is most appropriate to analyse the possible complexity of relationships among actors.[462]

3.2.2. Types, dimension and layers

Following *Signitzer*, public diplomacy can be divided into two types: hard public diplomacy conducted by governments and soft public diplomacy undertaken by non-state actors.[463] The focus of this analysis will therefore be on the second type. Connecting these types of diplomacy to *Nye's* dimensions of daily communication, strategic communication and long-lasting relationships,[464] daily communication which mainly concerns press work is part of hard public diplomacy. This also conforms to *Gilboa's*

458 *Tuch* (1990); *Gilboa* (2008); *Hocking* (2011).
459 *Nye* (2004), (2008); *Signitzer* (1995); *Manheim* (1994).
460 *Hayden* (2013).
461 *Melissen* (2007b); *Gilboa* (2008).
462 *Hocking* (2011).
463 *Signitzer* (1995).
464 *Nye* (2004), (2008).

framework of analysis which regards news management including advocacy and international broadcasting as closely linked to the practicing government. Strategic communication can be conducted by public and private actors whereas relationship-building is fostered by non-governmental actors only.[465] We therefore divide soft power public diplomacy into one-way communication and two-way communication. Others deny that one-way communication flows are part of public diplomacy.[466] However, the wider approach taken in this study includes propaganda into the framework. Following *Cowan* and *Arsenault's*, monologue can be part of the model but also two-way dialogic communication.[467] Two-way communication can be asymmetric in the case of persuasion and symmetric in terms of collaboration and mutual understanding.[468]

3.2.3. Addressees and networks

The addressees of public diplomacy differ according to the involved public diplomacy instruments. They can be the general public, journalists and media as well as specific disseminators, i.e. stakeholders of political, economic, scientific, cultural or civil societal influence. Among them are business leaders, youth groups, students, artists and non-governmental organisations. They may also include official representatives of the target state, such as members of parliaments, regional and local authorities or municipal institutions. Target audiences of public diplomacy may vary according to the structure of the target country, the possibility to access specific groups, windows of opportunity as well as the intended objective of the generator. *Hocking's* network model allows analysing the interchange between transnational and various public levels.[469] It will be looked at whichever is more central or dominant in the public diplomacy process and how resources are exchanged. Actor positions in the network, actor advantages as well as cooperation and competition among actors will be considered as far as data is available. Whether the connection between the actors is rather loose and resembles an "issue network" or is highly developed will be evaluated.

---

465 *Gilboa* (2008).
466 *Melissen* (2007b).
467 *Cowan/Arsenault* (2008).
468 *Grunig/Hunt* (1994).
469 *Hocking* (2007).

Table 3.1: Integrated model of public diplomacy[470]

Type	**Generators**	**Instrument/ Sample activity**	**Information flow**	**Dimension**	**Scope**	**Purpose**
Soft Public diplomacy	Governmental and non-governmental actors	– Political campaigns – Advertising campaigns	Monologue, one-way	Strategic communication, Propaganda	Mid-term (between few weeks and few months)	Proactive, dissemination of information
Soft Public diplomacy	Mainly non-governmental actors	– Scholarships – (Academic) Exchanges – Seminars – Conferences – Press Trips – Media Seminars – Cultural diplomacy – Think Tank events – Receptions	Dialogue, two-way: asymmetric and symmetric	Long-lasting relationships, Establishment of networks	Long-term (years)	Building favourable relationships and collaboration

3.2.4. Collaborative public diplomacy

While the model so far focuses on public diplomacy in monologue and dialogue form, it is necessary to also look at the practical aspects of public diplomacy and how it can be undertaken. This is often termed as cross-national collaboration. In contrast to *Cowan* and *Arsenault's* assumption, it is not a third form of public diplomacy however, but rather as *Riordan* points out part of dialogue-based public diplomacy. It can be especially found in projects of democracy building and conflict resolution and corresponds to the catalytic diplomatic activity described by *Hocking.*[471]

The following section will introduce official German public diplomacy concentrating on the Federal Foreign Office, the *Auswärtiges Amt* (AA). It is the main state actor of German public diplomacy and operates alongside the *Stiftungen*. It touches upon the question of who the originator of public diplomacy is and whether transnational actors are involved in the implementation of the public strategy. On this basis, I will analyse in chapter 5 whether the German political foundations are involved in this strategy.

470 Author's diagram.

471 *Cowan/Arsenault* (2008); *Riordan* (2007); *Hocking* (2011).

3.3. German public diplomacy: The Federal Foreign Office

In 2015, German public diplomacy was regarded as less developed compared to the public diplomacy ambitions of other states. The historical burden of terms such as propaganda and marketing during the time of National Socialism were reasons for the German reluctance.[472] Notwithstanding, the Federal Republic was active in the field of public diplomacy from its establishment onwards.

The German lack of approval in other Western countries after World War Two and the setup of *politische Öffentlichkeitsarbeit* (political public relations), the German variant of public diplomacy, accompanied the federal foreign relations from the beginning in 1949.[473] Government subsidised institutes were created with the intention to win back credibility and to reestablish foreign contacts remaining the main objective of German foreign cultural policy until the 1960s. [474] From the late 1950s onwards, the AA integrated also the German political foundations as intermediary organisations for their foreign cultural policy.[475] However, they never became proper mediating organisations (*Mittlerorganisationen*) as the official partner organisations for the AA in its implementation of cultural relations and education policy (*Auswärtige Kultur- und Bildungspolititk [AKBP]*).[476] The construct of the *Mittlerorganisations* stems from the idea that cultural policy should be decentralised and pluralistic.[477] Among these organisations are the *Goethe-Institut*, the *Deutscher Akademischer Austauschdienst (DAAD)*, the *Alexander von Humboldt-Stiftung* and the *Institut für Auslandsbeziehungen*. A successful example of exchange diplomacy is the Franco-German rapprochement which started in 1945 with the exchange of school children, later included town twinning, student exchanges, the proliferation of the *Goethe Institutes* and the *Instituts français* and the launch of the Franco-German TV channel, ARTE (Association Relative à la Télévision Européenne).[478] Another important element of German foreign cultural policy in the early times was the anti-communist activity against the German Democratic Republic (GDR) and the Soviet ideology.[479] Nothing less than

472 *Karten* (2008) p. 163; *Maaß* (2009) p. 25.
473 *Melissen* (2007b) p. 9.
474 *Karten* (2008) p. 163; *Schneider* (2007) pp. 157f.; *Kaiser* (1998) p. 200.
475 *Singer* (2003) p. 12 fn. 24.
476 See Ch. 5.1.2.; on the *Mittlerorganisations* and transnational actors see Ch. 2.1.
477 *Singer* (2003) p. 40; *Harnischfeger* (2007) p. 719.
478 *Cull* (2008) pp. 40ff.
479 *Singer* (2003) p. 11, fn. 19.

a public diplomacy campaign was the *Hallstein Doctrine* and its supporting information initiative. During the Cold War, the two German states competed for recognition in countries around the world and where "preoccupied by their Cold War en miniature".[480] Developed as a West German foreign policy concept in 1955, the doctrine stated that the establishment of diplomatic relations of third countries with the GDR was seen as "unfriendly act". Less a doctrine than a collection of emergency methods, it included a wide variety of responses, such as economic sanctions and the termination of diplomatic relations. According to Bonn, the Federal Republic was the only legitimate representative of the German state as the GDR had no democratic legitimacy.[481] It cannot be ruled out that German transnational actors where not only used to win back credibility but also to support the "cultural Cold War". Partnerships between governments and the private sector focused against communism and private organisations helped to give the illusion of political neutrality.[482] While in the 1950s West Germany had hold the better position by enjoying diplomatic relations with the main European Countries, East Germany had to be satisfied with the unofficial levels of diplomacy, such as chambers of commences.[483] At the end of the 1950s, the competition for diplomatic contracts shifted towards the developing countries of which many became independent from the colonial powers at that time. A trigger was the economic and development aid promised by both states. Although charitable thoughts were motives for the West German development aid, it was still used as a method to gain influence and friends due to the fear that population growth and poverty could promote communism.[484] Still, the concept of giving aid attached less value to ideology at that time and did not ask for political benefits in return. The politicisation of development assistance finally took place in 1961 shortly after the establishing conference of the non-aligned states in Yugoslavia. By cutting back development aid for states recognising the GDR, the *Hallstein Doctrine* was for the first time in-

480 *Gray* (2003) p. 226.

481 *Gray* (2003) p. 5; the term "Hallstein-Doctrine" goes back to the then state-secretary at the Federal Foreign Office *Walther Hallstein*, who is not the founder of the doctrine. It was created by *Wilhelm Grewe*, at that time head of the AA's political section.

482 *Scott-Smith* (2008) p. 182; *Singer* (2003) p. 40.

483 *Gray* (2003) p. 222.

484 AAPA B58-IIIB1 Bd. 387 23/10/1963, 26/10/1964, 20/05/1965; critically AAPA B58-IIIB1 Bd. 651 15/03/1965.

tensified.[485] Moreover, in 1961 the Federal Republic established the Ministry for Economic Cooperation back then provided with little power compared to the AA and the Ministry of Economics. By 1964 the AA had devised a strategy to link development aid and the *Hallstein Doctrine* more effectively by not just threatening to break diplomatic contacts but by involving "flexible measures" to withhold aid. However, in the following time the doctrine was applied less and less. It came to an end by the late 1960s due to the hesitation to use it. After 1970 the *Hallstein Doctrin* was given up completely.[486]

Against the background of "9/11", the troubled relations with the Islamic world and the "War on Terror" as well as the downturn of foreign perceptions, public diplomacy became more important in Germany and other countries in recent times.[487] In 2000, ambassador *Paschke* inspected 14 German embassies in Europe in order "to determine how the demands on our embassies in EU countries have changed".[488] The "*Paschke Report*" concludes that "embassies face new, additional challenges, particularly in the realm of public diplomacy" which targets foreign publics for explaining the German position in the European integration process and promoting Germany as an investment and business location. According to *Paschke*, public diplomacy was a number one priority and was "reaching out to people in the host country, actively communicating through ongoing dialogue with all sections of the informed public in order to generate interest in and understanding for both our European and bilateral concerns".[489] From 1998 onwards, the German government began to focus on the medial representation of Germany abroad which also concerned the AA's role and the involvement of new media and the internet. As one of the ministry's core tasks, it stressed the shaping of public opinion concerning decision makers in politics, economy and civil society of partner countries as well as in international organisations. Also, the *Mittlerorganisationen* should take part in this process. Media politics as part of AKBP aimed at the development of global networks and at the promotion of dialogue, exchange and cooperation. It also had the objective to prevent conflicts, promote democracy and free media.[490]

485 *Gray* (2003) pp. 116-39.
486 *Gray* (2003) pp. 225f.
487 *Maaß* (2011) p. 593; *Melissen* (2007b) pp. 6ff.
488 *Paschke* (2000); AA (2002a), author's translation.
489 Paschke (2000); commenting *Pamment* (2013) p. 15, *Melissen* (2007b) p. 11, *Hocking* (2007) p. 40.
490 BT (2002) pp. 1, 6f.; AA (2000a) pp. 8f., author's translation.

From 2003 onwards, the AA conducted a more systematic public diplomacy approach supported by several organisational modifications, such as the incorporation of the department of foreign press work into the AA as well as the establishment of a department for culture and communication mainly responsible for the German image cultivation abroad.[491] In recent times, the AA's public diplomacy aimed at "positioning Germany widely and as holistically as possible in the mind of the world population. A good image gives Germany political and economic (...) options. (...) To promote Germany means underlining important strengths without exaggeration and fraudulence. Hence, public diplomacy is only successful on a long-term basis when it has authenticity and is convincing".[492] Next to the economic objectives, such as representing Germany as research and investment location and the promotion of German products, Germany should be presented as reliable partner. Moreover, values should be furthered such as democracy and freedom.[493] The public diplomacy of the AA mainly addressed countries of strategic importance, not by the need for an image correction. Its geographic concentrations have changed over time. While in 1980, Western Europe was the most important target region, the AA focused in the last decade on Central-, East and South Europe. China, India and Japan and other strategic partners in Asia became new economical focal points. In the Arab and Islamic world, the Foreign Office concentrated on political and cultural dialogue. Addressees of public diplomacy were foreign governments and diplomats and broad levels of foreign population, such as journalists, scientists and other opinion leaders of civil society serving as disseminators. The main public diplomatic methods of the *Auswärtiges Amt* were political public relations, AKBP as well as location marketing and promotion of investment.[494] Political public relations contained the analysis of the German image abroad which subsequently found its way into the media work of the AA's headquarters and the missions abroad. This included, among others, the provision of information on Germany via print publications or online as well as journalists' exchange programmes.[495] In 2015, AKBP focused on imparting the German culture abroad and on promoting tolerance and democratic values as well as the prevention of conflict. This comprised activities such as international cul-

491 *Karten* (2008) pp. 163ff.
492 AA (2005) p. 193, author's translation.
493 *Karten* (2008) pp. 176f.
494 AA (2012a); *Karten* (2008) pp. 178ff.
495 *Bettzuege* (2007) pp. 240f.

tural dialogue, cultural exchange programs, and the promotion of the German language and of Germany as research location.[496] German cultural policy concentrated hence on culture as an end in itself but also on the promotion of other policy areas and image cultivation. Some mediating organisations differentiated between the two fields. Their attitude towards public diplomacy was often not very positive.[497] This might stem from the general idea that foreign cultural policy should rather be independent from authorities and distant from policy.[498] The German government named five strategies of AKBP: a dialogue approach, cultural understanding and value orientation, target group orientation, networking and public-private partnerships.[499] The AA but mainly the Federal Ministry for German Economic Affairs and Energy (BMWi) were active in location marketing and promotion of investment advertising Germany as a site for business. *Germany Trade&Invest* a government initiative and private company delt with attracting foreign investors, marketing and communication.[500]

In sum, despite its public diplomacy experience in the Cold War, in 2015 Germany was still a fairly new actor in this field and its ambitions were still relatively understudied.[501] The AA's rhetoric showed an explicit stance towards new public diplomacy emphasising network environments, dialogues and greater values which exceed mere interests. Still, the ambitions were also led by access to material resources and strategic importance. As *Pamment* outlined, Germany presented itself as a "benign mediator creating partnerships and dialogues in support of its policy goals".[502] A high amount of non-governmental actors was involved in the implementation of its public diplomacy.

496 AA at:http://www.auswaertiges-amt.de/DE/Aussenpolitik/KulturDialog/ZieleUndPartner/ZielePartner_node.html; AA (2015) p. 21.

497 *Schreiner* (2008) pp. 10ff.

498 *Harnischfeger* (2007) p. 719.

499 AA (2014) p. 8.

500 *Karten* (2008) p. 183; for details see AA at: https://www.auswaertiges-amt.de/de/aussenpolitik/themen/aussenwirtschaft/aufgaben-des-auswaertigen-amts; BMWi at: https://www.bmwi.de/Redaktion/DE/Dossier/aussenwirtschaftsfoerderung.html.

501 For case studies see e.g. *Pamment* (2013); *Ostrowski* (2010); *Zöllner* (2008); *Lange* (2007); *Gerz* (2005).

502 *Pamment* (2013) p. 30.

Conclusion

In 2015, the general public as well as politicians were increasingly critical of hard power's utility. The soft tackling of issues involving ideas had become more and more accepted and pushed forward. As *Hocking* stated, few actors nevertheless possessed this power which make others want what you wanted.[503] Public diplomacy whose key elements were values was thus one of the central instruments of soft power.[504] The concept offered a wider explanation of how diplomacy is undertaken in the 21st century. Still, little research has been conducted so far. Many empirical cases concentrated on the United States during the Cold War being therefore too one-sidedly focused and outdated. Research on actors other than governments has been even more limited.[505] Taking a constructivist starting point, helps focus on the public diplomacy as a process which includes various types of actors. We thereby return to what was originally defined as transnational interaction. Operations can take place in a network environment whereto actors bring various resources. Public diplomatic undertakings can be value-based and can include long-term relationship building, dialogue and collaboration. Constructivism allows here to consider ideational diffusion processes as the essence of public diplomacy. However, we do not assume that public diplomats only behave with integrity and further the common good. They might also be morally corrupt and manipulative in conducting questionable propaganda activities.

The next chapter will connect the outlined theoretical consideration of chapter 2 and chapter 3 to the methods of research used in this study. Theoretical and methodological aspects will be considered to generate knowledge on the research object of the German political foundations.

---

503 *Hocking* (2007) p. 35.
504 *Melissen* (2007b) p. 4.
505 *Gilboa* (2008) p. 56.

Chapter 4 – Research Methods

In this chapter the theoretical considerations of chapter 2 and 3 will be linked to the applied research methods. Furthermore, it outlines how research on the German political foundations was conducted. The consequences of a constructivist driven theoretical framework on the methodology of this work will be reflected. I focus on how the role of the German political foundations in international relations can be observed and understood under the premise of the established theoretical framework. Although I have a tendency towards a qualitative research strategy and its epistemological and ontological commitments, I do not see this as too deterministic. With the help of systematisations, we will gain some knowledge on the unanswered questions on the foundations' role in international relations.

The following chapter will outline the methodological strategy I adopt throughout the study and the phases of the qualitative research process. Furthermore, the research design and the chosen methodology will be presented. This includes considerations on the integrated model of diplomacy as outlined in chapter 3, the selection of cases, methods, data collection, as well as the aspect of coding.

This chapter was integrated when the study was already written up. Therefore, I take a retrospective look on the considerations to come.

4.1. Research strategy

The adopted research strategy is informed by several theoretical, epistemological and ontological assumptions as well as some practical considerations. Theory is understood here as elucidating observed regularities attempting to understand some part or facet of social life. During the earlier phase of the research, in which I focused on the literature on the German political foundations, I realised that it was not possible to use the background literature as an equivalent of a theory. There was neither an inconsistency within the studies nor was there an alternative approach to the existing findings to be provided which could have acted as driving force for the intended research project. A connection to international relations theory, transnationalism or the study of diplomacy was not established by the literature's authors. Nonetheless, the existing literature added momentum to this study as it brought up some relevant terms, such as "diplomacy" and "non-governmental organisations". This will be reflected upon in the relevant chapters.

The lack of literature and theoretical considerations as well as a deficiency of related knowledge in connection to the domain of the German political foundations did not allow a deductive study in logical sequences. For the aforementioned reasons, it was not feasible to first develop a hypothesis deriving from an underlying theory, then subsequently operationalise and determine the data collection process, confirming or rejecting the underlying hypothesis and finally feeding it back to the original theory. Instead, an inductive approach was used. I made use of an iterative method, where I intended to "draw generalizable interferences out of observations"[506] made during my research and where the result of my study could have a theoretical implication. This iterative approach was carried out by collecting data and then linking it to theoretical ideas afterwards instead of having a theory in mind prior to gathering the data. Following this procedure, my findings and observations continuously entered my theoretical considerations and the relationship between the two resembled a feedback loop. This means that the literature was already reviewed, and some interviews had already taken place before I established the connection to IR theory and transnational actors. And even more data was collected before I became aware of public diplomacy. This process will be outlined in detail below.[507] Like other qualitative researchers,[508] I was also interested in and preoccupied with the process which the German political foundations' activities followed over the course of time.

Despite the fact that I started with this iterative and inductive approach during the first years of my research, I proceeded deductively in the following time: The established public diplomacy model is the main theoretical outcome of this study.[509] However, I also tested it against the data and analysis afterwards.[510] This was necessary as the established model of public diplomacy would have had no connection to the international activities of the German political foundations otherwise. Without this link the model would have generated no knowledge with regards to the German political

---

506 *Bryman* (2016) p. 21.
507 See Ch. 4.2.
508 *Bryman* (2016) pp. 395ff.
509 See Ch. 5.
510 See Ch. 6 to 9.

foundations' role in international relations. Hence, it was necessary to bring them together.

Epistemologically, an interpretivist methodological stance of analysis guided the research. For this reason, I assume the impossibility of independent and external observation of realities and that social realities are socially constructed.[511] Unlike positivism, I consider social sciences as different from natural science such that human beings, their institutions and the social world are distinct from the logic of the natural order. Moreover, social action should be interpreted as achieving a "causal explanation of its course and effects".[512] It is therefore necessary to interpret the activities of people and their social understanding from their standpoint and to take up their values and ideas. In contrast to positivism, I do not support the idea of the objectivity of (social) science as meaning that research must be free of value. According to *Bryman*, interpretivism can lead to astonishing findings. He also underlines that interpreting social action does not mean to simply outline how interviewees understand their world. Researchers find further interpretations after he or she positions the interviewees' interpretation into a social scientific structure and expands upon them with reference to concepts, theory and literature of the field of study.[513] I put a lot of effort into outlining in detail the views and ideas of my interview partners.[514] I also interpreted and related their statements to the discussions in IR theory, the concepts of transnational actors and public diplomacy. I also derived from it the possible reasons of the foundations' tremendous public funding and thus their presence in the international political landscape.

Accordingly, in terms of social ontology and the underlying methodology, I assume that the German political foundations as social entities are constructions of their organisations' members. Unlike objectivism, I suppose that the German political foundations are not pre-given organisations with pre-given characteristics. Their organisational order and qualities are produced though active social interactions of social actors and through the reflections of the actors' perceptions. In this manner, social reality is constantly shifting. It is not an external and objective reality which exists independent from the involved social actors. This constructivist view in terms

511 See also *Haverland/Yanow* (2012) p. 403.

512 *Weber* (1947) p. 88.

513 *Bryman* (2016) pp. 27f.

514 See the case study chapters 8 and 9.

of the involvement of social actors in the social world has already been outlined in detail.[515]

The central research question of this work necessitates not only these theoretical, epistemological and ontological considerations but also a qualitative research strategy. The main question concentrates on the role of the German political foundations in international relations and the questions around their allocation to the transnational actors as well as their significant public funding. I am guided by questions which focus on understanding the reasons for the phenomenon of the German political foundations' international undertakings. I study why the German political foundations exist through looking at what they do and documenting the details of it. Although I outline the *Stiftungen's* and their activities' development over time,[516] our primary aim is not to reveal the causes of the phenomenon of the German political foundations. As already mentioned, there is not sufficient research on the matter of the German political foundations which would allow specifying variables in advance and testing hypothesises on these matters as a quantitative methodology would suggest. From the beginning of this research project, I looked at the rather general question of the role of the German political foundations. What would appear to be vague and lacking precision in the eyes of positivist research was necessary to grasp the meaning of the wide range of instruments, the complex organisational structure as well as the dimension of the foundations' activities. A narrower research question would have given no room for unanticipated meanings and prioritise my own preconceived ideas instead of the meaning-making of the interview partners. The elaboration of the question on the role of German political foundations was part of the research process. Further specification with the help of sub-questions took place after the first interviews with members of the German political foundations. Moreover, the detailing of the model of diplomacy happened in this phase of the research project. For these reasons, I give preference to a qualitative methodology and its underlying way of knowing.

In terms of contextualised meaning, I see myself as a researcher being positioned within the research situation. As will be shown below, the access to people, situations, collected data and gathered information was significantly influenced by my professional and personal life at that time. I finally give an interpretative answer to the foundations' role question by refining their position within the international arena with the help of the

---

515 See Ch. 2.2.2.

516 See especially Ch. 1.7 and 6.3.1.

previously developed model of public diplomacy.[517] This model is a conceptualised expectation of how the German political foundations work, which also allows for the drawing of some conclusions on why they are active. Moreover, the model itself is an outcome of which the applicability to the undertakings of the German political foundations will become clear throughout the next chapters. From a constitutive theories' starting point I try to understand how structure forms the German political foundations' personnel and staff members which, as social kinds, represent the foundations. The public diplomacy model and its special focus on the networking environment makes portraying this structure possible.

To enable the study of the German political foundations, I ontologically assume that states are important actors but, unlike rationalism, not the only objects in the international arena. However, before I clarify the relationship between state and non-state actors we step backwards and analyse what kind of objects the *Stiftungen* are and whether they are independent enough from state structures to classify them as entities in their own rights.[518] With constructivism I share the interest in social interaction and the relationships between states and other actors. The model of public diplomacy model and more specifically, the included considerations on networks in terms of relationships, resources, values and interests, help to examine communicative practices and social realities which are emphasised by constructivist authors. The disclosure of the relationship structure within the network can help to explain not only the social behaviour of the involved actors but also provide indicators for the reasons why such networks exist. Nonetheless, I note that this study is an initial cautious approach to a systematic assessment of the network and does not claim to be exhaustive.

I also try to shed light on how the German political foundations understand their role and, as social actors, how they view the world they navigate in. The idea is to understand the social actor's world by trying to look through his or her eyes.[519]

I do not reject the scientific methods of a quantitative methodology nor do I assume that the strict distinction is necessary. However, for answering the underlying research questions on the role of the German political foundations I needed a suitable and consistent research design, and I be-

517 See below Ch. 4.3.1.
518 See Ch. 5.1.
519 *Kurki/Wight* (2013) p. 27.

lieve that the methods stemming from qualitative methodology best reflect the purpose of this work.

Apart from these epistemological and ontological considerations, I do not deny the fact that practical considerations also played an important role in choosing the research strategy: I am interested in the views and underlying values of my interview partners. Moreover, there existed no literature from which to derive a connection between transnational activity and public diplomacy on the one hand, and the German political foundations activities on the other hand. This led to a rather explorative approach to carrying out the research project.

4.2. The qualitative research process

The qualitive research process followed an iterative strategy, where the specification of research question and additional theorising led to the collection of further data. In this section, I will detail the main steps of the process: As already outlined in the first chapter, I started with a general research question on the role of the German political foundations in international relations:

What role do the German political foundations have in international relations? Are rationalists correct in saying that states are the key international actors, or can it be demonstrated, as constructivists argue, that through the interaction with many different actors, the German political foundations as transnational actors have a significant impact? If the latter is the case, what is the reason for their substantial public funding?

I looked at IR theory and more closely at the position of transnational actors and their networking within the theoretical landscape. At the same time, I reviewed the available literature on the German political foundations. I found descriptions and studies on their international activities but mainly in the context of development assistance and/or development aid policies. From the first interviews with members of the *Stiftungen* and some short notes in the literature, I learned from the conflict management measures they undertook in some parts of the world and identified this practice as a newer field of activities for the German political foundations.

Despite some literature on democracy assistance I found that both fields, democracy assistance as well as conflict management, had little conceptualisation within the literature on the *Stiftungen*.

At this phase of the research I started to address several sub-questions, which I have already outlined before. They were connected to both democracy assistance and conflict management.

What makes the German political foundations democracy assistants? Do they follow a developmental or a political conception of democracy assistance? What ideas are diffused and are they different from those of official German policy? What do the foundations change? Are prerequisites established by the foundation for German companies?

Is conflict management implemented by the Stiftungen? If yes, what ideas are diffused and are they different from those of official German policy? What do the foundations change? Are prerequisites established by the foundation for German companies?

The definition of what was meant by both democracy assistance and conflict management and which activities and processes they comprised was rarely provided. Knowing this, I developed a structure consisting of categories for both concepts and a schedule for collecting data from documents and interviews.[520] I also discussed and substantiated which definitions were part of the concept and which aspects belonged to other concepts. At the time, I also chose two cases for studying both fields of activities.[521] In this phase of the research I selected relevant sites and subjects as a further step in the conducted qualitative research process.

Although I wanted to clarify whether and how the German political foundations were active in both fields and aimed at closing subject related knowledge gaps, it remained unclear at this point why such activities took place. I could not explain why those party-affiliated foundations in Germany had been chosen or had been allowed to conduct these tasks and as such why they were backed with these substantial public funds. One of the key findings at this phase of the research process was that I was unable to answer these questions.

While reading through the literature on the German political foundations, the term "diplomacy" appeared often, so I focused on the body of literature which dealt with transnational actors as diplomats and those operating in networks. I encountered public diplomacy. Public diplomacy and the German political foundations had not been brought together. In contrast to democracy assistance and conflict management, public diplomacy was not a declared "field of activity" or aim of the *Stiftungen*. In order to understand and build knowledge on the German political foundations

520 See Ch. 5.1. and 6.1. respectively.

521 See below Ch. 4.3.2.

in relation to public diplomacy I developed the following specific research question:

To what extent can German political foundations be considered as public diplomats? Are they independent generators of public diplomacy or do they work on behalf of the German government? Does their work substitute, supplement or conflict with traditional diplomacy? Who benefits and who loses from these activities? Do the foundations have advantages (e.g. resources) in comparison to other diplomatic actors? Are transnational networks established? If yes, who controls them?

In this phase of the project, I worked conceptually and theoretically towards developing the model of public diplomacy.[522] As with the concepts of democracy assistance and conflict management, I discussed and defined the notions in order to create a schema for future analysis. I also tried to clarify the hierarchy of the concepts of transnational actors, public diplomacy, democracy assistance and conflict management and their relations to each other and developed a categorisation.

This model brought several advantages with it: It allowed a return to the theoretical considerations in international relations on transnational actors. It made the operationalisation of their interaction processes possible. And it included a focus on social networks. Furthermore, it helped with linking together the concepts of democracy assistance and conflict management as they were summarised as practices of public diplomacy.[523] Finally, public diplomacy by this way became an indicator for the impact of the German political foundations as transnational actors and led back to the general research question on the role of the German political foundations as outlined above.

For each concept (that is public diplomacy, democracy assistance and conflict management) as well as for the countries' case studies I outlined the specific German official policy as well.[524] I aimed to identify possible connections to the German political foundations' activities in order to draw conclusions on the relationship between the *Stiftungen* and official actors, the independency of the foundations as well as the question of which values they diffused. In this context, I also encountered the conception of civilian power which I discuss in the following chapters.

In the time that followed, the main part of the collection of data as well as data analysis took place: in-depth interviews, the analysis of archival ma-

---

522 See Ch. 3.

523 See Ch. 4.3.1.

524 In chapters 4 to 9 a respective chapter on German policy can be found.

terial and official documents, the re-analysis of the existing literature on the German political foundations under the premise of the developed model of public diplomacy as well as the testing of the model with the qualitative data I collected.[525] Finally, in the last phase of the research process, I wrote up my findings and discussed them.

In the final chapter I presented a summary of the overall findings and related them back to the rationalist and constructivist approaches outlined in chapter 2 and the main research question. I concluded with the development of a hypothesis regarding the impact of the foundations connected to the reproduction of the conception of civilian power.

4.3. *Research design and methodology*

The research project was conducted as a case study design. It is based on qualitative research methods, as some deeper understanding on the social phenomenon and the socially constructed nature of reality is intended, with priority given to perceptions, meaning and ideas.[526] Quantitative research could not offer these insights. Moreover, I made use of systematisations deriving from the respective bodies of literature to operationalise the processes of public diplomacy, democracy assistance and conflict management. I carried out a collective case study where several cases were examined mainly to investigate some general phenomenon.[527]

In this subsection I will take a look at the model of public diplomacy as a theoretical outcome which was tested along the study. I than consider the selection of cases. Qualitative methods and data collection will be outlined afterwards. Finally, as part of the data analysis I will present the adopted coding technique.

4.3.1. The model of public diplomacy

The next chapters apply the integrated model of public diplomacy elaborated in chapter 3 to the international undertakings of the German political foundations. In chapter 5 I look at the question of whether the *Stiftungen* can be considered as public diplomats by analysing their independence

---

525 See in detail Ch. 4.3.
526 *Silverman* (2005) p. 10.
527 *Stake* (2000) pp. 437f.

and activities abroad. In chapter 6 and chapter 7 I reflect on the foundations' support in democracy and their conflict management as different modes how public diplomacy can be practiced correlating with the second and third mode of *Hocking's* network model and *Riordan's* findings on collaborative public diplomacy. Though identified as core activities of the *Stiftungen* by many authors, they have only partly been analysed systematically and never in a public diplomatic context. In the case study chapters 8 and 9, I bring those two practices and public diplomacy together.

The model of public diplomacy, the generated categories and concepts it entails, and its focus on collaborative and networked public diplomacy was used to make visible interaction processes between individuals from the German political foundations and others, which had not been studied in a structured way before.

Although the model is used here to study the international undertakings of the German political foundations, it can be applied for enquiring into the activities of other foundations, actors or organisations. It may also help to conduct research in other areas, different social settings or political contexts.

The model builds on the existing literature of public diplomacy, democracy assistance and conflict management and is used to systematically analyse the undertakings of the *Stiftungen*. Although this study has the broad characteristics of a qualitative research strategy, I included the element of a deductive approach, which is mainly employed in quantitative research by testing the German political foundations' activities against the model. However, this combination is not uncommon in the context of qualitative research design.[528]

I use the term "model" to illustrate that it is comprised of several concepts, such as transnational actors, which is especially relevant for the question of who generates public diplomacy as well as democracy assistance and conflict management as forms of collaborative public diplomacy. The concept of public diplomacy itself is also integrated into the model which consists of, among other things, a definition of generators, addressees, instruments and dimensions of public diplomacy. This structure is found in chapter 5, which deals more generally with the public diplomacy of the German political foundations, as well as in the specific case study chapters 8 and 9.

When developing the concepts of the model I followed *Blumer's* definition of sensitising concepts in the way that they deliver "a general sense of

---

528 *Bryman* (2016) p. 381.

reference and guidance in approaching empirical instances". *Blumer* contrasts sensitising concepts with definitive concepts. The latter consist of indicators representing the concept.[529] The integrated model of diplomacy includes the different varieties of public diplomacy and aspects I found in the literature. My idea was to build a model that comprises all identified characteristics to enable an initial stock taking on the public diplomacy of the German political foundations. The idea of this general formulation was to avoid overseeing important aspects of the foundations' activities in the context of public diplomacy. I also identified the concepts related to public diplomacy in order to differentiate public diplomacy activities from others.

Regarding the data analysis I adopted a syllogistic technique of subsumption, meaning I first defined the notions used within the model's concepts. I then considered these definitions as requirements for the presence of the respective concept. In a second step I looked for evidence in the collected data on the German political foundations' activities. In this context, I made use of coding as described below.[530]

4.3.2. Selection of cases

The cases of the two major party-affiliated political foundations, the *Konrad-Adenauer-Stiftung* and the *Friedrich-Ebert-Stiftung* were used. Both are comparable with regards to size, funding and staff members. They work in a wide international sphere and were able to offer enough relevant data to answer the research questions. With regards to the KAS, I considered their democracy assistance activities in the Southeast European countries, focusing especially on EU accession, while for the FES, I looked at conflict management in Southern Thailand. Although different in their focus, both fields of activities are assumed to be part of public diplomacy allowing some generalisation on their transnational interaction. Taking into account the foundations' normative backgrounds, variations can be stressed. The cases were not chosen on the basis of structural similarities of the involved countries/regions. The region of Southeast Europe offered an interesting case on how democracy assistance is carried out in the European context. Conflict management was particularly apt to be studied in Thailand, since interviews could be taken in the relatively safe environments of Bangkok and Chang Mai. Moreover, the field of the foundations' conflict manage-

529 *Blumer* (1954) p. 7.
530 See Ch. 4.3.4.

ment, relatively new in the foundations' activity portfolio, did not offer too many cases to be studied, as activities with an exclusive focus on conflicts rarely take place.

The case studies in chapters 8 and 9 connect the insights on public diplomacy and its characteristics of democracy assistance and conflict management gained in chapters 5 to 7 to the concrete cases of KAS's democracy assistance in Southeast Europe and to conflict management of the FES in Southern Thailand.

4.3.3. Methods and data collection

Data was collected using multiple methods. The techniques and tools used to carry out this research included the appraisal of the existing academic literature, official documents, archival material and those published by the German political foundations as well as in-depth interviews.

4.3.3.1. Method 1: Analysis of academic, official, archival and other material

Various textual data was examined. The sparse academic literature, mostly published in German, was investigated and served as a starting point in 2006 and 2007. I continued to collect material over the following years and in several different libraries at universities in Berlin, Nottingham and Brussels. However, studies connected neither public diplomacy nor transnational activity to the German political foundations. An exception as regards the latter is *Pascher's* doctoral thesis of 2002 analysing the foundations' adaptation to globalisation processes. She deals with the loss of state sovereignty, governance processes and the growing international influence of non-state actors and investigated the relations of the FES to the UN in the 1990s.[531] Furthermore, I took into account the political foundations' annual reports, evaluations and other material published by the *Stiftungen*.[532] The foundations made several unpublished internal documents available to me. Also, information on the foundations' online presence was

531 *Pascher* (2002).

532 The foundations' annual reports were inspected ever since the first report, as far as they were available. They are indicated in the footnotes as „[*Stiftung*] annual report [year]". They were not listed separately in the bibliography.

taken into consideration. In contrast to earlier works, which had almost completely relied on secondary literature, as primary literature was missing,[533] the material available from the German political foundations was sufficient. Still, details on the funding of single projects or (complete) evaluations of activities were veiled from the public. Moreover, various official documents from the German Bundestag and relevant material from the Federal Foreign Office (AA), the Ministry for Cooperation and Development (BMZ) as well as other ministries were investigated.[534] This was important, since the latter are the main financial backer of the political foundations' international activity. Their political concepts as regards the areas studied (public diplomacy, democracy assistance and conflict management) as well as the regions and countries studied (Southeast Europe and Thailand) were explored. In 2014 I spent several days studying the political archives of the AA and the German Bundestag to identify official primary sources and data on the beginnings of the foundations' international undertakings. The material, which is under a vesting period of 30 years due to its confidentiality, offered insights on the initial intention for the foundations' public funding and the foundations' relations to public bodies. In this context, the intensive efforts of the archives' staff members to make specific relevant material available, needs to be highlighted. Finally, media and press coverage in Germany and abroad was analysed, as well as the wealth of relevant information available on the internet.[535]

4.3.3.2. Method 2: In-depth interviews and others

The highly qualitative nature of interviews was used to overcome the hurdle of the sparse literature. Moreover, the individual beliefs of the *Stiftungens'* staff members as well as the values they attach to their activities were important for this work. Between 2009 and 2015 I carried out several in-depth and semi-structured expert interviews in Berlin, Bangkok and Chiang Mai which took between 2 to 3.5 hours. I used an open-ended questionnaire which allowed for deviation from the questions posed and flexi-

533 E.g. *Werner* (1982) p. 22.

534 In this context I thank Pascal Juretzko for his technical support and for providing his development of software to me which facilitated the review of the large volume of digital documents.

535 Online resources and websites have been accessed on 24/01/2016 unless specified differently.

ble responses to the topics raised during the interview. In addition, I also used unstructured interviews in the form of conversations where two or three questions were posed more generally. They lasted around 1 to 2 hours and were conducted at the beginning of the research project. The interviews were taken in person and either recorded using an audiotape recorder or notes were taken during the interview. Both types of interviews were transcribed afterwards. One interview was conducted as a telephone interview and another as written interview. The interviewees were foundations' staff members in the German headquarters including members of the executive boards, department heads, heads of divisions and foundations' representatives in the chosen countries. Also, people from the foreign ministry, specifically experts who had cooperated with the foundations, as well as scholarship receivers, were involved. The interviewees were given the opportunity to stay anonymous due to the sensitivity of the information provided. An interview's code number is mentioned in the footnote of the texts in order to create transparency. The possibility of interviewing foundations' partner organisations on site was not given to me, as travelling to them was either not possible due to the security situation (Thailand) or a language barrier existed. In light of the research question, these interviews, however, were not particular suitable on producing relevant data. I tried to use triangulation, entailing multiple methods and different sources in order to ensure credibility and accuracy in my interpretations.[536] In the Southeast European case study, I referred to an extensive evaluation of the KAS's activities, which had been carried out by an external evaluator in 2013. In the Thailand case study, I had interviews with the staff members from all active foundations as well as other people more directly involved in the activities of the FES, in order to consider other opinions.[537] However, the special role of the foundations' representatives in the context of the undertakings on site should not be underestimated. They are very much in control of information. I will discuss the representatives' role later on.[538] The cooperation of the interviewees was very positive as was the amount of time and effort spent responding to interview questions, establishing further contacts and providing additional material, even beyond the scope of the interview. During the research project I was given the opportunity to participate in discussions and conferences organised by the foundations. Systematic observation was not carried out, since limited

---

536 *Denzin* (1970) p. 310; *Bryman* (2016) p. 386.

537 *Becker* (1998) p. 91.

538 Ch. 7.

knowledge was expected to be gained from it for the answering of the research questions. Nonetheless, it helped to understand more broadly the environment in which the foundations operated. Furthermore, I could make some observations on the relations between the foundations and the members of parliament/government as well as the embassies, when working as a research assistant at the Protocol of the German Bundestag between 2007 and 2009, and as an intern at the German embassy in Nepal in 2005. I could draw upon these experiences in the research project.

I am aware that not only the values of my interview partners but also my own values might have influenced the conduct of my research. However, although I partly developed a close affinity with some interview partners due to the intensity and length of the interview situation, I tried to be self-reflective and mindful about such situations. There was also a personal development over the years that I studied the German political foundations. My own beliefs about the necessity and optimism of the transnational actors' potential in the international sphere changed and gave way to a more critical view.

4.3.4. Coding

As part of the analysis of the collected textual data and the data deriving from the interviews, I made use of coding, whereby I connected pieces of literature and the responses to the theoretical models and systematisations developed in this study.[539] I chose this process in order to be able to analyse the large volumes of collected data. I coded from the beginning of the reading onwards. By coding I mean that I indexed the textual material, such as academic, official and archival material as well as the interview transcripts. Firstly, I made use of more general codes in terms of concepts which I had already found in the literature. From the moment I had developed the model of diplomacy, coding became more detailed and specific. The terms I used for the index were those of the model and its notions or parts of them. I also used an index for the notions which I had differentiated from the model and public diplomacy beforehand. At this point of analysis, I also considered the conception of civilian power and its reproduction by the German political foundations as a more general theoretical idea and related it to the detailed codes and categories. In order not to lose the context by this process of fragmentation I went through the material,

539 *Bryman* (2016) pp. 581ff.

especially the transcribed interviews, several times and again when I wrote up the thesis.

Conclusion

The position of a constructivist-inspired qualitative analysis which borrows the aspect of testing a theory from a quantitative research design might seem arbitrary. However, it has become common to break down the qualitative and quantitative divide.[540] In this context, I believe that the contrast between quantitative and a qualitative analysis should not be overstated. Testing the generated theory throughout the research was necessary in bringing public diplomacy and the German political foundations together and generate knowledge on this connection. I was not interested in public diplomacy alone but in the context that it provided for the impact of the German political foundations in international relations. The testing was also necessary in order to develop a hypothesis on the civilian power reproduction of the German political foundations in the final summary of this study.

The next chapter applies the integrated model of public diplomacy as presented in chapter 3 to the international undertakings of the German political foundations. It looks at the question of whether the *Stiftungen* can be considered as public diplomats by analysing their independence and activities abroad. In chapter 6 and chapter 7 I analyse the foundations' support in democracy and their conflict management as different modes of public diplomacy having a networked and collaborative dimension. Though core activities of the *Stiftungen*, democracy assistance and conflict management have never been analysed systematically in a public diplomatic context. The subsequent case studies connect these insights to concrete cases of democracy assistance of the KAS in Southeast Europe and conflict management of the FES in Southern Thailand. The diffused values and policy ideas of the *Stiftungen* will be related to the official German policy and its rhetoric shedding lights on ideational differences and accordance.

---

540 *Bryman* (2016) pp. 621ff.

Part II: Public diplomacy and practice

Chapter 5 – The German political foundations: Public diplomats?

In the past, academic literature occasionally has set the German political foundations' undertakings in context within diplomatic activities. However, it remained very vague what form of diplomacy is conducted, how the *Stiftungen* undertake this activity or how it fits into the wider debate on public diplomacy. In being an under-theorised and disputed object in the IR discipline,[541] diplomacy might as well have caused this lack of attention. Still, several different authors already suggested a closer look at the *Stiftungens'* diplomatic activities assuming a broader notion of diplomacy involving states and transnational actors alike.

In the following chapter, the model of public diplomacy as presented before is applied to the foundations' foreign activities.[542] First, the chapter analyses whether the *Stiftungen* are indeed generators of public diplomacy or rather tools of the German state or other institutions. In a second step it is explored which public diplomatic instruments the German foundations make use of. Thirdly, in terms of a public diplomacy dimension, the chapter discusses possible propaganda activities and examines the foundations' operation in a network environment. The chapter addresses sub-research question 1[543] and tries to analyse more generally the potential of the German political foundations as public diplomats.

5.1. Generators

Who generates public diplomacy is closely connected to the question of whether the foundations are transnational actors or whether they are active on behalf of the German state (i.e. the ministries and parliament) or the

541 *Jönsson* (2002) p. 214.

542 See Ch. 3.2.

543 See Ch. 1.3.

political parties. It also touches upon the issue of the foundations being integrated in the political sphere as instruments of German foreign policy.

The literature often emphasises the autonomy of the German foundations from the state.[544] Still, reasons for this assumption are rarely given. On the contrary, when the associated party is in government the foundations are often perceived erroneously as semi-official bodies by many outside observers.[545] As we have seen above, the German political foundations were mainly state-sponsored.[546] The possibility is likely that they implemented only projects in the interests of the funder. In case of a direct control by means of binding specifications and monitoring, one can hardly speak of a particular *Stiftungs'* public diplomacy. Rather, they would be tools or instruments of a state public diplomacy and could, moreover, not count as transnational actors. Subsuming the German political foundations under the transnational actors' definition is difficult.[547] Whereas their "regular interactions across national boundaries" were clearly visible, their relationship with the German government posed problems. The FES, the FNS, the HBS and the RLS were registered NGOs at the United Nations in 2014. To the first three the "Roster" category was granted in 1979 (FES), 1993 (FNS) and 2004 (HBS). The RLS received the special consultative status in 2013.[548] The fact that government or political party members were often members at the affiliated *Stiftung*, does not contradict the UN's NGO definition.[549] While earlier works assumed that the foundations simply ranked among the NGOs,[550] increasingly authors considered them as QUANGOs.[551] As we have seen above, this not only implied the dependence on state funds but also a heteronomous activity on behalf of the German government. Consequentially, the foundations were precluded from being transnational actors.[552] Moreover, the affiliated political parties

544 E.g. *Klevenhörster/van den Boom* (2009) p. 61; *Smith* (2001) pp. 59f.; *Nölke* (2010) p. 395.

545 *Thunert* (2004) p. 79.

546 See Ch. 1.7.3.

547 See Ch. 2.1.

548 UN (2014); the Economic and Social Council (ECOSOC) recognises three categories of NGOs: (1) general consultative status NGOs concerned with most of the Council's work; (2) specialist NGOs concerned with a few fields and (3) "Roster" NGOs make occasional contributions to the Council (UN at: http://csonet.org/index.php?menu=30).

549 See Ch. 1.7.2. and 2.1.

550 E.g. *Krämer/Lehrke* (1996) p. 114.

551 E.g. *Schubert* (2005) p. 802; *Nuscheler* (1993).

552 See Ch. 2.1.

could exercise power over the *Stiftungen*. They were situated in the transition area between state and society and they were of great importance under German constitutional law.[553] In case of their control a foundations' public diplomacy "generatorship" would be inhibited. Both aspects need to be considered in the following subsection.

5.1.1. The Ministry of Development and Cooperation (BMZ)

In 2015, for their foreign activity the German political foundations received around 90 percent of their international funding from the BMZ aiming at their projects in the developing countries.[554] Still, the ministry's possibility to approve the foundations' activities was relatively limited. German development policy is implemented by different actors whose independence from the ministry varies tremendously. On the one hand, the German government initiates, funds and organises the development cooperation by making use of dependent implementing agencies (*Durchführungsorganisationen*) which belong to the QUANGOs.[555] They are so-called *verselbständigte Verwaltungseinheit* meaning "administrative unit made independent" which enjoy limited independence as to human and material resources and decision-making. The BMZ, however, has a conditioning control over the development political decision-making of these organisations as it pre-selects the possible projects and can object to the final projects' selection.[556] Such organisations are among others the *Deutsche Gesellschaft für Internationale Zusammenarbeit* (GIZ) and the *KfW Entwicklungsbank*. On the other hand, development projects are initiated and organised by independent NGOs partly backed by BMZ's funds. The latter includes the German political foundations, the church organisations as well as other NGOs.[557] In contrast to the implementation organisations, the German political foundations were not created to take on governmental tasks initially. Even though the beginnings of the foundations' international engagement partly coincided with the idea of the German government to support the foundations financially, their international activities

553 *Rudizio* (2006) p. 93; *Krebs* (2007) § 108 Rn. 25.

554 See Ch. 1.7.3.

555 BMZ at: http://www.bmz.de/en/what_we_do/approaches/bilateral_development_cooperation/players/implementing_organisations/index.html; see also Ch. 6.1.

556 *Glagow/Schimank* (1983) p. 151.

557 BMZ (2013a); BMZ at: http://www.bmz.de/en/what_we_do/approaches/bilateral_development_cooperation/players/index.html; *Glagow/Schimank* (1983) p. 162.

followed several years after their (re)establishment.[558] The international activities were initiated by political party members or, in case of the FES also by trade unions developing international relationships at that time.[559] The BMZ had a selecting control over their projects: The organisation first chose the possible projects which the ministry then could reject. However, the ministry was not able to determine contentwise binding requirements.[560] During the implementation of projects the foundations wrote mid-year and annual reports to the BMZ.[561] They were also supposed to constantly coordinate their activities abroad among each other and should inform the BMZ of the results.[562] As the ministry pointed out, the *Stiftungen* were not active *on behalf of* the German government but *with the approval of* the government. The foundations were also mostly independent from agreements resulting from bilateral development cooperation.[563] Still, the autonomy of all organisations from the ministry depends, as *Glagow* and *Schimank* point out, on its demand of funding and their availability of other resources. The *Stiftungen* did not have sufficient self-funds and the ministry financed their projects almost completely. However, the BMZ did not check the political imperative of projects. It was only responsible for the *pluralist* distribution of funds among the foundations. The quota was determined by the German *Bundestag*.[564] Each foundation had a certain amount of funding, literally on demand. In reality, the rejection of project proposals rarely happened in the history of the foundations' international activity.[565] Like the other independent NGOs receiving funding from the BMZ, the foundations were therefore relative autonomous. However, compared to the other NGOs the foundations were least dependent. Their relationship with the funding ministry was formal as the foundations did not have to negotiate their funding with the BMZ. They decided how and where to be active.[566] This formal independence permits to con-

---

558 See Ch. 6.3.1.

559 E.g. for the FES see *Von zur Mühlen* (2007) pp. 48ff.; for the KAS see *Beaugrand* (2003) pp. 43f.

560 BMZ (1973) p. 64; *Glagow/Schimank* (1983) pp. 152, 154f.

561 *Egger* (2006) p. 63 fn. 173.

562 BMZ (1973) p. 65; interview 3; critically *Schürmann* (1989) p. 55.

563 BMZ (1973) p. 64; BMZ at: http://www.bmz.de/de/was_wir_machen/wege/bilaterale_ez/akteure_ez/polstiftungen/index.html?follow=adword.

564 See Ch. 1.7.3.; *Glagow/Schimank* (1983) pp. 159, 161f., 174.

565 *Egger* (2007) p. 62 fn. 172 on lacking resources; *Glagow/Schimank* (1983) p. 162 on avoiding conflicts with the political parties.

566 *Glagow/Schimank* (1983) pp. 161ff., 174.

sider the foundations as GONGOs.[567] Elsewhere the *Stiftungen* have been termed as "mediation-NGOs". They acquired funds from the Northern donor and used them either for their own activity in cooperation with Southern NGOs or acted as a donor in relation to the Southern NGOs.[568] The term is misleading, however, as intermediary or mediation organisations are viewed as German *Mittlerorganisations*.

5.1.2. The Federal Foreign Office (AA)

In the last years the German political foundations received the remaining 10 percent of their international funding from the AA for projects in the industrialised countries and scholarships to foreign students. In 2015 the ratio between AA and BMZ had slightly shifted in favour of the AA since it was also responsible for EU candidates.[569]

The German political foundations were at times perceived as actors in German cultural relations and education policy *(AKBP)*. As already outlined, the AA implemented its AKBP with the help of *Mittlerorganisations* defined as QUANGOs.[570] Some criterions of the *Mittlerorganisations* could also be assigned to the *Stiftungen*: They were not obliged to follow implementation instructions and their projects were evaluated and monitored.[571] However, in contrast to the *Mittlerorganisationen*, the foundations were not bound by framework contracts and target agreements. Their independence in the projects' implementation was greater although also the *Mittlerorganisations* were partly automomous.[572] The German foundations were possibly not among the *Mittlerorganisationen* due to the understanding that cultural policy is rather non-political.[573] This criterion did not apply to the *Stiftungen*. However, an "intermediary"-function in AKBP was conceded to the foundations and the AA views them as "partners".[574]

---

567 See Ch. 2.1.; *Reimann* (2007) p. 93.
568 *Fahrenhorst* (2007) p. 72 fn.
569 See Ch. 1.7.3.
570 See Ch. 3.3. and 2.1.
571 Interviews 7, 3; KAS at: http://www.kas.de/wf/de/71.3712/; Egger (2007) p. 63 fn. 173; *Bartsch* (1998) p. 187.
572 AA (2011a) p. 19; *Renvert* (2011) p. 32; *Schreiner* (2008) p. 5.
573 *Harnischfeger* (2007) p. 719.
574 AA (2015) pp. 23, 164ff.; peripherally mentioning the foundations AA (2013) pp. 76, 88; see Ch. 5.2.3.

The AA also needed to agree to the projects authorised by the BMZ. The reason for the approval of the AA was rooted in the original issue of whether development aid was considered as part of foreign affairs.[575] The foundations' projects were examined regarding potential foreign political objections and their overlapping with other German organisations' projects. Since the beginning of the foundations' international activities, the AA established certain general rules in order to avoid that undertakings negatively affect the relations between Germany and the specific country. As a result, inner party debates of the specific affiliated German party were not supposed to be shifted abroad. Furthermore, the German foundations should not interfere abroad in political disputes on governmental power.[576] These guidelines, however, have left enough room for the *Stiftungen* to plan and implement their projects independently from the AA. Objections to projects were rarely made.[577] Despite regular meetings the coordination between the ministry and the *Stiftungen* was assumed to be not very formal.[578]

Despite their independence it was sometimes attested to the foundations to be instruments in German foreign policy. In his speech on the FES's 70th anniversary, then German President *Herzog* noted that "the foundations' commitment for the development of democratic and rule of law structures makes them one of the most effective and proven instruments of German foreign policy".[579] *Nuschler* considered the foundations as "diplomatic auxiliary forces" practicing a complementary "side foreign policy".[580] In several of her works, *Pogorelskaja* investigated the foundations' actor and instrument characteristics. She checked activities of the KAS and HSS in CSI and the Baltic States against the AA's concepts. According to her, the foundations contributed to the bilateral relations between Germany and the studied states and helped form new foreign political concepts.[581] As instrument they were recognised because they complemented official foreign policy by pre-political activities.[582] Some stressed the realisation of long-term political goals where the foundations as instruments offer advan-

575 AAPA B58-IIIB2 Bd. 304 7/03/1963.

576 BMZ (1973) p. 69; Bundeshaushaltsplan (2015) Kapitel 2302 Titel 68704.

577 *Bartsch* (1998) p. 187.

578 Interview 4; *Pogorelskaja* (2009a) p. 42.

579 *Herzog* (1995) p. 324, author's translation.

580 *Nuscheler* (1993) p. 231; *Ronge/Pascher* (1999) p. 189.

581 *Pogorelskaja* (1997) pp. 167f.

582 *Pogorelskaja* (2002a) pp. 33f.

tages.[583] While all these aspects might have an added value in the eyes of those conducting foreign policy they are, however, only helpful when the instrument can be controlled. Ultimately, also *Pogorelskaja* conceded that due to the impossibility to directly influence them, the foundations were not instruments in a classic sense.[584] To associate the foundations with "instruments" was therefore misleading. In fact, they offered different resources from which others profited which will be considered below.

5.1.3. The German parliament, the political parties and others

The German *Bundestag* controlled the German political foundations as it was in charge to provide the public funding to the foundations, which was distributed to the foundations via the ministries afterwards. The *Bundestag* also fixed the funds' allocation formula.[585] However, it only determined the amount conceded to the foundations but did not specify requirements for their activities. The pluralism of the foundations' affiliation to different political parties made governmental control difficult. Still, it did not preclude from the possibility that the party exercised control over the affiliated foundation's activities or that the foundation only implemented what is in the interest of the party. Some authors assumed that the *Stiftungen* are merely execution organs for a political party's foreign policy.[586] Since the foundations were important foreign political organisations for the political parties,[587] it was likely, though hard to prove that the foundation conducted certain activities in the service of the affiliated party. However, this did not occur through coercion and would contradict the ruling of the Constitutional Court terming the foundations' independence and autonomy from the political parties.[588] Exertion of influence rather took place informally and particularly through the personnel intertwining between party and foundation.[589] In this respect, *Pinto-Duschinsky* gave the glaring example of Chancellor *Kohl* and a CDU committee prohibiting a KAS publication which described emerging political groups in East Berlin in the early

583 *Mohr* (2010) p. 279.
584 *Pogorelskaja* (2009a) p. 26; (2002a) pp. 33f.
585 See Ch. 1.7.3.
586 *Bartsch* (1998) p. 192; *Mair* (2000) p. 131.
587 *Glagow/Schimank* (1983) p. 174.
588 BVerfGE 73, 1 of 14/07/1986 (Decision of the Federal Constitutional Court).
589 See Ch. 1.7.2.

weeks after the fall of the Berlin Wall.[590] At the time of writing, the informal interfering of the party seemed to be rather restrained.[591] Also the party's funding and that of the foundation were strictly separated.[592] Foundations' projects and events were planned and carried out independently.[593] Some authors assumed that especially the foundations' consulting activity prevented the foundations from becoming party instruments.[594] This is convincing as the foundation, compared to the affiliated party, had an advantage in knowledge and expertise on international subjects. Therefore, it was more likely that the party must trust the recommendations of the foundation than vice versa. Others assumed that foreign topics were rather uninteresting in terms of influence exertion as these did not help the domestic influence of the political party.[595] The prevailing ideational conformity of the foundation and the affiliated party in policy issues nonetheless remained but did not establish a link of control.[596] However, there were cases when the foundation's political position and that of the party were different. In 1999, the then government GREEN party supported the military intervention in Kosovo while the HBS opposed it.[597] In sum, the actual party's power of control over the foundation's foreign activities might have been only slightly pronounced due to the personal ties. However, this did not rationalise to view the *Stiftungen* as simple party instruments.[598] Rather the political party might have profited from valuable foundation's resources outside of the party's sphere of influence. Finally, the hybrid structure[599] of the *Stiftungen* in having connecting points to the affiliated political parties made them not only relative-autonomous from the public bodies but also, in reverse, from the political parties.

There were several other means of control of the foundations' activity. The funding ministries controled whether the financial support complied with the purpose of funding. The tax office verified the public utility of

590 *Pinto-Duschinky* (1991b) p. 223.

591 *Egger* (2007) p. 68 fn. 191.

592 See Ch. 1.7.4.

593 *Langguth* (1993) pp. 40f.; *Prechtl* (1996) p. 181.

594 *Mohr* (2010) p. 280.

595 *Egger* (2007) p. 68.

596 *Adam* (2012) p. 14; *Pascher* (2002) pp. 127ff. on a case of conformity of the FES and SPD on developmental political matters; differently *Wewer* (1987) p. 218.

597 *Bartsch* (2007) p. 282.

598 Similar *Egger* (2007) pp. 64ff.; *Pogorelskaja* (2002a) p. 30; *Nuscheler* (1993) p. 293; *Borchard* (2004) p. 95; *Bartsch* (2007) p. 282 with examples; differently *Werner* (1982) p. 31.

599 See Ch. 1.7.4.

the foundations' appropriations. Public utility, for example, was denied when foundations' funds were transferred to a political party. A statutory auditor, as prescribed by the funding ministries, reviewed and certified the regulatory and economic efficiency of the used funding.[600] However, these means did not deprive the foundations of their independence. Even when public funding was missing the foundations could finance some projects on their own. This was the case of the FNS's Tibet conference in Bonn in 1996, when funding was cut by the AA due to its supposed negative effects on the German Chinese relations. Ultimately, the FNS used other funding to hold the conference nonetheless.[601]

In sum, the German political foundations were generally able to generate their own public diplomacy as they were relative autonomous from the state institutions as well as the affiliated political parties. They were NGOs with the particularity to be state-funded which allowed terming them as GONGOs or as organisations "sui generis".[602] At the same time, they were different from QUANGOs as activity on behalf of the German government was missing. Since they regularly interacted across the German national boarder, they belonged to the transnational actors.

5.2. Addressees and instruments

Since 1962, the German political foundations' international activity was generally organised as project work and in cooperation with partner organisations.[603] The foundations deviated from this principle only for projects in the industrialised countries funded by the AA, when activities in the transition or developing countries were just about to be developed, when possible partner organisations lacked or when a specific development political mandate for their activity was missing (*Regieprogramme*).[604] In 1973, the involved partners in the developing countries were, according to the *German Bundestag*, trade unions, cooperatives, political parties, youth organisations, farmers' associations, journalists' associations and public institutions, such as broadcasting corporations, universities, governments and international organisations. Targets of the foundations' measures abroad

600 KAS at: http://www.kas.de/wf/de/71.3712/.

601 Der Spiegel, 24/1996 pp. 28f.

602 *Bartsch* (2007) p. 280.

603 BMZ (1973) p. 69; BT (1973) p. 41.

604 *Pogorelskaja* (2009b) p. 297.

were "political and social key groups".[605] The partner and target spectrum since then has hardly changed. Some new partner groups and individuals have been added, such as NGOs, think tanks and women's groups, business leaders and junior executives.[606] Partners and targets were not differentiated uniformly and often overlapped.[607] Partners termed as the "primary targets" paved the way for reaching a "secondary target audience".[608] While in the past, most of the foundations primarily targeted social and political elites, increasingly actors of civil society became a new focal point since the 1990s.[609] This shift coincided with growing use of funding from international organisations which possibly triggered the new primary target choice due to the organisations' imposed project conditions.[610] At the time of writing, the *Stiftungen* also increasingly targeted supranational and international organisations.[611]

Disputed aspects of the foundations' partner approach were the collaboration with political parties and high-level politics as practised from the very beginning of the foundations' international activities. In the 1970s and 1980s, the *Stiftungen* conducted almost aggressively the promotion of affiliated political parties, especially in Spain, Portugal and Latin-America. Sometimes the German foundations supported even parties devoid of any affiliation.[612] Such activities have decreased since then. For the activities in Eastern Europe in the 1990s the foundations targeted committees of the national parliaments and the respective fraction instead of the political party whose ideas did not match with the opinion of the respective foundation.[613] They also sought proximity to other party affiliated organisations, such as the British Westminster foundation as well as the Netherlands Institute for Multiparty Democracy.[614] However, political parties were still the key partners and targets for the majority of the German foundations

605 BT (1973) p. 41.

606 E.g. FNS (2013b) p. 19; FES at: http://www.fes.de/sets/s_fes_i.htm.

607 Explicitly FNS (2013b) p. 19.

608 *Pascher* (2002) p. 65.

609 Only the HBS had already targeted actors of civil society from the beginning of its international activities (*Pascher* [2002] pp. 65, 70); on cooperation with elites see KAS (2008a) p. 14.

610 FNS (2013a) pp. 101f.

611 *Pascher* (2002) p. 68.

612 *Pogorelskaja* (2009a) p. 45.

613 *Schneider-Deters* (2005) p. 112.

614 *Bartsch* (2007) p. 287.

and their "common denominator".[615] Although less practiced in the developing countries, the German political foundations tried as well to cooperate with governments even in countries where civil society partners could be found. The collaboration was particularly close when a political party previously supported by a foundation came into power. According to some authors, it was this desire to work with high level politicians differentiating the foundations from other non-state-organisations.[616] In this respect, they resembled lobby organisations. Apart from that, each foundation had a certain partner focus according to its political background.[617] The FES explicitly cooperated with trade unions, NGOs as well as academic and political consulting institutes.[618] The KAS referred to young professionals, media and public administration.[619] The FNS named regional networks, think tanks and NGOs.[620] The HBS concentrated on NGOs, women's organisations and other civil society actors, such as civil rights campaigners, the art scene and media.[621] The RLS gave attention to trade unions, women's organisations, social movements, research and educational institutions as well as international organisations,[622] while the HSS focused on associations and public administrations.[623] In the industrialised countries, the German political foundations did not apply the partner approach. Still, they remained focused on political, cultural as well as economic elites such as leaders of political parties, ministers, members of parliaments, economic decision makers, and important stakeholders from civil society, journalists

615 FES at: http://www.fes.de/sets/s_fes_i.htm; KAS at: http://www.kas.de/wf/de/71.3756/; FNS at: http://www.freiheit.org/Internationale-Politik/199c78/index.html (accessed on 28/09/2015); RLS at: http://www.rosalux.de/weltweit.html; HSS at: http://www.hss.de/internationale-arbeit/internationale-beziehungen.html; KAS even stressing political parties as partners for their media program: http://www.kas.de/wf/de/21.32/; lacking liberal and green parties led to a different partner focus of the FNS and the HBS in many countries. The RLS often faced the problem that many parties were already in cooperation with the FES (*Bartsch* [2007] p. 285).

616 *Pogorelskaja* (2009a) p. 47.

617 See Ch. 6.3.

618 FES at: http://www.fes.de/sets/s_fes_i.htm; FES annual report (1968) p. 12 on cooperatives and trade unions.

619 KAS at: http://www.kas.de/wf/de/71.3756/.

620 FNS (2013b) p. 4; FNS at: http://www.freiheit.org/Internationale-Politik/199c78/index.html (accessed on 28/09/2015).

621 C.f. HBS annual report 2012 pp. 4, 7, 8, 20, 45.

622 RLS at: http://www.rosalux.de/weltweit.html.

623 HSS (2014).

and think tanks' experts.[624] The list of international partners, as outlined, is not exhaustive and depended, evidently, on the involved instrument.

The German political foundations used several different medium and long-term public diplomacy instruments when being internationally active.[625] Abroad, the foundations carried out conferences, workshops, round tables, educational and expert seminars as well as discussion rounds. Moreover, they provided scholarships, organise exchanges, visitors' programs and deployments of experts to other countries. They also used certain media like publications and films, and they organised receptions. To a little extent, the German foundations supported their partners financially. However, this direct institutional funding was used less and less. Financial resources were made available, almost exclusively, via project financing.[626] These instruments, often overlapping, were generally used by all political foundations. What type of instrument was chosen depended on the country and what best served the respective project's objective.

5.2.1. Political dialogue

"Political dialogue" was an important foundations' work approach.[627] Its establishment coincided with the claim to create better economic, political and social framework conditions since in the 1970s many programs in the developing countries had failed.[628] Understanding political dialogue as a process of mutual exchange of information and ideas about options and activities in the development political arena,[629] it aimed at locating development bottlenecks and hindrances as well as finding suitable and necessary policies.[630] These dialogue processes wereexpected to generally take place at the highest political levels in the form of intergovernmental negotia-

624 E.g. FNS (2013b) p. 26; HSS at: http://www.hss.de/internationale-arbeit/internationale-beziehungen.html?tx_eepcollect_pi1[prozess]=add&tx_eepcollect_pi1[pid]=1150&tx_eepcollect_pi1[ctrl]=1392818881.

625 BMZ (1973) p. 70.

626 Interview 8.

627 Almost every political foundation maintained a division of political dialogue and analysis (c.f. KAS at: http://www.kas.de/wf/de/42.60/); *Pogorelskaja* (2009a) p. 40; *Pascher* (2002) p. 60.

628 *Lachmann* (2010) p. 265; see Ch. 6.1.

629 *Böhler* (1991) p. 129.

630 GTZ (1987) p. 2.

tions and discussions.[631] *Böhler*, on the contrary, assumed that the German political foundations' activities complemented these bilateral processes on an "operative level". The *Stiftungen* participated in political dialogue through the promotion of democracy aiming at developing political systems and at the strengthening of political parties, of law and order, of social and economic systems, of the role of media, of free elections, of the participation of minorities, of regional integration and of global governance.[632] Treating the foundations' activities in Eastern and Central Europe, *Schneider-Deters* stressed the replacement of the former political and civil education programs by political dialogue from the 1990s onwards targeting parliamentary, social and academic elites from other countries and in Germany. Political education had a negative connotation in the post-socialist states and signified ideological indoctrination.[633] For others, these dialogues were epitomes of the foundations' methods in the industrialised world.[634] The foundations' offices in the industrialised countries were mostly so called "International-political-dialogue-offices" (IPD). The IPD-departments interlinked different aspects of the foundations' activities where regional solutions were not appropriate, such as global and complex issues involving different partners and stakeholders.[635] Still, political dialogue even played an important role for the national work of the foundations where it concentrated on the dialogue between the general public and political actors.[636] In fact, political dialogue was a meta-level activity taking place in almost every country of activity focusing on the exchange of thoughts and experiences about political and social framework conditions and developments on national, regional and international level.[637]

5.2.2. Media programs

In the developing countries the German political foundations undertook media promotion programs considering media as part of a functioning

631 *Lachmann* (2010) p. 265.
632 *Böhler* (1991) p. 130, (2005) p. 8; KAS at: http://www.kas.de/wf/de/42.60/.
633 *Schneider-Deters* (2005) pp. 105ff.
634 *Nuscheler* (1993) p. 230; FES at: http://www.fes.de/sets/s_fes_i.htm.
635 *Mohr* (2010) p. 80.
636 FES at: http://www.fes.de/politischebildung/.
637 *Pascher* (2002) p. 60.

democracy.[638] Like political dialogue, media support coincided with the arising claims to improve the effectiveness of development cooperation in the 1970s. Since then it has been an instrument of the foundations' international activity.[639] Media seminars, journalists' trainings, radio programs, publications on media law or political opinion surveys, exchange programs for media professionals and the provision of grants were part of the foundations' media activities. In case of the KAS, the instrument included also the consulting of media providers, politicians and judges.[640] The KAS and the FES maintained regional media offices in addition to their country offices.[641]

5.2.3. Cultural diplomacy and scholarships

The German political foundations were also active in the field of cultural diplomacy. However, in the context of German AKBP (*Auswärtige Kultur- und Bildungspolititk)* coming closest to cultural diplomacy, other organisations, such as the Goethe-Institutes were more present.[642] According to *Pogorelskaja*, the foundations were only significant cultural actors when culture was understood broadly. However, they were in charge of foreign cultural political tasks from the very beginning of their activities.[643] In the *Konzeption 2000*, the framework for last decades' AKBP, the *Stiftungen* played a key role through the development of transatlantic and European cooperation, the support within the European unification process, the rapprochement of Central and Eastern Europe to these structures, and the performance of superregional and conflict prevention tasks.[644] Moreover, the foundations were active in several of AKBP's work fields: They supported professional and educational development through the provision of exchanges and seminars and established intercultural dialogues.[645] A small part of the foundations' activities comprised typical cultural programme

638 *Krämer/Lehrke* (1996); c.f. KAS at: http://www.kas.de/wf/de/21.32/; FES at: http://www.fes.de/sets/s_fes_i.htm; FNS (2013a) p. 26.

639 C.f. FNS (2013a).

640 KAS (2011) p. 5.

641 KAS at: http://www.kas.de/wf/de/21.32/; FES at: http://www.fesmedia.org/.

642 See Ch. 3.3. and 5.1.2.

643 *Pogorelskaja* (2009b) p. 299.

644 *Pogorelskaja* (2009b) pp. 301ff.; AA (2000).

645 AA (2011b) p. 40.

work, such as art exhibitions and readings.[646] Finally, the foundations awarded about 10-20% of all granted scholarships to foreign students from developing and transition countries.[647] A small amount of scholarships was given to foreign researchers.[648] In contrast to other AKBP actors, the foundations did not primarily pursue to transfer *German* culture. Still, through their activities they imparted German political culture abroad.[649]

5.2.4. Think tank activities and consulting

Around the world, the German foundations organised think tank events in partnership with other institutes and they were themselves considered as think tanks. Differentiating think tank activities from other foundations' activities was difficult. Typical think tank tasks were in-house academies, research and consulting units and study groups focusing on different types of policy and research. Moreover, the foundations lectured, published articles and books and organised conferences targeting research institutes and universities.[650] *Heisterkamp* identified four qualities of the *Stiftungen*: their hybrid character, their multifunctionality (i.e. think tank activity is not their only activity), their ideological orientation and a pluralistic labour division between the foundations resulting from the ideological background.[651] The *Stiftungen* were considered as advocacy think tanks although there were similarities with academic think tanks. Advocacy think tanks were characterised by thematic specialisation, a smaller number of permanent researchers, their networking with other experts and their activity as idea brokers instead of doing basic research.[652]

Closely related to the think tank activity, was the foundations' consulting activity often assessed as their core competence. While the think tank activities mainly took place in Germany, consulting was relevant at home and abroad. Consulting activities in the developing countries concerned the drafting of law, and the strengthening of public administrations, parlia-

646 C.f. KAS annual report (2013) p. 79.
647 See Ch. 1.1.
648 FES (2012a) p. 1.
649 *Dakowska* (2002) pp. 287, 288, 290; *Pogorelskaja* (2009b) p. 300.
650 *Thunert* (2004) pp. 78ff.; *Stone* (2004) p. 6; *Weilemann* (2000) p. 169.
651 *Heisterkamp* (2014) pp. 466ff.
652 *Thunert* (2003) p. 31; *Heisterkamp* (2014) pp. 486ff.

mentary committees and the judiciary.[653] This was closely connected to democracy assistance.[654] Consulting was also practiced in the industrialised countries and related to political dialogue.[655] On the European level the foundations consulted members of the EU parliament. The KAS, for instance, had been especially active in the drafting process of the EU Constitution by organising joint meetings with the EVP-ED Fraction at the EU Parliament, helping to coordinate and to find a position in the process.[656] The foundations' political orientation was surprisingly regarded as advantageous since the consulting foundation was expected to know the subject and those in receipt of advice. On the other hand, the foundation was not, in contrast to the party or fraction, devoted to actual trends.[657]

5.2.5. Political campaigning, advertisement and monologue instruments

The German political foundations were not involved in political or advertising campaigns. Their activities abroad were also not limited to a short period of time which became particular apparent in the establishment of international offices. In terms of monologue instruments, the foundations published books, articles, studies, conference papers and other material. The treated national and international topics arose from the specific political focus of the foundation and did not aim at advertising Germany directly. The material was introduced through seminars, conferences and consulting activity to the respective audience and did not, in this way, remain completely monologue.

In sum, the German political foundations were mainly active with dialogue public diplomacy instruments and covered the full range of activities as defined in the systematisation of public diplomacy as outlined in chapter 3. This included asymmetric communications, such as consulting but also symmetric communication in the form of political dialogue and cultural diplomacy.

653 BMZ at: http://www.bmz.de/de/was_wir_machen/wege/bilaterale_ez/akteure_ez/polstiftungen/index.html?follow=adword.

654 See Ch. 7.

655 *Thunert* (2007) p. 346.

656 *Pogorelskaja* (2009a) pp. 128f.

657 *Borchard* (2004) pp. 92f.

5.3. Dimensions

Of the public diplomacy dimensions the *Stiftungen* were often confronted with the accusation of promoting propaganda. In addition, networking was associated with their international activity.

5.3.1. Propaganda

In the developing and emerging countries, the criticism of interference was voiced from time to time. It could even manifest itself in investigations against the *Stiftungen* and their staff members or the disposed closing of offices. Recent cases were the questioning of KAS's and FES's staff members in Moscow by the Russian prosecution and tax investigation in 2013 as part of President Putin's action against NGOs, "Western influence" and "foreign agents".[658] Search of premises of the KAS's office in Egypt were carried out in 2011, when the then Egyptian government incriminated the *Stiftung* and several other NGOs to be foreign financed illegally.[659] In 2012, the government reproached the KAS and other institutions for being involved in a conspiracy against Egypt with the result that several KAS's staff members were prohibited to travel and, in 2013, convicted in absentia to several years of imprisonment. Also, the closure of the office was ordered.[660] The impediment of the foundations' activities has also taken place in other places like Abu Dhabi.[661] Of criminal infiltration and subversive activities the KAS, FES, FNS and HBS were accused by the Turkish prosecution in 2002 as they had been supported the prevention of gold mining in the region of Bergama. The Turkish court finally acquitted them in 2003.[662] Difficulties occured no matter whether Germany and the respective country are friendly states. For example, Israel discussed a maximum tax rate of 45 percent for political NGOs receiving money from foreign governments in 2012 which was traced back to a feeling of intrusion into internal affairs by Israel.[663]

---

658 *Brössler*, Süddeutsche Zeitung, 05/04/2013 and 26/03/2013.
659 Süddeutsche Zeitung, 30/12/2011.
660 *Ehrhardt/Hermann*, Frankfurter Allgemeine Zeitung, 06/02/2012; Die Welt, 04/06/2013.
661 *Pöttering*, Financial Times Deutschland, 11/06/2012.
662 HIP 13/11/2002; Frankfurter Allgemeine Zeitung, 04/03/2003.
663 *Von Mittelstaedt/Neukirch et al.*, Der Spiegel, 06/02/2012.

Conversely, the German foundations rationalised their interference. Chairman of the KAS *Pöttering* deemed necessary the external intervention of the *Stiftungen* in terms of cooperative partnerships with members of civil society. The prevention of the foundations' work by foreign governments would therefore direct against the country's own civil society. With the activities of the *Stiftungen* in the 1970s in Spain, Portugal and Greece as well as later in Eastern Europe and with the successful development of these countries, *Pöttering* rationalised the foundations' course of action.[664]

In the academic literature the problem of propaganda wasrather discussed under the premise of transparency and control. Most of the authors criticised the lacking clearness of projects, the partly obscure financing and the missing parliamentary control of the foundations' undertakings.[665] Although in the last two decades the publication of annual reports with balance sheets, articles and background information had increased, vagueness still existed in terms of detailed information on single projects as well as objectives, partners and financing. The FES, for instance, published some of their project evaluation reports, a conclusive list of reports was missing, however.[666]

The *Stiftungen* made no secret of this secrecy. In 2013, the FNS, for instance, published on their homepage that the reform process in Burma increasingly allowed them to work *openly* in the country, which implies that undercover activities had been taken place before.[667] The foundations rationalised the imprecision regarding project details and information on partners with the sensitivity of their work as increased transparency could lead to loss of trust and governmental implications for partners. Furthermore, the maintained contacts generally established over several years or even decades could suffer from the publicity.[668] In some regions, the foundations' activity might have only been possible because of discretion and nondisclosure. Nonetheless, it conflicted with their public financing and control over funds. The foundations' reluctance led also to the fact that

664 *Pöttering*, Financial Times Deutschland, 11/06/2012.

665 *Wewer* (1987); *Pinto-Duschinsky* (1991a) p. 35; *Mohr* (2010) p. 299, pp. 294ff.

666 FES at: http://www.fes.de/international/inhalt/evaluierung.htm; an author's request on the availability of other reports was denied pointing to their public inaccessibility (12/03/2014).

667 FNS at: http://www.freiheit.org/Stiftung-fuer-die-Freiheit-verstaerkt-Praesenz-in-Myanmar/617c21369i/ (accessed on 28/09/2015).

668 Indicated by the findings from the conducted interviews; e.g. HBS annual report (2012) p. 14 on activities in Belarus.

conducting interviews was often the only source for research.[669] In former times, the AA had pointed out to the foundations that they should avoid giving the information to their partners that their financial means stem from German public resources.[670] At the time of writing, this practice could not be confirmed anymore. As an interview partner assured, project partners generally knew about the sources of funds.[671]

According to the AA's requirements of non-interference, the *Stiftungen* must not get involved into internal political battles abroad which included the assistance in electoral campaigns.[672] Especially their Latin-American activities in the 1970s and 1980s are viewed as examples of this requirement's violation.[673] In Chile, the first democratically elected president after the *Pinochet* era in 1990, *Patricio Aylwin*, had close relations to the KAS.[674] From time to time, the subject was still a matter of discussion.[675] In some countries the *Stiftungen* seemed to work underground when they did not receive the respective permissions, like in Belarus.[676] Also the foundations' support of underground organisations fighting against the respective foreign government was officially proscribed by the AA.[677] However, it could not be ruled out that in autocratic regimes the foundations sought contacts and assisted groups that were politically outlawed by the respective government. Moreover, the foundations' project secrecy would not make sense if partners must not fear reprisals from their governments for cooperating with the foundations. Despite the ministry's binding rule of non-interference, the *Stiftungen* are institutions of a Western democracy. As *Pogorelskaja* precisely summarised, most of their foreign activities could be ultimately viewed as interference into internal affairs.[678] It depended on the involved states and their relations to the Western World whether they regarded the activities as propagandistic. From time to time, the foundations were even suspected of being henchmen of the Federal Intelligence Service. At the end of the Franco dictatorship in Spain in the 1970s, the German political

669 Authors' personal experience; similar *Mohr* (2010) p. 297 fn. 832.
670 BMZ (1973) p. 65.
671 Interview 8.
672 BMZ (1973) p. 69; Federal budget of 2015, Kapitel 2302 Titel 68704.
673 *Pogorelskaja* (2009a) p. 46.
674 *Von Mittelstaedt/Neukirch et al.*, Der Spiegel, 06/02/2012.
675 E.g. on an assumed KAS's election campaign support in Nicaragua in 1990 (BT [1990]).
676 *Von Mittelstaedt/Neukirch et al.*, Der Spiegel, 06/02/2012.
677 *Pogorelskaja* (2009a) p. 41.
678 *Pogorelskaja* (2009a) p. 47.

foundations financially supported political parties. It was assumed that for this purpose the intelligence service had created a secret fund, which was allocated by the Federal Chancellery.[679] Although such practices could not be confirmed, they were difficult to rule out. Still, they rationalised suspicion and mistrust. On the contrary, the foundations' relative autonomy and heterogeneity impeded an instrumental use of the foundations for propaganda purposes. Moreover, there were generally several foundations active in one country, each promoting different objectives, partners and groups in society. This pluralistic approach and the fact that the foundations mainly supported dialogue instruments spoke against the assumption of propaganda.

5.3.2. Networks

The literature on German public diplomacy, so far, had not considered the network building of the *Stiftungen*. The foundations, on the contrary, were aware of their network operations. However, they mainly focused on their international contacts only.[680] Also the Foreign Office considered from the very beginning of the foundations' international activities, the foundations' capabilities to establish contacts in a German and foreign networking environment.[681] The foundations' networking has also been increasingly acknowledged by researchers studying the *Stiftungen*, but in most works it usually remained a side-effect. The findings either focused on the international relationships[682] or referred to cooperation with link-minded civil society organisations.[683] Others found networking among political, economic and cultural elites only relevant for the foundations' transnational and European activities.[684] Very rarely, the foundations' networking was mentioned in the context of democracy assistance, like in case of the foundations' activities in Central, Eastern and Southeast Europe.[685] In a diplomatic context *Renvert* mentioned public diplomacy and transnational network-

---

679 *Pogorelskaja* (2009a) p. 162; differently *Von zur Mühlen* (2007) p. 65.

680 C.f. FES at: http://www.fes.de/sets/s_fes_i.htm; KAS at: http://www.kas.de/wf/de/71.3756/.

681 AAPA Zwischenarchiv 118163 30/11/1973.

682 C.f. *Pascher* (2002) pp. 71ff.

683 *Thunert* (2004) p. 79; *Nuscheler* (1993) p. 232.

684 C.f. *Bartsch* (1998) p. 3.

685 *Pogorelskaja* (2009a) pp. 127f.

ing of the foundations in the USA.[686] Also *Schneider-Deters* conceded to the German foundations an important role in "civil diplomacy" when establishing networks in the framework of the political dialogue instrument.[687]

5.3.2.1. Relationships

The German political foundations had strong foreign interlinks as they addressed various levels of society and politics ranging from foreign governments and administrations, political parties, civil society organisations, researchers, students and executives. Each foundation was part of an international party organisation or a similar umbrella organisation connecting members with a common political background.[688] Furthermore, the *Stiftungen* liaised constantly with the German embassies and the other foundations' representatives abroad in order to coordinate their activities.[689] At times, the foundations cooperated with other German organisations abroad, such as the *Goethe Institute* or the GIZ.[690] Further relationships, for example with EU or UN bodies, were established on supra-national level.

In Germany, the German political foundations were first of all linked with their affiliated parties on organisational and personnel level.[691] If the political party was in power, the foundation also maintained contacts to the highest political level ranging from the ministries to the chancellery. Similar contacts existed on the *Land* level. Interaction also occurred with the German *Bundestag* and the responsible departments in the funding ministries. The German universities and external researchers were interlinked with the foundations: Several foundations' researchers taught at universities. Research was also contractually outsourced by the foundations to other researchers. Relationships between the foundations and German students were, similar to those with international students, established through the provision of scholarships. Also mentoring programs between former and current fellows were organised and contacts existed to the ad-

686 *Renvert* (2005) p. 7.
687 *Schneider-Deters* (2005) p. 111.
688 *Pinto-Duschinsky* (1991a) pp. 42ff.; *Mohr* (2010) pp. 147ff.
689 Interview 2, 4; *Pogorelskaja* (2009a) p. 40; *Schmidt*, Frankfurter Allgemeine Zeitung, 23/03/2011.
690 FNS (2013a) p. 53; *Pogoreslkaja* (2009b) p. 303 fn. 22; *Schneider-Deters* (2005) p. 115.
691 See Ch. 1.7.2.

vising professors of the supported students.[692] Public events in Germany organised by the foundations also helped to link the German general public and interested civilians to the network of relationships.[693] Due to different thematic work focus and affiliation to partners who were poles apart, each foundation established dissimilar relationships.

The stability of the relationships in Germany stemmed from the fact that the foundations were an integral part of the German political landscape resulting mainly from the time factor. The *Stiftungen* were mostly (re)created in the early years of the Federal Republic and could develop and adapt simultaneously to Germany's political conditions. Also, their abroad activities were almost as old as the foundations themselves. With their world-wide offices at least one foundation could always be found in a region.[694] Continuity of projects and long-term partnerships were regarded as very important by all political foundations and estimated as the key to trusting and firm relationships.[695] Stability and personal contacts were further enhanced by the foundations' overseas representatives. They generally stayed several years in one place, which allowed coordinating projects intensively. It was also a main task of the offices establishing contacts with future partners and keeping follow up contacts with former partners.[696] The international offices usually employed local staff members, who further provided valuable entry points into the foreign societies contributing to stability.[697]

Despite their public funding, the *Stiftungen* enjoyed a great amount of independence from the public bodies and political parties in Germany as we have seen above. Partner organisations abroad might have been financially dependent on the foundations although financial dependence had decreased in the last decades.[698] Also scholarship holders were financially dependent on the foundations. The dependency was yet relativised as there were generally several different foundations offering scholarships. The influence of the foundations also ended with the selection procedure. In the party internationals or similar organisations, the German foundations hold

---

692 Interview 8; Weilemann (2000) pp. 183f.; FES at: http://www.fes.de/studienfoerderung/ehemaligen-netzwerk.
693 *Thunert* (2004) p. 83; *Bartsch* (2007) p. 287.
694 See Ch. 1.7.1., 6.3.1.
695 Interviews 8, 13; c.f. FES (2012b) p. 2; FES (2012c) p. 1; KAS at: http://www.kas.de/wf/en/42.9/; FNS (2013b) p. 10.
696 KAS (2008a) p. 14; *Schürmann* (1989) p. 140.
697 BMZ (1973) p. 71.
698 See Ch. 5.2.

a strong position due to their financial basis which was more solid than that of other members.[699]

While the majority of relationships between the foundations and others was characterised by cooperation, competition had been especially relevant in former times. In 1982, *Werner* stated that the foundations often competed with the official German diplomats abroad which then caused irritations in the partner country. Moreover, the reputation as well as the influence of the foundations was sometimes assumed to be higher than that of the official diplomats.[700] The archival material of the 1960s showed a great scepticism of the German embassies in Latin America towards the activities of the political foundations. They overly indicated possible conflicts of interferences since the foundations worked with high-level politics and the opposition.[701] Also later material showed that embassies were concerned about the activities of the foundations from time to time. In 1980, for example, the German embassy criticised a conference with leftwing and revolutionary organisations which was organised by the FES in El Salvador.[702] Furthermore, critics outlined that the foundations competed abroad.[703] Their support of different political groupings would lead to political confusion and pointless development actions neutralising each other.[704] The foundations were supposed to coordinate their activities on site.[705] At the time of writing, it seemed that both relationships embodied fewer contests. The foundations and the embassies seemed to depend on each other. Both had access to different resources of which the other was in need. Projects were sometimes even implemented as joint-projects. Information on the foundations could also be found on the German embassies' websites.[706] Conflicts between the foundations and the funding ministries were rarely known. The actors seemed to share a common sense about political usefulness and allowance of projects.[707] The foundations' different partner focuses, and the distinct party affiliation generally led to separate spheres of activities and little relations among the foundations. At times,

699 *Pinto-Duschinsky* (1991a) p. 42; *Mohr* (2010) p. 147.
700 *Werner* (1982) pp. 27f.; *Von zur Mühlen* (2007) pp. 70f.; similar interview 4.
701 AAPA B58/1 Bd. 872.
702 AA (1980a).
703 *Schürmann* (1989) pp. 55f.
704 *Werner* (1982) p. 30.
705 BMZ (1973) p. 65.
706 Similar *Pogorelskaja* (2009a) p. 42.
707 *Bartsch* (2007) p. 281.

the foundations even collaborated.[708] Also funding competition did not take place due to the fixed allocation formula.[709] The relations to the German GIZ were ambivalent.[710] They were marked by cooperation as well as competition. Conflicts resulted recently from the extension of the GIZ's activities.[711] Despite some common declaration intending a clear dividing line between the activities of both organisations, the foundations' mistrust did not fully dispel.[712]

In sum, the German political foundations maintained many relationships to public and private actors, abroad as well as in Germany. The relationships were generally stable and primarily independent characterised by competition and cooperation.

5.3.2.2. Resources, values and interests

In the context of the established relationships, we could identify various resources which the foundations provided to other network members and from which they profited in turn. This included financial resources, knowledge, information, moral authority and networking capabilities.

Financial resources were assigned to the German political foundations from the German *Bundestag* and allocated through the funding German ministries. Further capital was given to them by supranational organisations.[713] The *Stiftungen* made these financial resources available for their activities. Limited direct financial support was given to some partners.

From partners abroad as well as their observations and experiences, the foundations accessed information on the country and its political, social and economic situation. The foundations' international offices all over the world provided the necessary infrastructure for this task. In this gathering of information, the foundations were similar to embassies. The foundations' representatives prepared regular country reports which did not only concern the project but also information on the country's political, economic and social development which was also sent to the BMZ.[714] Research

708 Interview 13; *Pascher* (2002) p. 88; KAS (2008a) p. 15; differently *von Borries* (2007) p. 199.
709 See Ch. 1.7.3; *Egger* (2007) p. 70.
710 See Ch. 6.2.1.
711 KAS (2008a) p. 14; *Bartsch* (2007) p. 286; FNS (2012a) p. 102.
712 *Mohr* (2010) pp. 288f.
713 See Ch. 1.7.3.
714 BMZ (1973) p. 73; *Egger* (2007) p. 63 fn. 173.

and country information provided by the foundations were also sources of information when official travelling and foreign visits to the German *Bundestag* were prepared.[715] Furthermore, the foundations' abroad offices produced material concerning current political topics published on the foundations' websites. Information was processed, and knowledge was used for the foundations' think tank and consulting activities. Research was also provided by the foundations' scholarship holders and often publicised on the foundations' websites.[716] Through their coordination abroad all foundations exchanged experiences and information informally.[717] As outlined above, the German embassy and the foundations' country offices were in close contact on the projects. The foundations were able to offer information on aspects that were generally not available to the German embassies due to the partners they cooperated with. The foundations could maintain contacts with various actors of civil society and to even doubtful opposition groups without being bound to official diplomatic guidelines. For other activities, the foundations bought expertise from others, who were not foundations' employees but indentured for the specific task.[718] Expertise that the foundations needed sometimes came from other German organisations, such as the GIZ.[719]

The regular meetings of the foundations with the German ministries did not only concern the foundations' international projects but also conceptual questions of development policy.[720] While foundations' staff members participated at conferences and departmental meetings of the ministries, ministerial staff members were also regular participants in working groups initiated by the foundations.[721] Moreover, foundations' staff members often were invited to committee meetings of the German *Bundestag* when their practical experience or special knowledge as experts on a country's or region's matter was necessary.[722] Finally, the political party profited from the affiliated foundation's expertise, research and collected information

---

715 Author's personal experience.

716 FES (2012a) p. 2.

717 Interview 3.

718 Interview 1; c.f. FES at: http://journalistenakademie.fes.de/trainer.php; Ch. 9.

719 *Schneider-Deters* (2005) p. 114.

720 BMZ at: http://www.bmz.de/de/was_wir_machen/wege/bilaterale_ez/akteure_ez/nros/index.html.

721 *Bartsch* (1998) p. 187; *Pogorelskaja* (2009a) pp. 40ff.; e.g. ministerial staff members participating at the FES's working group on European integration in Brussels: http://www.fes.de/sets/s_gekr.htm.

722 Author's personal experience; *Bartsch* (1998) p. 186.

presented in elaborated form. This became particularly valuable for political parties in opposition since their access was closed to such information resources the ministries provided to governing parties.[723] This processing of information and knowledge from abroad to actors in Germany has been described as "feedback effect" and international knowledge transfer. [724]

The *Stiftungen* possessed furthermore significant networking resources, which included not only being nationally and internationally well connected but also the capability to establish and moderate such networks.[725] For the partners abroad not only funding and expertise of the foundations were important, but also the contact network that the foundations created.[726] Official travels of German parliamentarians, parliamentarian groups as well as of committees and of the presidium of the German *Bundestag* often included visits with the foundations' representatives abroad. Regularly the foundations' representatives were referred to regarding information on suitable interlocutors abroad.[727] Also the members of the affiliated political parties were interested in the networks established by the foundations. They were guests and speakers at conferences and seminars organised by the foundations abroad.[728] Still, the foundations did not only focus on networks among politicians or on connecting politicians with other actors. They were able to multidirectionally interlink various levels of politics and society formally or informally: Foreign elites, think tanks and civil society groups were brought together with German experts, members of civil society and politicians in visit or educational programs.[729] At the same time, the foundations also tried to connect similar partners from different countries.[730] Partners from developing and transformation countries were also brought together with actors from the industrialised countries.[731] The instrument of political dialogue was the epitome for this networking. But also, the other instruments implemented by the foundations, not necessar-

723 Interview 4; *Weilemann* (2000) p. 185.

724 C.f. *Bartsch* (2007) p. 287; *Borchard* (2004) p. 93.

725 Similar *Böhler* (2005) p. 7.

726 C.f. FES (2012d) p. 2; *Pascher* (2002) p. 75.

727 Interviews 2, 4, 13; author's personal experience; *Weilemann* (2000) p. 184; AA (1980b).

728 Interview 8; *Pascher* (2002) p. 92.

729 E.g. FNS's visitors' program: http://www.freiheit.org/Informations-und-Besuchs programme/430c159/index.html (accessed on 28/09/2015).

730 C.f. FNS (2013b) p. 19.

731 E.g. FNS (2013b) p. 26; HSS at: http://www.hss.de/internationale-arbeit/internat ionale-beziehungen.html?tx_eepcollect_pi1[prozess]=add&tx_eepcollect_pi1[pid]=1150&tx_eepcollect_pi1[ctrl]=1392818881.

ily abroad, contributed explicitly or implicitly to the establishment of these networks. Also the think tank activity "adds up to a widely diversified network".[732] Similar to the information and knowledge resources, the affiliated party profited from these contact possibility and channels of communication especially when being in opposition.[733] Moreover, the foundations sought to constantly extend their network of contacts but also to involve contact persons more closely in the network even when their actual interaction was terminated. The FES, for example, tried to establish researchers and young professionals who had received a scholarship as experts in their home countries or region afterwards.[734] Foreign scholarship holders were also relevant as they often became future decision makers. The then Nepali prime minister *Sher Bahadur Deuba* was, for instance, a former FES's scholarship holder.[735] The disseminator approach as practiced by the foundations helped to broaden the network and integrate new participants and scholarship holders could function as "door-openers". The establishment and expansion of the network added furthermore to the knowledge and information resources, as described above. Finally, the foundations seemed to be aware of their networking competence when they changed their educational provisions to political dialogue measures.[736] Their potential of being well connected had also been realised by other international actors. Its access to foreign partners and political actors was, according to the FNS, its comparative advantage when carrying out projects in cooperation with the EU, the UN and the GIZ.[737]

Another important resource that the foundations provided was their moral authority. From the very beginning of the foundations' establishment, they used the term "foundation" despite its legal incorrectness. This affix created a false appearance about the financial situation, but it was also beneficial for the foundations' image.[738] It is likely, that the philanthropic representation was helpful when working with groups which were rather critical of states' structures. As the fact of state funded foundations was not even much known to the German public, it can be expected that the origins of funds were not always a matter of discussion when establishing contacts abroad. We can assume that the foundations profited from the

732 *Weilemann* (2000) p. 184.
733 Interview 4.
734 FES (2012a) p. 2.
735 *Pascher* (2002) p. 76.
736 See Ch. 5.2.
737 FNS (2013a) p. 101.
738 See Ch. 1.7.2.; *Vieregge* (1977a) p. 31.

perceived governmental independence which contributed to a larger network and increasing information as civil society actors could be involved.[739]

The exchange of resources among the foundations and the different actors was not necessarily caused by a common interest. It could match but it could also be diverse. The *Stiftungens'* activities broadly aimed at fostering social stability and the improvement of political circumstances in the developing and transition countries.[740] With most of their partners abroad as well as with the affiliated political party in Germany, the foundations evidently shared a highly developed sense of value which rooted in a common political attitude. Whether these common values and policy interests were shared as well with the German government needs to be assessed for the field of activity as well as the specific region the foundations are active in. *Glagow* characterised the relation between the ministries and the *Stiftungen* as led by conformity of interest. The ministry could not influence these interests as they were "domestically opportune".[741] We will come back to this assumption later on.

In sum, we could see that the foundations largely operated in a cooperative networking environment where ideational and material resources were exchanged. This is a preliminary inventory. We have not found answers to the type of transnational network the foundations mainly operated in nor to the ideas diffused by them. This will be analysed in the following chapters.

Conclusion

The German political foundations were transnational actors. As public diplomats they mainly implemented dialogue instruments and established relationships with various foreign and domestic actors with which they exchanged resources. In contrast to propaganda, creative communication accepts pluralism.[742] It was this overall pluralistic context of various political preferences and different ideas in which the political foundations must be seen. We will return to these ideas in the following chapters.

739 Similar AAPA Zwischenarchiv 118163 30/11/1973.

740 *Bartsch* (1998) p. 3.

741 *Glagow* (1990) p. 174.

742 *Melissen* (2007b) pp. 18f.

We also saw that the foundations were relatively independent actors. When the foundations started their international activities in the 1960s and public funding was granted to them, it had happened at the expense of public control. At the time of writing, even the limited existing abilities to exercise influence on the foundations' work were mostly not performed by the German ministries. In particular, the evaluations of projects did not serve as instrument of control but rather seemed to help gathering information on the country. The political parties, in contrast, were not allowed to control the foundations' activities officially. Recently, the foundation's independence was further enhanced when starting to acquire additional funds from other supranational donors which originally resulted from diminishing national funding. Consequently, the *Stiftungen* could not be considered as tools of a "public" public diplomacy. Still, the foundations' organisational autonomy was granted intentionally by the public bodies. As we have seen above, German public diplomacy was characterised by many different semi-public and private actors. Although they were involved in German public diplomacy, they did not have to implement the AA's public diplomacy strategy.[743]

We can assume that the outsourcing of certain undertakings to the *Stiftungen* had happened since only the foundations were able to fulfil certain tasks or at least to fulfil them more easily. The proposed network image where resources are exchanged, and which is characterised by labour division offers an explanation on the advantages which resulted from it, especially for the German government. The establishment of contacts and the dissemination of information between civil society actors abroad and actors in Germany had been rarely possible if the foundations were not a node in the network structure. Since a wide variety of actors could not be reached and this could not be compensated by other actors, the German political foundations had a gate keeper function. In this context, each foundation established its own network. International partners of other foundations were generally respected and not headhunted.[744] Moreover, in cases of a power shift in a certain country already established contacts between former opposition groups and the German foundations could be helpful for the official German diplomacy.[745] An interview partner gave a concrete example: After the political change in Indonesia in 1998/9 when

743 See Ch. 3.3.; *Karten* (2008) p. 178.

744 *Pascher* (2002) p. 77.

745 *Pogorelskaja* (2002a) pp. 35f.; *Renvert* (2011) p. 35; *Nuscheler* (1993) p. 237; *Mair* (2000) p. 133.

President *Suharto* was ousted from power, the Federal Foreign Office did not have sufficient contacts to the following *Bacharuddin Jusuf Habibie*. Regular meetings with the *Stiftungen* and the German embassy took place to fill the gap.[746] Certainly, the foundations depended on the fact that partners abroad could be found. However, they were flexible enough to find them other partners and work fields when originally desired connections could not be established in the first place. Recently, this problem had been experienced by the German political foundations in some countries participating in the Arab Spring from 2011 onwards. Here, the greater transformation processes led to gaps in the desired partner landscape.[747] While the foundations' network connections and resource exchange was visible, the actual use of information and communication channels resulting from the network could hardly be verified. There were cases in which such pathways could be confirmed. *Pinto-Duschinsky* gave the drastic example where Chancellor *Kohl* (CDU) circumvented the Foreign Minister *Genscher* (FDP) in the months before the German reunifications by using KAS's representatives in some foreign capitals as "alternative channels of high-level politics" due to tensions between the foreign ministry and the chancellery.[748]

In the literature on the practical aspects of public diplomacy, it was suggested that the promotion of civil society as well as the struggle against terrorism and the prevention of conflict presented apt examples of how public diplomacy can be undertaken.[749] They are collaborative forms of dialogue public diplomacy. In the following chapters, we will analyse the activities of the *Stiftungen* in the context of both concepts.

746 Interview 4.

747 *Schmidt*, Frankfurter Allgemeine Zeitung, p. 3, 23/03/2011.

748 *Pinto-Duschniksky* (1991b) p. 222.

749 See Ch. 3.2.4.

Chapter 6 – The German political foundations: Democracy assistants?

Public diplomacy has several practical aspects. As already outlined, development assistance in transition and developing countries can be regarded as one such initiative aiming at the building of social relationships.[750] Also institution building has been mentioned.[751] Moreover, a "soft" nation building approach can be among such activities described as a long-term process where the creation of civil society and a strong middle class is enhanced.[752] In such practical forms of public diplomacy, transnational actors are central as they either perform a supporting role or are part of state-non-state joint initiatives leading to a catalytic diplomatic activity.[753] Sometimes, the involvement of official diplomats is even considered inappropriate and the participating of transnational actors as simply more effective especially when civil society is promoted.[754] Also the literature on non-state actors has highlighted these comparative advantages.[755] Both, the public diplomatic and the non-state perspective consider the establishment of networks in the development political context.[756]

The German political foundations have been identified as being involved in democratisation processes. The literature on public diplomacy mentioned briefly their networking activities in this context.[757] However, the diplomatic literature did not systematically introduce the development political concepts. Thus, the following chapter starts from the concept of democracy promotion in the form of democracy assistance as this comes closest to the activities of the *Stiftungen*. It also takes up the connected concepts mentioned by the diplomatic literature. In order to understand the overall position of the *Stiftungen* in the framework of these activities,

750 See Ch. 3; *Cowan/Arsenault* (2008) pp. 21ff.; *Riordan* (2007) p. 191; *Zaharna* (2009) describing development aid as public diplomacy's second-tier relationship-building (p. 94).

751 *Hocking* (2011) p. 230.

752 *Riordan* (2007) pp. 184f.

753 *Hocking* (2011) p. 230.

754 *Riordan* (2007) pp. 186, 190.

755 C.f. *Biekart* (2001) p. 257.

756 *Basu* (2011) pp. 406, 408ff.; *Riordan* (2007) pp. 191, 193.

757 *Riordan* (2007) p. 191.

German development policy and its democracy promotion component is briefly introduced. Afterwards, the undertakings of the *Stiftungen* are analysed as regards the preceding considerations. We conclude with the actor advantages and benefits for the German government that stem from the construct of the foundations' international activities.

6.1. Democracy promotion and assistance

Defining democracy directly is almost impossible. It refers broadly to the form of government in which all eligible citizens participate equally. It has various forms.[758] The promotion of democracy in many countries has been policy rhetoric for the last 100 years.[759] According to the modernisation theory dominating the development policy debate in the 1950s and 1960s, democracy was, in short, an automatic result of economic growth. Development policy therefore concentrated on the latter. In the 1990s it was discussed that democracy was reversely a condition for development although this was not entirely supported by scientific evidence. Nonetheless, the support of democracy and human rights in the following time became a central goal of the development and foreign policy of the OECD and of most democratic states, including Germany. It based on an ethical and normative understanding of development policy and the peaceableness of democratic states among each other.[760] Since then, aiding countries mainly use three instruments for the promotion of democracy abroad:[761] The first mechanism is political conditionality which either sanctions the violation of human rights or democratic principles by refusing the award of payments (negative approach) and rewards positive developments by dept reliefs and favourable loans (positive approach). The second instrument is the use of positive measures, namely democracy assistance. It encompasses methods by transnational actors to help the electoral process, to assist democratic state institutions and to support civil society. The latter focuses on free and fair election (campaigns), the ability for citizens to vote, a party system where few major parties are bound to democratic values and mod-

758 *Buchstein* (2006) p. 47; *Richter* (2009) pp. 34ff.

759 *Carothers* (2006) pp. 3f.

760 *Schmidt* (2013a) pp. 280f. referring to *Russett* (1993) regarding the democratic peace approach; *Nuscheler* (2005) pp. 423f.; *Burnell* (2000a) p. 3.

761 *Burnell* (2008) p. 283 with details; *Burnell* (2000a) pp. 6-10 on the definitional distinction of democracy promotion and assistance.

erate ideological affiliation, a written constitution, the separation of powers and the rule of law, an active and diverse civil society articulating interests as well as independent media and trade unions (see *table 6.1*).[762] Examples for this instrument are the sensitizing of public employees, such as policemen, military, security forces and judges for human rights, the support of NGOs being active in the fields of democracy or human rights, the assistance of journalists and vulnerable groups.[763] It also includes the support of democratic parliaments, the building up of political parties and the monitoring of elections.[764] Often these political activities are viewed as intrusion into the sovereignty of the state.[765] The third instrument of promoting democracy is the imposition of democracy by force. It is not very popular due to few successful examples, such as post-war Germany and Japan.

Table 6.1: Democracy assistance: objectives and modalities[766]

Sector	Sector Goal	Type of Aid
Electoral process	– Free and fair elections	– Electoral aid
	– Strong national political parties	– Political party building
State institutions	– Democratic constitution	– Constitutional assistance
	– Independent, effective judiciary and other law-oriented institutions	– Rule of law aid
	– Competent, representative legislature	– Legislative strengthening
	– Responsive local government	– Local government development
	– Pro-democratic military	– Civil-military relations
Civil society	– Active advocacy bodies and NGOs	– Building civil-society organisations and NGOs
	– Politically educated citizenry	– Civic education
	– Strong independent media	– Media strengthening
	– Strong independent unions	– Union building

In democracy assistance a distinction is made between the developmental and the political approach. The first conception understands democracy

762 *Carothers* (2006) pp. 86f.
763 *Schmid* (2002).
764 *Schmidt* (2013a) p. 281.
765 *Schmid* (2002).
766 *Carothers* (2006) p. 88, (1999) p. 88; *Burnell* (2008) p. 284.

broadly which is achieved through incremental and long-term change processes on various political and socioeconomic levels. The political approach, in contrast, mainly looks at elections and political liberties. It hopes to gain dominance over non-democratic trends and to become a catalyst in focusing on central political processes and institutions.[767]

Democracy promotion has points of contact with good governance, a contested reference concept in development policy first coined by the World Bank in the 1990s. It defines governance "as the manner in which power is exercised in the management of a country's economic and social resources of development. Good governance, (...) is synonymous with sound development management".[768] After 1990, different international organisations refined the concept. Until today the term is used non-uniformly. It centres on the characteristics of the rule of law, the accountability of governments, the effectiveness and efficiency of governance, transparency and participation.[769] Good governance is a condition for development cooperation but also its aim.[770] In fact, it tries to establish universally structural characteristics historically developed in the West. As this can collide with the developed structural traits in the recipient countries, it is often pleaded for a "bottom-up"-understanding centring on civil society which presents the root for the democratic "super-structure".[771] This requirement is also reflected in the democracy assistance model as presented above (see *table 6.1*). Capacity development as a flexible process to build and enhance

767 *Carothers* (2009) p. 5.

768 World Bank (1992) p. 1.

769 Rule of law has the following requirements: the law accordance of the government, an independent court system, constitutional rights to investigate and supervise the executive and administrative powers and equality before the law (OECD [1995] p. 14). Accountability concerns those of governmental institutions (and the private and civil-society sector) to the public and their institutional stakeholders. Effectiveness and efficiency ensure that processes and institutions achieve results that satisfy the societal needs using the available resources in the best way. Efficiency also covers the sustainable use of environmental resources. Transparency means that decisions are taken and enforced in a manner that follows rules and regulations. Information is freely available and directly accessible to those who will be affected by such decisions. Participation is the partaking in the governance process of men and women either directly or through legitimate intermediate institutions (UN [2009a]). Good governance can also include the controlling of corruption and the reduction of excessive military expenditure (OECD [1995] pp. 14-22).

770 *Schmidt* (2013b) pp. 285f.; *Seifert* (2009) pp. 16f.

771 *Lapins* (2007) pp. 19f.; *Schmidt* (2013b) pp. 288f.

organisational and professional competencies in third countries[772] is closely connected to democracy assistance when it comes to the furthering of political institutions and civil society organisations.

The definitional separation of democracy assistance from state-building is difficult.[773] Although democracy assistance has a stronger focus on the support of civil societies whereas state-building is more directed to reforms and the establishment of non-existing but essential state functions, both modalities mostly overlap. State-building is more holistic in contrast to democracy aid for the state sector. It does not concentrate on "democratic" state structures only but also on welfare state and security components.[774] It can involve the construction of institutions from scratch, while democracy assistance tries to reshape existing institutions. Democracy assistance does not particularly aid the executive state power. Authoritarian or totalitarian countries often have an overly powerful executive which is supposed to be counterbalanced.[775] The modernisation of the executive, in contrast, is a state-building component.[776] The main difference is that state-building focuses on failed and fragile states only.[777] It aims towards the following targets: the stabilising of existing structures and institutions, their reform if not transformation or their (re)construction.[778] This is why it is often dis-

---

772 *Tayyar* (2013) p. 214.

773 *Burnell* (2000a) p. 12; *Stütz* (2008) p. 23.

774 On the modalities see *Schneckener* (2007) p. 10. State-building is sometimes assumed to be a part of nation building (*Hippler* [2004] p. 23). *Stütz* (2008), however, convincingly argues that both are different strategies: while state-building focuses rather on the "visible, organisational and technical side of the state", nation building comprises the support of civil society, culture and patriotism (p. 21).

775 *Carothers* (2006) p. 159.

776 *Schneckener* (2007) p. 9.

777 *Lambach* (2014); *Smith* (2008). State-building originally focused on failed states. In 2008 it was extended by the OECD (2008b) to fragile states (*Grävingholt/Gänzle/Ziaja* [2009] p. 5). Neither fragility nor failure is used uniformly (*Preuß* [2013] p. 310). In general, fragility exists when the state's institutions have lost or insufficiently developed in central remits their control, allocative functions and their capability to act which often causes a rapid or creeping process of the loss of legitimacy (*Schneckener* [2007] p. 7). A fragile region or state has weak capacity to carry out basic governance functions and lacks the ability to develop mutually constructive relations with society (OECD [2014b] p.18). State failure refers to circumstances of less than a complete state collapse where basic state functions are not fulfilled anymore. (*Doornbos* [2008] pp. 251f.). It is therefore situated between state collapse and fragility.

778 *Schneckener* (2007) p. 9.

cussed in the context of peace-building and viewed as being at the interface between security policy and development policy.[779] In contrast to a state formation happening directly or indirectly on the impulses of the respective population, state-building involves external actors which implement measures straightly.[780] The range of measures and the influence of external actors on the process vary from mere consulting activities to a complete state function's substitution.[781] For the aim achievement state-building concentrates on short periods of time.[782] This is different from a political approach of democracy assistance focusing on longer periods and from democracy assistance as "whatever helps democratisation directly or indirectly, sooner or later".[783]

Although until today democracy is on the development political agenda of most countries, the subject was not treated with priority by the main international forums from 2000 onwards.[784] The "war on terror" in the aftermath of 9/11 also relativised U.S. ambitions in democracy promotion and led to a primacy of military and security policy including friendly relationships with non-democratic states.[785] Although it is assumed that democracy can help combating terrorism in the long run, its promotion may cause conflicts due to changes unintended by the established elite.[786] Another challenge to the promotion of democracy is that some donor countries often do not intend political reforms and therefore diminish the efforts of the democracy focused donors.[787]

---

779 See Ch. 7; c. f. *Debiel/Lambach/Pech* (2007) p. 15.

780 *Stütz* (2008) pp. 21ff.

781 *Schneckener* (2007) p. 5.

782 *Stütz* (2008) p. 23.

783 *Burnell* (2000a) p. 12.

784 An exception is the Warsaw declaration of 2000 establishing the Community of Democracies. It aims at strengthening democracy world-widely (https://www.community-democracies.org/). The UN's *Millenium Development Goals* of 2000, in contrast, did not specify binding targets for democratisation (UN [2000a] pp. 6f.); likewise, the OECD Paris declaration on aid effectiveness (OECD [2008a]); *Schmidt* (2013a) p. 282.

785 *Burnell* (2010a) p. 12.

786 *Sœrensen* (2008) pp. 83f.

787 A prominent example is the cooperation between the oil-rich Angola and China (*Schmidt* [2013a] p. 282).

6.2. *Promoting democracy in the context of German development policy*

The promotion of democracy is a component of German development policy which is influenced by various actors and in the responsibility of a range of ministerial departments. As a cross-border policy, development policy is an integral part of foreign policy and therefore undoubtedly associated with its diplomatic, strategic and normative goals and instruments. Through the involvement of non-state actors in the policy implementation, it also takes place on the transnational level.[788]

6.2.1. Germany's development policy

German development policy in terms of an overall conception did not start before 1956, while development aid to third countries was already conceded to Germany after the establishment of the Federal Republic in 1949. In contrast to other countries, such as the USA, Great Britain and France, Germany was rather late coming. Colonial policy could not result in development policy.[789] In 1952, Germany for the first time contributed to the UN's "Extended support program". In 1956, the German *Bundestag* established a fund of 50 million *Deutsche Mark* at the Foreign Office (AA) for the assistance of the developing countries. The federal ministry for economic cooperation and development (BMZ) was established in 1961.[790] Over time, German development policy followed the international trends.[791] In the beginning development policy was understood as a diplomatic instrument only and used for the containment of communism. It aimed at hindering the recognition of the GDR in the developing world.[792] As the treaties with the countries of Eastern Europe *(Ostverträge)* and the termination of the *Hallstein Doctrine* diminished the need for this kind of policy, trade became a new focal point in times of the German

---

788 *Bodemer* (2002) p. 236.

789 *Dennert* (1968) pp. 26f., especially experts and knowledge on the developing countries were missing (p. 31).

790 BMZ on its history at: http://www.bmz.de/de/ministerium/geschichte/index.html#t1.

791 *Ihne/Wilhelm* (2013) pp. 13-7 referring to the classification of UN development decades: 1961-1970 development through growth; 1971-1980 strategy for basic needs; 1981-1990 lost decade – ineptness; 1991-2000 sustainable development; 2001-2010 global human security (p. 17).

792 See Ch. 3.3.

"economic miracle". From 1969 onwards, development policy showed some innovations and gained some independence from the foreign political agenda. In times of the first oil crisis, development policy stagnated first and finally focused increasingly on conflict management. With the end of the Cold War, security political interests and geo-strategy became temporarily less important.[793] The changed political situation in the 1990s triggered several international conferences and allowed to concentrate further on the conditions in the developing countries. Especially the requirement of good governance came to the centre of attention.[794] At the same time, the budget made available to the BMZ shrank while private direct investments increased.[795] In 2000 the UN members ratified the Millennium Declaration including development political core objectives (MDG) defined by the OECD, the World Bank, the IWF and the UN. It focused on the fight against poverty, peace-keeping and environmental protection.[796] As a national support program the German government adopted the *Aktionsprogramm 2015* in 2001 aiming among others at more coherence between the different policy areas.[797] Finally, globalisation and the events of 9/11 led Germany to concentrate recently on global structural policy.[798] Development policy was understood in such way that it was incorporated in global processes and had increasing responsibility.[799] Subjects like capacity and institution building in order to strengthen the developing countries' ability to act have been put in the centre. Also, cooperative solutions with the help of non-state actors and global policy networks were preferred.[800] A recent focal point has also become the dealing with fragile states.[801]

In 2015, German development policy was a cross-cutting subject with many different actors involved. The ministry of finance (BMF) was responsible for the developing countries' dept relief and partly for the multilateral development cooperation funds. The ministry of economy (BMWi) ad-

---

793 *Bodemer* (2002); *Nuscheler* (2007) pp. 674f.

794 *Nuscheler* (2007) p. 679.

795 *Andersen* (2005) pp. 46f.

796 For details see UN at: http://www.un.org/millennium/declaration/ares552e.pdf; *Martens* (2006) p. 217.

797 Bundesregierung (2001); BMZ (2003); *Nuscheler* (2005) pp. 579-89 for details.

798 *Ihne/Wilhelm* (2013) p. 17; CDU/CSU/SPD (2013) p. 180.

799 *Klemp* (2001) p. 13.

800 *Nuscheler* (2007) pp. 680f.

801 BMZ (2013b) pp. 2, 8, 15f.; AA/BMVg/BMZ (2012); *Debiel/Lambach/Pech* (2007) p. 10.

ministered the policies of trade and raw material. The AA was mainly in charge for representing German development policy abroad and emergency assistance, while the competence for global environmental policy laid at the federal ministry for the environment, nature conservation, building and nuclear safety (BMU). The main actor was the BMZ. It administered around half of the public development cooperation funds.[802] Its core tasks concerned program work, international consultations and negotiations with the developing countries about projects carried out by implementation organisations.[803] The work of the BMZ was controlled by the German *Bundestag* where the technical competence laid at the Committee for economic cooperation and development (AwZ).[804] For 2014 the BMZ had 6,44 Billion Euro available.[805] In 2013, it received 6,29 Billion Euro which equalled 2,03 percent of the federal budget.[806]

German development policy was roughly divided into financial (FZ) and technical cooperation (TZ).[807] FZ was capital assistance and comprised financial resources given to the developing countries for their economic and social development. It was the most important development political tool in terms of volume and was mainly in the responsibility of the *KfW Entwicklungsbank (Kreditanstalt für Wiederaufbau)*.[808] TZ aimed at capacity development and the transfer of technical, economic and organisational knowledge to a large part implemented by the *GIZ (Gesellschaft für Internationale Zusammenarbeit)* which involved the preparation, training and post-

802 *Nuscheler* (2007) p. 673; *Andersen* (2005) pp. 55f.

803 *Andersen* (2005) p. 57; 4.1.

804 Despite the official control of the AwZ, in reality the federal budget committee restrains the work of the ministry (*Nuscheler* [2007] p. 673).

805 German federal government at: http://www.bundesregierung.de/Webs/Breg/DE/Themen/Entwicklungspolitik/1-EntwicklungspolitikGrundsaetzliches/engagement_bundesregierung/_node.html.

806 German federal budget law.

807 The proportion between FZ and TZ was in 2011 at around 61 (FZ) to 38 (TZ) percent measured in terms of BMZ's ODA payments (BMZ [2013] p. 30f).

808 The *KfW* founded in 1948 originally aimed at giving loans for the reconstruction of Germany after World War Two. In 2015, it had several different branches. Since 1961 the *KfW* is responsible for German financial cooperation abroad. The *KfW Entwicklungsbank* mainly cooperated with foreign state institutions (https://www.kfw-entwicklungsbank.de/Internationale-Finanzierung/KfW-Entwicklungsbank/Aufgaben-und-Ziele/Unsere-Arbeitsweise/), while the *DEG (Deutsche Investitions- und Entwicklungsgesellschaft)* a subsidiary of the *KfW* assisted the private sector in developing and transition countries.

ing of development aid workers.[809] The other actors in this field were the *Stiftungen*, the church organisations, many NGOs as well as certain ministries on the Land-level.[810] The following figure shows the payments in thousand Euros and the distribution in percent of BMZ's official development assistance (ODA) funds among actors of TZ of 2010:

Figure 6.1: Bilateral BMZ's ODA funds to actors of German TZ in 2010[811]

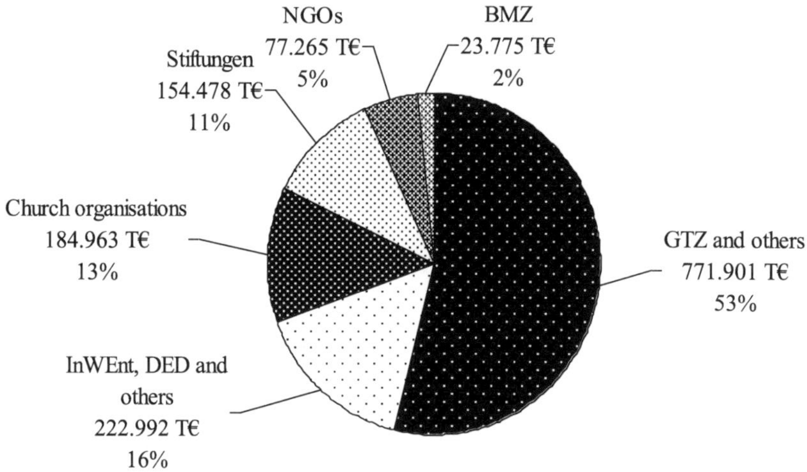

In 2015, Germany had a prominent donor position. Internationally it ranked among the top three donors of development assistance. However, it

809 BMZ at: http://www.bmz.de/de/was_wir_machen/wege/bilaterale_ez/akteure_ez/durchfuehrungsorga/index.html; the *GIZ* was founded in 2011 and was a merger of the *GTZ (Gesellschaft für technische Zusammenarbeit)*, the *DED (Deutscher Entwicklungsdienst)* and *InWEnt (Iinternational Weiterbildung und Entwicklung gGmbH)*; it was intended to improve the cooperation between technical and financial assistance (*Goldmann* [2006] p. 1010; c.f. Die Zeit of 28/12/2006).

810 See BMZ for details on the involved actors at: http://www.bmz.de/de/was_wir_machen/wege/bilaterale_ez/akteure_ez/index.html; most of the NGOs as well as the church organisations active in development cooperation were joint together in *VENRO (Verband Entwicklungspolitik deutscher Nichtregierungsorganisationen e.V.)* which had 120 members (as of 4/09/2015) (http://venro.org/mitglieder/mitgliederdatenbank/). The *Stiftungen* were not part of *VENRO*.

811 BMZ (2013b) pp. 30f.

continuously spent only a small part its national income on ODA.[812] Moreover, the amount of actors led to an exceeding fragmentation of development cooperation.[813] Others understood, in contrast, the number of actors as a German particularity giving a lot of flexibility and enabling a differentiated approach of development work.[814] In the aftermath of the *Paris Declaration on Aid Effectiveness* in 2005 determining the main conditions for effective development cooperation,[815] Germany merged several implementation organisations.[816] However, problems of coherence still existed in 2015.[817] Moreover, a lack of strategy and an over-reliance on the implementation organisations had been attested to the BMZ.[818] Furthermore, the term "projectits" was coined for the lack of geographical foci and too many single projects.[819] Recently, Germany began to concentrate on certain topics and reduced the number of cooperating countries.[820]

6.2.2. Promoting and assisting democracy in the German context

Little research on German democracy promotion has been conducted so far and the German ambitions have generally not been described as very ambitious.[821] However, from the 1990s onwards, Germany has developed an "increasingly explicit stance" towards democracy promotion.[822] In 1991 the BMZ determined five indicators political conditionality should be orientated towards which were kept up by the following German govern-

812 OECD (2014a) p. 226. In 2009, Germany spend 0,35% of its GNI on ODA. It promised to increase the ODA payments to 0, 7% in 2015 (OECD [2010] p. 53). This was reconfirmed in the coalition contract of December 2013 (CDU/CSU/SPD [2013] pp. 89, 181).

813 OECD (2005) p. 87; OECD (2010) p. 20.

814 BMZ at: http://www.bmz.de/de/was_wir_machen/wege/bilaterale_ez/akteure_ez/durchfuehrungsorga/index.html; *Nuscheler* (2007) p. 678f.

815 The declaration was further specified in the Accra Agenda For Action of 2008 (http://www.oecd.org/dac/effectiveness/parisdeclarationandaccraagendaforaction.htm; OECD [2008]).

816 BMZ at: http://www.bmz.de/de/was_wir_machen/ziele/ziele/parisagenda/paris/index.html; OECD (2010) pp. 13f.

817 *Nuscheler* (2007) p. 678.

818 OECD (2010) pp. 20, 66ff.

819 OECD (2005) p. 87; *Nuscheler* (2005) p. 499.

820 BMZ at: http://www.bmz.de/de/was_wir_machen/ziele/ziele/parisagenda/paris/index.html; OECD (2010) p. 13f.

821 *Wolff* (2013) pp. 478ff.

822 *Lapins* (2007) p. 8; *Wolff* (2013) p. 484.

ments (*Spranger* criterions).[823] It included the respect of human rights, citizens' participation in political processes, granting of legal security, market-oriented economic order and the orientation of the state towards development. In 1992, the AA created a democracy promotion facility focussing on election observer missions.[824] In its defence policy guidelines of 1992, the Federal Ministry of Defence (BMVg) considered the promotion of democracy in "Europe and world-wide" as one of the "vital security interests".[825] From 1992 onwards, the BMZ began to prefer democracy assistance over imposing sanctions.[826] According to the German government, democracy assistance became a foreign political focal point in 1998.[827] From 2006 onwards, democracy and the rule of law finally received a prominent role in the overall German political agenda.[828] Priorities were electoral aid, educational work, the promotion of political participation and media as well as the support of constitutional bodies.[829] In 2008, "democracy, civil society and public administration" became one of the 11 areas for the BMZ's technical and financial development cooperation.[830] As of 2014, 33 developing countries have agreed on this field of activity focusing on long-term political reform processes.[831] The defence policy guidelines of 2011 defined the fostering of democratic values as a security interest.[832] This was also in line with Germany's "value-oriented" foreign policy referring to the values and norms of international law and human rights law.[833] Also the German

823 *Spranger* was then Minister of the BMZ (BT [1991] p. 3873); *Betz* (1996) p. 204; *Schmidt* (2013a) pp. 280f.

824 *Rüland/Werz* (2002) p. 81.

825 BMVg (1992) II. 8 (7).

826 *Betz* (1996) p. 208.

827 Bundesregierung (2004) p. 37.

828 *Lerch* (2007) pp. 9f. with details; in the security political context see BMVg (2006) p. 16.

829 Bundesregierung (2006) p. 38; Bundesregierung (2010) p. 14; electoral observer missions are practiced multilaterally by the AA (http://www.auswaertiges-amt.de/DE/Aussenpolitik/Friedenspolitik/Krisenpraevention/2_Demokratisierungshilfe/Demokratisierungshilfe_node.html).

830 For the other focal points see BMZ (2008) p. 9; OECD (2010) p. 36. In 2009 Germany spent EUR 388 Mio. on the specific focal point (Bundesregierung [2010] p. 14).

831 BMZ at: http://www.bmz.de/de/was_wir_machen/themen/goodgovernance/demokratie/arbeitsfelder/index.html.

832 BMVg (2011) p. 5.

833 AA at: http://www.auswaertiges-amt.de/DE/Aussenpolitik/Schwerpunkte/Schwerpunkte_Aussenpolitik_node.html.

government's coalition treaty of 2013 stressed the strengthening of democracy.[834]

The multitude of actors, typical for German development policy in general, could also be found as regards to the promotion of democracy: The AA was responsible for the support of elections and parliaments, international democracy conferences, human rights diplomacy, political dialogue, sanctions and coordination in the European CSFP (common foreign and security policy). The BMZ was in charge of the long-term democracy assistance measures.[835]

Since the 1990s also good governance played a major role in the German promotion of democracy.[836] As regards to democracy, the BMZ promoted the following approaches: (1) the enforcement of the political systems' capacity such as the (regional) parliaments in their legislative; (2) control and representative functions; (3) the support of the preparation and conduction of elections; (4) the strengthening of democratically legitimised institutions on all levels; and (5) the promotion of the institutionalised participation of civil society in political processes.[837]

The German democracy assistance was characterised as retentive as towards a *political* approach. As regards political conditionality, Germany preferred a "soft" course of action focusing on consultations, dialogue and long-term approaches for the exertion of influence. In the past, only few sanctions have been practiced.[838] This course of action was very much in line with Germany's role as a "civilian power" and the normative guidelines stemming from it. Democracy promotion by an ideal-type civilian power has four features: (1) it follows an "abstract and broad notion of universal values and rights"; (2) it views democratisation as a long-term and

---

834 BMZ (2012) p. 4; CDU/CSU/SPD (2013) p. 180.

835 Bundesregierung (2010) p. 14. In terms of democracy assistance measures the AA mainly supported constitutional organs, election aid including education for voters and election workers and local election observers as well as independent media (AA at: http://www.auswaertiges-amt.de/DE/Aussenpolitik/Friedenspolitik/Krisenpraevention/2_Demokratisierungshilfe/Demokratisierungshilfe_node.html); *Schmidt* (2013a) p. 281.

836 BMZ (2009) pp. 11ff.: These areas are: the protection and respect of human rights, democracy, rule of law and media support, gender equality, administrative reforms and decentralisation, good financial governance, transparency in the raw materials area, and the fight against corruption; BMZ at: http://www.bmz.de/de/was_wir_machen/themen/goodgovernance/index.html.

837 BMZ (2009) p. 13; BMZ (2010); BMZ at: http://www.bmz.de/de/was_wir_machen/themen/goodgovernance/index.html.

838 *Lerch* (2007) p. 9; *Betz* (1996) p. 208.

complex process; (3) it prefers "pragmatic strategies of (institutional) cooperation and inclusion"; and (4) it is restrained in interfering in other countries affairs. At the same time, democracy assistance complied with what was perceived to be Germany's material interest as regards an export-oriented economy.[839]

6.3. Democracy assistance of the German political foundations

In 2015, the German political foundations played a key role in democracy assistance. Authors have highlighted that even European democracy assistance was driven by the activities of the German *Stiftungen*.[840] Others outlined that the overall origins of democracy assistance laid with the German foundations which were equipped with many offices all over the world already in the 1990s.[841] Often the German *Stiftungen* were termed as institutions of democracy assistance par excellence,[842] as they were "the oldest, most experienced and biggest actors in international democracy assistance".[843] Their activities differed principally from that of other German developmental actors in TZ, whose activities were mainly socially oriented, impartially and driven by altruistic motives. In their joint declaration of 1998, the *Stiftungen* determined to give developmental aid with their projects and programs and to contribute to the development of democratic, liberal and constitutional structures committed to human and civil rights.[844]

6.3.1. Historical overview

The history of the German political foundations' international activities went through the same phases as German development policy in general. Their international activity started properly with the establishment of the BMZ in 1961.[845] In 1957, the FES had already cooperated with the organi-

839 *Wolff* (2013) pp. 487, 479; see also Ch. 7.2 for details on Germany as a civilian power.
840 *Carothers* (2010) p. 13.
841 *Burnell* (2000b) p. 36.
842 *Erdmann* (1996) p. 143; *Philipps* (1999) p. 80.
843 *Mair* (2000) p. 128; *van Wersch/de Zeeuw* (2005) p. 11.
844 FES/KAS/FNS/HSS/HBS (1998) p. 3.
845 *Mair* (2000) p. 129; *Pinto-Duschinsky* (1991a) p. 33.

sation of anti-communist trade unions (ORIT) in Latin America. The impulse for these activities came from SPD party members and the trade unions.[846] From 1962 onwards, the BMZ granted public funds to the FES, the KAS and the FNS on a regular basis for projects in the developing countries concerning civic education *(gesellschaftspolitische Bildung)* and the promotion of social structures *(Sozialstrukturhilfe)*. Some grants already came from the AA at that time.[847] As reasons for the establishment of the foundations' international activity were considered the long-tradition of foreign political funding dating back to *Bismarck*, the German practice to outsource governmental tasks to non-public bodies and the approval of the U.S. when German foreign political possibilities were still limited.[848] In the aftermath of the Nazi-dictatorship, it was more innocuous for German politics to internationally operate by means of non-governmental organisations than on governmental level avoiding the impression of imperialistic nostalgia.[849] While in the beginning the foundations mainly implemented individual projects, the international and developmental activities systematically expanded in the following time.[850] Due to limited resources, the foundations' activities were restricted to the short-term sending of German representatives abroad, invitation of representatives from the developing countries to Germany and training measures in Africa, Asia and Latin America. It was not until 1964 and 1965 that offices abroad were established.[851] In 1973, the principles between the German government and the *Stiftungen* defined several development political tasks of the *Stiftungen*. They were supposed to contribute to social equality, political participation and the strengthening of economic independence through the cooperation with partners in the developing countries.[852] Although development aid at that time was rather technical, it aimed at gaining the upper hand in the bloc confrontation. In this hustle the foundations were useful to the Ger-

846 *Von zur Mühlen* (2007) p. 49.

847 *Pinto-Duschinisky* (1991a) p. 34. The other political foundations were not established at that time. The HSS started its international engagement in 1973, the HBS, then *Stiftungsverband Regenbogen*, followed in 1989 and the RLS in 2000. The AA's funding for the activities in the industrialised world started in 1974.

848 *Pinto-Duschinisky* (1991a) p. 34.

849 *Wagner* (1994) p. 220.

850 *Böhler* (2005) p. 4.

851 *Von zur Mühlen* (2007) pp. 66f. highlighting the then pioneering role of the FES (p. 69).

852 BMZ (1973) p. 63.

man government.[853] They pursued an approach to support social justice, national independence and to improve the economic and social conditions. Political participation was rather not part of their ambitions. At that time already, the political foundations began to move outside of the defined limits. In the 1980s several foundations supported different political groups and governments in South Africa during apartheid and in the political struggles in Latin American.[854] The end of the Cold War brought a stronger political focus and more independence since the foundations were now "no longer part of the great game". Similar to international development policy focusing on good governance and political conditions in the early 1990s, the foundations paid increased attention to the promotion of political participation.[855] A new regional focal point at that time became East Europe. In this context the foundations' international work was extended from the developing and industrialised countries to the transition countries.[856] Some assumed that the foreign political importance of the *Stiftungen* diminished with the fall of the iron curtain due to the lack of instrumental use by German foreign policy.[857] Others, on the contrary, assumed that the German foundations helped to maintain Germany's role as civilian power.[858] We will return to these considerations in the following chapters.

6.3.2. Literature review

The early literature on the German political foundations did not treat their international activities or still less their democratisation activities. An exception is *Watson's* work of 1976 mentioning that "the new German democracy intends to teach democracy to autocratic countries".[859] With the increase of studies on the foundations' international activity from the 1980s onwards, development became the focal point. Moreover, the significance of the *Stiftungen* for German foreign affairs was a matter of discus-

853 See also Ch. 3.3.; *Von zur Mühlen* (2007) p. 71; on former technical development cooperation of the FES see annual report (1969) p. 18.
854 *Mair* (2000) pp. 132f. with details.
855 *Mair* (2000) p. 133.
856 *Nuscheler* (2005) p. 466; *Egger* (2007) p. 6; like other NGOs, the foundations were also integrated in CSCE-processes (*Pogorelskaja* [1997] pp. 29f.).
857 *Mair* (2000) p. 133.
858 *Wolff* (2013) p. 488, see Ch. 6.2.
859 *Watson* (1976) p. 3.

sion. The first work focusing exclusively on the *Stiftungs*' international activity by *Werner* in 1982, looked at the relevance of the *Stiftungens*' international activity for both the political parties and German politics.[860] In 1985, *Forrester* concentrated on the geographical distribution of development projects and showed for each foundation some regional preference, target group and fields of activity.[861] While the literature written in the 1980s was initially more descriptive, detailed case studies on the foundations' activities in the developing countries came up in the following years. *Kress's* substantial analysis of 1985 looked at the FES's and KAS's cooperation with political partners abroad and compared their activities in Venezuela. In 1989, *Schürmann* analysed the KAS's activity in India. However, these works did not contain cross references between German policies and the activities of the German foundations. *Wagner*, in contrast, investigated the German foundations' foreign and development policy in Latin America in 1994. He looked at conditions, advantages and disadvantages describing the foundations' autonomous activities as "semi-official" and concluding that the *Stiftungen* were of elementary importance for German Latin-American relations.[862] He lastly predicted a shift of the foundations' activities from South America to East Europe in the future,[863] which matched with the actual development.

From the 1990s onwards, the literature on the *Stiftungens*' international undertakings began to focus on the up-coming democracy promotion. In 1991, *Pinto-Duschinsky* dealt with U.S. and German foreign political aid.[864] In this context, he investigated the German foundations' activities and some U.S. organisations' set up in the 1980s on the German model. According to *Pinto-Duschinsky*, political aid was the building of democracy. It forwarded donor government's interests, impacted on the donor country's political life and was highly cost-effective, unlike economic or military assistance.[865] In the increasing use of non-governmental organisations by development and foreign ministries and the up-coming of public diplomacy

860 *Werner* (1982) p. 22.
861 *Forrester* (1985).
862 *Wagner* (1994) pp. 167, 218, 220.
863 *Wagner* (1994) p. 221.
864 *Pinto-Duschinsky* (1991a). Another article of 1991 dealt with the German foundations and party finance in Germany. *Pinto-Duschinsky* analysed extensively the foundations' role within the German party system while illustrating aspects of the foundations' party links. He also studied the legislation governing the political funding in Germany (*Pinto-Duschinsky* [1991b]).
865 *Pinto-Duschinsky* (1991a) pp. 54ff.

he saw a reaction to the changing forms of international relations. The considerable number of independent states and the influence of political parties, unions and pressure groups made it essential for governments to enter the political arena in foreign countries.[866] He concluded with the prediction that "payments for foreign politics will be increasingly significant instruments of modern diplomacy and development aid".[867] In 1996, *Mehler* published a short article on chances of support programmes for democratisation in West Africa and the *Stiftungens*' contribution.[868] *Erdmann* looked at the foundations' democracy assistance activities in South Africa and Chile.[869] In his work in 2000 *Mair*, resuming the results of his cross-sectional comparison on democracy assistance carried out three years before, took a close look at the foundations' democracy assistance in sub-Saharan Africa[870] supporting *Pinto-Duschinsky's* argument[871] that foundations' projects were often more political than they seemed.[872] In 2002 *Pinto-Duschinsky* mapped foreign sources of political funding in Latin America, focusing on the activity of the KAS giving grants to partner organisations.[873] He dealt with the legitimacy of giving money to politicians in foreign countries and established the link between democracy promotion and interference.[874] In the following time, authors happened to be interested also in certain aspects of democracy assistance. In 2006, *Erdmann* published two analyses on political party aid. One dealt extensively with the German foundations' party aid in Africa,[875] while the other one looked more generally at issues in international party promotion.[876] *Erdmann* understood party aid as synonym of party assistance which is part of the democracy assistance spectrum.[877] *Burnell's* article forged links between globalisation and democratisation through international party aid refer-

866 *Pinto-Duschinsky* (1991a) p. 62.
867 *Pinto-Duschinsky* (1991a) p. 63.
868 *Mehler* (1996); see also *Eyinla* (1999) surprisingly titled the "West German political foundations" 9 years after the reunification although not taking a historical perspective.
869 *Erdmann* (1996) pp. 157ff.
870 *Mair* (2000), (1997).
871 *Pinto-Duschinsky* (1991a) p. 38.
872 *Mair* (2000) p.135.
873 *Pinto-Duschinsky* (2002) pp. 248-50.
874 *Pinto-Duschinsky* (2002) p. 227.
875 *Erdmann* (2006a).
876 *Erdmann* (2006b).
877 *Erdmann* (2006b) p. 123.

ring to the *Stiftungen* among others.[878] Moreover, *Böhler* discussed the foundations' political dialogue activities, in his view, virtually a synonym for democracy assistance.[879] He outlined especially the networking function of the foundations as well as their value orientation when promoting democracy.[880]

Several studies took account of the foundations' turn towards the countries in East and Central Europe. At the same time, more researchers happened to be interested in how the *Stiftungen* contributed to German and European foreign relations and how they practiced diplomacy in the transition countries.[881] In 1999 *Philipps* treated the foundations' activities of in Central-East Europe as "ideal-typical activities" in the field of democracy assistance though concluding with mixed results and supporting a rather limited ability of the foundations to "export" democracy.[882] As already mentioned, in 1997, *Pogorelskaja* investigated the foundations' activities in the Commonwealth of Independent States (CIS) and the Baltic States. She connected them to aspects of German foreign policy concluding that the foundations improved the bilateral relations with these states while party interests were rather secondary.[883] Also the instrumental and actor characteristic of the *Stiftungen* in German foreign policy *Pogorelskaja* discussed in 2002.[884] Due to the current process of denationalisation and interdependences *Pogorelskaja* presumed that the role of the German *Stiftungen* in German foreign policy was about to increase.[885] In 2006, *Progorelskaja* explored the German political foundations' role in the EU policy towards the East European Countries (CEECS) and the CIS presenting exemplary the foundations' activities in Russia.[886] *Pogoreskaja* assumed that the German foundations could enrich European foreign and security policy, if they got deeper involved into the European neighbourhood policy.[887] In 2009, she

878 *Burnell* (2006).

879 See Ch. 5.2.1. for details.

880 *Böhler* (2005); on the German foundations' political dialogue in Latin America, see (1991) p. 128.

881 An exception is the work of *Renvert* (2005) treating the non-developmental activities of the foundations in the U.S.A, for details see Ch. 6.3.1.

882 *Philipps* (1999) pp. 80, 92.

883 *Pogorelskaja* (1997) pp. 167, 14.

884 For details see Ch. 5.1.2.; *Progorelskaja* (2002a); *Pogorelskaja* (2002b) dealt with the foundations' activity as part of the German domestic and foreign policy as well as their activity in the new German Federal Countries.

885 *Pogorelskaja* (2002a) p. 38.

886 *Pogorelskaja* (2006) p. 17.

887 *Pogorelskaja* (2006) pp. 22f.

also treated the foundations' activities in the context of German foreign cultural policy[888] and conflict prevention[889]. In 2002, *Dakowska* studied the impact of the EU enlargement process on the identity of Polish political elites providing case studies on the activities of the KAS and the FES particularly active in the field of transnational communication. *Dakowska* considered the foundations as transmitter of political culture since they enabled contacts between the CEEC and European parties which played an important role in the pre-accession period.[890] In 2005, she concentrated on the foundations' civic education in Poland[891] and treated the FES's activity in Poland between 1971 and the "peaceful revolution" accompanying the German policy towards East Europe.[892] In 2007, *Egger* analysed in detail the activity of the FES in Mexico and Poland and their adaption to the transformation in East Europe highlighting that the foundation became successfully accustomed to the new contexts.[893] As already outlined, *Schneider-Deters* treated the shift of the foundations' activities away from civil education towards political dialog and civil diplomacy in East and Central Europe.[894] He saw the specific potential of the foundations in the promotion of the convergence of Russia and the former Soviet republics at the European Union. He compared the foundations' democracy assistance to U.S. NGOs' activity in this area.[895] The work of *Mohr* of 2010 offered several regional case studies of the foundations' democracy assistance addressing extensively the current issues around these activities.[896] In 2012, *Renvert* outlined in a short article the difficulties of the foundations' democracy assistance in the Arab world and in the recent transformation processes.[897]

In the last decade, there has been an increasing amount of descriptions of themselves by the German *Stiftungen* treating their international activi-

888 *Pogorelskaja* (2009b); see Ch. 5.2.3.

889 *Pogorelskaja* (2009a); see Ch. 7.3.

890 *Dakowska* (2002) pp. 287, 288, 290; However, in this work the spotlight is rather on European politics and less on the German foundations. The same can be said for *Dakowska* (2005a).

891 *Dakowska* (2005b).

892 *Dakowska* (2005c); for a short portray of the foundations' activities in Central Eastern Europe after 1989 see also *Pratsch-Hucko* (2004).

893 *Egger* (2007) p. 362.

894 See Ch. 5.1.

895 *Schneider-Deters* (2005) p. 108. A similar comparison was outlined by *Koschel* (2005) on democracy assistance in Serbia.

896 *Mohr* (2010). Short case studies on the foundations' democracy assistance in Russia, Bolivia and Turkey can be found at *Wolff* (2013) pp. 484ff.

897 *Renvert* (2012).

ties which are more self-reflected than earlier publications. In 2003, *Beaugrand* chronicled the founding of the KAS with the help of contemporary witnesses' reports giving detailed historical insights.[898] *Von zur Mühlen*, a historian who had worked for the FES from 1975 onwards dealt with the beginnings of the FES's international activity and treated the period until the Cold War. It is a substantive work with several years of research in the FES's archive.[899] His work is part of a series of books published since 2007 on the history of the FES's international work offering numerous country case studies and including internal documentation.[900] In 2005 and 2006, the KAS treated its media encouragement and the rule of law support.[901] Other publications treated its party cooperation in Central, East and Southeast Europe providing a helpful overview on the party support activities in fourteen countries.[902] An extensive presentation of the FES's cooperation with political parties and liberation movements in Africa gave *Vinnai* in 2007.[903] The foundations' integration in foreign and development policy in the context of globalisation was also recognised by authors of the FES.[904]

898 *Beaugrand* (2003); see also on this matter *Beaugrand* (2005), *Hennig* (1998).

899 *Von zur Mühlen* (2007).

900 See *Adam* (2012) concerning the FES's democracy assistance in the developing countries in general; more specifically *Muñoz Sánchez* (2013) studied the activities of the FES at the end of the Franco dictatorship in Spain; *Ehrke/Römpczyk* (2013) concentrated on the activities in Serbia and the Baltic States; *Hofmann/Vinnai/Benzing* (2011) looked at Indonesia, Tanzania and Central America, *Werz/Hofmann/Bussiek* (2014) studied the cases Venezuela, Vietnam and Zimbabwe which posed challenges to the FES's democracy assistance; the FES's activities in the emerging countries of Chile, India and South Africa were the subject of *Wille/Treydte/Vinnai* (2010); *Spanger/Reddies* (2011) treated the FES's undertakings in USSR/Russia and China. The activities in Turkey were discussed by *Schumacher* (2012); two thematic areas of democracy assistance were treated: *Ritter-Weil/Treydte* (2013) looked at the FES's promotion of gender and media policy, while *Eckl/Hofmann* (2012) studied the FES's cooperation with trade unions and the promotion of economic and social development; *Veit* (2013) constituted an exception to the above works. He treated the FES's non-developmental activities in the northern hemisphere from 1989 onwards.

901 KAS (2005), (2006).

902 *Fischer-Bollin* (2006); KAS (2007d).

903 *Vinnai* (2007). Further publications on the KAS's development cooperation are *Thesing* (1987), (1997), *Krieger* (1983); see *Meier-Walser* (2004) and *Kahane* (1998) for interviews with members of the foundations on the international activities.

904 *Hillebrand/Optenhögel* (2001).

Until the time of writing, the literature on the *Stiftungen* was still sparse and mostly written in German. [905] Some authors assumed that the foundations preferred to keep a low profile as they operate in very sensitive surroundings.[906] This is an impression which the author can confirm as regards the conducted case studies.[907]

6.3.3. Geo-political regions

In former times, the *Stiftungen* seemed to "distribute" countries amongst each other.[908] The FES in the 1980s had its regional focal point of the activity in Southeast Asia (ASEAN-countries) and the Iberian Peninsula. The KAS focused on Latin America. The FNS concentrated mainly on Africa and Latin America. The HSS, back than new in the international field, initially gave attention to Africa and became then active in the Pacific and Latin America complementing the work of the KAS.[909] Despite these key regions the foundations had offices in other countries. In the 1990s the FES concentrated mainly on sub-Saharan Africa, Latin America and Southeast Asia. The KAS named Latin America as regional focal point, while the FNS focused on East Europe and Southeast Asia and the HBS on East Europe and sub-Saharan Africa. These indications by the foundations also corresponded with the regional distribution of the foundations' international offices.[910] In 2013, the regional dissemination was only partially consistent with that of the 1990s.[911] The FES had most of their offices in Europe (29 offices). So, did the KAS (22 offices). The focal points of the

905 *Werner* (1982) p. 22; *Forrester* (1985) p. 60; *Erdmann* (2006a) p. 181; *Egger* (2007) p. 5.
906 *Mair* (2000) p. 128.
907 See Ch. 8 and 9.
908 See *Werner* (1982) pp. 11, 14, 18, 20; *Forrester* (1985) p. 47.
909 *Forrester* (1985) p. 51.
910 *Mair* (2000) p. 135, (1997).
911 It was difficult to receive information on the distribution of funds per region as the foundations' annual reports generally did not outline such information with exception of the FNS (c.f. FNS annual report [2013] p. 66) and the HBS (c.f. HBS annual report [2013] p. 3). In former times such information had been included in the annual reports (see c.f. KAS annual reports in 1977-1993); *van Wersch/de Zeeuw* (2005) gave the annual project expenditure for all political foundations by region: 23 % to Eastern Europe and Euro-Asia, 22% to Central and South America, 21% to Asia, 20% to Africa and 14% to North Africa and the Middle East (p. 22).

FNS in the 1990s could still be confirmed as regards East Europe (6 offices) and Asia (9 offices) though the Middle East/North Africa (6 offices) was also important. The former HBS's focus on East Europe was still obvious in the spread of offices (8 offices) while in sub-Saharan Africa there was almost the least number of HBS's bureaus. The regional distribution of the youngest of the foundations, the RLS, was relatively balanced. The HSS had a regional focus on Asia regarding the distribution of offices (21 offices). The shifted focus towards the countries in East, Southeast and Central Eastern Europe, which had already been noted by the literature,[912] could be thus confirmed. A comparison between the numbers of offices in West, Central and South Europe and those in Southeast, East and Central Eastern Europe showed about twice as many offices in the latter region (see *figure 6.2*). Besides their country offices, the foundations often had regional offices. This allowed especially the smaller foundations to ensure project work in countries where they did not have a local office.[913] Several foundations could be generally found in one country.

Figure 6.2: Number of foundations' offices in European countries in 2012/13[914]

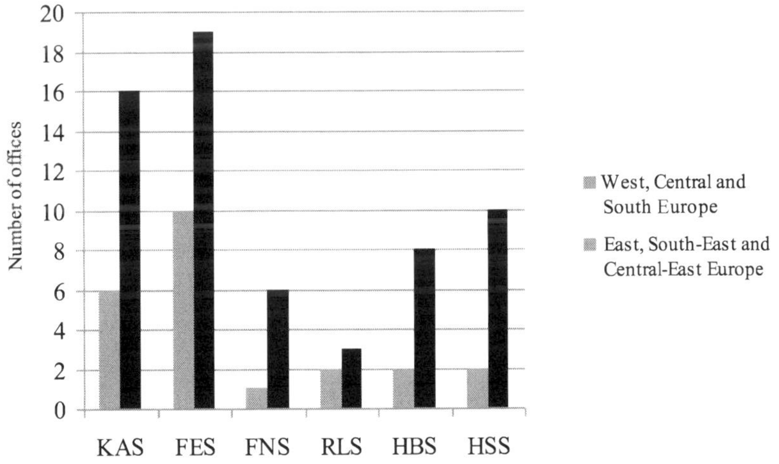

912 *Bartsch* (2007) p. 288.

913 The FNS, for example, was active in 72 countries (FNS annual report [2013] p. 58) although the actual amount of offices was at 47 country offices and 7 regional offices (FNS [2013a] p. 9).

914 Author's diagram, see for the sources fn. 915. The region Southeast, East and Central Eastern Europe included Russia, Belarus and the Caucasus.

The overall distribution of all foundations' offices was relatively balanced (see *figure 6.3*). Most of the total numbers of foundations' offices were in Europe (26%) followed by Asia (25%). In sub-Saharan Africa the proportion of foundations' offices was at 18%, in Latin-America at 16% and in the region of North-Africa/the Middle East at 12%. The share of offices in North America was at 3%. Also, the ODA grant distribution provided to the foundations by the BMZ in 2010 per region confirmed this finding (see *figure 6.4*).

Figure 6.3: Regional distribution of all German political foundations' international offices in 2012/13[915]

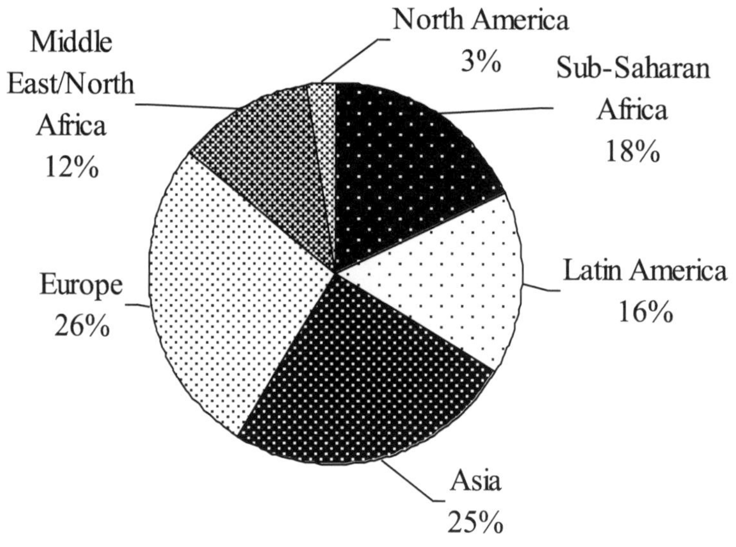

915 Author's diagram, sources: KAS annual report (2013) p. 100; FES annual report (2012) pp. 80f.; FNS at: http://www.freiheit.org/Internationale-Politik/199c78/index.html# (accessed on 28/09/2015); RLS at: http://www.rosalux.de/weltweit.html; HBS annual report (2013) p. 3; HSS annual report (2013) pp. 84f. The region "Europe" includes Russia, Belarus and the Caucasus. Turkey counted for the Middle East. It was not differentiated between different types of offices. It included regional and thematic offices alike as long as they were not in the same place with other offices of the same foundation. The foundations' headquarters were not considered.

Figure 6.4: Regional distribution of ODA funds provided to the foundations by the BMZ for 2010 [916]

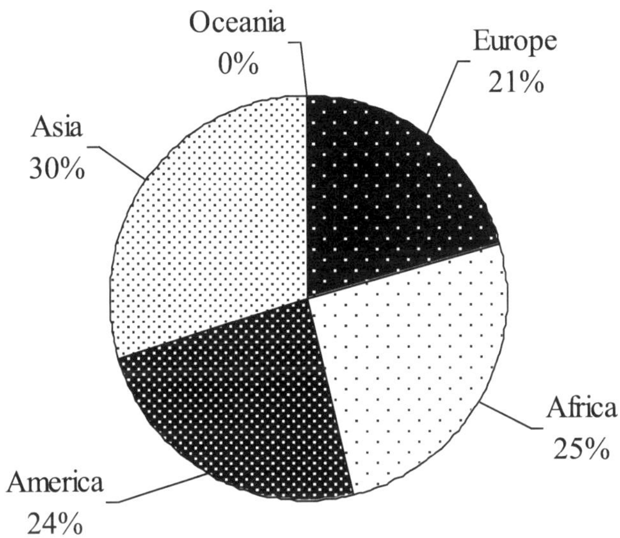

6.3.4. The *Stiftungens'* democracy assistance objectives

In the past, the *Stiftungen* assisted democracy in the developing, emerging and transition countries using, as outlined, consulting and dialogue-oriented instruments.[917] According to the BMZ, the foundations' developmental tasks were "the sustainable promotion or establishment of democracy and civil society. That involves strengthening the key institutions in a democratic social order, such as parliaments, political parties and an independent judiciary, as well as promoting good governance and opportunities for civil society participation".[918] As a consequence, foundations' international ac-

916 Author's diagram on the basis of BMZ (2013b) pp. 30f. The BMZ chose slightly different regions than the foundations and did not give any further specifications.

917 *Bartsch* (2007) p. 284.

918 BMZ at: http://www.bmz.de/en/what_we_do/approaches/bilateral_development_cooperation/players/political_foundations/index.html.

tivities could be found in every democracy assistance sector.[919] According to the above definition, the foundations were thus "ideal-types" of democracy assistants.[920]

Until the 1990s, democracy assistance was not the only developmental activity of the *Stiftungen*. Around one third of funds were dedicated to the support of social structures which the BMZ financed from an additional budget title.[921] The participation of broad levels of society was purposed by means of supporting self-help organisations and cooperatives.[922] Especially at the outset of activities in a country, it enabled contacts and acquired some insights on the country before working with higher political levels.[923] It was mainly due to the financial cutbacks in the 1990s that the foundations refrained from this approach.[924] In 1997, the payments for social structural projects were ceased. Ongoing and new projects in this field weresince then funded by the BMZ's regular budget item available to the *Stiftungen*. These funds allowed tackling development political objectives beyond democracy assistance, such as the fight against poverty, as long as projects intened to change political structures.[925] The support of social structures though still important for German development policy, was generally assigned to other organisations.[926]

Since the beginnings of the *Stiftungens*' international activities, the specific focus on democracy assistance sectors has often changed and was determined by the geo-political regions.[927] Although each foundation's partner focus influenced the used measures, there was no clear distribution of sectors among the foundations. The improvement of the electoral process has always been on the agenda of the German political foundations. It was mainly evidenced by their party aid. The foundations' intense cooperation with political parties, a unique characteristic in comparison with other German actors in this field, was already touched.[928] The *Stiftungen* general-

919 It is impossible to define how much of the assistance was allocated for which sector as neither the ministries nor the *Stiftungen* provided data on such aspects; similar *Erdmann* (2006a) p. 191.

920 See definition at Ch. 6.1.

921 *Erdmann* (2006a) p. 189; BMZ (1973) p. 67; Federal budget, Kapitel 2302 Titel 68703.

922 BMZ (2004a).

923 *Egger* (2007) pp. 52f.; *Wagner* (1994) p. 182.

924 *Hellwig* (1998) p. 155; *Egger* (2007) p. 53.

925 *Böhler* (2005) p. 9.

926 BMZ (2011a) p. 7.

927 *Mair* (2000) p. 134.

928 See Ch. 5.2.

ly practiced a "partisan approach" when supporting political parties which implies the assistance of ideologically affiliated political parties.[929] Since the beginnings of their international activities, the *Stiftungen* supported political parties dating back to the late 1950s in Spain. In 1973, the FES was even involved in the establishment of the Portuguese socialist party.[930] In the 1970s, party collaboration was at the foundations' agenda in Africa. In the decades that followed, the foundations paid less attention to party aid in Africa until it became a primary focus from the mid-1990s onwards.[931] In the 1980s, the foundations supported heavily political parties in Latin America. From 1989 onwards, then flourishing political parties in Central Eastern Europe were assisted.[932] Soon afterwards, the foundations focused on fraction and members of parliament.[933] In recent times, the direct financial support of political parties abroad as well as the financing of election campaigns is, however, not permitted for the German *Stiftungen* according to the Federal budget law.[934] Nonetheless, some authors noted the direct funding of political parties' institutes in order to circumvent this regulation.[935] Also campaigns were supported indirectly. In Central Eastern Europe, for example, the foundations offered programs to affiliated party members in order to learn about successful campaigning as well effective media for the respective affiliated partners.[936] Moreover, activities of the foundations have also been noted as regards electoral aid. During the 1990s, the AA collaborated with the *Stiftungen* in Africa. The foundations were in charge of the technical preparation.[937] Recently, there were also cases when the foundations monitored elections with local partners.[938] Moreover, the *Stiftungen* assisted state institutions abroad. They helped to professionalise key democratic institutions and concentrated on constitu-

929 *Erdmann* (2006b) p. 134; *Mair* (2000a) p. 140.
930 *Von zur Mühlen* (2007) pp. 203, 209.
931 *Erdmann* (2006a) pp. 188f., (2006b) pp. 130f.
932 *Philipps* (1999) p. 83, the foundations also chose social and economic partners in addition.
933 *Schneider-Deters* (2005) p. 112.
934 Federal budget, Kapitel 2302 Titel 68704.
935 *Pogorelskaja* (2009a) pp. 44f.; *Mair* (2000) p. 142; *Philipps* (1999) giving the example of the Czech Klaus foundation only founded to implement projects with the KAS (p. 83).
936 *Philipps* (1999) p. 85.
937 *Betz* (1996) p. 212; *Mehler* (1996), p. 27.
938 FES (2005c) p. 28 referring to the presidential election in Madagascar in 2001.

tional advice, on the support of legislators, and the judiciary.[939] The foundations also focused on minority rights.[940] The promotion of the rule of law was a priority of the KAS. In Chapter 8, we will analyse these activities in detail. Also, the other foundations implemented rule of law measures.[941] Moreover, the foundations improved professionalism in communal politics and public administration.[942] Although civil-military relations were rarely mentioned in the literature and the foundations' publications, the activities of the FES in Thailand as presented in Chapter 9 show such aid. Also, *Mohr* noticed an explicit focus of the HSS on military issues and the military's role in democracies.[943] Finally, the German political foundations were active in the civil society sector. In the early 1990s, similar to the international trend in democracy assistance, the foundations focused on civic education.[944] While some authors observed a shift from the promotion of self-help organisations to the enhanced support of elites by focusing on managers, decision makers and disseminators from the mid-1990s onwards,[945] this trend cannot be confirmed.[946] As already outlined, the support of NGOs and other civil target groups was part of all foundations' partner portfolios. Moreover, they also backed young professionals, women's and youth organisations, academics, medium companies and economic associations among others.[947] Despite the tendency to work with governments, the conducted interviews showed a substantial flexibility regarding the choice of partners which also depended on the available partner structure in the country. As already outlined, the support of the free press

939 *Mair* (2000) p. 134, (1997); *Bartsch* (2007) p. 284; for the foundations' support of judicial and legislative authorities in Africa during the 1990s see *Erdmann* (2006a) pp. 188f., (2006b) pp. 130f.; for the FES and the KAS the improvement of parliaments' activities in West Africa see *Mehler* (1996) p. 27.

940 *Philipps* (1999) on the foundations' activities in Central Eastern Europe.

941 C.f. the FES activities (*Adam* [2012] p. 430).

942 See *Philipps* (1999) p. 85 on the foundations' activities in Central Eastern Europe.

943 *Mohr* (2010) p. 117.

944 *Erdmann* (2006a) pp. 188f., (2006b) pp. 130f.; *Mair* (2000) p. 134 referring to *Mair* (1997).

945 *Egger* (2007) pp. 51-4 stating, however, that this was not the case for the HBS and the FNS who continuously support self-help organisations (fn. 140); *Hellwig* (1998) p. 155; *Pascher* (2002) p. 111; *Böhler* (2005) p. 5.

946 *Pascher* (2002) p. 65 and *Pogorelskaja* (2009b) p. 297 assuming, on the contrary, a shift towards the cooperation with civil society organisations and broad levels of society.

947 See Ch. 5.2.; see *Merz* (2006) for activities with youth organisations in Palestine.

and media was part of the foundations' international activity.[948] In the beginning the support of trade unions was practiced by most foundations. Recently, it was a key component in the FES's democracy assistance due to their affiliation with the Federation of German trade unions (DGB).[949] However, direct financing of unions as well as of labour disputes were prohibited for the foundations.[950]

The overall politicisation of foundations' activities abroad was what differentiated the foundations from other actors in this field. While *Forrester* in the 1980s still differentiated between the "foundations' political activity" and their "developmental activities",[951] from the 1990s onwards, most of the foundations' activities were finally considered as political. Even projects seemingly or declared non-political often had political intent.[952] "Civil education" was the label and budget item for all foundations' activities financed by the BMZ, hence, mainly all types of democracy assistance apart from electoral aid which was financed by the AA.[953] The foundations did not strictly separate between the democracy assistance sectors. The KAS's rule of law support, for instance, also included the support of NGOs.[954] There were also meta-aspects which were relevant for all work areas. The FES, for instance, focused on the promotion of women and gender equality as a cross-cutting issue.[955] Also the foundations' IPD-departments in the industrialised countries served indirectly the democracy assistance program, as they included stakeholders from the developing countries in dialogue processes.[956]

The foundations' characteristics in development cooperation were the long-term presence of the foundations' field representatives, the long-term

948 See Ch. 5.2.2; on media the foundations' media support in general *Krämer/ Lehrke* (1996) and in the context of German development policy see *Leusch* (2013) pp. 260f.; for media support in Africa in the 1980s see *Mehler* (1996) p. 27, *Erdmann* (2006a) pp. 188f., (2006b) pp. 130f. and in Central Eastern Europe in the 1990s see *Philipps* (1999) p. 85.

949 FES annual report (2012) p. 84; FES (2005c) p. 68.

950 German federal budget law.

951 *Forrester* (1985) pp. 55, 59.

952 *Pinto-Duschinsky* (1991a) p. 38; *Pogorelskaja* (2009a) p. 29.

953 German federal budget law: The budget item is named "politische Bildung" which can be translated as "civil education".

954 KAS (2013d).

955 FES (2005c) pp. 33ff.

956 *Mohr* (2010) p. 238; see Ch. 5.2.1.

partnerships and short-term initiatives as well as their value orientation.[957] They also undertook activities that went beyond the democracy assistance spectrum and were rather part of a state-building approach. It included, among others, approaches for decentralisation and the modernisation of public administration,[958] security sector reforms,[959] economic strengthening,[960] and the support of human rights.[961] Nonetheless, the foundations' undertakings did not only take place in fragile or post-conflict states and had a strong focus on the support of civil societies which speaks against an emphasis on state-building. Despite their short-term measures, the foundations expected actual changes to happen in a long period of time.[962] They thus supported, like the German government, a developmental approach to democracy assistance as they concentrated on long-term processes of political development.

Conclusion

Certain actor advantages and benefits for German politics stem from the construct of the German political foundations' democracy assistance.[963] Moreover, the foundations also had comparative advantages over other actors in the field of democracy assistance. Already in 1982, *Werner* judged that the foundations' independence led to a wider frame of action for the foundations. While governments were obliged to work together with other governments, the foundations could choose from a wide range of partners to cooperate with.[964] High versatility and flexibility have been attested to the foundations for their developmental activities. They were able to take advantage of windows of opportunity and to work in difficult political sur-

957 *Mair* (2000) pp. 136, 140; Adam (2012) p. 14; similar *Burnell* (2006) p. 75; *Lerch* (2007) p. 10.

958 BMZ (2010) p. 22 on KAS's activities; this was also a focal point for the HSS (2014b).

959 See Ch. 7.3.2.

960 In line with their liberal tradition, the FNS supported cooperatives and self-help organisations and similar to the KAS enterprise federations. (Mohr [2010] p. 116); the support of market economy was a focus in East Europe (*Bartsch* [1998] p. 189); critically *Schneider-Deters* (2005) p. 118.

961 FES (2005c) pp. 77ff.; FNS (2013b) p. 7.

962 *Rüland/Werz* (2002) p. 84.

963 See also conclusion Ch. 5.

964 *Werner* (1982) pp. 26 f.; see also *Wagner* (1994) p. 170; *Kress* (1985) p. 8 quoting BMZ (1983).

roundings, like in Sudan or Myanmar.[965] They enabled the establishment and the keeping of contacts with opposition leaders and members of liberation movements which might come into power and which could not be achieved by official diplomats, which were too sensitive for the formal arms of government and which could be undoubtedly viewed as intrusion.[966] This ability to operate in "a grey zone" as well as to cultivate lasting and close partnerships has been stressed as a major advantage.[967] Moreover, the ability to choose either political or civil society partners was advantageous for the foundations. In case the countries' political development did not allow the cooperation with political actors or the cooperation was politically difficult, the withdrawal to civil society actors helped to keep a "foot in the door".[968] A recent example was the democracy assistance activity of the *Stiftungen* in Tunisia in 2011. Despite the foundations long-standing presence in Tunisia before the start of the Arab Spring in 2010, the KAS, HSS and FNS had problems to find partners as the existing political parties were mainly leftist. In contrast to the FES, which collaborated with *Mustapha Ben Jafaar*, founder and leader of the *Forum démocratique pour le travail et les libertés* (FDTL) and since 2011 president of the constituent assembly, the other foundations concentrated on enterprises and market economic matters, and in case of the KAS, additionally on interreligious dialogue. At the same time, the foundations' ability to rapidly react to short-term political changes became apparent. With little administrative effort and with additional means from a German governmental fund ad hoc created for the democracy assistance in North Africa, the subject became immediately part of the foundations' international portfolio.[969]

Since different foundations' representatives usually complemented each other's activities by focusing on different political parties, Germany advantageously "can hope to gain a friend as head of the government no matter

965 *Erdmann* (2006a) p. 193; *Bartsch* (2007) p. 283.

966 *Pinto-Duschinsky* (1991a) p. 45; *Forrester* (1985) p. 57; *Bartsch* (2007) p. 282; *Wolff* (2013) pp. 481, 485.

967 *Mair* (2000) p. 148.

968 *Pinto-Duschinsky* (1991a) pp. 39f.; *Bartsch* (2007) pp. 284f.; *Mair* (2000) p. 143; *Mohr* (2010) noted this course of action for the foundations' activities in China (p. 263).

969 BMZ on the democracy assistance fund at: http://www.bmz.de/20120914-2; c.f. FNS annual report (2013) p. 21f.; *Schmidt*, Frankfurter Allgemeine Zeitung, 23/03/2011; also the AA provided additional means to the foundations for the democratisation processes in North Africa and the Middle East: see Federal budget, Kapitel 0501 Titel 68721; BMZ (2011b) pp. 8, 31.

who wins".[970] At the same time, this construct contributed to a pluralistic society enabling the exchange of different views and productive political discussions.[971] The foundations also focused on different values: The FES was dedicated to social democratic values, the FNS to liberal values and both, the KAS and the HSS to Christian and federal democratic values. The HBS felt bound to ecological and emancipatory values and the RLS to social and participatory values.[972] In this respect, the legitimate support of democratic pluralism was a positive outcome.[973] Furthermore, the outsourcing of activities which were originally tasks of the ministry to the foundations was advantageous for the government as regards efficiency. The costs of government employees were generally higher in contrast to staff members of the foundations. Moreover, the parliamentary control of the ministry did not apply to the foundations' undertakings.[974] Another benefit for the German government deriving from the foundations' international activities was the protection of international relations on a long-term basis.[975] A change of government in Germany did not lead to the termination of successful foundations' projects abroad.[976] This bore comparison with the concept of public administrations in relation to the varying governments. In contrast to other organisations active in democracy assistance, the foundations' budget was assumed to be the highest.[977] While the fact that Germany had not been among the colonial powers was a disadvantage at the beginning of German development policy, for the democracy assistance activities it was helpful as activities appeared rather "neutral".[978] According to the then Federal Minister for Economic Cooperation and Development, *Dirk Niebel*, the German political foundations were the important backbone of the German development work.[979] At the same time, they were considered as "Germany's most powerful diplomatic asset".[980]

---

970 *Pinto-Duschinsky* (1991a) p. 45.

971 *Wagner* (1994) p. 170 f.; *Pogorelskaja* (1997) refered to a „bridging function" of the foundations in this context (p. 28).

972 *Mair* (2000) p. 134; RLS at: http://www.rosalux.de/weltweit.html.

973 *Pinto-Duschinsky* (2002) pp. 248-50.

974 *Glagow/Schimank* (1983) pp. 164f.

975 *Kress* (1985) p. 144.

976 Interviews 13, 14; *Schürmann* (1989) p. 178.

977 See Ch. 1.7.3.

978 On the credibility of the German foundations in contrast to U.S. organisations in Central Asia see *Schneider-Deters* (2005) p. 110 and *Watson* (1976) p. 6.

979 Süddeutsche Zeitung, 30/12/2011.

980 *Pinto-Duschinksy* (2002) p. 250.

Development policy is a multi-purpose system including various interests.[981] It allows that actors take different roles. It is highly political[982] and can be therefore easily made subject of a public diplomacy portfolio. As ideal types of democracy assistants, the German political foundations simultaneously supported a collaborative public diplomacy approach which focused on values and dialogue processes. The above consideration on democracy assistance will be connected to public diplomacy in the case study on the KAS's rule of law program in Southeast Europe.[983]

981 *Nuscheler* (2005) pp. 433ff., 674. The U.S. policy, for instance, has termed development policy as transformational diplomacy in 2006, see *Vaïsse* (2007) pp. 27ff.

982 *Basu* (2011) pp. 406, 408ff.

983 Ch. 8.

Chapter 7 – The German political foundations: Conflict managers?

The literature on the practical aspects of public diplomacy does not only highlight democracy assistance as one such form.[984] It also looks at transnational actors' supportive role in peace-building and other peace-maintenance activities in international conflicts as a catalytic diplomatic activity.[985] Public diplomacy's mediating role has also been stressed when it comes to conflicts among different values such as Western and Islamic ideals.[986] Moreover, the bridging of social and political divides and the transformative strength of dialogue in conflict management processes through trust-building collaborative activities has been highlighted.[987] In these cases, the affinity of public diplomacy and track two diplomacy, in which third parties can operate as facilitators or mediators,[988] is striking.[989] The idea that dialogue processes can help to mitigate, prevent and solve conflicts can furthermore be found in concepts of foreign cultural policy.[990]

While conflicts until the end of the Cold War were mainly such clashes between states or alliances, the security situation of the 21st century's multipolar system is much more complex, ranging from transnational and regional conflicts to various intra state disputes and classic two-state-conflicts. The prevailing opinion assumes that these situations require compre-

---

984 See Ch. 6.

985 *Hocking* (2011) p. 230. At times, the connection between public diplomacy and international conflicts is understood differently. *Pratkanis* (2009), for instance, analysed the use of public diplomacy in terms of social influence and strategies used to legitimise activity or to change the enemy's opinion among others (p. 111).

986 *Riordan* (2007) pp. 180ff.

987 *Cowan/Arsenault* (2008).

988 *Azar* (2002) pp. 23, 27; *Kelman* (2002) p. 91.

989 See Ch. 3.1.; *Cowan/Arsenault* (2008) p. 26. Track two diplomacy as the unofficial representative's interaction which aims at conflicts' transformations refers mainly to three different processes: to problem-solving workshops and meetings among conflicting parties, the influence of public opinion and cooperative economic development to support the peace process (*Montville* [1990] pp. 163ff.; *Bolewski* [2007] pp. 39f.).

990 AA (2000) p. 1, (2013) p. 5.

hensive and networked proceedings which are based on military and civil components and the involvement of various state and non-state actors. Current conflict management consequently faces a broad range of tasks and covers a long period of time.[991] The modern conflict situation and the assumed dependence between development, peace and democracy also renewed interest in development cooperation[992] as democracy assistance can help to stabilise a conflict situation.[993] Instability, in turn, is often viewed as a central reason for missing development successes.[994] The international community frequently discusses this interdependence in connection to its own security.[995] High competence and flexibility has been attributed to transnational actors when dealing with the recent conflict situations.[996] In some fields, such as humanitarian aid and early warning, governments and IOs almost completely depend on non-state actors.[997]

Supportive functions have been increasingly but still rarely attributed to the German political foundations. As will be shown, they undertook a wide range of conflict management activities. The chapter's first section offers a systematisation of the management of international conflicts shedding light on the establishment of complex approaches and defining transnational actors' general activities and concrete measures along the conflict management cycle. The subsequent section summarises the official German ambitions in this field at the time of writing. Finally, the German political foundations are put in these contexts. Their activities are analysed according to the established framework and illustrated with several examples.

---

991 *Kloke-Lesch/Poeschke* (2013) pp. 306f.; *Major/Schöndorf* (2011) p. 1.

992 C.f. UN Secretary General (2011), see also Ch. 6.1. Peace can be defined as the "facilitation of non-exploitative, sustainable and inclusive social relationships free from direct and indirect violence and the threat of such violence" (*Mac Ginty* [2008] pp. 15ff., 24).

993 See Ch. 7.1.2; *Burnell* (2000a) p. 12.

994 *Klingebiel* (2013) p. 23 quoting World Bank (2011); BMZ at: http://www.bmz.de/de/was_wir_machen/themen/frieden/friedensentwicklung/index.html.

995 *Kloke-Lesch/Poeschke* (2013) p. 292; *Beswick* (2011) p. 1913; critically *Bermeo* (2010) pp. 83f. Security can be either defined as "absence of danger" or as the "persistence of worths over time" (*Frei/Gaupp* [1978] p. 5).

996 *Stephenson* (2011) p. 403. There is also a dark side of non-state actors' involvement in conflicts. A strand in the literature deals with armed and violent actors (c.f. *Schneckener* [2006]). Others stress the conflict's intensification by them (*Barak/Cohen* [2014] p. 10).

997 *Eberwein* (2011) p. 375; *Roth/Klein* (2007); *Bakker* (2001).

7.1. Crisis and conflict management

Since the end of the Cold War the security field has enlarged revealing space for transnational actors to become involved. From their traditional humanitarian and developmental role, they expanded their position to the management of conflicts corresponding with the increase of liberal peacebuilding, the finding of dependence between development and conflict, a greater interest in the affected society and a modified definition of state sovereignty.[998]

7.1.1. Comprehensive approaches

Comprehensive approaches emerged in the last decade to the successful international management of conflicts, assuming that civil, political and military instruments need to be used together or sequentially.[999] They are supposed to ensure legitimacy and coherence among the expanded number of actors involved. While comprehensive approaches are used on the international level, the coordination of different interdepartmental policy areas on the national level is termed as whole-of-government approach.[1000]

The establishment of comprehensive approaches coincided with an expanded concept of security: While security during the Cold War mainly referred to that of states, individual security has increasingly come to the fore becoming particularly apparent in the principle of human security.[1001] Moreover, the averting of danger made way for precaution and risk management often highlighted in preventative crisis management concepts. While before the 1990s security mainly referred to military threats, humanitarian aspects became central in the following time relating to human

998 *Goodhand/Walton* (2012) pp. 430ff. Due to the non-uniformly application, I use conflict and crisis interchangeably. Conflict inherent in every social relationship is a socially constructed reality created through interaction inseparable from the cultural frameworks in which it has emerged (*Lederach* [1995] p. 9). In accordance with the peace definition (fn. 991), it can be defined as a system or action of exploitation, exclusion, and of limited opportunity and direct violence (*Mac Ginty* [2008] p. 59).

999 Exemplary NATO (2006), OECD (2006).

1000 *Major/Pietz/Schöndorf/Hummel* (2011) p. 43.

1001 First mentioned in the Human Development Report of UNDP in 1994, human security puts development policy in the centre of security political considerations (*Major/Pietz/Schöndorf/Hummel* [2011] p. 12).

rights. Security was furthermore extended from the national territory to the international space, often referring to global security as world society's security.[1002] Moreover, internal and external security became increasingly connected.[1003] Internal security is generally very institutionalised by means of cooperation among security services and refers to the political system's protection against internal enemies while external security relates to outside threats.[1004] The multilateral cooperation of states and various other actors in order to avert to various threats is termed as "co-operative security".[1005]

Comprehensive approaches and the broad notion of security are also relevant in the international discussions on the "responsibility to protect" (R2P) aiming at protecting human beings from strong violations of human rights and at humanitarian law.[1006] In 2001 the International Commission of Intervention and State Sovereignty defined R2P as a principle formulating three responsibilities: to prevent such a situation, to react to it and to reconstruct.[1007] Subsequently, the UN outlined a list of situations, such as genocide, war crimes and ethnic cleansing in which R2P applies.[1008] UN General Secretary Ban Ki Moon added three pillars of R2P in 2009: (1) the responsibility of the state to protect its own population, (2) the responsibility of the international community to help states meet this requirement through international assistance and (3) the timely and decisive response in case of the state's failing including military intervention and, as ultimate rationale, the use of force.[1009] Since then the UN Security Council referenced R2P in several cases, such as South-Sudan, Syria and Libya, but only in the context of pillar one.

1002 *Daase* (2010).

1003 *Endreß/Petersen* (2012).

1004 *Rausch* (2005b) p. 886.

1005 *Von Bredow* (2006) pp. 9f.

1006 R2P is part of the debate on humanitarian interventions defined as the protection of human rights of people who are nationals and/or residents of a country by another country or a group of countries through threats or the use of force (EP [1994] p. 3). R2P is wider as it includes components of prevention, reconstruction and non-military reaction. On the discussion whether R2P is a principle, concept or norm, see *Rudolf* (2013) pp. 12ff. China and Russia generally reject R2P referring to Article 2(7) UN Charta (*Masala* [2008] p. 23). On R2P as great powers' instrument see *Mallavarapu* (2013).

1007 ICISS (2001).

1008 UN (2005) p. 31 (§§ 138f); UN (2006).

1009 UN (2009b) pp. 8f.

The application of comprehensive approaches becomes apparent in the international dealing with fragile states combining democracy assistance and military intervention. Complex approaches can also be found in the literature on diplomacy. They assume that state diplomacy alone is not able to transform conflicts and stressing the importance of transnational actors. This is particularly apparent in *Hocking's* catalytic diplomacy model.[1010] Collaborative approaches focus on long-term and dialogue processes, the building of capacity in civil society, the enhanced public support and structural development.[1011] Also approaches which combine development, diplomacy and defence have been identified aiming at stabilising the recipient country and gaining its acceptance while donors pursue military interests.[1012]

7.1.2. Transnational actors' instruments in conflicts

In conflict situations transnational actors take various peace-supporting activities comprising some general tasks and concrete measures along the conflict management cycle. Civil approaches, collaborative public diplomacy and track two diplomacy generally stress transnational actors,' advocacy networks' and epistemic communities' establishment of trust-based and communicative relations, dialogic interactions as well as information and ideas exchange among conflict parties.[1013] Moreover, the informal diplomatic function of think tanks was highlighted offering neutral spaces of interaction for those searching for conflict resolution policies which can cover public and private actors' networks.[1014] Also transnational actors' policy work in conflicts was mentioned aiming at winning over governments and international institutions. It comprises agenda-setting, campaigning, coalition building and the generating of knowledge through analytical skills and information accessed on-site.[1015] The latter is also relevant in the non-

---

1010 *Hocking* (2011) p. 230.

1011 *Davies/Kaufman* (2002); *Cowan/Arsenault* (2008).

1012 *Amos* (2014) p. 147.

1013 *Heinrich/Lange* (2009) p. 254; *Azar* (2002) p. 23; *Cowan/Arsenault* (2008); *Hocking* (2011) p. 230; *Mbabazi/MacLean/Shaw* (2005); *Simon* (2002); *Bolewski* (2007) coined the term soft-track-two diplomacy (p. 39).

1014 *Stone* (2011) pp. 244f.

1015 *Hocking* (2011) p. 230; *Goodhand/Walton* (2012) pp. 434f. A typical example is the successful International Campaign to Ban Landmines (*Stephenson* [2011] pp. 399f.).

state actors' involvement in early warning defined as the methodical gathering and analysis of information on the crisis in order to foresee violent developments offering policy options to decision makers and institutions.[1016] Capacity building in affected civil societies, the promotion of public support for the peace processes and the encouragement for justice were furthermore indentified as transnational engagement in conflicts.[1017]

All these transnational actors' general tasks are also conspicuous in concrete measures along the conflict management cycle. According to the ideal-typical model of *Major/Pietz/Schöndorf/Hummel*, there are four different phases of a (potential) crisis to which actors can react with specific measures (see *table* 7.1).[1018] In the first phase, crisis prevention measures are involved as the situation is peaceful or at least armed conflicts do not occur. In the second period, actors can react to the crisis with mediation and intervention instruments. In the following phase, in which an armed conflict has broken out, crisis management refers to conflict transformation measures, while the later fragile post-conflict phase makes tools of peace consolidation necessary. Measures can often be used in several phases and at times overlap.[1019] As the conflict's process is circulating, the last phase potentially leads into the first period. In practice, the phases are difficult to determine. Frequently in the same region the peace and conflict situation varies tremendously.[1020] The whole conflict management cycle is ideally guided by certain principles, such as R2P, human security, do-no-harm, local ownership and UN resolution 1325 on the involvement and protection of women in conflict processes.[1021] There are several actors involved in the management of crisis: The EU and the UN are potentially active in all phases of a conflict. While the OECD implements measures in the field of crisis prevention and peace consolidation, NATO can step in when it

1016 *Bakker* (2001) pp. 264f., 267, 272.

1017 *Goodhand/Walton* (2012) pp. 433ff.

1018 *Major/Pietz/Schöndorf/Hummel* (2011) p. 6; for a similar systematisation on transnational actors' instruments see *Fischer* (2006) pp. 6ff.

1019 In Afghanistan (as of 11/2014) the multilateral peace enforcement ISAF mission was for example combined with the political United Nations Assistance Mission mainly active in peace-building. Parallel to this, the Operation Enduring Freedom US-led and without a UN mandate was active.

1020 *Schaller/Schneckener* (2009) p. 10.

1021 See Ch. 7.1.1. "Do-no-harm" refers to the necessary conflict sensibility as external intervention might cause negative effects. "Local ownership" stresses the importance of local actors to be involved in the crisis management phases in order to ensure sustainability (*Major/Pietz/Schöndorf/Hummel* [2011] pp. 10f.).

comes to escalation and armed conflicts.[1022] Moreover, states are multilaterally and bilaterally involved in the management process as well as transnational actors whose activities and available instruments are particularly important for the analysis of the German political foundations' conflict management.

The conflict prevention instruments implemented in the first phase of the conflict attempt to resolve conflicts with peaceful measures and low costs.[1023] Despite the importance of conflict prevention for most international actors' agendas, timely action is often missing as seen in Rwanda and Kosovo in the 1990s and in Darfur in 2004 and 2005.[1024] A positive case is the implementation of the UN preventative deployment force in Macedonia in 1995.[1025] In the prevention phase transnational actors implement the instruments of small arms control, political missions, reforms of the security sector (SSR), and election observation. Small arms control comprises measures to prevent illegal access to small weapons and to improve the control of legal arms trade.[1026] Political missions are a collective term for primarily civilian missions by international organisations including a wide variety of different measures such as humanitarian action, human rights monitoring, development work, peace-building and traditional diplomacy. Often political missions follow peace-keeping operations.[1027] SSR aims at transforming the dysfunctional bodies responsible for internal and external security and involving primarily military and police institutions, the respective political levels, the jurisdiction and the intelligence services.[1028] Election observation, closely connected to democracy assistance (see Ch. 6.1), refers to the monitoring of the electoral process by ex-

1022 NATO, however, assumes its activity even "before and after the crisis" (NATO [2010] pp. 7f.). On the problematic relationship between these IOs see *Giegerich* (2012) pp. 95f., 102; *Yost* (2007) pp. 88f.

1023 It is disputed whether conflict prevention only applies to situations in which the conflict is not yet broken out (*Gareis* [2006] pp. 208f.) or also when the conflict's reoccurrence should be avoided (*Varwick* [2002] p. 5). The latter assumption is convincing when, as outlined, the conflict's process is understood as a cycle.

1024 *Naumann* (2001).

1025 *Gareis* (2006) pp. 211f.

1026 *Major/Pietz/Schöndorf/Hummel* (2011) p. 35; for details see *Bob* (2014) pp. 133ff., see *Stephenson* (2011) pp. 401f. for examples.

1027 *Gowan* (2010) pp. 2f.

1028 *Hänggi* (2005); *Bryden* (2006) p. 23.

ternal and local actors stemming from the idea that elections help democratically stabilise conflictive situations.[1029]

During the conflict's second phase, transnational actors mediate and intervene through multidimensional peace-keeping and conflict resolution. Peace-keeping involves international troops stationed in the conflict region. In contrast to peace-building, where certain actors are supported to strengthen capacity locally, it is a neutral approach.[1030] Traditional peace-keeping bases on Chapter VI of the UN Charter and requires the conflicting parties' approval. There are several other forms like peace enforcement and observer missions.[1031] In multidimensional approaches traditional peace-keeping is supplemented by a civil component, such as election monitoring or the training of police forces. For traditional and multidimensional peace-keeping, UN troops (Blue helmets) are deployed using force for their self-defence.[1032] Transnational actors' conflict resolution covers activities trying to diplomatically and dialogically end the conflict through mediation and good offices. Mediation is the structured, results-oriented decision-making process for a mutually agreed solution. Good offices provide the logistical prerequisites for direct talks of the conflicting parties.[1033] Both are also part of track two diplomacy.[1034] As outlined by works on public diplomacy, part of conflict resolution is also collaboration in which participants from different (conflicting) countries work together on projects of general interest.[1035]

In the transformational conflict phase, civil actors offer humanitarian aid and can participate in multidimensional peace-keeping and civil-military co-operations (CIMIC). Humanitarian aid is defined as a life-saving activity in armed conflict focusing on the short-term relief to those in need

1029 *Kühne* (2010) p. 3; *Kumar* (2000).

1030 *Schaller/Schneckener* (2009) pp. 11f.

1031 Peace enforcement, frequently a UN-led mission regulated by Chapter VII UN Charter allowing the use of weapons, aims at the termination of fighting by use of compulsive acts, at the separation of the parties of conflict even against their will and at securing the respect of the ceasefire (*Schaller/Schneckener* [2009] pp. 10f.). The forces are not UN troops and come from the involved countries. Observer missions are typically smaller unarmed operations.

1032 *Page Fortna* (2004) p. 270.

1033 *Liese* (2005) pp. 549f. For transnational actors active in conflict resolution the term CROs (Conflict resolution organisations) was coined (c.f. Amos [2014] p. 146).

1034 *Berridge/James* (2003) p. 260; *Goodhand/Walton* (2012) p. 433; see Ch. 3.1. on track two diplomacy.

1035 See Ch. 3.1.1.

including the provision of shelter, food and health services.[1036] It bases on the principles of non-interference, neutrality, impartiality and independency.[1037] CIMIC was defined in the context of NATO missions and has three core functions: the establishment of civil-military relations in general, the civil forces' support through insights into the civilian situation, and the support of civil institutions and actors to increase the acceptance of the forces on-site.[1038]

The last phase of the conflicts' peace consolidation offers the most instruments for non-state agents. An important task is peace-building as a cross-cutting measure comprising several means which can also be used independently.[1039] It was first mentioned in 1992 in the UN Agenda for Peace of the then general secretary *Boutros Boutros-Ghali* referring explicitly to the consolidation phase after the armed conflict ended. This temporal determination has gained ground in the literature and political practice.[1040] In 2005 the UN created the Peace-building Commission elaborating strategies for conflict-affected countries and coordinating the funding members.[1041] The Peace-building Fund established in 2006 provides financial resources to countries emerging from conflict.[1042] Peace-building aims at the removal of wars' political, economic, social and psychological consequences and focuses on the conflicts' structural reasons. It mixes security-political and development-political approaches with a central focus on local capacity building.[1043] The security dimension of peace-building includes the measures of disarmament, demobilisation and reintegration (DDR) and the establishment of efficient political, legal and penal structures including SSR. While disarmament and demobilisation generally make a military component necessary, the reintegration of former combatants is part of civil actors' long-term engagement.[1044] Peace-building's political dimension attempts to build political institutions focusing on the rule of law, the observance of human rights, free elections and the estab-

1036 *Eberwein* (2011) p. 363; *Rodon/Serrano/Giménez* (2012) p. 367.
1037 *Kloke-Lesch/Poeschke* (2013) p. 300.
1038 *Paul* (2008) p. 3.
1039 *Major/Pietz/Schöndorf/Hummel* (2011) p. 6.
1040 UN (1992) Sec. 55ff. Peace-building is partly used as a generic term for peace enforcement, peace-keeping (*Doyle/Sambanis* [2000] p. 781) and peace-making (*Berridge/James* [2003] pp. 200f.).
1041 UN at: http://www.un.org/en/peacebuilding/mandate.shtml.
1042 UN at: http://www.unpbf.org/who-we-are/.
1043 *Schaller/Schneckener* (2009) pp. 10f.
1044 *Major/Pietz/Schöndorf/Hummel* (2011) p. 26; *Bryden* (2006) p. 23.

lishment of political parties. The socio-economic dimension includes economic recovery, the rebuilding of infrastructure, the promotion of the economic, health and educational sectors and the combat of criminal structures.[1045] In the context of the psycho-social dimension, the reintegration of refugees and war victims, the dealing with war crimes, reconciliation and transitional justice processes can be initiated. Reconciliation has several linked components, such as the healing of survivors, retributive or restorative justice and the seeking for publicly recognised truth and reparations.[1046] Transitional justice embraces judicial and non-judicial measures against the violation of human rights including institutional reforms, truth commissions and the establishment of victims' organisations.[1047] Partly the literature assumes a fifth dimension of peace-building, integrating the neighbouring regions into the peace process and promoting the conflict countries' (re)integration into the international structures and markets.[1048] Part of the conflict's consolidation phase are furthermore democracy assistance,[1049] the establishment of international tribunals and police missions as well as the before mentioned political missions, conflict resolution, small arms control, election observation and CIMIC. International tribunals cover the international criminal court (ICC) and other tribunals limited in time and region. They are not completely recognised by the international community. Transnational actors often lobby for the tribunals' establishment or offer networked support.[1050] Police missions assist the security forces in crisis states and help creating internal security. Their scope has been continuously extended in the last decades to consulting and training for police forces, prosecution, frontier protection, and SSR.[1051]

1045 World Bank (1998) p. 4; UNDP (2008) p. 5.

1046 *Bloomfield* (2006) p. 11.

1047 *Zupan/Servaes* (2007) p. 4.

1048 *Schaller/Schneckener* (2009) p. 11.

1049 See Ch. 6.1.; *Major/Pietz/Schöndorf/Hummel* (2011) mentioned "democracy promotion" (p. 25) but refered to democracy assistance.

1050 *Hellwig-Bötte* (2013); *Stephenson* (2011) pp. 400f.

1051 *Major/Pietz/Schöndorf/Hummel* (2011) p. 38.

Table 7.1: Conflict management cycle and transnational actors' instruments[1052]

Conflict's phase	Conflict management	Transnational actors' instruments
Peace/absence of armed conflict	Conflict prevention	– Small arms control – Political missions – SSR – Election observation
Escalation	Mediation, Intervention	– Multidimensional peace-keeping – Conflict resolution
Armed conflict	Conflict transformation	– Multidimensional peace-keeping – Humanitarian aid – CIMIC
Fragile post-conflict phase	Peace consolidation	– Democracy assistance – DDR – Peace-building – International tribunals – Small arms control – Conflict resolution – Political missions – Police missions – SSR – Reconciliation and transitional justice – Election observation – Economic recovery – CIMIC

7.2. German conflict management

German security policy from the unification onwards referred to a "transfer of stability". It purposed the export of security and focused on conflict management as the violation of the German territorial integrity was no longer at risk. In 1994, the Federal Constitutional Court's ruling which followed the "out of area debate" on the German Armed Forces' deployment outside the NATO territory in the context of the Gulf War in 1991, brought significant changes. The ruling, in short, confirmed under consti-

1052 *Major/Pietz/Schöndorf/Hummel* (2011) p. 6. The systematisation originally included possible instruments of all involved actors.

tutional law the German participation in combat and armed UN and NATO missions with parliament's approval.[1053] While Germany had already participated in smaller UN-lead missions since the 1960s, its involvement in international military operation increased from 1994 having a strong focus on the determent of violence in Southeast Europe. As a consequence, the role of the German Armed Forces changed from a deterring to an intervention force while politically Germany followed the strategy of integrating its Eastern neighbours into the international structures.[1054] As of 2014, the most important missions regarding size and amount of involved German soldiers were the ISAF mission in Afghanistan of 2001 and the KFOR mission of 1999, UN-mandated, and NATO-led peace enforcement missions.[1055]

Despite this increasing military course of action, Germany has been partly characterised as a "through and through pacifist nation"[1056] which is, however, not convincing. As already touched, Germany is a classic civilian power[1057] which aims at civilising politics accepting cooperation, preferring non-military over military means and striving for supranational structures to deal with obstacles.[1058] In Germany, this is rooted in the experiences of the Second World War and National Socialism, the German div-

1053 BVerfGE 90, 286 of 12/07/1994 (Decision of the Federal Constitutional Court) so called "Blue-helmet-ruling"; Der Spiegel 29/1994 pp. 23ff. According to Article 24(2) German Constitution "with a view to maintaining peace, the Federation may enter into a system of mutual collective security". A collective security system is a multilateral institution of universal or regional scope offering security to its members in case of interstate aggressions (*Rudolf* [2005] p. 443). In order to comply with the German constitution, the system needs to have a defensive character (*Jarass* [2000] § 24 GG, 20). The notion of defence was increasingly widened in the last couple of years. Concisely is the famous statement of then defence minister *Peter Struck* in 2004 that "Germany's security is not only but also defended in the Hindu Kush" (BT [2004] p. 8601). Since 2005 the requirement of parliamentary approval to international armed missions is governed by the Parliamentary Participation Act. For details on the on-going debate see BPB (2014).

1054 *Hellmann* (2007) pp. 610ff., (2013) p. 54; precisely on the conflict in Yugoslavian wars and the German military involvement see *Callic* (2007) pp. 474ff.

1055 As of August 2014, 3640 German soldiers participated in 17 UN, NATO and EU peace operations, see the Federal Armed Forces at: http://www.bundeswehr.de/portal/a/bwde/!ut/p/c4/04_SB8K8xLLM9MSSzPy8xBz9CP3I5EyrpHK9pPKUVL3UzLzixNSSKiirpKoqMSMnNU-_INtREQD2RLYK/.

1056 *Bender* (2008) p. 4. Extensively on the question of German pacifism *Delgaard-Nielson* (2006) p. 142.

1057 See Ch. 6.2.

1058 *Maull* (1990/91) pp. 92f. referring to the soft power concept (see Ch. 2.3.2).

ision and the connected foreign political guidelines of the allies.[1059] Before and after the unification, Germany felt bound to the normative principles of the Western democracies, its foreign political predictability and the reliability to its partners. It is more oriented towards economic growth and social prosperity and less towards territorial expansion and becoming a great power.[1060] Since the end of the Cold War and until the time of writing, Germany has been repeatedly criticised by its partners for its military reluctance.[1061] The German reserve towards the Iraq War led to a tremendous crisis in German-U.S. relations. Although this reluctance was consistent with the conception of civil power,[1062] other approaches interpreted the situation differently. According to the realist idea of Germany as the European central power, due to its geographic position, the size of its population, the strong economy and its cultural influence, Germany preferred an open conflict with the U.S. and increasingly militarised in the last two decades.[1063] This perspective, however, overlooks that German politicians, journalists and researches generally tended to avoid using the term "power" when referring to Germany.[1064] Also the German public was generally sceptical about military interventions.[1065] In 2013, *Guido Westerwelle* still referred to a "culture of military reluctance" as the core of Germany's foreign policy.[1066] From a constructivist perspective *Risse* argued that civilian power, multilateralism and European and pro-Western orientation are components of the German foreign political identity guiding the political preferences.[1067] Consequently, *Risse* viewed the debates on the German rearmament and the participation in international military operations as

---

1059 *Lapins* (2007) p. 7.

1060 *Maull* (2007) p. 76.

1061 *Gathmann/Medick/Weiland/Wittrock*, SPIEGEL Online, 27/08/2013; *Braun*, Süddeutsche Zeitung, 25/08/2014; *Joffe*, Die Zeit, 30/01/2014.

1062 *Maull* (2007) pp. 79, 81.

1063 *Baumann* (2007) pp. 69f.; *Schwarz* (1994) pp. 10f.; *Münkler* (2015).

1064 *Bender* (2008) p. 4; *Hacke* (1993) termed Germany a "world power against its will".

1065 SWP/GMF (2013) p. 42; *Hellmann/Wagner/Baumann* (2014) pp.185f.; *Rattinger* (2007) p. 317.

1066 *Friedrichs*, ZEIT Online, 15/01/2013.

1067 *Risse* (2007b) pp. 50, 55 referring to *Wendt* (1999); similar *Hellmann/Wagner/Baumann* (2014) pp. 200f. *Risse* (2007b) defines national identity as a sense of belonging to an imaginary community in a concrete territorial space which refers to the community's characteristics and the differences vis-à-vis other groups (p. 52).

debates on the German identity.[1068] The German support of international military operations was not a break with the conception of civilian power since it was different from a pacifist policy renouncing the use of military means. Moreover, Germany has always preferred political over military solutions. *Risse* convincingly regarded the confrontation with the U.S. as a clash of the two components, civilian power and Western orientation, with the first prevailing.[1069] Others stressed that Germany develops towards a "civilian-military" power taking account of the increasing military involvement in the last decades.[1070] However, the German abstention to the resolution of a no-fly-zone in Libya in 2011 throws doubts on this assessment.

In line with its foreign political identity, Germany at the time of writing is mainly multilaterally engaged in international conflict management[1071] taking as a basis a broad notion of security.[1072] It followed the peace imperative, as peace enjoys a priority position in the German constitution. [1073] Its preamble outlines that the adaption of the basic law is "inspired by the determination to promote world peace".[1074] In recent times the government perceived state conflicts, cross-border organised crime and terrorism, poverty, struggles for resources, and the effects of climate change as threats[1075] and preferred a comprehensive approach coordinating the relevant areas of foreign, security, developmental, economic, financial and environmental policy. It understood conflict according to the conflict cycle.[1076] Multifaceted crisis management with emphasis on the civil component was outlined in the government's action plan for "civil crisis prevention, conflict resolution and peace consolidation" *(Aktionsplan)* of 2004.[1077] Moreover, the "networked security" approach was summarised in the

1068 *Risse* (2007b) p. 54.
1069 *Risse* (2007b) pp. 58f.
1070 *Algieri* (2011) p. 134.
1071 AA at: http://www.auswaertiges-amt.de/DE/Aussenpolitik/Friedenspolitik/Krisenpraevention/Grundlagen/Ueberblick_node.html; *Major/Pietz/Schöndorf/Hummel* (2011) p. 5.
1072 BMZ (2005) p. 8.
1073 *Naumann* (2009) p. 11.
1074 Basic Law of the Federal Republic of Germany, 23 of May 1949, last amended by the Act of 21 July 2010.
1075 AA (2010a) p. 22; Bundesregierung (2004) pp. 5f.
1076 AA (2010a) p. 16; AA at: http://www.auswaertiges-amt.de/DE/Aussenpolitik/Friedenspolitik/Krisenpraevention/Grundlagen/Ueberblick_node.html; *Flechtner* (2007) pp. 9f.; *Rühle* (2008) pp. 7, 10.
1077 Bundesregierung (2004) preceded by the concept of 2000 (see Bundesregierung ibid. XVI).

"White paper on security policy and the future of the German armed forces" *(Weißbuch)* published by the Ministry of Defence in 2006 assuming that military and civil means were equally important and multilaterally used for the achievement of broad security.[1078] *Aktionsplan* and *Weißbuch* are not coherent, however. The *Aktionsplan* did not refer to military means whereas "networked security" seemed to include measures across departments but was often rejected by civil society actors due to its military origin. In practice, undertakings were not sufficiently coordinated among the different ministerial departments.[1079] Civil components were mostly financially and personally underequipped and subordinated to the military missions[1080] which in turn lacked evaluation and legitimacy as the parliamentary decisions deviated from public opinion.[1081] Often Germany offered compensation for its military nonparticipation to partners being involved in battles.[1082] The *Aktionsplan* outlined 161 civil activities with long-term implementation scope,[1083] recognised the "Do no harm" concept[1084] and established connections to democracy assistance.[1085] However, it did not use notions uniformly. Prevention, for example, referred to the whole conflict cycle.[1086] Moreover, it lacked concrete measures[1087] and included too many aspects not necessary part of a conflict prevention portfolio, such as the reactive fight against terrorism.[1088] Despite these issues and although Germany turned to conflict management rather late, it has continuously

---

1078 BMVg (2006) p. 25, also mentioned in the government's coalition treaties of 2009 (CDU/CSU/FDP [2009] p. 123) and 2013 (CDU/CSU/SPD [2013] p. 122).

1079 *Major/Schöndorf* (2011) p. 3; *Naumann* (2009) p. 13.

1080 *Nachtwei* (2008) p. 6.

1081 *Gareis* (2011) pp. 151f.; BPB at: http://sicherheitspolitik.bpb.de/index.php?page=deutsche-beteiligung-an-friedensmissionen.

1082 *Bittner/Geis/Lau/Bernd/Wurmb-Seibel*, Die ZEIT, 01/04/2013.

1083 Bundesregierung (2004). Three reports were published on the *Aktionsplan's* implementation: Bundesregierung (2006), (2008) and (2010).

1084 Bundesregierung (2004) pp. 6f.

1085 Bundesregierung (2004) p. 37. Already in 1980, the independent German North-South Commission had outlined the interdependence between development and stability (*Brandt* et al. [1980] p. 13)].

1086 Bundesregierung (2004) p. 6; similar BMZ (2013c) p. 31.

1087 *Major/Schöndorf* (2011) p. 3.

1088 Bundesregierung (2004) p. 18; *Nachtwei* (2008) p. 6; *Dückers/Mehler* (2011) p. 269.

expanded its policy.[1089] In summer 2014, the *Bundestag* agreed to an increase of appropriations in the field of conflict prevention.[1090]

Apart from the AA's general support of UN missions through membership dues and civil personal, its contribution to the UN peace-building fund[1091] and its engagement in the Peacebuilding Commission which it chaired in 2010,[1092] the AA additionally backed conflict management measures implemented by other IOs and NGOs. Since 1999 the government-supported Ifa-project *(Institut für Auslandsbeziehungen)* "Zivik" constitutes the interface between the government and the implementing NGOs.[1093] In 2014, the AA's conflict management focused on the rule of law, transitional justice, the support of women and the reintegration of child soldiers and former combatants.[1094] Concrete measures were the training of police forces, the formation of judges, SSR and the reinforcement of the civil society.[1095] Moreover, the AA supported single democracy assistance projects concerning constitutional bodies, election aid and election monitoring.[1096] Additional funding was provided for projects supporting the democratic transition in North Africa and the Middle East.[1097] German AKBP[1098] was assigned the role to mediate between cultures through dialogue processes, to be active in early warning and to establish intercultural competence.[1099]

1089 Bundesregierung (2012a) p. 22; *Dückers/Mehler* (2011) p. 266.

1090 More than one third of the AA's budget was assigned to the protection of peace and stability. It covered 1,46 Billion Euro, an increase of 120,35 Million Euro compared to 2013. Almost 400 million Euros alone were provided for the subsection "humanitarian aid and crisis prevention" (Federal budget 2014, Kapitel 0501 Titelgruppe 03); *Hausding*, Das Parlament, 30/06/2014.

1091 AA at: http://www.auswaertiges-amt.de/DE/Aussenpolitik/Friedenspolitik/Krisenpraevention/Massnahmen/Massnahmen_node.html.

1092 AA (2012b) pp. 35f. It was partly viewed as consolation for the permanent seat on the UN Security Council see *Schneckener/Weinlich* (2006) p. 21.

1093 Bundesregierung (2004) p. 45.

1094 AA at: http://www.auswaertiges-amt.de/DE/Aussenpolitik/Friedenspolitik/Krisenpraevention/Massnahmen/Massnahmen_node.html.

1095 AA at: http://www.auswaertiges-amt.de/DE/Aussenpolitik/Friedenspolitik/Krisenpraevention/Massnahmen/Rechtsstaatlichkeit_node.html.

1096 AA (2010a) p. 32; AA at: http://www.auswaertiges-amt.de/DE/Aussenpolitik/Friedenspolitik/Krisenpraevention/Massnahmen/Wahlbeobachtungen_node.html.

1097 AA at: http://www.auswaertiges-amt.de/DE/Aussenpolitik/RegionaleSchwerpunkte/NaherMittlererOsten/Umbrueche-TSP/Projekte/111125_TP_Foerderung_node.html.

1098 See Ch. 3.3.

1099 AA (2014) pp. 5, 7, (2011a) p. 15, (2000) p. 1; *Singer* (2003) pp. 49ff.

The AA gave a special emphasis to the intercultural dialogue with the Islam.[1100]

The BMZ complemented to the *Aktionsplan* and outlined its cross-sectoral concept on crisis prevention, conflict management and peace support in 2005[1101] which was replaced by the concept on "Development for peace and security, Development political commitment in the context of conflict, fragility and violence" in 2013.[1102] In 2008, crises prevention and peace development were termed as focal points of Germany's development policy. So was the promotion of democracy and civil society.[1103] In 2014, projects of the BMZ focused on democracy, rule of law, good governance, human rights, promotion of the economy, protection of the resources and the environment, education, SSR and strengthening of the civil society.[1104] Along the conflict's phases the BMZ promoted dialogue processes on various levels, government consulting, peace conferences, local peace projects, economic recovery and reconciliation.[1105] The BMZ-funded Civil Peace Service (ZFD) established in 1999, internationally seconded civil experts to partner organisations for conflict resolution tasks.[1106] Crisis management was also connected to a cultural and dialogue dimension in terms of intercultural acceptance and understanding.[1107]

Since 2005 the German government explicitly supported R2P[1108] and was member of the "group of friends" an informal union of states at UN headquarters supporting R2P as a principle.[1109] The literature, however, criticised the German reluctance and a lack of coherence in this field.[1110]

1100 AA (2010b) p. 3.

1101 BMZ (2005) pp. 5, 8.

1102 The BMZ referred to the whole-of-government approach on fragile states (see Ch. 6.2.1) and on the peace and state-building goals of the High Level Forum on Aid effectiveness in Busan in 2011, see BMZ (2013c) p. 11.

1103 BMZ (2008) p. 9; OECD (2010) p. 36; see Ch. 6.2.2.

1104 BMZ at: http://www.bmz.de/de/was_wir_machen/themen/frieden/krisenpraevention/index.html.

1105 BMZ at: http://www.bmz.de/de/was_wir_machen/themen/frieden/friedensfoerderung/index.html, http://www.bmz.de/de/was_wir_machen/themen/frieden/konfliktbearbeitung/index.html.

1106 ZFD at: http://www.ziviler-friedensdienst.org/en.

1107 Bundesregierung (2004) p. 48; *Maaß* (2009) p. 29; AA (2014) p. 7.

1108 AA (2012b) pp. 36f., (2012b) p. 29; BT (2011b) pp. 3f., (2010) p. 22.

1109 BT (2011a) p. 17750.

1110 *Brenner* (2012) pp. 66f.

Moreover, the German government felt bound to UN resolution 1325.[1111] In 2012, it adopted an action plan for the resolutions' implementation establishing the principle as cross-cutting theme[1112] and continuously reported on respective German measures.[1113] Furthermore, it focused on the concept of human security highlighting human rights and the security of people in conflict regions.[1114]

For the management of conflicts, Germany established certain national structures.[1115] Since 2004 the inter-ministerial steering group on civil crisis prevention *(Ressortkreis Zivile Krisenprävention)* coordinated activities and ensured the *Aktionsplan's* implementation. The advisory board for civilian crisis prevention *(Beirat für zivile Krisenprävention)* created in 2005 involved civil stakeholders from the fields of human rights, developmental and security policy. The parliamentary subcommittee on civilian crisis prevention, conflict management and integrated action established in 2010 enabled the study of the subject in the *Bundestag*. It cooperated with the steering group. Moreover, the Centre for International Peace Operations (ZIF) set up in 2002 strengthened German civilian capacities for international peace operations including the recruiting, training and deploying of civilian specialists and election observers as well as some academic activity.[1116] The Working Group on Peace and Development (FriEnt) founded in 2001 included BMZ's staff members and eight non-governmental members and sought to pool information and capacities through public events, expert meetings, publications, training measures and advice.[1117]

1111 UN (2000b), AA at: http://www.auswaertiges-amt.de/DE/Aussenpolitik/Menschenrechte/Frauenrechte/Frauen-Konfliktpraevention_node.html, critically *Hentschel* (2010) p. 46.

1112 Bundesregierung (2012b).

1113 Bundesregierung (2014).

1114 Bundesregierung (2004) p. 57; BMZ at: http://www.bmz.de/de/was_wir_machen/themen/frieden/friedensentwicklung/index.html; *Kloke-Lesch/Poeschke* (2013) p. 293.

1115 AA at: http://www.auswaertiges-amt.de/DE/Aussenpolitik/Friedenspolitik/Krisenpraevention/NationaleStrukturen_node.html.

1116 AA (2012b) pp. 34f.; AA at: http://www.auswaertiges-amt.de/DE/Aussenpolitik/Friedenspolitik/Krisenpraevention/Massnahmen/Wahlbeobachtungen_node.html; ZIF at: http://www.zif-berlin.org/en/about-zif/what-we-do.html.

1117 FriEnt (2011).

7.3. Conflict management of the German political foundations

Since the beginning of their international undertakings, the German political foundations have been active in countries of latent or acute conflicts. Scholars, however, did not become interested in this matter until the late 1990s. The attention grew simultaneously to the topic of civil conflict management on the German political agenda.[1118] In 2015, conflict prevention, civil conflict management, the fight against terrorism and the dealing with fragile states were tasks increasingly assigned to the *Stiftungen* and mostly compatible with the existing foundations' approaches. New strategies had been partly adopted as well. In this context, the foundations also profited from additional funding made available by the German government.[1119]

7.3.1. Literature review

Since the late 1990s the German political foundations' conflict management and peace activities appeared more often in the literature but selectively and mainly in context of democracy assistance.[1120] In 1999 *Ronge* and *Pascher's* article treated the foundations' contribution to peace assuming that interaction on multiple levels builds trust.[1121] According to them, the foundations were able to modify and compensate foreign policy when working in countries of underdeveloped official diplomacy due to dictatorships or revolutionary regimes. The foundations furthermore mediated in cases of violent situations within one country, exemplified in Latin America, or in conflicts between two or several states, such as Israel and Palestine. Moreover, through the active participation in UN summits, the foundations influenced a global peace policy.[1122] In 2000, however, *Mair* still identified a foundations' disinterest in conflict management when many other actors had entered the domain already. He mentioned lacking capacities as a reason but stressed that the foundations' democracy assistance, such as the provision of dialogue and discussion floras, already covered

1118 *Schmidt* (2007) p. 542.
1119 FNS (2013a) p. 101; *Bartsch* (2007) pp. 284, 289.
1120 C.f. *Böhler* (2005) p. 11; *Bartsch* (1998) p. 189.
1121 *Ronge/Pascher* (1999) p. 190f.
1122 *Ronge/Pascher* (1999) pp. 192ff.

much of conflict management.[1123] In 2005 *Renvert* studied the foundations' activities as regards the crisis between Germany and the USA due to the intervention in Iraq.[1124] *Renvert* saw an "early warning system" in the work of the foundations allowing to harmonise political tensions and to identify ways of cooperation.[1125] An increased significance of the foundations in preventing intrastate and regional conflicts was noticed by *Pogorelskaja* in 2006.[1126] In 2007 the foundations' activities were mentioned briefly in the context of development cooperation with non-state armed groups exemplified by activities of the KAS in the Democratic Republic of the Congo and of the HBS in Afghanistan.[1127] In 2009 *Pogorelskaja* identified foundations' conflict management as a trend in the foundations' international activity mentioning negotiations, mediation and "structure-oriented" long-term conflict prevention defined as democracy assistance.[1128] She noted a dense network of offices in the conflict regions of the Middle East and North Africa.[1129] Other regional focal points were Afghanistan, Central Asia and the Caucasus. She concluded with a case study on the foundations' activities in Uzbekistan lacking, however, specific measures in conflict management.[1130] Some descriptions of themselves by the German *Stiftungen* have mentioned their peace-supporting activities. *Hennig* referred to the KAS's contribution to discussions on security structures and conceptions, and their democracy assistance in conflict regions such as Cambodia, Thailand, Yugoslavia, Pakistan, Indonesia and Nigeria.[1131] In 2005 *Wahlers* showed the intention to strengthen the KAS's support of peace and security in the future.[1132] *Gerster* outlined the KAS's support of the reconciliation processes between Israel and Germany which started in 1980 mainly through media and educational projects and later through think tank and consulting activities.[1133]

1123 *Mair* (2000) p. 148.

1124 *Renvert* (2005) p. 3; see Ch. 5.3.2.

1125 *Renvert* (2005) pp. 9, 23.

1126 *Pogorelskaja* (2006) p. 16.

1127 *Grävingholt/Hofmann/Klingebiel* (2007) p. 83.

1128 *Pogorelskaja* (2009a) pp. 140ff. Prevention in her definition, however, seemed to cover also dispute settlement and conflict transformation.

1129 The findings of Ch. 6.3.3. on the offices' distribution do not particularly support this argument although the territories' size was not set in relation.

1130 See Ch. 6.3.4.

1131 *Hennig* (1998) pp. 398, 400.

1132 *Wahlers* (2005) p. 49.

1133 *Gerster* (2005).

7.3.2. The conflict management objectives of the *Stiftungen*

The German political foundations' democracy assistance in conflict regions has always supported peace on an overall level.[1134] Nonetheless, projects with a clear conflict perspective increased from 2000 onwards.[1135] In 2007 the KAS outlined a stronger focus in their international work on security threats caused by fragile states and terrorism among others.[1136] However, it did not become a central task.[1137] At the time of writing, the FES had emphasised the importance of its conflict management[1138] and regards peace and security as a cross-cutting field[1139] and strategic goal.[1140] Also the FNS had more explicitly integrated conflict prevention and resolution to its activity portfolio in the last decade.[1141]

The foundations' conflict management was closely related to the German official ambitions. The government recognised the important role of the *Stiftungen* and referred to them in several documents. In 2005 the BMZ stressed the long-standing experience of the foundations (and other organisations) and their independently developed peace-building strategies.[1142] In 2013 it highlighted the foundations' active shaping of peace and security referring to their network and partner structures.[1143] The foundations were also integrated in the respective national conflict management structures. Since its establishment in 2005, representatives of every political foundation participated in the *Beirat für zivile Krisenprävention* offering expert advice to the *Ressortkreis Zivile Krisenprävention*. Moreover, the FES and the HBS were founding members and part of *FriEnt* established in 2001.[1144] The FNS joined *FriEnt* in 2003, resigned from an institutional activity a couple of years later but still cooperated on a project basis in 2014.[1145]

The foundations' conflict management activities concerned three broad areas: general peace-supporting activity on the international and regional

1134 Interview 14.
1135 C.f. FES (2002) pp. 8f.
1136 KAS (2008c) p. 13.
1137 Interview 12.
1138 Interviews 11, 13, 17; FES (2009a) p. 1.
1139 FES (2012f) p. 1.
1140 FES annual reports (2011) pp. 32f. and (2013) p. 25.
1141 FNS (2013b) pp. 21, 23.
1142 BMZ (2005) p. 15.
1143 BMZ (2013c) pp. 25f.
1144 BMZ (2013c) p. 26; FriEnt at: https://www.frient.de/frient/mitglieder.html.
1145 FNS (2013a) p. 73. Also, the KAS was not a FriEnt member but the FriEnt homepage referred to some KAS's activities and publications in 2014.

level as well as in Germany, concrete measures along the conflict management cycle of conflicts between two or several countries or within one country, and crisis management which involved Germany as a conflicting party.

7.3.2.1. General tasks

First of all, the *Stiftungen* initiated political dialogue on security policy and peace support and channelled information on international and national discussions.[1146] One such example was the German-Chinese symposium on global security issues and cooperation organised by the KAS and its Chinese partners in 2007 in Beijing.[1147] At the recurring Asia-Europe Roundtable co-organised by the FES since 2000, ASEM (Asia-Europe Meeting) members discussed cooperation in conflict management and other global aspects.[1148] At the annual European Strategic Forum, politicians and experts exchanged on developments in European security policy. Security dialogue was also initiated by several foundations between the USA, Europe and Russia.[1149] In 2011 the KAS, the FES, the HBS and the FNS organised a joint program for Afghan civil society actors prior to the International Foreign Ministers' Conference on Afghanistan which aimed at formulating policy recommendation. The results were presented on the Civil Society Forum in Bonn.[1150] Information from these international fora was channelled in national and regional debates through the foundations' country offices. They fed back regional and national perspectives to the foundations' supranational offices.[1151] Peace and security dialogues among politicians, researchers and scholarship holders were also offered by the foundations in Germany.[1152] The *Stiftungen* were furthermore involved in policy work. An early example is the foundations' cooperation with the Conference on Security and Co-operation in Europe (CSCE) in the

---

1146 C.f. KAS (2007b) p. 13.
1147 KAS (2007a) p. 13.
1148 FES (2010) p. 2.
1149 FES (2012f). On the initiation of Russian-German security political dialogues: FNS (2013a) p. 98, HSS annual report (2013) p. 47, FES (2002) p. 36.
1150 FES/KAS/HBS/FNS (2011); the Afghanistan Forum at: http://www.afghanistan-forum.org/.
1151 FES at: http://www.fes.de/GPol/inhalt/sicherheitspolitik.htm.
1152 See also Ch. 5.2.1.; FES (2012f) p. 2.

mid-1990s when NGOs where allowed to participate in the process.[1153] The foundations' participation in UN summits was already mentioned.[1154] They were also involved in lobbying for conflict management in Germany.[1155] In 2008, the KAS, for example, intended to convey more intensely the necessity of the international deployment of German Armed Forces and to help produce respective arguments.[1156]

The foundations were also involved in conflict analysis, knowledge-generating and the processing of information. The offices in the industrialised countries monitored and analysed the developments on the international level, such as the UN and the EU.[1157] On the occasion of the German membership in the UN Security Council in 2010/2011, the FES, for instance, started a series of publications on matters of the Council.[1158] The country offices in the conflict regions offered analysis and studies on concrete cases, such as the study on decentralisation conducted by the FNS and Centre for Policy Alternatives after the civil war in Sri Lanka in 2010.[1159] Furthermore, findings in the form of policy papers and outcomes from the dialogues were published on the website and disseminated to decision makers.[1160] The FES, for example, channelled the results of the experts' interchange in Afghanistan in 2012 and 2013 to the respective politicians on-site, in Germany and Europe.[1161] Experiences from their conflict management were also treated in seminars with politicians, researchers and business experts in Germany.[1162] Already in the mid-1990s, the FES was a founding member of the UN initiative "Lessons Learned and Best Practice Unit" in New York which elaborates best practices in UN peace missions. Since then, the FES focused on the creation of interregional networks to transfer conflict experiences.[1163] In partnership with the Stockholm international peace research institute the FES also organised re-

1153 *Pogorelskaja* (1997) pp. 29ff.

1154 See Ch. 7.3.1.; *Ronge/Pascher* (1999) pp. 194f.

1155 Bundesregierung (2006) p. 93.

1156 KAS (2008c) p. 13.

1157 FES (2012f).

1158 FES annual report (2011) p. 33; FES at: http://www.fes.de/gpol/inhalt/unsc.htm.

1159 FNS (2013a) p. 61.

1160 C.f. BMZ (2007) p. 44.

1161 FES at: http://www.fes-afghanistan.org/pages/projects/reinforcing-peace-and-security.php.

1162 C.f. FES (2002) p. 67.

1163 FES (2002) p. 78, experiences from Macedonia and Kosovo were transferred to the Middle East's conflict (p. 79).

search-supported regional dialogues between emerging countries and troop-providing countries on challenges of peace operations.[1164]

The foundations also furthered the establishment of regional early warning systems.[1165] However, early warning on-site was surprisingly not assigned to the foundations. The *Aktionsplan* mentioned explicitly the German embassies,[1166] whereas the potential of the German *Stiftungen* in terms of analysis capacity, the necessary access to the civilian population and the embassy-like infrastructure was not highlighted.

The foundations were finally active in capacity building. In 2014 the KAS and its partners offered a capacity building program in Senegal for stakeholders from the public, the non-public and the academic sector being involved in conflict management. It was part of the AA-supported ifa-program "zivik".[1167] The KAS also organised a recurring academic training module on conflict management together with Bar-Ilan University in Akko, Israel.[1168] Also the RLS focused on conflict management capacity building in the Middle East.[1169] In 2005 the FES, the AA and a local NGO organised a project treating the tolerance of religious and non-religious teachers and students[1170] and a summer school on conflict prevention and religion for girls of a Koran school in Tadzhikistan.[1171] Seminars in conflict management were also offered by the foundations to individuals in Germany.[1172] Apart from these general tasks, the foundations made use of other methods as well. The RLS, for instance, regularly organised festivals and cultural events to support peace in the Middle East and Bosnia-Herzegovina.[1173]

1164 FES at: http://www.fes.de/GPol/inhalt/konfliktbearbeitung.htm; SIPRI at: http://www.sipri.org/research/conflict/pko/new-geopolitics-of-peace-operations; FES (2002) p. 18.

1165 C.f. FES (2010).

1166 Bundesregierung (2004) pp. 59, 64.

1167 See Ch. 7.2.; KAS at: http://www.kas.de/senegal-mali/de/publications/30574/.

1168 KAS at: http://www.kas.de/israel/de/publications/38011/; KAS (2014c).

1169 RLS annual report (2005/2006) p. 49.

1170 Bundesregierung (2006) p. 58; FES at: http://www.fes.de/GPol/inhalt/projektbeispiele.htm; FES (2002) p. 43.

1171 BMZ (2007) p. 45.

1172 C.f. FNS (2013b) p. 28.

1173 RLS annual report (2005/2006) p. 49; RLS at: http://www.rosalux.de/news/40519/kultur-des-friedens.html.

7.3.2.2. Concrete measures

In 2015, the *Stiftungen* implemented most of the outlined transnational actors' instruments along the conflict management cycle. However, it cannot be confirmed that instruments were strictly implemented in the respective conflict management phases. Often instruments were combined or overlapped. Especially the FES and the HBS were very active in this field but also the other foundations undertook such tasks, even if mainly in a democracy assistance context. The establishment of the KAS's rule of law program in Southeast Europe, for example, was originally initiated to help peace and secure consolidation.[1174]

The principles which ideally guide conflict management activities were important for the *Stiftungen*. Explicitly mentioned was the do-no-harm tenet[1175] which was particularly apparent in the FES's PCIA (Peace and Conflict Impact Assessment) methodology, applied since 2002 and in accordance with the BMZ's strategy.[1176] PCIA focused on conflict sensitivity and the monitoring of the impact of activities. The conflict was analysed first, and the project work was adapted to the findings. Afterwards, the conflict dynamic was monitored, and project adjustments were made. On the basis of long-term case studies, also methodical guidelines were established.[1177] Furthermore, the foundations critically monitored the international coordination processes in the context of human security.[1178] Moreover, the foundations' partner approach furthered the principle of local ownership.[1179] The foundations also focused on R2P and the protection and involvement of women in conflict regions. In 2007 the FES and FriEnt, for example, organised a workshop on R2P.[1180] A discussion on the Asian and European perspective on R2P was organised by the KAS in Shanghai in 2011.[1181] In 2014 the HBS held a conference together with other organisations as regards the safety of women in countries of the Arab

---

1174 *Auga* (2007) p. 8; see Ch. 8.
1175 FES at: http://www.fes.de/GPol/inhalt/projektbeispiele.htm.
1176 BMZ (2005) pp. 20f.; see also Ch. 9.
1177 *Abirafeh* (2005) p. 10; FES at: http://www.fes.de/gpol/en/pcia.htm; on PCIA see *Pfaffenholz* (2005).
1178 Interview 11; FES at: http://www.fes.de/GPol/inhalt/nichtstaatliche-gefaehrdun gen.htm; see Ch. 9.2.1.
1179 Interview 10; see Ch. 5.2.
1180 Bundesregierung (2008) p. 89.
1181 KAS at: http://www.kas.de/china/de/events/47323/.

Spring.[1182] In 2004 it supported an Israeli women NGO in their activities to integrate gender mainstreaming in the Israeli conflict management.[1183] In 2002 the FES organised an international women peace conference in Angola. The subject was also continuously treated in a symposium in Germany.[1184] The HBS and the FES were also founding members of the German Women's Security Council, a network of German women organisations and researchers to further the implementation of UN resolution 1325 in Germany.[1185]

Of the instruments in the conflict prevention and peace consolidation phase, the *Stiftungen* undertook small arms control, SSR and election observation. The FES made disarmament and arms control a special focus in their peace support activities[1186] and supported UN and regional programs in this field.[1187] In 2010, for example, it co-organised a conference on small weapons control together with the UN Institute for Disarmament Research and the Geneva Centre for Security Policy and arranged a conference on humanitarian disarmament in 2014.[1188] Regarding SSR, the FES supported the democratic integration of the security sector and targeted political decision makers to implement reforms.[1189] The foundations' activities also included educational programs for police forces and civil-military dialogues[1190] which showed overlaps with the instruments of police missions and CIMIC. The KAS, for example, organised a dialogue program between military officers and politicians in West Africa in 2007. A continuous program educated officers in rule of law.[1191] Election observation was mainly covered by other German actors. Nonetheless, it was closely connected to the foundations' democracy assistance. Examples could be found in the monitoring of elections with local partners and capacity build-

1182 Bundesregierung (2014) p. 50. For another HBS's conference see Bundesregierung (2007) p. 41.
1183 *Aharoni* (2007) pp. 263, 273 fn.
1184 FES (2002) pp. 70f.
1185 *Çalişkan* (2007) p. 295 fn.
1186 FES (2012f) p. 1.
1187 FES at: http://www.fes.de/gpol/en/disarmament.htm.
1188 FES at: http://www.fes-globalization.org/geneva/documents/06Apr2011_Final%20Programme_UNIDIR%20FES.pdf, http://www.fes.de/GPol/pdf/Berlin-Sessions-Invitation.pdf.
1189 FES (2012f) p. 1.
1190 FES at: http://www.fes.de/GPol/inhalt/projektbeispiele.htm; BMZ (2007) p. 46; FES (2002) pp. 52f.
1191 KAS (2007a) p. 13; on foundations' SSR engagement see also Bundesregierung (2006) p. 121 and *Bartsch* (2007) p. 284.

ing.[1192] In 2014 the KAS, for instance, co-organised several workshops for poll watcher in Tunisia. Participants were supposed to further train other poll watchers subsequently leading to several thousands of trained individuals.[1193] In 2001 the FES supported a radio and TV campaign in the run-up of the presidential election in Benin which was directed against election corruption and aimed at mobilising voters.[1194]

Of the transnational instruments which are ideally implemented in the conflict escalation and consolidation phases, the *Stiftungen* undertook conflict resolution through dialogue creation, track two diplomacy and collaboration. Particularly important in this context was the foundations' political dialogue instrument and the establishment of vertical relationships and horizontally among different types of actors.[1195] Moreover, the foundations acted as mediators in bringing together the conflicting parties or offering exchange platforms.[1196] In 2012 the FES furthered the Afghan experts' dialogue including the neighbouring countries on peace policies for the time after the withdrawal of the ISAF-troops. Four policy groups of ambassadors, civil servants, military generals, parliamentarians, leading civil society figures, researchers and media people from Afghanistan, Central Asia, India and Pakistan were formed. Additional expertise came from China, Turkey, Iran and Russia. The different stakeholders within one group and the different regional groups interacted with each other.[1197] The results were outlined in a joint declaration presented at the UN headquarters in 2013.[1198] For many years the HBS and the FNS had been active in fostering dialogues between the ethnically and territorially conflicting groups and

1192 See Ch. 6.3.4; Bundesregierung (2006) p. 118.

1193 KAS at: http://www.kas.de/tunesien/de/publications/36054/.

1194 FES (2002) p. 47, see (2010a) p. 2 on an academic workshop on this matter.

1195 See Ch. 5.2.1.

1196 C.f. FES at: http://www.fes.de/GPol/inhalt/projektbeispiele.htm; FES (2012f) on security political "trialogues" between Afghanistan, Pakistan and India (p. 1); FES (2002) on the creation of intra-state dialogues among youth organisations in Nigeria (p. 16) and among conflicting parties in Sudan (p. 17).

1197 FES (2012e). On regional dialogue initiation in Mali see FES annual report (2013) p. 25. In this context the FES also mentioned Track 1,5 (http://www.fes-asia.org/pages/reinforcing-peace-and-security.php). Track 1,5 bridges track one and two. It is defined as "unofficial intervenors working with official representatives of the conflict parties" (*Nan/Druckman/El Horr* [2009] p. 66). This applies largely to the foundations' dialogue initiation in conflicts as government members were often involved.

1198 FES (2013); FES annual report (2013) p. 25; *Maiello*, Huffington Post, 14/02/2014.

societies in the Southern Caucasus.[1199] In 1998 the HBS supported a women-NGO and the environmental ministry in Somaliland. Both thereafter cooperated horizontally in the form that the ministry was allowed to use the NGO's technical infrastructure and in turn defended the NGO from other ministries' tutelages.[1200] An interesting early example is a trilateral conference between politicians from the U.S. State Department, the AA and a Cuban delegation including *Ricardo Alarcón*, then vice foreign minister of Cuba, organised by the FNS in 1987 in Germany which treated the different political positions and cooperation possibilities. According to the FNS, the Cuban side had contacted the FNS in order to win them over to the conference organisation and to establish a contact to the U.S. side with the help of the then Foreign Minister *Genscher*, a member of the FNS-affiliated Free Democratic Party.[1201] The KAS was particularly active in Asian ethic-religious conflicts.[1202] In cooperation with the Philippine Centre for Islam and Democracy, for instance, it published academic works on the subjects.[1203] The FNS organised study trips for Israeli and Palestine parliamentarians and staff officers to create channels of communication between them.[1204] FES's activities could furthermore be found in collaboration where conflict parties' experts cooperated on specific technical projects of general interest and regional cooperation was furthered.[1205] Between 2001 and 2006 the FES organised the Jerusalem Berlin Forum where Israeli, Palestinian and German experts worked out common solutions in water management and regional planning among others.[1206] In 1999 it initiated an EU-funded joint agreement on public administrative cooperation, such as health, education and fight against crime in the West Bank's and Israel's border region. Further consulting was offered to the parties from the region of "RegioTriRhena" at the Southern Upper Rhine where France, Switzerland and Germany cooperated in the field of communal policy.[1207] In 2002 the FES facilitated the exchange among governments, parliamen-

---

1199 HBS at: http://www.boell.de/de/2013/11/20/buero-suedlicher-kaukasus-tbilisi; *Kaufmann* (2007) p. 307; FNS (2013b) p. 21, (2013a) p. 61, the FNS was also active in dialogues in South Asia.

1200 *Fahrenhorst* (2007) p. 83.

1201 FNS (2013a) pp. 92f.

1202 KAS (2006) p. 77; see Ch. 7.3.

1203 KAS (2013e) p. 24.

1204 FNS (2013a) p. 99.

1205 FES (2002) p. 14; FES at: http://www.fes.de/gpol/en/project_examples.htm.

1206 FES (2009a) p. 1.

1207 FES (2002) pp. 19f.

tarians and researchers of the conflicting Azerbaijani, Georgian and Armenian to foster economic cooperation in the South Caucasus.[1208] Also consulting was offered by the FES. Since 2004 it advised the ECOWAS (Economic Community of West African States) initiative on a common democratic security architecture.[1209]

As regards instruments in the peace consolidation phase, the *Stiftungen* were active in democracy assistance and peace-building, in particular DDR, SSR, reconciliation and transitional justice and economic recovery. They also lobbied international tribunals and advocated small arms control and monitored elections, as already outlined. The foundations' democracy assistance was extensively presented previously.[1210] To differentiate strictly between democracy assistance in conflict regions and such in the rest of the world was difficult as it generally aimed at eliminating structural conflict causing deficits. The *Aktionsplan* of 2004 and the subsequent reports stressed the foundations' long-term relations with politics, political elites and civil society actors and their media promotion helping to stabilise a peaceful situation.[1211] In the context of conflict, it mainly involved the capacity building.[1212] Measures were the foundations' fostering of civil society structures, to be empowered for mediating in conflicts, their rule of law engagement and constitutional assistance.[1213] Also, the foundations' media strengthening was relevant, aiming at deactivating or defusing conflicts.[1214] In 2004 and 2005 the FES supported the elaboration of several radio programs by Iraqi journalists on the elections in Iraq and its broadcasting all over Iraq.[1215] Workshops for Afghan parliamentarians were also offered to overcome ethical divides.[1216] Democracy assistance in conflict regions covered most of peace-building's political and security dimensions. The foundations' activities in the context of DDR could also be found. Since 2012 the HSS had been engaged in dialogue programs in Columbia between the FARC-guerrilla fighters, the Columbian government and the

1208 FES (2002) p. 30.

1209 FES (2009a) p. 2, (2005c) p. 42; *Bartsch* (2007) p. 289.

1210 See Ch. 6.3.

1211 Bundesregierung (2004) pp. 38, 44, 47, (2006) pp. 39, 62, (2008) pp. 47f., 75, (2010) pp. 15, 43; FES (2005b) p. 3.

1212 *Major/Pietz/Schöndorf/Hummel* (2011) p. 25.

1213 C.f. *Pascher* (2006) p. 16.

1214 FES at: http://www.fes.de/GPol/inhalt/projektbeispiele.htm.

1215 FES (2009a) p. 2.

1216 FES (2009a) p. 2, (2002) on activities in Bosina-Herzegovina and Croatia (pp. 40f.).

peace commission focusing on demobilisation, and reintegration of former fighters.[1217] Also minority rights were strengthened. The FES's regional office in Southeast Europe monitored such rights and furthered consulting activities of local organisation towards the respective public bodies.[1218] Although the foundations were not active in economic recovery as such, they, however, helped to strengthen the economic sectors as already outlined.[1219] Closely connected were the foundations' activities in environmental protection. In 2002 the FES, for example, furthered economic and environmental regional cooperation among conflicting parties in Central Asia where a conflict over water was expected.[1220] The HBS organised several conferences on the connection between nature conservation and crisis management in 2002 and 2003 in Berlin.[1221] Regarding the psychological and social dimension of peace-building, foundations' undertakings in the field of refugee reintegration, reconciliation and transitional justice could be found. Together with the Centre for the Study of Violence and Reconciliation in South Africa the FES held a workshop with UN mediators, governmental and non-governmental participants at the international conference "Building a Future on Peace and Justice" on the importance of reconciliation in 2007.[1222] Reconciliation was also combined with SSR or media capacity building when integrating public security forces or journalists.[1223] The FES, for example, initiated dialogues and used media work to facilitate the return of refugees in Bosnia-Herzegovina and Croatia after the Balkan war.[1224] The foundations also organised transitional justice conferences,[1225] were active in human rights[1226] and furthered truth commissions. In 2005 the FES's annual human rights award honoured the heads of the Chilean and Peruvian truth commissions.[1227] The Columbian truth commission was supported with monitoring[1228] and the Indonesian truth commission

1217 HSS annual report (2013) p. 56.

1218 FES (2009a) p. 1.

1219 See Ch. 6.3.4.; Bundesregierung (2006) p. 41; *Eckl/Hofmann* (2012) on the FES's engagement.

1220 FES (2002) p. 32.

1221 Bundesregierung (2006) p. 53.

1222 *Brounéus* (2007) p. 3; Bundesregierung (2008) p. 52.

1223 FES at: http://www.fes.de/GPol/inhalt/projektbeispiele.htm.

1224 FES (2002) p. 26.

1225 C.f. the FES: *Avello* (2008) p. 16, KAS (2007c).

1226 C.f. KAS (2007) p. 20, FES (2005c) pp. 77ff., FNS (2013b) p. 7.

1227 FES (2005a).

1228 FES (2009a) p. 2.

was encouraged with a study trip to South Africa.[1229] As already outlined, the foundations were active in integrating neighbouring countries in peace processes. The foundations furthermore lobbied international tribunals. In 2010 the FES, the International Centre for Transnational Justice (ICTJ) and the Moroccan Centre for Human Rights conducted a training session on the International Criminal Court with members from the Moroccan Coalition for the ICC and journalists.[1230] In 2008 the ICTJ and the FES organised a series of events aiming at raising awareness for the Special Tribunal for Lebanon.[1231]

There were only few transnational activities along the conflict management cycle where the foundations' engagement was completely missing. The *Stiftungen* were neither involved in humanitarian aid as they did not carry out short-term life-saving tasks, nor in cases of multidimensional peace-keeping, presumably because the foundations' activities were not politically neutral.

7.3.2.3. Conflicts in German foreign relations

The *Stiftungen* were also involved in managing political conflicts which involved Germany as a conflicting party.[1232] The foundations' maintaining of relations with foreign opposition groups outside of the Federal Foreign Ministry's reach and official adequacy and with countries of underdeveloped diplomatic relationships was already mentioned.[1233] Furthermore, the foundations fostered dialogue processes between Germany and Israel. In this context, the HBS also focused on cultural events, exhibitions and readings.[1234] Moreover, the foundations established intercultural dialogue with the Islam.[1235] Some authors observed an increase in the foundations' activities in the Middle East from 2005 onwards coinciding with an intensified German political interest in the region and dialogues with the Muslim world.[1236] For many years, the KAS had been particularly active in estab-

1229 FES (2002) p. 53.
1230 Coalition for the ICC at: http://www.iccnow.org/?mod=newsdetail&news=4605.
1231 ICTJ (2008) p. 5.
1232 C.f. *Renvert* (2005).
1233 See Ch. 5.3.2.2.; *Ronge/Pascher* (1999) p. 192.
1234 HBS at: http://www.boell.de/de/navigation/naher-mittlerer-osten-5289.html.
1235 Bundesregierung (2008) p. 43, (2010) p. 39; *Bartsch* (2007) p. 289.
1236 *Steinbach* (2007) p. 504.

lishing religious dialogues in Germany and internationally. Since 9/11 the engagement had been further enhanced.[1237] Often these dialogue processes were put in the context of democracy and political participation. In 2013 the KAS implemented the project "Muslims in state and society world wide" which brought together workshop participants from different countries in Istanbul, Singapore and Casablanca discussing the relationship of religion, culture and politics and including activities with the Muslim community in Germany.[1238] Since 2006 the office of the KAS in Turkey organised trainings for imams of the Turkish religious authority. They were prepared for their work in German Muslim communities.[1239] Finally, the *Stiftungen* as already outlined, helped smoothing the U.S. German relationship during the political crisis from 2002 onwards.[1240]

Conclusion

The potentials which stemmed from the German political foundations' activities in conflict management were mainly congruent with those outlined for democracy assistance. This included high flexibility and the opportunity to establish contacts and work with groups unreachable for official diplomats.[1241] Especially the foundations' diverse partner structures on-site and their duality between the state and non-state sphere made them being accepted by different types of conflicting actors.[1242] This was ideal, since the difference between state and non-state actors in conflict regions is often blurred.[1243] Not being bound to work with one type of actor only, allowed the establishment of trustful and communicative relations horizontally and vertically. According to the FES, conflicts could only be managed when the political level was integrated in the process as it needed to enable the necessary reforms.[1244] The FES's activities in Central Asia in 2005 and 2006 therefore concentrated on such conflicts which the govern-

1237 KAS (2007b) p. 16.
1238 KAS annual report (2014) p. 12.
1239 KAS (2013e) p. 7.
1240 *Renvert* (2005).
1241 See conclusion Ch. 6; c.f. BMZ (2005) p. 15; FES (2002) p. 12 on the establishment of unofficial contacts and the completion of official diplomacy.
1242 See Ch. 5.2.
1243 *Fahrenhorst* (2007) p. 83.
1244 FES (2002) p. 12.

ments themselves wanted to avoid.[1245] At the same time, conflict management extended the foundations' foreign working relationships as it allowed integrating governments in complex conflict management approaches which were rather unwilling to take part in democracy assistance programs.[1246]

The foundations' democracy assistance as practiced for several decades equiped them well for taking on conflict management tasks. For the foundations, it was rather old wine in new bottles as most of their developmental activities easily fit in the new context. Nonetheless, they added additional conflict-focused activities. As the review on the foundations' conflict management has shown, most of the transnational instruments used in conflicts were covered already. In its focus on civil conflict management, also the German government had identified the foundations' potential in peace and security. It highlighted their long-term international experience and global networking.[1247] The foundations had hence expanded their sphere of activity and influence from development to security policy.[1248] Since it is to be expected that war and violent conflicts will increase in the future,[1249] equally the foundations' role in effective conflict management will continue to gain importance.

For overall development policy, authors observed a movement towards conflict-relevant humanitarian aid in the 1990s, an increased politicisation and its integration in broad security concepts.[1250] The "securitisation" of development[1251] and the fact that transnational actors are taken in for different strategic purposes might be one side of the coin.[1252] The renewed interest in development, on the contrary, led to an increase in necessary initiatives.[1253] Finally, these changes paved the way for conflict management to become part of collaborative public diplomacy approaches. In chapter 9 we will connect conflict management to public diplomacy.

1245 BMZ (2007) p. 43.

1246 *Pogorelskaja* (2009a) p. 150.

1247 BMZ (2013c) p. 26.

1248 *Grimmel/Jakobeit* (2009) p. 216.

1249 *Gareis* (2006) p. 225.

1250 *Roth/Klein* (2007) p. 9.

1251 *Beall/Goodfellow/Putzel* (2006) pp. 52f.; critically *Kloke-Lesch/Poeschke* (2013) p. 300, *Dückers/Mehler* (2011) p. 268 and *Brock* (2004) p. 324.

1252 *Roth/Klein* (2007) p. 13 quoting former U.S. foreign minister *Powell* on NGOs' strategic purposes in Iraq.

1253 *Gareis* (2006) p. 221.

Part III: Case studies

Chapter 8 – Practising public diplomacy through democracy assistance: The rule of law program of the Konrad-Adenauer-Stiftung in Southeast Europe

In the following chapter, I look in detail on the rule of law program (RLP) of the *Konrad-Adenauer-Stiftung* (KAS) in Southeast Europe. The case aims at illustrating how public diplomacy in the catalytic and collaborative form of democracy assistance was practised by the *Stiftung*. It allows getting some detailed insights into the status of the network surroundings and on the common values of network members as it compares the objectives and activities of the RLP against German policy formulations. More generally, it reflects on the KAS's impact as a transnational actor.

The chapter starts with an overview on the framework in which the RLP operated, before I shed light on the KAS's public diplomacy in the context of the RLP. The chapter bases mainly on an in-depth interview conducted in 2014, several other interviews, an evaluation of the RLP in 2013 as well as other material which the KAS kindly made accessible to me. The evaluation of the RLP was carried out on behalf of the KAS by *Otto Luchterhandt*, professor for public and Eastern European law at the University of Hamburg.[1254]

8.1. Southeast Europe and Germany

The KAS's RLP in Southeast European[1255] covered the former Eastern bloc countries of Rumania, Bulgaria and Moldova (as part of the USSR), the former Yugoslavian states and Albania. The following subsection outlines perceptions of the political situation, the region's deficits and the KAS's relations to the aid organisations on site. It then looks at German policy towards the region which often had similarities with European policy. After-

1254 *Luchterhandt* (2013).

1255 The region is not clearly defined. Sometimes, it is used interchangeably with the countries of the Western Balkan or includes Turkey and Ukraine.

wards, the ambitions of the German political foundations in Southeast Europe are briefly outlined, while the last subsection introduces the KAS's RLP in Southeast Europe followed by an excursus on the overall RLPs' conception.

8.1.1. Political situation and aid organisations

In 2014, the political conditions in Southeast Europe the interview partner at the KAS described as diverse: Albania was very isolated in the region before the 1990s. Bulgaria and Rumania were geostrategically significant and hence the first to be integrated into the EU (European Union). Moldova had declared its independence even before the break-up of the Soviet Union, while the Yugoslavian countries experienced conflicts during the 1990s. In common these countries underwent political, social and economic transformation processes. The interview partner stressed the astonishing progress in the last decades. It included democratic constitutions, elections and institutions. He mentioned the long-term and complicated processes which were necessary for the proper parliaments' functioning, the constitutional jurisdiction to fight for recognition, and the difficulties in executive institution building. As challenging, he regarded the economies' transformation due to missing management experience and the old elites often gaining advantage from the privatisation at the general public's cost. Furthermore, political parties which could have been addressed by the KAS or other organisations were nonexistent. The political parties already developed were little ideologically programmatic, oriented towards the interests of certain groups and hence differed considerably from Western parties. Despite major advances, the transformation process was, according to the interview partner, not completed and substantial deficits, especially regarding the rule of law were still persisting.[1256] These deficits were: a weak civil society and an underdeveloped media sector due to former state's oppression of private initiative; high demands towards the state and low individual political and social engagement paradoxically combined with renouncing the state and political parties, having few members, a strong leader fixation and a weak democratic structure; underdeveloped political oppositions as counter-elites to the Communist Party regimes and a low propensity to deal with the past; the former state bureaucracy with a rather "tactical" attitude to democratic principles and the rule of law and which

1256 Interview 8; similar *Luchterhandt* (2013) p. 48.

enriched itself during the transformation processes; problems to establish rule of law principles as elites lacked conviction; and political clientelism due to the ruling political parties' tendency to fill posts in the executive with their adherents.[1257]

Many international organisations were active in Southeast Europe in 2014. Partly they were state-controlled, like USAID, which consulted with large expenditures. Although the interview partner stressed the indispensability of many organisations, he gave rise to the concern that they did not send consistent messages. U.S. organisations, for instance, had different ideas than the KAS. At times, too much aid was available. Strange and "patchwork-like" solutions were developed originating from U.S. and European influence. To partners on site the KAS communicated to follow the European advice rather than what was recommended by the Americans since they desired the integration into the European Union. The situation among the organisations was described as competitive.[1258] The main rule of law focused international organisations active in the region were USAID, the American Bar Association, the Council of Europe's Venice Commission, the EU and the OECD. Other German organisations were the GIZ *(Gesellschaft für Internationale Zusammenarbeit)*, the IRZ *(Deutsche Stiftung für international rechtliche Zusammenarbeit e.V.)*, and the other *Stiftungen*.[1259]

8.1.2. Germany's policy

In the past, German foreign policy towards the Southeast European countries was characterised by the German division and the East-West conflict. While the GDR already had economic and military relations with the region before the Berlin Wall Fall, intense policy of the unified Federal Republic yet had to develop.[1260] The relocation of the German Parliament from Bonn to Berlin in 1991 was viewed as swing towards the region.[1261] The relationships with Bulgaria, Rumania and Moldova developed smoothly. Rumania had a significant German minority which for the most part left the country after 1989. Still, it was challenging to remove the East-

1257 *Luchterhandt* (2013) pp. 16f.
1258 Interview 8.
1259 *Luchterhandt* (2013) p. 31.
1260 *Dauderstädt* (2007) p. 422.
1261 *Dauderstädt* (2007) p. 426.

ern neighbours' fears of a unified and powerful Germany, to advocate their interests and, simultaneously, to maintain good relations with the Soviet Union/Russia.[1262] Until recently, the Eastern EU integration and affiliation led to tensions.[1263] German-Yugoslavian relations were already intense before the Wall Fall: Germany was the most important Yugoslavian trading partner, many foreign workers in Germany came from Yugoslavia, which was also a popular German travel destination and supported by the German government.[1264] In the Yugoslavian crisis starting in 1991, Germany took an active role. Since the situation increasingly required military engagement, it finally led to a redefinition of German foreign and security policy and to foreign political identity changes.[1265] Also the German-Albanian relations were characterised as sympathizing since the 1990s including cooperation, active governmental exchanges and German assistance in the Albanian transformation and Euro-Atlantic integration.[1266]

Over the last decades, German policy supported all efforts to integrate or link the countries of Southeast Europe into the EU and to expand the NATO eastwards in order to secure a peaceful neighbourhood,[1267] reduce migratory pressure and tap new sales markets.[1268] With the focus on trade, aid and integration, Germany also exhibited the characteristics of a civilian power.[1269] Its political and economic motivations in Southeast Europe con-

---

1262 *Colschen* (2010) pp. 201f.; *Gareis* (2006) p. 75; *Dauderstädt* (2007) p. 428; *Bos* (2007) p. 456.

1263 *Caspari*, ZEIT Online, 28/08/2014.

1264 *Calic* (2007) p. 468.

1265 *Calic* (2007) p. 480; see Ch. 7.2. In the Bosnian War between 1992 and 1995 Germany showed strong involvement, especially in the elaboration of the Dayton peace agreement. In 1992 it supported the international airlift to Sarajevo as part of the UN Protection Force and was involved in measures to control the embargo against Serbia and Montenegro and in patrolling the Bosnian airspace in 1993. The ruling of the Federal Constitutional Court in 1994 brought legitimisation for the German involvement in international peace missions and a reorientation regarding a German military engagement. The NATO operation "Allied Force" in 1999 was Germany's first combat mission. Germany became an equal partner in the following NATO-led KFOR mission, the UN-lead UNMIK mission and in other stabilisation missions on the Balkan from 2000 onwards (*Calic* [2007] pp. 470-9).

1266 *Milo* (2008) p. 70.

1267 BT (2011c) pp. 3, 5; *Colschen* (2010) p. 201; *Dauderstädt* (2007) pp. 432f.

1268 *Colschen* (2010) p. 188.

1269 *Dauderstädt* (2007) p. 435; *Tewes* (1997) spoke of civilian power with *Gestaltungsmacht* (creative drive); see also Ch. 6.2 and 7.2.

sequentially coincided.[1270] In recent times, German foreign policy was mainly driven by EU politics and the stabilisation and association process (SAA).[1271] It supported the European Instrument for Pre-Accession Assistance (IPA) helping financially the accession efforts and supporting all in all reforms, capacity building, development, employment, education, agriculture and regional cooperation since 2007. Of the countries covered by the RLP the resources were available to Albania, Bosnia Herzegovina, Kosovo, Macedonia, Montenegro and Serbia.[1272] Also German foreign cultural relations and education policy (AKBP) supported the EU integration process.[1273] A particular emphasis the AA put on regional cooperation in Southeast Europe in order to avoid the former reactive crisis management.[1274] On the German EU Council and G8 presidency's initiative in 1999, the Stability Pact for Southeast Europe was established covering the former Yugoslavian countries, Bulgaria, Rumania and Moldova and allowing for an EU membership prospect.[1275] It was replaced by the Regional Cooperation Council (RCC) in 2008 and was part of the Southeast European Cooperation Process (SEECP).[1276] Bulgaria and Rumania became EU member states in 2007. In 2013 Croatia accessed the EU. However, the European Commission still systematically assed the Bulgarian and Rumanian progress in judicial reforms and the fight against organised crime and corruption (benchmarking) at the time of writing.[1277] Since 2009 Moldova was part of the EU's Eastern Partnership policy. As a component of the EU's Eastern Neighbourhood policy, it aimed at politically associate and economically integrate the former countries of the USSR with the EU.[1278] In this context, the German government supported particularly civil society organisations and their interlinking with NGOs in the EU at the time

1270 *Staack* (2007) p. 95.

1271 CDU/CSU/SPD (2013) pp. 156, 165; BT (2011c) pp. 3f.; *Janning* (2007) pp. 747, 753; *Caspari*, ZEIT Online, 28/08/2014.

1272 EU Regulation No 231/2014, Article 3.1 and Annex I.

1273 AA (2014) p. 11.

1274 BT (2011c) p. 5.

1275 *Calic* (2007) p. 479.

1276 BT (2011c) p. 5. As of January 2015, it covered 46 members, organisations and institutions (RCC at: http://www.rcc.int/pages/14/structure).

1277 On this so-called "Cooperation and Verification Mechanism" see EC at: http://ec.europa.eu/cvm/index_en.htm; for Croatia the EC renounced benchmarking mechanisms (*Palokaj*, euobserver 16/11/2010).

1278 Council of the EU (2009) p. 6.

of writing this study.[1279] Although Moldova was not a key state for German politics,[1280] the relations had been recently intensified, according to the AA.[1281]

During the early transformation processes, the German government offered multilateral assistance and bilateral credits to Southeast Europe. Under the coordination of the BMZ, it also provided advice to Rumania and the Yugoslavian countries which had been recognised developing countries. The consulting first focused on economic activities. Therefore, critics assumed the elaboration of a German trade facilitating social market economy. Over time, it was replaced by the political cooperation of the German political foundations.[1282] Legal advisory came also from the IRZ, a Justice Ministries' initiative created in 1992 and funded governmentally and by the EC. It supported rule of law based and democratic constitutional structures and the harmonizing of national with EU law.[1283] For the non-developing countries in the region, such as Bulgaria, the AA and the BMWi coordinated the consulting assistance between 1994 and 2005 in the so-called "TRANSFORM" program.[1284] At the time of writing, Germany's bilateral development cooperation covered Albania, Serbia, Kosovo, Bosnia Herzegovina and Moldova.[1285] Much assistance took place in European development cooperation formats.[1286] Overarching developmental objectives in Southeast Europe were EU orientation, good governance, conflict prevention, the fight against corruption, and job creation. Political focal points were the promotion of economic activity, public administrative and judiciary reforms and the infrastructure's modernisation.[1287] In the context of

---

1279 AA at: http://www.auswaertiges-amt.de/DE/Europa/Erweiterung_Nachbarschaft/Nachbarschaftspolitik/Oestliche%20Partnerschaft.html; Council of the EU (2011) p. 2, (2009) p. 10.

1280 *Bos* (2007) pp. 456, 467.

1281 BT (2011c) p. 19; AA at: http://www.auswaertiges-amt.de/sid_329E5AB6408C1CB6571D1B4A47E52427/DE/Aussenpolitik/Laender/Laenderinfos/Moldau/Bilateral_node.html.

1282 *Dauderstädt* (2007) pp. 430ff; see Ch. 8.1.3.

1283 IRZ at: http://www.irz.de/index.php/en/about-us.

1284 BMZ at: http://www.bmz.de/de/was_wir_machen/laender_regionen/Mittel-Ost-und-Suedosteuropa/transform/index.html. Since 2005 the TRANSFORM successor program concerns Russia, Belarus and Ukraine (BMWi at: http://www.bmwi.de/DE/Presse/pressemitteilungen,did=201520.html).

1285 BMZ (2013b) p. 27.

1286 For details see BMZ at: http://www.bmz.de/de/was_wir_machen/laender_regionen/Mittel-Ost-und-Suedosteuropa/eu_programme/index.html.

1287 BMZ at: http://www.bmz.de/de/was_wir_machen/laender_regionen/Mittel-Ost-und-Suedosteuropa/index.html; BT (2011c) p. 20.

judicial foreign affairs, the Federal Ministry of Justice and Consumer Protection (BMJV) promoted rule of law and democratic structures in the region including expert exchanges, legislative support, conferences and seminars for foreign jurists. Thematically it concentrated on the spread of human rights and criminal law principles and, considering the German economy, on commercial and corporate law.[1288] In the "Alliance for German law" the BMJV and the major German professional organisations advertised Germany as a legal location mainly through the initiative "Law – Made in Germany".[1289]

The CDU (Christ-Democratic-Union) the KAS is affiliated to and ruling party since 2005 supported EU orientation and stabilisation in the region. It welcomed the former EU enlargement and highlighted the EU's responsibility towards the Balkan and East European countries. Although stressing also the EU's integration ability, it emphasised the necessity of good neighborly relations, cooperation agreements and partnership treaties.[1290]

8.1.3. Landscape of the German political foundations

In 2014, all the German political foundations were active in the countries of Southeast Europe with partly overlapping work fields. Apart from the RLS, they all focused on the EU integration process next to other thematic areas.[1291]

The KAS aimed at bringing the Southeast European countries closer to the Euro-Atlantic structures and supported accession strategies through specific measures. It gave assistance in the democratic and economic transformation processes and focused on political and socio-political dialogue as well as regional cooperation.[1292] It maintained offices in all countries of the region except for Montenegro which was supported from the Serbian

---

1288 BMJV at: http://www.bmjv.de/DE/Ministerium/Abteilungen/EUInternationale Zusammenarbeit/INT-KOR/_doc/Zielgerichtete_Justizau%C3%9Fenpolitik.html?nn=1471926 (accessed on 20/09/2015).

1289 BMJV at: http://www.bmjv.de/DE/Ministerium/Abteilungen/EUInternationale Zusammenarbeit/INT-KOR/_doc/Das_Buendnis_fuer_das_deutsche_Recht.html?nn=1471926 (accessed on 20/09/2015); http://www.lawmadeingermany.de/; CDU/CSU/SPD (2013) p. 154.

1290 CDU (2007) No. 328-30.

1291 On the *Stiftungens'* activities in East Europe compared to other regions see Ch. 6.3.

1292 KAS at: http://www.kas.de/wf/de/71.4785/.

office.[1293] In addition, it had a regional media program and a rule of law program. The latter will be analysed extensively in the following sections.

The activities of the FES in Southeast Europe focused on a just society, innovation, progress and democracy. Important work fields were elections and parliaments, economic and social policy, working relationships and social dialogue, education and media policy, communal policy and regional development, protection of minorities, foreign and security policy and challenges of globalisation. It fostered regional dialogue on these subjects. With view to the SEECP, it promoted the European integration, good neighbourly relations and cooperation.[1294] The FES held as many country offices in the region as the KAS and an additional regional office.[1295]

Contacts of the FNS to the region already dated back to the 1970s.[1296] With its consulting, dialogue and educational activities, the FNS focused on the economic transformation and liberal conceptions. It assisted the rapprochement with the EU, furthered cooperation and concentrated on freedom, human rights, democracy and market economy.[1297] The FNS supported among others, liberal parties, associations, institutions, disseminators, individuals and media representatives.[1298] The regional office in Sofia coordinated the activities in Central, East and Southeast Europe, South Caucasus and Central Asia. The sub-regions offices in Bulgaria and Serbia were responsible for Southeast Europe and the Western Balkans.[1299]

The HBS mainly supported democracy and the rule of law. It assisted the development of civil society, the dealing with the past and the countries' European integration. A focus was on the economies' environmental transformation, urban development and the protection of common resources. It targeted journalists, jurists and political scientists. Methodologically, the HBS initiated media debates and workshops. It consulted reform-minded

---

1293 KAS annual report (2013) p. 100.

1294 FES (2011a) pp. 6ff., (2011b); FES at: http://www.fes.de/international/moe/index.htm, http://www.fes.de/international/moe/in_moe/progr_so.htm.

1295 FES at: http://www.fes.de/international/moe/in_moe/moe_so.htm, http://www.fessoe.de/.

1296 FNS (2013a) p. 62.

1297 FNS (2013b) pp. 20f.

1298 FNS (2013a) p. 66.

1299 FNS at: http://www.msoe.fnst.org/webcom/show_article.php/_c-1559/i.html; The Bulgarian office was also responsible for Macedonia, Rumania and Moldova (FNS at: http://www.freiheit.org/webcom/show_article.php/_c-218/i.html [accessed on 29/09/2015]). The Serbian office also covered Montenegro, Kosovo, Albania, Bosnia-Herzegovina und Croatia (FNS at: http://www.freiheit.org/webcom/show_article.php/_c-221/i.html [accessed on 29/09/2015]).

political parties and focused on the consolidation of the Green political spectrum. It also offered analysis and education measures and supported regional networking. In Southeast Europe the HBS had offices in Serbia, Bosnia Herzegovina and Croatia. The office in Belgrade also coordinated activities in Montenegro and Kosovo. [1300]

The RLS was committed to trade union representation of interests, antifascism, feminism, democratisation of the education system, strengthening of alternative political discourses and the support of critical research. Primarily, its activities targeted civil society organisations and social movements, trade union initiatives, schools and educational institutions, leftist academic and cultural institutions and researchers.[1301] It also aimed at transnational networking of leftist initiatives, the critical coming to terms with the past of the left-leaning political parties and academic discussions on the redefinition of a modern leftism. The activities of the RLS in Southeast Europe started in 2002 and were further expanded to almost all Southeast European countries coordinated by the regional office in Serbia.[1302]

The activities of the HSS primarily focused on EU integration and crisis' prevention. They directed to the establishment and consolidation of democratic, rule of law based and civil society institutions targeting public administrations, police forces and judiciaries. Methodologically, the HSS offered education, seminars, trainings and interregional cooperation facilitating conferences. The HSS had five offices in Southeast Europe and activities in all countries of the region.[1303]

8.1.4. The rule of law program of the KAS

The KAS's RLP in Southeast Europe started its work in 2006. Originally, it concentrated on five countries and was extended successively. As of May 2015, it covered Albania, Bosnia-Herzegovina, Bulgaria, Croatia, Kosovo,

---

1300 *Fischer* (2011) p. 3; HBS at: http://www.boell.de/de/2013/11/20/regionalbuero-suedosteuropa-belgrad (accessed on 20/09/2015).

1301 RLS (2011) pp. 7f.; RLS at: http://www.rosalux.de/weltweit/osteuropa/suedosteuropa/themenschwerpunkte.html (accessed on 20/09/2015).

1302 RLS at: http://www.rosalux.de/weltweit/osteuropa/suedosteuropa.html (accessed on 20/09/2015).

1303 HSS (2015); HSS at: http://www.hss.de/internationale-arbeit/regionen-projekte/europa.html.

Macedonia, Montenegro, Republic Moldova, Rumania und Serbia.[1304] The office was located in Bucharest and existed alongside the KAS's country offices. In 2014, it comprised a director and four Rumanian local employees.[1305] Its annual budget amounted to 419.000 Euros in 2012.[1306]

Since the beginnings in 2006, the RLP had a strong European perspective concentrating of EU integration and the resolution of democracy and rule of law deficits. It was clear to the KAS that the countries of the Western Balkans only had an integration prospect in case they overcame these deficiencies. The program was supposed to send a signal of assistance to the Southeast European countries in their transformation processes. Since the RLP had already been established in other parts of the world, a program in the immediate sphere of European influence appeared necessary to the KAS. The program was organised regionally due to the comparability of the countries' rule of law issues and in order to improve the respective information exchange among them.[1307] Rumania's importance in the region, its forthcoming EU accession and its stability in contrast to the former Yugoslavian states were reasons for establishing the office in Bucharest.[1308]

The overall objective of the RLP was therefore the EU integration and EU corresponding legal orders and cultures.[1309] Sub-targets oriented towards the RLP's objectives world-wide[1310] were the consolidation of democratic institutions through cooperation with constitutional courts and consulting of democratic institutions' representatives, the modernisation of constitutions, constitutional jurisdictions, substantive and procedural laws, the strengthening of the public administration, judicial independence, human and minority rights, the counteraction of corruption and the dealing with the past.[1311] Moreover, the RLP focused on the promotion of the European ideal and the strengthening of regional cooperation and law-oriented networks.[1312] Several aspects were considerably different in South-

1304 The initial countries covered by the RLP were Rumania, Serbia-Montenegro, Macedonia and Croatia (*Luchterhandt* [2013] p. 28). For the RLP's website see: http://www.kas.de/rspsoe/en/.

1305 Interview 8.

1306 *Luchterhandt* (2013) p. 40.

1307 Interview 8.

1308 *Luchterhandt* (2013) p. 50.

1309 KAS at: http://www.kas.de/rspsoe/en/about/.

1310 See excursus below.

1311 Interview 8.

1312 *Luchterhandt* (2013) p. 19.

east Europe from the other regions where the KAS's RLPs were active: the high level of political conflict, the post-communist or post socialist transformation processes and the efforts to join the EU.[1313]

The RLP generally pursued long-term goals although some activities had medium- or short-term objectives, such as the revision of a certain law.[1314] Although it was an internal requirement that equal weight needed to be given to the objectives, the matter of dealing with the past had never played a significant role, not every objective was equally important in each country and activities in Rumania were more strongly developed.[1315] The RLP's directors also had some flexibility with regard to the choice of activity which recently had led to an increase in regional projects. Still, the types of activities were relatively steady and those of 2013 and 2014 were almost identical.[1316]

Excursus: rule of law programmes

In 1991 the KAS established the first RLP in Latin America. In 2006 the RLPs for Sub-Saharan Africa, Southeast Europe and Asia started their work.[1317] In 2013 the RLP in North Africa and the Middle East followed.[1318] The programmes were designed as regional sector programmes complementing the other KAS's international undertakings. They were supervised by fully qualified German lawyers at offices in Bucharest, Nairobi, Mexico City, Bogota, Singapore and Beirut coordinated from the KAS's headquarters in Berlin.[1319] The KAS defined four general objectives of the RLPs: (1) promoting rule of law structures and institutions; (2) the division of powers including a strong and independent judiciary and an executive

1313 KAS (2008b) p. 25; *Luchterhandt* (2013) p. 17.

1314 Similar KAS (2014a).

1315 The evaluation mentioned as reasons for the imbalance limited resources, political issues, a low propensity to participate in some countries and inequalities in the countries' development (*Luchterhandt* [2013] pp. 18, 28). Croatia's integration in the program, for example, was weak (ibidem p. 28). Little interest in the RLP was also attested to Albania, Kosovo and Montenegro (ibidem p. 39).

1316 Interview 8.

1317 KAS annual report (2006) p. 36.

1318 KAS annual report (2013) p. 13.

1319 KAS (2015a), (2008) p. 4.

bound to the law; (3) strengthening fundamental and human rights; and (4) reinforcing respective regional cooperation and networks.[1320]

The regional approach was driven by the insight that rule of law reform processes often ran regionally parallel, such as the Southeast European constitutional reforms after 1998 and those of Latin-American criminal proceedings in the mid-1980s. A catalyst for the set-up of the RLPs were the *Spranger* criterions of the German government which had highlighted the rule of law, among others.[1321] According to the KAS, the approach across countries also helped to work on topics which could not be addressed publicly on the national level and regional networking among experts also strengthened the self-help.[1322] The rule of law support had a high priority in its international work since development and security needed stable democracies as said by the KAS.[1323] While the KAS's guidelines nonetheless did not mention the rule of law, the foundations' common declaration considered rule of law engagement.[1324]

The instruments involved in the RLPs did not deviate from those generally used by the *Stiftungen* and included conferences, seminars, workshops, panel discussions, trainings, the publication of research, studies and other material, visiting programs in Germany, scholarships and consulting.[1325] As target groups and partners, the KAS mentioned private and public sector individuals such as legal practitioners including judges, lawyers, prosecuting attorneys and judicial staff officers, legal scholars, members of the parliaments, legislative committees, ministers and civil servants from the ministries' of justice and internal affairs. The KAS also sought cooperation with professional associations of lawyers, political parties, NGOs, church associations and media representatives.[1326]

Next to the RLPs, the KAS maintained several other regional sector programs, such as media and regional dialogue programs mostly developed in 2010. As of 2015, the KAS had 19 such programs world-wide.[1327]

1320 *Luchterhandt* (2013) p. 17; KAS (2008b) p. 9.
1321 Interview 14; see also Ch. 6.2.2.
1322 KAS (2008b) p. 10.
1323 KAS (2015a).
1324 FES/KAS/FNS/HSS/HBS (1998).
1325 KAS (2015a), (2008) p. 11.
1326 KAS (2015a).
1327 See KAS's annual reports between (2009) and (2013); (2014) pp. 100f.

8.2. The practice of public diplomacy through democracy assistance?

The following section looks in detail on how the KAS was public diplomatically active in the context of its RLP in Southeast Europe whilst applying the integrated public diplomacy model.[1328] I traced the communicative process either taking place as one-way communication or within a network surrounding where connected actors brought various resources and shared values and interests. Afterwards, it is set in connection to the collaborative and catalytic public diplomacy form of democracy assistance adopting the systematisation of chapter 6. Finally, I consider the impact of the KAS as a transnational actor in the region.

8.2.1. Generator

In the context of the RLP in Southeast Europe, the KAS showed the ability to generate public diplomacy. The KAS was autonomous in the decision over measures and their implementation and the case did not reveal a dependence link on German state institutions or the affiliated CDU. The RLP, like the other foundations' activities was funded over the Federal Budget. In 2014, it did not receive international backing and was therefore not bound by respective requirements. Although the KAS's RLP office had contacts with the German embassies in the region, they were not allowed and had not tried to give instructions. At times, the KAS consulted with the embassies as regards a measure.[1329] One example, however, was found where the *Stiftungen* became part of an AA's public diplomacy initiative: In 2013 the German embassy in Sofia held together with the KAS, the FNS and other German organisations a series of cultural events in North Bulgaria with the intention to present a multifaceted image of Germany and to highlight cooperation.[1330] The example is still not appropriate to prove the KAS's instrumental use by the AA's public diplomacy initiative measured by the overall amount of KAS's activities.

The KAS's headquarters left the RLP free reign over decisions and it acted independently from the KAS's country offices in the region. The decision on implementing a measure was taken by the RLP's director and the

1328 See Ch. 3.2.
1329 Interview 8.
1330 AA (2014) p. 56.

whole implementation procedure was in his hands.[1331] Although in all measures the KAS cooperated with local partner organisations,[1332] activities were conducted as *Eigenmaßnahmen* implying the KAS's involvement in some form, for instance through the provision of seminar's speakers, and the measures' (partially) financing. Each measure's costs generally did not exceed 15.000 Euros.[1333] The RLP's office collected project proposals until the 30th of September of each year and selected 30. Afterwards, it submitted them for the headquarters approval which normally consented. Partly, the director of the office had promoted certain measures to be implemented by partners. But he also appreciated the proposals of the partners often having more exact information on issues on-site. Follow-up measures were implemented in the subsequent year when the KAS considered their appropriateness.[1334]

The interview partner estimated that partners perceived the KAS neither as part of official diplomacy nor as an extension of the state but as civil society organisation. He associated the term public diplomacy with the KAS but objected that it was a term known to insiders.[1335]

8.2.2. Addresses and instruments

Of the three groups public diplomacy can target, that is the general public, the media and specific disseminators, the RLP in Southeast Europe addressed mostly the last group. Its work mainly focused on a law-oriented audience.[1336] The evaluation described the target group as broad and the activities as elite-focused.[1337] For the media sector's support the KAS had established a specific regional program in 2005 located in Sofia.[1338] The instruments involved in the RLP only slightly differed from those generally used by the foundations.

The RLP was organised as project work in cooperation with partner organisations. Civil society actors were important partners. In 2014, the ratio

1331 Interview 8.

1332 KAS at: http://www.kas.de/rspsoe/en/about/.

1333 *Luchterhandt* (2013) pp. 25, 37.

1334 Interview 8.

1335 Interview 8.

1336 See excursus above; KAS at: http://www.kas.de/rspsoe/de/about/ on target groups, http://www.kas.de/rspsoe/de/about/partners/ on concrete partners.

1337 *Luchterhandt* (2013) p. 18.

1338 For details see KAS at: http://www.kas.de/medien-europa/en/.

of civil society partners and partners from the state was relatively balanced with a slight preponderance of the non-state sector.[1339] The overall partner choice was considered as challenging and the KAS had to assess potential partners closely. Selection criteria were the potential partner's rule of law support and reliability. The interview partner also referred to the foundations' public funding why partners had to ensure correct accounting. It was often difficult to estimate whether potential partners pursued serious targets or whether they depended on invisible actors.[1340]

The RLP showed particularities regarding the cooperation with political parties and high-level politics which were different from the general findings made before.[1341] Cooperation with high-level politics was "legitimised" in the RLP as for rule of law topics they were the natural target group. Furthermore, it was difficult for the KAS to find suitable political parties to cooperate with and even to alternatively cooperate with parliament's committees and fractions. Political party structures were not comparable to those of German political parties. Legal political or domestic affairs spokesperson were missing to be supported systematically and the strong parties' hierarchy hindered the development of expertise.[1342] The often-changing committees' compositions furthermore impeded the parliamentarians' responsibility for respective issues.[1343] Rule of law structures, moreover, could not be discussed on a party-political basis having the effect that the KAS even cooperated with rather left-leaning organisations. The KAS was nonetheless pleased with partners being politically affiliated.[1344]

The RLP's instruments corresponded to the medium- and long-term public diplomacy instruments and were broadly situated within dialogues, discussions and the transfer of knowledge. The RLP organised around 30 conferences, seminars and workshops per year which took place successive-

1339 Interview 8; similar *Luchterhandt* (2013) pp. 20, 26.

1340 Interview 8.

1341 See Ch. 5.2.

1342 Interview 8; a similar experience was made by other foundations in the region: The FNS originally tried to support liberal parties. Since they often did not have continued existence, it started to focus on a broader target group (FNS [2013a] p. 66). An evaluation on the HBS's activities even highlighted the advantage of missing political partners as partners perceived the *Stiftung* as neutral, unbiased and pluralistic possessing the ability to bring together people of different social background (*Fischer* [2011] p. 4).

1343 The evaluator already had suggested further integrating chairman of the parliamentary committees into the RLP (*Luchterhandt* [2013] p. 21).

1344 Interview 8.

ly in the Southeast European countries. Activities in Germany of the RLP did not happen except for some part of the Rumanian junior lawyers' program. Parallel measures were not carried out as the RLP's director attached importance to sit in on every activity.[1345]

The political dialogue instrument was most important for the RLP and a meta-level work approach which included the other instruments. The RLP followed a political, value- and dialogue-based approach in contrast to a rather technical and advisory method when promoting the rule of law.[1346] It thereby focused on the political fields of law such as combating corruption, the dealing with the past and minority rights. With value orientation it meant the focus on peace, freedom, equality, democracy and the rule of law.[1347] The approach was highlighted as the KAS's "unique selling position" and contrasted with the capacity building and training measures of other actors in the field.[1348] Only one example was found where the RLP had offered technical support: In 2012 together with the GIZ it supported the Serbian parliament in publishing a manual about how to draft legislation. According to the KAS, it had wanted to push the cooperation with Serbia difficult to be integrated into the RLP.[1349]

Elements of cultural diplomacy were visible in the RLP. It organised cultural events and an annual human rights festival. Scholarships were granted to students in the region by the country offices but the RLP organised certain events for former and current legal scholarship holders.[1350] Moreover, it can be believed that the RLP imparted German legal culture in the region as the German legal system was a framework of reference in activities and high-ranking German lawyers and legal institutions were integrated in the program.[1351] The KAS also linked its rule of law engagement to an assumed world-wide interest in German legal culture.[1352]

The RLP was also active in think tank events and consulting. It organised conferences with think tank partner organisations, such as the Romanian Centre for European politics (CRPE), the Romanian Expert Forum (EFOR) and the Serbian Centre for Advanced Legal Studies (CUPS). Some cooperation took place with universities, such as with the Serbian

1345 Interview 8.
1346 Interview 8.
1347 *Luchterhandt* (2013) pp. 19f., 22; FES/KAS/FNS/HSS/HBS (1998).
1348 Interview 1.
1349 *Luchterhandt* (2013) p. 20.
1350 *Luchterhandt* (2013) pp. 26, 33.
1351 See Ch. 8.2.3.1.
1352 KAS (2008b) pp. 5f.

Singidunum University's affiliated faculty of European law and political science.[1353] The RLP also offered on its website serial country reports and analysis of political events connected to the rule of law.[1354] The KAS's RLP was also involved in legal consulting of democratic institutions' representatives focusing on EU corresponding legal orders.[1355] Consulting could also be found as regards the region's stabilisation: In 2012, the RLP organised advisory meetings with Kosovan and Serbian actors on rule of law solutions for the relations between them.[1356]

Due to the regional media program, the RLP did not undertake media activities. However, one workshop on media and transitional justice in 2013 was found.[1357] Also monologue public diplomacy instruments were rare. The RLP produced certain material, such as studies and books as well as the above-mentioned serial publications but mostly as result of a dialogue instrument. One monologue example is the translation of significant decisions of the German constitutional court into some of the regional languages.[1358] Other monologue instruments, such as political campaigning and advertisement could not be found.

8.2.3. Dimensions: Propaganda and network

The promotion of the rule of law and the direct cooperation with judicial institutions as practised in the KAS's RLP was highly political. The KAS was aware that rule of law aid could be perceive as propagandistic or international intrusion. It had also dealt with manipulations, the tendency to mendacity and the lack of credibility, aspects the literature often connected to propaganda.[1359] According to the KAS, its political affiliation and value-based dialogue approach created credibility on site.[1360] It also assured that it did not force the German legal culture onto the countries, put bluntly

---

1353 KAS at: http://www.kas.de/rspsoe/de/about/partners/; the evaluation, however, noted some underrepresentation of legal professors in the RLP's activities (*Luchterhandt* [2013] p. 21).

1354 KAS at: http://www.kas.de/rspsoe/de/publications/.

1355 Interview 8.

1356 KAS (2012).

1357 KAS (2013b).

1358 KAS (2014a), (2008) p. 6.

1359 KAS (2008b).

1360 KAS (2008b) p. 4.

German interests and avoided hidden agendas.[1361] In this context, it outlined that "rule of law helps the recipient country to improve their development opportunities. At the same time, it is in the German economic and security political interest when counting on stable and democratic partner countries under the rule of law".[1362] The KAS's involvement in internal political battles or criticism by the recipient countries could not be noted. The promoted EU affiliation was mostly also intended by the governments of the Southeast European countries. This was different from other regions where the political ideas of the KAS and those of the respective countries collided. According to the interview partner, the RLP did not cooperate with secret services and transparently presented its partners and events on its website. Also, the KAS's affiliation to the CDU was known to the partners. Despite missing financial information, former activities could at least be found several years past. During the conducted interview the atmosphere was very cooperative, and the requested information was disclosed. What finally spoke against a propaganda dimension in the KAS's RLP was what has been generally noted for the *Stiftungen*: the KAS's relative autonomy, the implementation of mostly dialogue instruments and the pluralistic approach of several *Stiftungen* offering different solutions to rule of law issues.[1363]

The networking dimension, in contrast, was well recognizable in the RLP's case. It also enjoyed a prominent position in the RLP's activity portfolio although it referred to the linking of actors in the region only and did not consider the KAS as an important node. The following subsections analyse the relationships as well as the exchanged resources and common values and interests of the network participants. We conclude with the attempt to specify the overall network surrounding.

8.2.3.1. Relationships

In 2014, diverse relationships to local, foreign and German actors existed in the context of the RLP. Most of them were stable, independent, characterised by cooperation. Although the local relationships mainly concerned the legal sector in the Southeast European countries, diverse state actors, NGOs, students, academics and professional organisations were included.

1361 KAS (2008b) p. 6.
1362 KAS (2008b) p. 5, author's translation.
1363 See the findings of Ch. 5.

Relationships with media people and political party members were underdeveloped, yet.[1364] Intensive contacts on site existed also to the KAS's country offices and the regional media office, to German embassy members, to the other *Stiftungen* and German organisations, such as IRZ, GIZ and the German church organisations as well as to foreign organisations.[1365] With the U.S. think tank Freedom House in Rumania the RLP, for instance, had held a workshop on the fight against public procurement criminality in 2012.[1366] It also cooperated with the Chinese Scheherazade foundation.[1367] The KAS had contacts and cooperated with foreign embassies and supranational levels.[1368] Examples were a round table event in Rumania on the inclusion of Roma people organised by the RLP, the Slovakian embassy and the EU commission in 2014[1369] and a speech of the RLP's director on the UN anti-corruption strategy for Central and Eastern Europe at the US embassy to Rumania in 2015.[1370]

The RLP profited from the wide variety of contacts which existed between actors in Germany and the KAS. German politicians of the CDU at the federal and the state level participated in the RLP's conferences and events and senior officials of the German ministries showed interest in the program.[1371] The RLP's director had also political contacts on the German local level due to his former membership at the Lübeck parliament and the *Landtag Schleswig-Holstein* for the CDU. These contacts were also used for the RLP.[1372] A conspicuous aspect in the RLP was the integration of high-ranking German lawyers and German institutions in the RLP's activities. Judges of the Federal Constitutional Court had been, for instance, guest speakers at the Rumanian and Moldavian Courts during book presentations of significant German decisions translated to Rumanian.[1373] The Federal Anti-Discrimination Agency's director, *Christine Lüders*, visited the RLP in the context of conference on the 10th anniversary of the Rumanian

1364 See Ch. 8.2.2.
1365 Interview 8.
1366 Freedom House at: http://www.freedomhouse.ro/ISEC/en/index.php/about/the-project; KAS (2013a).
1367 KAS at: http://www.kas.de/rspsoe/de/publications/39331/.
1368 Interview 8.
1369 KAS (2014b).
1370 KAS (2015b).
1371 Interview 8; see exemplarily KAS at: http://www.kas.de/rspsoe/de/publications/22880/: In Rumania the parliamentary state secretary at the interior ministry *Ole Schröder* hold a lecture on the fight against corruption in Germany in 2011.
1372 Interview 8.
1373 See *Schluckebier* (2013); *Kessal-Wulf* (2014).

Anti-Discrimination Agency.[1374] NGOs in Germany, moreover, occasionally established contacts to the RLP and German academics participated in activities on site.[1375]

Initially, the RLP's relationships depended on the KAS's country offices. The RLP was even directed by the Rumanian office in the first year. Afterwards, it increased its activities and independence. Additionally, it referred to the existing links of the country offices to actors on site.[1376] The relationships' stability was central, since the KAS considered important continuity and long-term partnership prospects. In Rumania and Bulgaria, the KAS remained active beyond 2007 although the aim of the EU membership was already achieved. According to the evaluation, the partners highly acknowledged it, especially because other international organisations prevailingly had left the country.[1377] Furthermore, the RLP's office in Rumania was an important guarantor of stability. It was an important point of contact for the partners. RLP's undertakings were also easier to be organised than in other countries leading to a preponderance of activities in Rumania. Moreover, the employment of local staff members and the permanent German representative contributed to the stability of contacts.[1378]

Although the overall situation among donor organisations on site and especially with USAID was characterised as competitive,[1379] the KAS's relationships with other actors were mainly cooperative. Joint-measures were implemented with the German embassy.[1380] Intensive cooperation could also be found with the KAS's country offices and the media office in Southeast Europe.[1381] The country offices were supposed to generally focus on all aspects of the countries' political development while the RLP specifically directed to legal issues for which extensive legal knowledge of a person being in the law was deemed necessary.[1382] Still, both showed conceptual similarities in the support of the countries' rapprochement with the

1374 KAS at: http://www.kas.de/rspsoe/de/publications/31288/.

1375 Interview 8; KAS (2012) p. 1.

1376 *Luchterhandt* (2013) pp. 27f.; most of the country offices in the region existed since the 1990s. The Albanian and the Moldovan offices both started their work in 2009 (KAS annual report 2009 p. 77).

1377 *Luchterhandt* (2013) p. 24.

1378 Interview 8.

1379 Interview 8; although USAID had more general program focusing on democracy, human rights and governance future overlapping was expected (*Luchterhandt* [2013] p. 31).

1380 Interview 8.

1381 KAS (2008b) p. 9, (2012), (2013b).

1382 Interview 8.

EU, the dealing with the communist past, political party cooperation or parliamentary assistance, the consulting in constitutional reform processes (in Bosnia Herzegovina) and the explicit cooperation with rule of law actors (in Albania).[1383] To avoid activity overlaps, coordination took place. Direct, e-mail and telephone contacts with the other directors were frequent.[1384] Annually, the offices' staff members in the region met to discuss the KAS's overall activities. Also, the other German political foundations' activities on site and those of the RLP partly corresponded as they equally circled around EU affiliation, stabilisation, democratisation and the rule of law.[1385] However, the RLP's in-depth and explicit specialisation on the rule of law stood out. The KAS exchanged views with other German *Stiftungen* and occasionally met with them. One such instance was the German embassy periodically inviting the foundations.[1386] The FES in Rumania and the RLP both maintained a partnership with the National Association of Judges but a competitive situation between them the interview partner did not confirm. Several times in the past, the KAS and the FES even had organised joint conferences in the field of justice.[1387] According to the evaluator, also the other *Stiftungen* were willing to cooperate with the RLP.[1388] Remarkably, the missing approach of different political partners in the region did not equally result in increased competition among the foundations. Also, the relations with the other German organisations, the interview partner described as cooperative. Projects were carried out together with the German catholic and protestant churches. With the GIZ the RLP had a joint-project in Serbia at the time of the interview and the IRZ was an occasional conversation partner.[1389] Both, the IRZ and GIZ followed a technical and advisory approach and the GIZ concentrated on civil and commercial law which led to activities and partners other than those of the

---

1383 This information stems from the KAS's country offices' websites in Albania (http://www.kas.de/albanien/de/about/), Bosnia Herzegovina (http://www.kas.de/bosnien-herzegowina/de/about/), Kosovo (http://www.kas.de/kosovo/de/about/), Croatia (http://www.kas.de/kroatien/de/about/), Macedonia (http://www.kas.de/mazedonien/de/about/), Rumania and Moldova (http://www.kas.de/moldau/de/about/). Information on this matter was missing for Serbia/Montenegro (http://www.kas.de/serbien/de/about/) and Bulgaria (http://www.kas.de/bulgarien/de/about/).

1384 Interview 8.

1385 See Ch. 8.1.3.

1386 Interview 8.

1387 *Luchterhandt* (2013) p. 31.

1388 *Luchterhandt* (2013) p. 22.

1389 Interview 8.

RLP. In case of overlapping, for example with the IRZ in supporting public law reforms in Moldova and with the Venice Commission regarding constitutional reform processes, activities were coordinated.[1390]

8.2.3.2. Resources, values and interests

Within the framework of the aforementioned relationships, the RLP and the other actors exchanged resources and, to a high degree, shared values and policy interests.

Financial resources received over the Federal Budget the RLP used for the activities on site. One fourth was made available directly to the partner organisations on side.[1391] Partners often had some financial means and contributed moreover with human resources and labour. Financial support of political parties was not allowed and did not take place, whereas the co-operation with politicians or party foundations was possible.[1392] The evaluator attested to the RLP a shortage in human, physical and financial resources.[1393]

Information resources were accessed by the KAS through the partners on site and from its own experiences. Partners generally had an advantage in knowledge on the local situation. All RLPs exchanged experiences at regular meetings in Berlin. Information was also exchanged with the German embassies and the other foundations.[1394] The KAS's country offices provided logistical resources and information through the monitoring of the political situation and indentified suitable partners for the RLP especially for measures in other countries than Rumania. In turn, the country office benefitted from the RLP's measures in its country.[1395] Necessary expertise was also bought from other actors.[1396] The information collected was further

1390 *Luchterhandt* (2013) pp. 31f.

1391 *Luchterhandt* (2013) p. 25.

1392 Interview 8; see also Ch. 6.3.4.

1393 *Luchterhandt* (2013) p. 29.

1394 Interview 8.

1395 *Luchterhandt* (2013) pp. 27f.

1396 Exemplarily, the KAS and the Bulgarian interior ministry commissioned the Max Planck Foundation for international peace and the rule of law to carry out a study on best practices for fighting corruption in the Danube region (*Hensgen* [2013]). The RLP's supported also a study of Zenith, a Macedonian think tank, on the European political conditionality in the region (*Nechev* et. al. [2013]).

processed in analysis of the situation on site and was used for the reports to the KAS's headquarters and the German ministries. The headquarters assessed and compared the information to that of other RLPs.[1397]

The RLP, moreover, had significant networking resources. Promoting the cooperation between the Southeast European countries was one of the RLP's objectives and viewed as a condition for the program's sustainability. According to the evaluation, the KAS was able to interlink actors at the constitutional and other courts, rule of law-oriented NGOs, qualified junior lawyers and former scholarship holders in the region. Many nodes already potentially existed through the country offices and before the RLP's establishment.[1398] Challenging was considered in this context to arouse the countries' interests in each other.[1399] The evaluation also mentioned the linguistic differences between them.[1400] The KAS also connected partners from the different RLPs world-wide.[1401] As outlined, the KAS invited German politicians and legal actors to the region, established connections to their foreign counterparts and tried to further political cooperation. Also, the KAS's visit and educational program in Germany and the RLP's Rumanian junior lawyer program focused on the relationship building between actors from both countries. The KAS's approach of its own participation in the measures and the inclusion of local partner ensured the necessary contacts on site and the integration of German actors. Since the director of the RLP attended the measures, he also had some control over the establishment of contacts. Furthermore, the office located on site was obviously important for the networking as the RLP had most of its local contacts and activities in Rumania, whereas in other countries the RLP depended on the country offices and the integration of actors was more challenging.

The KAS furthermore provided moral authority in the context of the RLP. The KAS's affiliation to the CDU was known to the partners and therefore often associated it with Chancellor Angela Merkel. At the same time, it was perceived as civil society organisation. The interview partner saw an advantage of promoting rule of law as a German organisation as the highly respected German Constitutional Court, the good institutional setup, the professional parliament and the profound substantive and procedural law allowed "products to sell well" and increased credibility when advo-

1397 *Luchterhandt* (2013) p. 33.
1398 *Luchterhandt* (2013) pp. 30, 51.
1399 Interview 8.
1400 *Luchterhandt* (2013) p. 29.
1401 KAS (2008b) p. 11.

cating these aspects in Southeast Europe. He also stressed that Germans were considered on site as competent and reliable.[1402] According to the KAS, Germany also served as a role model owing to the successful GDR's legal integration.[1403] Often this German model character was viewed in dissociation to the US model.[1404]

Apart from the exchange of resources, the RLP's network was characterised by shared policy interests and values of the involved actors. As already outlined, values were particularly highlighted in the RLP's work approach. The RLP's objectives moreover fitted almost "template-like" with the German and EU integration policy towards the region. Also the KAS traced the RLPs' world-wide initiation to the beginnings of German development policy's conditionality and the emphasis on political criteria in the aiding countries[1405] as well as the international agendas attaching increasing importance to the rule of law from the 1990s onwards.[1406] In Southeast Europe these considerations were reflected also in the EU enlargement policy.[1407] With the takeover of the BMZ's consulting assistance in the region, the *Stiftungen*, as outlined, became an integral part of the German policy.[1408] The interview partner explained the RLP's engagement by the desire to assist the countries in meeting the admission conditions and becoming equal members.[1409] Concrete accordance can be found with the policies of the BMZ and of the European's IPA in the support of public administrations' and judiciaries' reform processes, the fight against corruption (BMZ) and regional and territorial cooperation (IPA). The RLP's objectives were also consistent with the BMJV's policy although the ministry emphasised civil and economic law while the RLP did not promote economy-related legal fields and focused on public law. Both furthered standards in criminal law. Moreover, the countries covered by the RLP were those of the EU's Stability Pact, largely consistent with the IPA countries and with the EC's benchmarking as regards Bulgaria and Rumania. Moreover, the German

---

1402 Interview 8.

1403 KAS (2008b) p. 5, (2012) p. 2; IRZ at: http://www.irz.de/index.php/en/about-us.

1404 See Ch. 6 conclusion; *Schneider-Deters* (2005).

1405 Known as the "Spranger-criterions", see Ch. 6.2.2.

1406 KAS (2008b) p. 3.

1407 In 1993 the European Council had outlined rule of law as one of the conditions for the EU's eastward enlargement in its "Copenhagen Criteria" (European Council [1993] § 7A.iii).

1408 See Ch. 8.1.

1409 Interview 8.

government meant exactly the countries covered by the RLP when referring to Southeast Europe.[1410] The engagement of the KAS was furthermore in line with the CDU's political program stressing cooperation treatments and EU membership prospects. With the visiting German politicians, the RLP also shared conservative values. With actors from German legal institutions the RLP had in common the worthwhile goal of the rule of law. German and international organisations on site either shared the political interest in the EU integration or the focus on the rule of law. Local partners the RLP chose when they supported the rule of law. Although it is uncertain whether other local actors and addressees associated with the network shared these mutual values and interests, the governments of the Southeast European countries largely supported the EU integration.

8.2.3.3. Types of transnational policy network

The network in which the RLP operated in 2014 did not corresponded to the outlined ideal-typical forms of transnational policy networks.[1411] Although it came closest to the Global public policy network, attributes of other network types could be found and led to a mixed character. The network resembled a transnational advocacy network (TAN) only in terms of the common issues circling around the rule of law deficits in the region. The prerequisite of a campaign was missing as the situation's improvement could not be achieved in a foreseeable period. Contrary to TANs, the network also linked actors on site which often did not have anything to do with each other, included the public sector and exchanged more resources than information only. Furthermore, the connections furthermore resembled a transnational executive network due to links with civil servants on site and in Germany. However, the KAS was not part of the German public administration and, according to the interview partner, was not perceived on site as government official. Moreover, due to the integrated professionals and experts, the network had similarities with a global knowledge network (KNET). Knowledge generation, the informing of policy, its application and networking itself played an important role. Also, the measures involving research, networking, advice and consulting in the policy making process were consistent with those of the RLP. German public bodies supported the RLP leading to a semi-official position. The RLP also con-

1410 See BT (2011c).

1411 See Ch. 2.3.1. and 3.1.1.

trolled resources and was internationally experienced. However, experts and professionals were not the only network's participants. The KAS also lacked scientific neutrality particularly highlighted in its value-based approach and combined political affiliation which was, though secondary but still important for the KAS. Finally, the RLP's network was trisectoral, as it included public sector officials, civil servants and civil society professionals similar to a Global public policy network (GPPN). Still, the included individuals, such as students and scholarship holders did not appear in the GPPN terminology. Due to the missing economic sector, the network could not be termed as a tripartite global governance network. GPPNs consider international actors while the current case involved mainly national and local actors and did not have a supranational character. Whether the deficit in the rule of law was a shared problem existing over crossboarders, according to the GPPN's definition, depended on the perspective of the involved actor. For the KAS it was a regional phenomenon and part of the supranational integration policy why it furthered regional cooperation. The national countries, in contrast, were often not interested in it. They obviously deemed the processing of the rule of law deficit as something to be managed on the national level which complied with the EU's practice of integrating national countries in contrast to regions.

Loose couplings and issue networks have been suggested forms of interaction between state and non-state actors in the context of public diplomacy.[1412] Unlike these types, the public-sector presence in the current network was relatively high and interaction between the non-state and the state actors was strong. In contrast to the issue network, it existed among most actors a common policy objective and the permeability of the network in terms of new actors' inclusion was rather low due to the RLP's selection procedure. The integration of the established network into the policy making process was ambivalent as several processes came into question: In the Southeast European countries the influencing of partners directly involved in policy making was difficult due to the lack of collaborating political parties and chairmen of parliamentary committees. This and the fact that the KAS as a transnational actor dominated the setting, spoke for the issue network. In Germany, the KAS was strongly involved in the policy making process. As outlined in Chapter 5, it consulted formally with the respective German ministries and delivered expert opinion at the parliamentary committees. It also actively implemented the policy of the BMZ in Southeast Europe. In this respect, the network appeared to be a policy community

1412 See Ch. 3.1.1.

actor.[1413] The internationalised policy environments of multilevel governance and self-regulatory, private regimes, where the public sector is more strongly involved compared to the loose coupling were still not appropriate to characterise the current case's interactions. Both assume a highly institutionalised form of cooperation among actors and a certain degree of formality, which neither in Germany nor in Southeast Europe could be found.

8.2.4. Assisting democracy?

In the model of democracy assistance, the state institutions' support allows for rule of law aid directed at other countries' legal systems. It aims at an independent and effective judiciary and other law-oriented institutions.[1414] In this context, *Carothers* itemised firstly the reforming of institutions including judicial reforms, legislative strengthening, retraining of prosecutors, police and prison reform, bolstering public defenders and introducing alternative dispute resolution; secondly, the rewriting of laws, such as modernisations in criminal, civil and commercial laws; thirdly the upgrading of legal professionals including the strengthening of bar associations and legal education; and finally the increasing of legal access and advocacy aiming at the support of law-oriented NGOs, public interest law reforms, legal media training and the support of legal aid clinics.[1415]

The RLP's activities in 2014 focused on all four fields of rule of law assistance: It aimed at the consolidation of institutions and furthered constitutional jurisdiction. In the public sector the KAS mainly cooperated with constitutional courts and association of judges. Its collaboration with parliaments also intended the legislatives' strengthening. It also focused on the modernisation of public and procedural laws and on legal education as it targeted legal scholars and professional legal organisations.[1416] In 2015, it had also initiated a program to further the knowledge transfer on the rule of law in grammar schools.[1417] Through its partnerships with law-interested NGOs, the RLP was also active in assisting the advocacy sector.

1413 See Ch. 2.3.1.

1414 See Ch. 6.1., for a definition of the rule of law see also Ch. 6.1.

1415 *Carothers* (2006) p. 168. Legislative strengthening is often treated as a separate aid category (see Ch. 6.1). *Carothers* included it here, as it has a dual position serving both the rule of law situation and the political process.

1416 Interview 8.

1417 KAS at: http://www.kas.de/rspsoe/de/publications/40687/.

The RLP's democracy assistance ambitions were not restricted to rule of law aid only, although aid in the state institutions' sector prevailed and the judiciary's support was most significant.[1418] The RLP irregularly supported electoral processes. It had, for instance, organised penal discussions in order to confront politicians with critical questions of the audience. However, election aid was rather a country offices' task and elections were not supported technically. In the context of the democracy assistance' political party building, the KAS looked for contacts to them and acted as an advisor, although, as already outlined, it proved difficult.[1419] The modernisation of constitutions and the furthering of the division of power were RLP's objectives and part of democracy assistance's constitutional aid. In Bosnia-Herzegovina, for instance, the RLP had helped elaborating a constitutional commentary available in the local languages and in English and drafted by domestic and foreign experts in 2010.[1420] The RLP also focused on local political development. The office had established contacts between Serbian mayors and the association of German cities and towns.[1421] The RLP's cooperation with NGOs and other civil society actors finally can be viewed as aiding democracy assistance's civil society sector.

The RLP's long-term involvement and the focus on long-term political and social reform processes in the region were in line with the developmental democracy promotion approach. Still, the RLP's activities even approximated the wider approaches of state-building[1422] and conflict management:[1423] The RLP's objectives of human rights protection, of comprehensively supporting transformation processes and the strengthening of public administrations were part of a state-building approach. Also, the RLP's focus on combating organised crime complied with the state-buildings' security component and peace-building. According to the interview partner, the KAS cooperated with police forces in this context which referred to the instrument of security sector reforms. The RLP's dealing with the past regarding war crimes and totalitarianism complied with peace-building, reconciliation and transitional justice. Also, the RLP's strategy to further integrate the region into the EU and the fostering of regional cooperation corresponded to peace-building. According to the partner organisa-

1418 Interview 8.

1419 Interview 8; see Ch. 8.2.2.

1420 *Steiner/Ademović* (2010); KAS at: http://www.kas.de/rspsoe/de/publications/19629/.

1421 Interview 8.

1422 See Ch. 6.1.

1423 See Ch. 7.1.

tions, the RLP was able to bring together political and legal actors of different views to talk to each other in cases of domestic tensions[1424] which can also be viewed as dialogic interaction among conflicting parties. Although state-building is generally focused on a short-term aim achievement and the RLP, in contrast, adopted a long-term approach integrating elements of both state-building and conflict management, this was justified as the stability of most of the countries in the region was not sufficient.[1425]

8.2.5. Impact of the KAS

In chapter 2 I reflected on the difficulty of measuring the impact of transnational actors by policy outcomes and their influence on the policy making process. To causally link the RLP's activities to political results in the Southeast European countries was equally impossible. I found one such success story the KAS credited itself with: During the Rumanian political crisis in 2012, the constitutional court, which had cooperated with the KAS for many years, had held a key position to end the conflict between the political camps as it had to decide about the referendum on the president's removal. It was not awed by the intimidation attempts of one of the political camps. This was virtually celebrated as the victory of the rule of law.[1426] Still, to trace back this success to the RLP's engagement only is doubtful. Although the interview partner believed that the RLP had initiated social reform processes and positive changes, he also regarded as particular difficult to change and encourage thought processes and to become one of the crucial socialisation factors among all the other aspects of influence.[1427] Also the evaluation stressed the RLP's positive effect on the region's modernisation and EU integration.[1428] However, to fully meet the needs in rule of law activities, the funds had to be increased by ten times or more.[1429] Cooperation with political parties and parliamentary committees

1424 *Luchterhandt* (2013) p. 20.

1425 According to the World Bank (2015), Kosovo and Bosnia Herzegovina were fragile states. In the fragile states index of the Fund for Peace of 2014 Serbia, Moldova and Bosnia ranked as "high warning" fragile states, in Macedonia and Albania the situation was "warning", while Montenegro, Romania, Bulgaria and Croatia counted as "less stable" (see https://fragilestatesindex.org).

1426 *Luchterhandt* (2013) p. 36.

1427 Interview 8.

1428 *Luchterhandt* (2013) pp. 23, 34.

1429 *Luchterhandt* (2013) p. 21.

also showed the difficulties of the KAS to offer expertise and exercise influence on the agenda setting process. The interview partner and the evaluation both concluded that it was all about a *progress* towards the defined RLP's objectives and not about the actual aim achievement by the RLP's activities alone.[1430] Nonetheless, the evaluation regarded the RLP as the most important external rule of law program, at least in Rumania.[1431] The KAS tried to overcome this difficulty of measuring causal results by focusing on the proper implementation of measures. The interview partner referred to the concept of sustainability including the subject's relevance for the respective country and the production of a certain result. In the follow-up of a conference, for example, an academic work, a thesis paper or the initiation of a network was a necessary requirement.[1432]

Consequently, considering the KAS's impact in the region in light of policy changes or development effects did not lead to results. While it was also methodological difficult to trace back how information and experiences gathered in the context of the RLP influenced German policies towards the countries in Southeast Europe, the RLP was, as demonstrated, strongly involved in implementing parts of the German policy. Furthermore, with its focus on aid and EU integration it supported indirectly Germany's role concept of a civilian power. To view the RLP as a sheer executive organ for German politics, however, is misleading since its activities often went beyond the respective policy implications. In 2014 the BMZ, for example, was only partially active in Southeast Europe due the focus on specific countries and the fact that some states were not defined as developing countries. In these cases, the ministry relied on other actors, such as the *Stiftungen*. Especially in rule of law aid, state actors were not apt for the task and the *Stiftungens*' undertakings were often the only possibility when the claim of interference was to be avoided.[1433] Still, the fragmented German foreign policy making process which included different departmental

1430 *Luchterhandt* (2013) p. 23. During the monitoring failed project were not found. The evaluation identified several beneficial factors for target achievement among others: the KAS's long-term presence, the experiences of the country offices with potential partner organisations before the RLP started, the manageable size of the measures, the integration of local staff members and their insights into the societies on site (see *Luchterhandt* [2013] pp. 24f. for details).

1431 *Luchterhandt* (2013) p. 36.

1432 Interview 8.

1433 Similar KAS (2008b) p. 4.

responsibilities[1434] also apparent towards Southeast Europe did not allow speaking of the KAS as a vicarious agent for *the* German policy. Interests of economic policy, for example, promoted by the BMJV could not be found in the RLP.

According to the point of view taken here and understanding impact as the establishment of communication channels and operation in networks, sheds a completely different light on the KAS's impact. Within the established RLP's network, the KAS took a central position as it controlled the exchange of resources and was therefore more dominant than the involved state actors. The KAS was also mainly involved in the network's building and maintained a bridging function which can be viewed as an "example of mattering" itself.[1435] The case showed furthermore a high flexibility of the KAS to adapt its activities to the domestic conditions in the region. With abandoning its world-wide practised approach of predominantly working with affiliated partners and focusing on law-oriented addressees instead, the KAS bypassed the problem of missing partners with a political background akin to the KAS. From a more general perspective, the RLP also intensified the links between Germany and the countries of Southeast Europe on different levels. Also, the interview partner believed that the activities of the RLP contributed to the bilateral relations.[1436] Whether the RLP positively impacted the image of Germany and its law in the region as assumed by the evaluator[1437] is difficult to verify, in contrast. Although the KAS did not plan in the near future the establishment of other RLPs world-wide and the progress in Southeast Europe was slow, the interview partner was cautiously optimistic regarding future developments in the rule of law field and pleaded for a committed continuation of work in the region.[1438]

Conclusion

With the case of the KAS's rule of law program in Southeast Europe I tried to illustrate the public diplomatic undertakings of the *Stiftungen*. It

1434 *Rudizio* (2006) p. 486; *Tewes* (1997) p. 96; *Maull* (2015) p. 226; *Weller* (2007) p. 210.
1435 *Noortmann/Arts/Reinalda* (2001) p. 302.
1436 Interview 8.
1437 *Luchterhandt* (2013) p. 34.
1438 Interview 8.

showed that the KAS predominantly planned activities for the long-term, mainly used dialogue instruments and purposed especially the building of favourable relationships.

The RLP was organised as a sector program. It showed several particularities which translated into the public diplomacy approach. Due to the focus on the rule of law, the public diplomacy's addressees were limited to specific disseminators while simultaneously the target groups were extended to politically non-affiliated partners and high-level politics. It secured the KAS's own ability to act in countries were political partners were missing as partnerships were defined through the specific topic. It also legitimised the cooperation with state actors on site, something desired by the *Stiftungen*.[1439] The balance between the German political foundations, on the contrary, was disrupted. Although competition between the KAS and the other foundations could not be noted, the adopted target group concept neutralised the unwritten partner pluralism among the foundations which I consider at least partly as a guarantor against propaganda activity.

The network surrounding mainly determined the KAS's impact on site. Not only exchanged the KAS resources with various actors, it also actively built networks, mainly controlled the links between actors and acted as a gate keeper. Especially the RLP's office in Rumania and the long-term KAS's activities in the region positively impacted the network building. The network was characterised by a mixed character and features of different transnational policy networks. It showed a high degree of shared values and policy interest among actors, but German and European policy interests were put to the fore. Although the KAS acted independently from governmental guidelines, it implemented large parts of German policy in the region and indirectly extended the official margin for manoeuvre through its cooperation with a wide variety of actors which otherwise could have not been reached easily by governmental actors. This also happened intentionally as the KAS frequently referred to German politics when justifying its undertakings on site. Although the KAS appeared as a civil society organisation abroad, it disguised neither its affiliation to the German ruling party nor the fact that it was a political organisation purposing political changes. Finally, the case of the RLP showed moreover that the KAS mixed several catalytic and collaborative public diplomacy forms. Neither did it limit its democracy assistance to rule of law aid only nor did it strictly differentiate between democracy assistance and conflict management tasks.

1439 See Ch. 5.2.

Activities were rather adapted flexibly to the perceived necessities and possibilities on site.

Chapter 9 – Practising public diplomacy through conflict management: The Friedrich-Ebert-Stiftung in Southern Thailand

The following chapter aims at illustrating how German political foundations are active in the field of conflict management. This is shown in the case of the Friedrich-Ebert-Stiftung (FES) and its ambitions to further peace in the Southern regions of Thailand where violence, without much international perception, is the order of the day. The chapter is based mainly on fieldwork conducted in Thailand in 2009. It also includes more recent material. The chapter starts with an overview of the framework in which the FES operated in Thailand in 2009. Afterwards, we look more closely at the FES's public diplomacy ambitions in the context of its conflict management in Thailand's deep South.

9.1. Thailand and Germany

The kingdom of Thailand is the only Southeast Asian state without a colonial history. The revolution of 1932 led from absolute to constitutional monarchy as well as to power struggles between concurring groups of armed forces and of social elites. Since World War Two, Thailand has seen all manner of different forms of government, ranging from military dictatorships to electoral democracy. At the time of the interviews, seventeen constitutions and charters had been in power since that time. They all approved the monarchy. Most of Thailand's numerous post-war governments were controlled by the military and periods of parliamentary democracy alternated with military governments.[1440] At the time of this study, King *Bhumipol Adulyadej* had been ruling Thailand since 1946.[1441] He was the world's longest-serving monarch and was assumed to be the world's richest royal.[1442] He was the head of state, the supreme commander of the armed

1440 *Nohlen* (2002) p. 788.

1441 *Bhumipol* died on 13th October 2016.

1442 CIA (2010).

forces and the highest Buddhist dignitary. He also confirmed the prime minister, who was elected by the House of Representatives.

The 1997 constitution was widely hailed as a landmark in democratic political reform. It included electoral innovations, an increase in checks and balances, the establishment of the constitutional court and the explicit recognition of human rights.[1443] At the time of the interviews, Thailand's constitution was that of 2007, which had replaced an interim constitution formed in 2006 after an army-led coup. It provided for a bicameral parliament. Members of the House of Representatives were elected on a proportional party list by popular vote. The Senate consisted partly of representatives of the 76 Thai provinces; the other part was appointed by a committee and consisted of members who were not allowed to be political party members and mainly belonged to the social and military elite.

In the 1980s, Thailand experienced an economic boom and became one of Southeast Asia's economically leading countries, making the leap from a developing to a threshold country.[1444] It managed to recover from the 1997 Asian financial crisis by 2001.[1445] In 2002 the Federal Foreign Office (AA) considered Thailand a small "tiger economy".[1446] Thailand is a founding member of the Association of Southeast Asian Nations (ASEAN), the Asian Pacific Economic Cooperation (APEC), and the ASEAN Free Trade Area (AFTA). In 2009, at the time of the interviews, the political situation in Thailand was one of conflict; this situation grew out of control soon thereafter.

The following sections will give an overview of the political situation in Thailand at the time of the interviews and the challenges faced by the German political foundations, the situation in the Southern provinces, the official relations between Germany and Thailand, and the landscape of the German political foundations on site. The sections consider the perceptions of the interview partners.

9.1.1. Political situation and aid organisations

In 2009 Thailand experienced conflicts between the political camps of *Thaksin Shinawatra*, former prime minister of Thailand (the "Reds") and

1443 *Banpsirichote* (2004) p. 244.
1444 *Nohlen* (2002) p. 789.
1445 LOC (2007) pp. 7f.
1446 AA (2002b) p. 3.

the conservative elite in Bangkok (the "Yellows"). *Thaksin*, a telecommunications businessman and one of the wealthiest people in Thailand, ruled from 2004 to 2007, a time dominated by gross violations of the rule of law and by clampdowns on Muslim dissenters in the Southern provinces.[1447] The "Reds" were mainly rural workers supporting the pro-*Thaksin* People Power Party (PPP) led by Prime Minister *Samak Sundaravej*. *Thaksin* fled from Thailand in 2008. The "Yellows", supporters of the People's Alliance for Democracy (PAD), were for the most part a loose grouping of royalists, businessmen and the urban middle class, led by media mogul *Sondhi Limthongkul* and *Chamlong Srimuang*, a former general with close ties to the king.[1448] During the 2008 PPP government, protests and violence did not relent and led to the occupation of the two international airports by members of the PAD. From late 2008 onwards, *Abhisit Vejjajiva* was prime minister and leader of the opposition Democrat Party (DP), associated with the "Yellows".[1449] Political instability continued in 2009. The pro-*Thaksin* United Front for Democracy against Dictatorship (UDD) stormed the ASEAN Conference in Pattaya and violence escalated in Bangkok. In the months that followed, the internal affairs situation calmed down after the government initiated a military intervention, but protests resumed in 2010.[1450] The military intervened several times. In 2013, during the governmental term of *Thaksin's* sister *Yingluck*, who had been elected in 2011, protests flared up again and were ended by a military coup in 2014.

Although most Thais saw the king as the source of stabilisation and modernisation, the king's political role was not undisputed.[1451] Since the beginning of his reign, a coup d'état had taken place every six years. Most of them were supported by the throne when the acting civilian government became too democratic or its independence seemed to be no longer tolerable for the monarchy.[1452] The "Yellows" feared for their privileges since the king was too ill to exercise his authority, whereas the "Reds" acted with increasing confidence, supported with money and video messages by the exiled *Thaksin*.[1453] At the time of the interviews, the human rights situation in Thailand was characterised by limits on freedom of expression and an assembly curtailed by emergency decrees issued after violent demonstra-

---

1447 *Rüland* (2009) p. 118; *Handley* (2006) pp. 424, 444.
1448 BBC Profile, 13/07/2012.
1449 ai (2009) p. 454; CIA (2010); *Köckritz*, Die Zeit, 15/04/2010.
1450 *Doherty*, The Guardian, 12/04/2010.
1451 *Head*, BBC, 5/12/2007.
1452 *Handley*, Die Zeit, 16/04/2009.
1453 *Köckritz*, Die Zeit, 15/04/2010.

tions in 2008. Restrictions on the media had also increased. Moreover, the number of people charged with lese majesty had augmented substantially in 2008 and 2009 with drastic sentences of imprisonment.[1454]

In 2009 the Friedrich-Ebert-Stiftung (FES), the Konrad-Adenauer-Stiftung (KAS), the Heinrich-Böll-Stiftung (HBS) and the Friedrich-Naumann-Stiftung (FNS) had offices in Thailand. They faced several challenges. Firstly, it was complicated to openly address problems, as this was not part of Thai culture. Communication of unpleasant, negative or conflictive issues was avoided and often meant a loss of face.[1455] Thais tended to prefer indirect communication, which set hurdles for the aid organisations.[1456] However, the occupation of the airport in Bangkok in 2008 and the storm of the ASEAN conference in 2009 damaged Thailand's international reputation, which in turn opened up the situation for assistance from abroad.[1457] Secondly, working conditions were very restrictive. Only nine international organisations were accredited at the TICA (Thailand International Development Cooperation Agency), a department in the Thai ministry of foreign affairs. Of the *Stiftungen* only the FES and the KAS held accreditation, whereas the other German foundations, bilateral actors and NGOs had to work in a grey area. The German foundations which were not accredited at the TICA regretted not having official status. They had to re-register every second year at the Thai Ministry of Labour. In the beginning a lot of persuasion had been necessary to become registered. Over the years, the relationship to the authorities had improved, but comprehensive reporting to the public bodies was still necessary.[1458] Thirdly, the political crisis in Thailand created different framework conditions every couple of months.[1459] The organisations were forced to constantly adapt to the changing situations and new governmental actors.[1460] During times of military governments, it was more difficult for the *Stiftungen* to maintain their activities as they were often restricted.[1461] Fourthly, the political crisis had led to a severe polarisation within the party landscape and society at large, which made the work of the *Stiftungen* more complicated. It was often not

1454 ai (2009) p. 455; HRW (2010) p. 356.
1455 Interviews 1, 2, 3.
1456 Interview 1.
1457 Interview 3.
1458 Interviews 1, 2, 3.
1459 Interview 1.
1460 Interview 3.
1461 Interview 3; e.g. The Guardian at: http://www.theguardian.com/world/2015/jan/30/thailands-military-junta-forces-cancellation-of-press-freedom-conference.

known which side the local partner supported, and partners refused to enter dialogue with the other camp. Being viewed as partial, getting caught between the camps and being forced to adopt a clear position was considered as challenging.[1462] Finally, the language barrier was considered a major challenge for finding partners. Only the Thai elite spoke English. It was therefore necessary to have an office in Thailand with Thai staff members.[1463]

Apart from the four political foundations, several other German aid organisations were active in Thailand in 2009. Technical assistance came from the *Deutscher Entwicklungsdienst* (DED), the *Internationale Weiterbildung und Entwicklung gGmbH* (InWent) and the *Gesellschaft für technische Zusammenarbeit* (GTZ). All three became the *Gesellschaft für Internationale Zusammenarbeit* (GIZ) in 2011.[1464] Some consulting organisations which were assumed to be spin-offs of the GTZ also worked on site. For German financial assistance, the *Deutsche Entwicklungsgesellschaft* (DEG) was active.[1465]

9.1.2. The conflict in Southern Thailand

In 2009, the conflict in Thailand's Southern provinces of Narathiwat, Yala, Pattani, Satun and Songkhla, mainly inhabited by Muslims of Malay ethnicity, smouldered.[1466] Between 2004 and 2009 thousands of people were killed in bombing attacks and confrontations between Muslim insurgents and the Thai government. Whether the insurgents were separatists, terrorists or criminal groups was unknown. In 1902, after Siam, the former Thailand had annexed the independent Muslim Sultanate Patani, violent excesses already took place. In the 1970s and 1980s militant groups fought for separation. In the 1990s violence slackened but in the middle of 2001 several assassinations of policemen led to an upsurge in violent behaviour. Experts began speaking out about an escalation of violence in 2004; that year 18 schools were set on fire and several bombs exploded in Narathiwat. Moreover, several insurgents who had attacked police and military stations were shot by the Thai military when a mosque in Pattani was stormed.

1462 Interviews 1, 3, 4, correspondingly 2.

1463 Interview 3.

1464 See Ch. 6.2.1.

1465 Interviews 2, 3.

1466 For a detailed timeline see *Wagner* (2007) pp. 36ff.

One hundred and seven militants were killed. Furthermore, 78 protesters suffocated to death while being moved to a military camp handcuffed and stacked on top of each other in a van.[1467] By 2010 the number of deaths had reached around 4000 with another 6500 injured.[1468] Targets belonged to all different kind of groups, such as policemen, soldiers, officials, teachers, students, farm workers, local businessmen, monks and Muslim clerics.[1469] The rhetoric around the conflict was charged with conspiracy theory.[1470] Several reasons behind the conflict can be identified, however. Firstly, the culture, the language (Jawi, a Malay dialect) and ethnicity of the Thai Muslims had not been taken into account by the Thai government, which provided a breeding ground for separatist movements. In the 16th and 17th century the Muslim Sultanate Pattani was the centre of Islam in Southeast Asia and particularly important both politically and economically. Armed conflict with Siam had occurred in earlier centuries. Despite the reign of Siam, Pattani had kept its political and economic structure until the early 20th century. Some scholars therefore connected a historical reason to the conflict.[1471] Secondly, the social, economic and educational situation in the Southern regions was viewed as a reason for the conflict. It was characterised by poverty and unemployment as well as a lack of subsidies for educational institutions.[1472] One interview partner assumed that economic interests such as the access to oil and gas fields as well as smuggling in the border regions to Malaysia could be a catalyst.[1473] Thirdly, the Southern provinces were often exposed to radical policies of assimilation in the last decades. *Thaksin*'s policy had furthered this by dissolving the Southern Border Provinces Administration Centre (SBPAC), the responsible authority for the Southern regions and a stabiliser, and attributing the responsibility to the police.[1474] *Thaksin* also closed ranks with the Bush administration, which inspired sympathy for Al-Qaeda among young people in the Southern provinces, according to some observers.[1475] Finally, the unclear

1467 *Heiduk/Möller* (2004) p. 2.
1468 *Möller* (2011) p. 7.
1469 AA at: http://www.auswaertiges-amt.de/DE/Aussenpolitik/Laender/Laenderinfos/Thailand/Innenpolitik_node.html; ai (2009) p. 457.
1470 *Askew* (2007) p. x.
1471 *Möller* (2011) p. 12.
1472 *Wagner* (2007) pp. 9ff.
1473 Interview 3.
1474 *Möller* (2011) p. 12; critically on the role of SBPAC *Askew* (2007) p. 67; SBPAC resumed work in 2006.
1475 *Heiduk/Möller* (2004) p. 3.

legal situation, the lack of legal security and the violations of human rights were blamed for the smouldering of the conflict. In 2004 the government had proclaimed martial law in numerous Southern districts, which was still in force in 2009, giving impunity to soldiers and police officers. The government did not take disciplinary action in cases of violation of the law. Arbitrary arrests, detentions, torture, and killings of people in the Southern regions seemed to be carried out systematically.[1476] Also, the Act on Internal Security of 2008 gave wide powers to the Thai military and security forces. Its application to the insurgency in Southern Thailand remained unclear but it restricted fundamental rights, the overriding of civilian administration, and did not require the declaration of a state of emergency.[1477] In 2009, there was limited access to the Southern regions. The AA issued a travel warning, as attacks against state institutions and private individuals happened on a daily basis.[1478] The conflict was believed to be one of the most dangerous in Southeast Asia.[1479]

Of the German political foundations, the FES, the KAS and the FNS were active in Southern Thailand. Activities were kept low-profile in order to avoid appearing as interfering actors from abroad. The Thai government was assumed to have no interest in conflict handling through the UN or other international actors. However, foreign actors were tolerated within a limited framework.[1480] Other international organisations such as the ASIA Foundation were also involved in managing the conflict. The military putsch in 2006 had opened up the situation in the Southern regions for foreign actors and an increase of actors was noticed.[1481]

9.1.3. Germany's policy

Political cooperation between Germany and Thailand dates back to 1858 when the Hanseatic cities signed commercial contracts with the kingdom of Siam. Over the following decades, German merchants and experts wielded great influence in Siam's economic life and occupied influential

1476 HRW (2009); HRW (2010) p. 358.

1477 ai (2009) p. 456; HRW (2010) p. 357.

1478 AA at: http://www.auswaertiges-amt.de/diplo/de/Laenderinformationen/Thailand/Sicherheitshinweise.html (accessed on 16/05/2010).

1479 Interview 3.

1480 Interviews 3, 4.

1481 Interviews 3, 6.

positions in developing a modern infrastructure.[1482] During World War Two, the Thai prime minister had sympathy for the German *Reich* and supported Japan and the Axis in order to regain land taken by France and Great Britain in 1919. However, the following *Thai Seri* movement joined the Allies in 1944. During the bloc confrontation, Germany's policy towards the Southeast Asian countries was first characterised by winning back its political ability to act and, until the early 1970s, by the *Hallstein doctrine*.[1483] With the end of the Cold War, normative principles became increasingly important in German and other Western foreign policies, leading to conflicts in the EU-ASEAN dialogues of the 1990s.[1484] In its Southeast Asia concept of 2002 the AA stressed democracy, rule of law and human rights as preconditions for internal and external stability and development and as a central objective. Instruments of the German government in the region were consulting and supporting institutions, civil society organisations and the security sector. According to the AA, the government was directly active through public relations and development policy, and indirectly via support for German NGOs and the *Stiftungen*.[1485] Furthermore, the AA emphasised peace and regional stability. It showed interest in convincing the ASEAN states of the importance of regional confidence building and collective conflict prevention referring to a broad notion of security, with Thailand and Singapore playing leading roles.[1486] As instruments the AA suggested imparting German experiences in dialogue, civil and military training programmes, conferences for conflict prevention, and institutional consulting for the civil control of armed forces, as well as the support of structural reforms. Further key objectives in the strategy were advancing environmental cooperation and continuing development assistance although financial aid to Thailand had already been stopped due to Thai economic development. Finally, the AA stressed cultural and academic relations, mentioning in particular the awakening of interest in Germany and conveying an up-to-date image of Germany. In this context, it highlighted the support of the *Stiftungen* and other organisations. The strategy also emphasised the development of regional security structures, the *Stiftungen*'s consulting assistance, political dialogue and development

1482 AA at: http://www.auswaertiges-amt.de/DE/Aussenpolitik/Laender/Laenderinfos/Thailand/Bilateral_node.html.

1483 *Stoffers* (2014) p. 185f.; *Rüland* (2007) pp. 560f.; see Ch. 5.3.

1484 *Rüland* (2007) p. 563.

1485 AA (2002b) p. 7.

1486 See Ch. 7.1.1.

cooperation.[1487] The German government's political concept of 2012 on partnership with new players mentioned further confidence-building measures in regional security organisations such as ASEAN.[1488] This increased focal point on regional security also corresponded with the ambitions of the EU in Southeast Asia. While in the 1990s the EU's political focus was on trade, security political aspects increasingly came on the agenda from 2000 onwards. Since then, cooperation between the EU and ASEAN on this matter has improved.[1489]

Between 2005 and 2015 some cooperation between Germany and Thailand existed in terms of military and police training as regards the role of the military in a democracy.[1490] The German government withdrew from the cooperation in 2006 and resumed activities in 2008.[1491] Diplomatic contacts were also restricted during the time of the military coup; high-level political and economic dialogue was continued when Thailand returned to democracy.[1492] In 2009, German-Thai relations were considered to be very good.[1493] According to the German government, along with its EU partners it kept an eye on democratic deficits and the political situation and broached the issue of political participation at a higher political level. It also referred to the *Stiftungen* for the long-term accompanying and furthering of the democratic process.[1494] In 2012 both countries celebrated the 150th anniversary of their bilateral relations, leading to further intensification of contacts, cooperation, academic exchanges and cultural events.[1495]

With the Thai economic upswing, foreign trade with Germany grew steadily from the 1980s onwards.[1496] The Southeast Asia strategy of 2002 highlighted German foreign economic interest in the region although it was less dominantly articulated than in the preceding Asia concept of

1487 AA (2002b) pp. 8ff.

1488 Bundesregierung (2012a) pp. 24, 65: it referred to the Aquis of the OSCE (Organisations for Security and Co-operation in Europe) and included mainly military information exchange. It defined new players as economic motors and key regional players (p. 5).

1489 *Dosch* (2004) p. 13; KAS at: http://www.kas.de/wf/de/33.34546/.

1490 *Rüland* (2007) p. 565.

1491 BT (2010b) p. 8.

1492 AA at: http://www.auswaertiges-amt.de/diplo/en/Laenderinformationen/01-Laender/Thailand.html (accessed on 16/05/2010).

1493 Interviews 1, 3, 6, 7; *Rüland* (2007) p. 570.

1494 BT (2010b) p. 2.

1495 BT (2013) p. 51.

1496 AA (2002b) p. 5.

1993.[1497] The German economic interest in Southeast Asia declined after the financial crisis and shifted to East Asia. Culture relations between the two countries based on an agreement signed in 1984. In 2011, the main organisations active in Thailand were the Goethe Institute, the German Academic Exchange Service (DAAD) and the Alexander von Humboldt Foundation. The development cooperation between Germany and Thailand started in the 1960s.[1498] In 2004, the BMZ considered Thailand as an "anchor country", a term referring to states with a special regional impact in terms of economy and politics and increasing importance in the management of global challenges and international processes. The assistance approach combined elements of development cooperation and foreign policy.[1499] Although Thailand increasingly transformed itself from a recipient into a donor and German development assistance ended in 2011, Germany still financed technical cooperation projects in Thailand focusing on climate change and energy, sustainable consumption and production, regional integration in Southeast Asia, and joint development cooperation for third countries.[1500] Still, Thailand was not among the 57 partner countries of German development assistance and therefore lacked the opportunity for intensive cooperation.[1501] In 2011 the BMZ's fields of cooperation in Asia were economic and ecological development, education, good governance and health.[1502] It planned to further integrate German civil society organisations as dialogue partners and critical catalysts. In this context, it stressed the particular role of the *Stiftungen* and their consulting and dialogue instruments on the political level to further democratic and rule of law-based institution building.[1503]

1497 *Rüland* (2007) p. 570.

1498 Interviews 3, 2; *Rüland* (2007) p. 568; AA at: http://www.auswaertiges-amt.de/DE/Aussenpolitik/Laender/Laenderinfos/Thailand/Bilateral_node.html.

1499 OECD (2010) p. 35 fn.; BMZ (2004b) p. 5.

1500 AA at: http://www.auswaertiges-amt.de/DE/Aussenpolitik/Laender/Laenderinfos/Thailand/Bilateral_node.html.

1501 OECD (2010) pp. 33f. Between 1997 and 2001 Thailand still ranked 19 among the 143 receiving countries of German bilateral assistance (OECD [2010] p. 114).

1502 BMZ (2011b) p. 9.

1503 BMZ (2011b) p. 14.

9.1.4. Landscape of the German political foundations

In 2009, the FES, the KAS, the FNS and the HBS maintained offices in Thailand and determined the political landscape of the *Stiftungen*.[1504] In addition to their offices in Thailand, most of them maintained regional offices in Southeast Asia concentrating on regional issues and organisations such as ASEAN. Activities of both types of offices usually did not overlap.[1505] In the case of the HBS and the FNS, the location of the regional offices and their Thai offices coincided. The landscape of the *Stiftungen* was therefore considered as more significant compared to other countries.[1506] The Hans-Seidel-Stiftung (HSS) and the Rosa-Luxemburg-Stiftung (RLS) either worked from an office in Singapore in the Thai rural areas (HSS) or had no declared activities in Thailand (RLS). All the German foundations held workshops and seminars and issued publications. Some of the *Stiftungen* intensified their activities in the field of organising conferences and training sessions. They all implemented measures mainly in collaboration with local partners.

Activities in Thailand of the FES dated back to the early 1970s, coinciding with the start of its international activity. In the very beginnings, the FES did not have an office on site. As was the case in other Southeast Asian countries, its activities started with the support of newly formed trade unions and in the field of employment and social policy. In the 1980s, the main emphasis was on gender questions and Thailand became one of the FES's offices working with gender issues. Furthermore, so-called "WISO-projects", grassroots-oriented advisory projects in the field of economy and social policy, took place. From 1992 onwards and parallel to Thailand's democratisation process, activities increased concerning the democratisation of institutions. They remained the focus until the time of the interviews. In 2009, the FES was active in three main areas: (1) The promotion of democratic institutions and processes based on social and progressive democracy with social elites taking a key role in shaping it. Within this working area one project line supported the access of women and young people to politics, and another project line dealt with the role of the media in democracy; (2) the contribution of instruments and methods to conflict transformation and the promoting of knowledge on the Southern conflict

---

1504 The following sections use deviating interview codes. This takes account of data's sensitivity.
1505 Interview 5.
1506 Interview 7.

and its parties; and (3) the implementation of economic and social human rights. This area included the promotion of trade unions and addressed the interests of employees and economic migrants from Burma. As regards the second focal point of conflict management, the FES had implemented an extensive EU-funded project in addition to its regular activities. In 2009, the FES office regularly consisted of seven people (six Thai, one German), with four working on content-related matters. In addition, three people were working on the EU project. One of them was an external German consultant.[1507]

The KAS had been active in Thailand for almost as long as the FES. In 2009, one of the KAS's areas of interest was the promotion of the people's political participation. In collaboration with the secretary of the national assembly and the senate, local political leaders were trained to improve their exchange with voters. Furthermore, the KAS promoted the rule of law by encouraging the Thai administration and constitutional court. Both courts were still relatively new achievements. Study programmes were offered to Thai administrative law judges in Germany and German lawyers offered short-term training courses. The German administration court served as a model. In the case of the constitutional court, consulting took place on the constitutional complaint and decisions were translated into English. Moreover, the topics of regulatory policy and security policy had become focal points for the KAS in 2009. In addition to public bodies, partners of the KAS were civil society organisations and Thai universities. In the absence of Thai think tanks, the KAS supported academic projects. Around 200 measures were implemented annually. The Bangkok office and its partners decided annually which measures to carry out. The plan was then adjusted quarterly. The KAS's headquarters in Berlin had to approve measures. However, a rejection had not occurred in recent years. In earlier times, programmes were tailored to people in rural areas and Bangkok's elite. In 2009, the KAS focused on the Thai middle class and political development was given priority over rural development. In addition to a German representative, the KAS's office employed six Thai staff members.[1508]

The FNS's activities in Thailand began in 1975. In 1999, the office moved from Singapore to Bangkok. In 2009, it was one of seven regional offices that the FNS maintained worldwide and covered the region of Southeast and East Asia including Thailand, the Philippines, Malaysia,

1507 Interview a.
1508 Interview d.

Cambodia, Indonesia, South Korea and North Korea. Moreover, projects in China and Burma were managed from there. For a period of three to five years, liberal political principles were formulated by the FNS's headquarters in Berlin. From 2008 to 2011, the FNS's work focused on "freedom and property", "freedom and civil society" and "freedom and the rule of law". In Thailand, the main fields of interest were democracy, rule of law and economic freedom, with democracy as the key topic. It concerned mainly cooperation with political parties, e.g. the Thai Democrat party.[1509] It also covered activities with the Thai electoral commission, the council of civic education, the municipality of Bangkok and civil society organisations. As for rule of law and economic freedom, the FNS undertook activities with the Thai legal reform commission and cooperated with local think tanks. Conflict management in Southern Thailand was also a topic. Over the years, the activities of the FNS in Thailand changed. In the beginning, projects were more driven by "classic" development policy. The first project of the FNS in Thailand, for instance, involved water buffalo banks in Chiang Mai. Political dialogue, though part of the FNS's prior activities, was further developed and a "strategy for the promotion of organised liberalism and liberal thought" was adopted in the early 1990s. The desire to stand out from activities that could also be undertaken by the GTZ was one of the reasons for changing the portfolio. From then on, technical assistance was only given when there was a political context or when it was the only possibility to be active at all. In 2009, the FNS's activities in border regions between Thailand and Burma, for example, concerned ethnic minorities. They were considered as very basic, including the fight against poverty, infrastructure development and the organisation of village communities. In earlier times, political assistance had included more institutional assistance and financial backing for partners. At the time of the interviews, the emphasis was on collaboration with networks and action groups. In their partner choice, the FNS attached importance to ideological affiliations. Measures were planned annually with partners. Cooperation also took place with other organisations, such as the United Nations Development Programme (UNDP), the European Union, the GTZ, and the British embassy. In 2009, the FNS's office had between 20 and 25 staff members.[1510]

1509 Between 2000 and 2010 the percentage of costs for measures with the Thai DP or partners affiliated to the DP was however, only at around 14% compared to all measures of the FNS in Thailand (see BT [2010b] p. 11).

1510 Interview b.

In 2009 the HBS worked from Chiang Mai, a city in the north of Thailand. The regional office was founded in 2000 to implement projects in Thailand and Burma. At the time of the interview, it was about to move to Bangkok. The idea for the office in Chiang Mai was derived from the HBS's wish for decentralisation as the other *Stiftungen* were active in Bangkok. Moreover, Chiang Mai was considered an intellectual centre. However, the HBS remained very isolated, which prompted the decision to move to Bangkok. Regional cooperation with partner organisations had already started in the 1990s. In 2009, the main areas of interest were democratisation, climate, ecology and sustainable development. As regards democratisation, the HBS supported information democracy, media, and people's opportunity to select from a diverse range of non-monopolised information services. Concerning climate, ecology and sustainable development, the HBS furthered reform efforts that aimed at overcoming institutional problems and providing greater transparency. A special focal point was nuclear energy, which was partly introduced in Thailand as clean energy, whereas the HBS tried to counteract this trend. At the time of the interview, the area of climate was expanded while democracy was hardly emphasised. The HBS did not work directly with Thai political partners and did not support a political party. There was no Green political party counterpart. The HBS mainly worked with civil society organisations and cooperated with the GTZ. Similar to the FNS, the HBS had started more as a sponsor and had focused on basic development cooperation. It was also considered part of the Green ideology to give money and let partners decide what to do with it. This had changed due to imposed conditions by the BMZ and the work had become more political. The interview partner used "cross-linker" and "bridge-builder" to describe the role of the HBS at that time. Methodologically, the HBS conducted more meetings, events and publications and less capacity building measures like trainings and seminars. In 2009, the office had 12 staff members of whom two were German/Austrian.[1511]

In sum, the German political foundation in Thailand had very different focal points, which mainly was a result of different political backgrounds. Some overlaps existed as regards activities in the Southern conflict. We also saw that activities focused less on institutional funding and had become more political over the time, although affiliated political parties were mostly missing. Technical development assistance and direct financing re-

1511 Interview c.

mained an area of retreat when other activities were not possible. Apart from the HBS, all foundations worked with political actors in Thailand.

9.2. The practice of public diplomacy through conflict management?

The following sections apply the integrated model of public diplomacy to the FES's ambitions to further peace in the conflict in Southern Thailand.[1512] It will shed light on whether the FES's was a generator of public diplomacy. Moreover, it will identify the instruments used and targets addressed. It then takes a close look at the network environment, including resources and sharing values and interests. Subsequently, we connect the activities to collaborative and catalytic public diplomacy practised as conflict management. Finally, we consider the impact of the FES as regards these activities.

9.2.1. Generator

In the context of the activities concerning the Southern conflict in Thailand, the FES appeared as a generator of public diplomacy as it implemented its projects autonomously and independent of the German ministries and the affiliated SPD.

The FES had been active in Southern Thailand since 1990. In the beginning, the focus of its undertakings was on democratic development and political education. Cooperation took place with an informal network of Muslim opinion leaders. Activities in the form of seminars were not too intense and did not concern the conflict. The established contacts were helpful when the conflict flared up in 2004. The FES first focused on the protection of human rights. Depending on the approval of TICA, the FES organised some human rights activities in the following time. After an interruption of the work, FES resumed the activities in 2005. At that time, the Southern activities of the FES were not very systematic. Thereafter, the FES arranged seminars with women and youth organisations as well as the university. These groups were selected in order to avoid political sensitivity and to reach civil society beyond the Muslim and male-dominated partner network. In 2006 the conflict was systematically analysed using the Peace and Conflict Impact Assessment (PCIA) methodology. The analysis took as

---

1512 See Ch. 3.2.

a starting point the methodological guidelines for socio-political cooperation programmes in the context of conflicts developed by the FriEnt Group at the BMZ.[1513] From 2007 onwards, several of the identified topics and measures were chosen to work on the conflict. In 2008, the FES and the FNS were selected to implement an EU-funded project in the Southern region lasting 18 months. The FES had been invited by an EU office/delegation in Bangkok to submit a proposal for the project. The funds were part of the EU instrument for stability (ifs) launched in 2007, which aimed at reacting to political crisis in third countries in the short-term and warding off global threats in the long run.[1514] For the FES, the office in Thailand was the first to apply for ifs funds. By the end of 2009, the project was nearly complete. In addition to the EU project, the FES kept up its former activities funded by the BMZ, which had, in part, already concerned the conflict.[1515] The funding period for the BMZ project lasted three years. In this timeframe, particular objectives had to be achieved. According to the BMZ's guidelines, the foundation's activities had to be monitored and evaluated. Although some financing for activities in Thailand could generally come from the AA, in 2009 those funds were not issued to the *Stiftungen*.[1516]

In contrast to other German organisations in Thailand, the *Stiftungen* did not operate under the auspices of the embassy. Meetings and coordination between the German embassy and the *Stiftungen* took place but the *Stiftungen* were not accountable to the embassy regarding project details. The relationship between the foundations and the German embassy was considered to be good.[1517] According to the interview partner, the FES also operated independently of the affiliated SPD. The main areas or overall objectives were suggested by the office in Thailand and discussed with the specific country section at the FES's headquarters in Berlin. These objectives were further substantiated by specific targets that were defined annually. The regional office was not involved in this process, concentrating instead on regional issues.[1518] The national office was autonomous although synergy effects between the regional work and the national work were supposed to be enabled. In 2009, the FES had departed from the procedure of

1513 Interveiw a; *Wagner* (2007) p. 5 referring to *Hasemann/Hübner-Schmid/Dargatz* (2005); see Ch. 7.3.2.2 on PCIA and Ch. 7.2 on FriEnt.

1514 See ifs at: http://eeas.europa.eu/ifs/index_de.htm.

1515 Interview a; see Ch. 9.1.3.

1516 Interviews 1, 2, 3, 6.

1517 Interviews 1, 2, 3, 4, 7.

1518 Interview 5.

having partners hand in annual activities since several years. It consulted with partners and defined measures itself. The main motivation behind the shift was to improve the overall quality of projects, for instance considering conflict sensitivity and gender integration. The measures were conducted as *Eigenmaßnahmen* and involved contributions of the FES.[1519]

According to the interview partner, the organisations on site did not consider the FES as a governmental instrument but rather as an academic organisation. Its public funding was not concealed. The activities of the FES were associated with civil diplomacy and track two diplomacy. According to the interview partner, civil diplomacy concerned the activities which had a foreign political dimension, such as consulting and official visits from Germany. Track two was understood as an informal track used parallel to official diplomacy that targeted decision makers and those having an impact on them.[1520]

9.2.2. Addressees and instruments

The FES's activities were characterised by a broad approach and were focused on all three target groups of public diplomacy: the general public, the media and specific disseminators. The main groups were civil society organisations, individuals with a key social role, academics, journalists and members of trade unions. Civil society in Thailand was assumed to be weak and state-controlled. Its organisations did not have enough resources to work independently, and so the FES often undertook tasks which in other countries were conducted by partners. In the Southern regions, the FES could hardly fall back on existing partners when it started the activities based on the conflict analysis. Furthermore, the FES addressed public actors, such as personnel from the Thai ministries and parliamentarians as well as stakeholders from the military and security sector. The FES considered the latter two to be crucial for a conflict solution. In the Southern region the FES also worked with women, young people and journalists. Methodologically, the FES used trainings, seminars, workshops, events and publications. In 2009, the FES conducted 60 to 70 measures annually in the context of the BMZ project. As regards the EU project, it implemented

1519 Interview a; see Ch. 8.2.1. on *Eigenmaßnahmen*.
1520 Interview a.

around 20 measures, including small training sessions of 15 to 20 people and large events with up to 300 participants.[1521]

The FES's activities concerning the conflict consisted of several broad areas which could be mainly subsumed under the public diplomacy's political dialogue and media instruments. Firstly, the FES created dialogue forums, mainly between the Southern partner network and decision makers in Bangkok. This interchange concerned the Thai government's Southern policy and conflict resolution strategies. Often the FES established first contacts. This component was funded by the BMZ. The second field of activities concerned woman and young people from the South and their role in conflict transformation. Organised female communities, their leaders and other interested women participated in meetings and programme development where their role as de-escalators was taken into account. These activities also had some capacity building and educational elements and included study tours where women from the South could engage in exchange with other women leaders and organisations and experience multicultural environments.[1522] Young persons were important addressees for the FES as their potential for radicalisation was high because of trauma, frustration and unemployment. Through youth camps, the FES intended to further community involvement, life skills, confidence building and mutuality. Networking was also enabled, bringing youth groups of different backgrounds together.[1523] The third field of the FES's activities was the application of participatory dialogue methods. Thai institutions and organisations, such as the King Prajadhipok's Institute (KPI) and the Peace Academy, focused on programmes in the South and were trained by the FES and an external consultant in participatory dialogue methods, such as "Open-space", "Worldcafé" and "Future Search". These measures were supposed to enhance capacity for dialogue and further the focus on common issues and mutual understanding, as well as to find a consensus.[1524] In 2009, these measures were the unique feature of the FES and differentiated them from the other *Stiftungen* and organisations in Thailand.[1525] The second and the third activity components were part of the EU-funded project. In all three fields of activities the FES operated as a dialogue facilitator between different social and political groups in Thailand. Dialogue was often

1521 Interview a.
1522 Interviews a, 6; FES (2009b) pp. 17ff.
1523 Interviews a, 6; FES (2009b) pp. 21ff.
1524 See FES (2009b) pp. 32f. with details.
1525 Interviews a, 6.

combined with capacity building. Another component, which can be considered political dialogue but had points of contact with consulting, was about to be developed by the FES in 2009. It was part of the FES's democracy assistance working line and concerned dialogue forums on security sector governance amongst the Thai military, the police, civil society, the Thai National Security Council, the senate and stakeholders from the South. Activities were organised with the Geneva Centre for the Democratic Control of Armed Forces (DCAF). The FES offered political assessments and contacts while DCAF provided the expertise on the matter. As regards the public diplomacy instruments, media activity could be identified. The FES's activities had a strong focus on objective media coverage and the deescalating role of the media. The FES cooperated with both the mass media in Bangkok and with local reporters in the South. The activities consisted of trainings for journalists and study trips where journalists were sent abroad. One group, for instance, was sent to India in order to experience a diversified multilingual media landscape free from control and mostly uncensored. Cultural diplomacy as well as think tank activities could not be identified in the context of the FES's conflict management. Few monologue instruments could be found in the form of publications, such as a handbook with guidelines on conflict-sensitive journalism published in Thai.[1526]

9.2.3. Dimensions: Propaganda and network

Propagandistic or strategic communication in terms of advertising or campaigning could not be identified in the activities of the FES. However, the case showed how the assessment of interference depended on the perception of the host country. In 2009, the FES enjoyed relatively wide-ranging trust of decision makers at all political levels in Bangkok. It was the first organisation to be officially permitted to work in the South. In former times, the Thai government had been more suspicious, as already outlined. For decades, the FES had also worked with trade unions, which were perceived as subversive by the Thai authorities. Furthermore, there was no interest in international supporting measures, and foreign activities in the Southern regions had always been mistrusted. The Thai government was mostly displeased that foreigners interfered in internal problems. This was also reflected in development cooperation: topics such as gender, HIV and

1526 FES (2009b) p. 10f.; interview a.

technology were welcomed, while politically sensitive issues like statehood, democracy, sovereignty, internal political processes and the role of the monarchy were very difficult to address.[1527] This also included the Southern conflict. After having won the trust of the authorities, the FES had tried to be active without much publicity. According to the interview partner, it was not the intention of the FES to tell Thai society how to resolve the conflict but instead to enable dialogue. In other areas, the FES was sometimes asked to "postpone" seminars, although measures were not vetoed. The FES also knew that it was under constant observation by the authorities. In 2009, the political situation was very tense and insecure.[1528] As outlined by an interview partner, foundations' political activities were viewed as relatively undesirable by the Thai authorities, and so the word "political" of "political foundation" often remained silent.[1529]

In contrast to the propaganda dimension, the networking dimension in the activities of the FES could be recognised. However, it was limited to actors from Thailand. Actors in Germany were hardly included.

9.2.3.1. Relationships, resources, values and interests

In 2009, various stable and independent relationships existed between the FES and local and foreign actors on site that were mainly characterised by cooperation and coordination. As already outlined, the FES interacted strongly with various Thai public bodies and higher political strata. The relationship between TICA and the FES in 2009 was described as friendly and cooperative. TICA regularly arranged information events for the accredited organisation. Organisations generally had to notify of their work in advance and to report afterwards. The weak civil society and political party landscape made it difficult for the FES to establish partnerships and develop relationships. Civil society organisations had no clear vision about their issues and aims. It was difficult to find partners with capacities at the average European or international level. Especially smaller organisations were missing. The interview partner explained this by citing a lack of financial resources and complicated approval procedures. Particularly in 2009, partners practiced increasingly strong self-censorship. During the

1527 Interviews a, 2, 6.
1528 Interview a.
1529 Interview 2.

measures, FES's staff members were generally present, thus contributing to the stability of the relationships on site.[1530]

In 2009, the FES also had relationships with German actors on site. All the German foundations participated in regular coordination meetings organised by the GTZ; the atmosphere was described as very good and strong information exchange existed. A representative of the German embassy also attended those meetings.[1531] Although the KAS and the FNS were also active around the Southern conflict, the topics of interest and activities were different from each other. However, when partners overlapped, coordination took place. Cooperation among the foundations hardly ever occurred.[1532] According to one interview partner, the raison d'être for each of several different foundations was otherwise not justified.[1533] The relationship between the FES and the German embassy was considered to be good.[1534] In the years before the interview, the embassy seemed to have reduced its prejudices against the *Stiftungen*.[1535] In the past, German ambassadors had interfered in stronger ways. The interviewee traced this development back to the work of several high-ranking German politicians who had emphasised the role of the *Stiftungen* abroad, and several studies which focused the attention to the *Stiftungen* and their importance as instruments of foreign affairs. However, contacts with the embassy often depended on the political position of the ambassador.[1536]

German politicians and members of the government rarely came to the FES's office in Thailand. Contacts between 2004 and 2009 were limited to several committees of the German *Bundestag* and a state secretary. The conflict was not in the focus of the visits. According to the interview partner, it had not found its way into their general consciousness. At the time of the interviews, the first official visit to the region had been initiated by the Thai foreign ministry for the ambassadors of the EU.[1537] Other interview partners reported a lack of interest from the German side. Although German officials and institutions requested information about Thailand from the *Stiftungen*, inquiries to the offices were not numerous.[1538] In many cas-

---

1530 Interview a.
1531 Interview 1.
1532 Interview a.
1533 Interview 1.
1534 Interviews a, 7.
1535 Interview 7.
1536 Interview 4.
1537 Interview a.
1538 Interviews 1, 2.

es, they concerned the whole Southeast Asian region. One interview partner assumed that the lack of interest was related to the German government's Asia strategy, which focused on China.[1539] However, the interest of other German actors in the activities and assessments of the FES was relatively strong. Visits and enquiries came from academics, other organisations active in development cooperation, policy consultants, and educational institutions. German media showed increased interest when the political situation changed. The interview partner estimated that there were about 50 to 60 annual visits to the office. The FES did not foster business contacts. At times, interchange occurred in the context of the trade union activities. Strong relationships also existed between the FES's office in Thailand and other FES's offices and divisions working in fields where Thailand was affected. This included global issues, EU politics, the international trade union activity of the FES and bilateral measures which concerned Thailand and other countries. Here the FES in Thailand cooperated with the respective country offices.

The aforementioned relationships were mainly cooperative or, in case of the other foundations, coordinative, at least. However, the situation for aid organisations in the Southern regions was characterised by strong competition. An interview partner even mentioned an overload of measures for the local population.[1540] At the end of 2009, USAID announced that it planned to invest 36 million US dollars for conflict resolution activities in the Southern regions in the following years. It was suspected that trust which existed towards the FES and other foreign actors would diminish and the large US investment would be considered as interference by the authorities. On the other hand, it was feared that FES's partners were poached with higher remuneration.[1541]

In the context of the relationships, various resources were exchanged. The findings did not deviate significantly from the general findings on the foundations' resource exchange.[1542] The FES obtained financial resources from the BMZ and the EU, which were used for the measures on site. The guidelines were strict, and the foundations were not allowed to conduct institution building. The FES received a wide range of information resources from civil society and political partners. As regards the conflict, the FES

1539 Interview 4.

1540 Interview 6.

1541 From 2010 onwards the USAID program SAPAN was active in the Southern provinces (see USAID [2012]).

1542 See Ch. 5.3.2.2.

was able to maintain contact to the local population in the Southern regions as well as to Thai stakeholders of the military and the police. Both groups were unreachable for the German embassy, as it had to be selective in its cultivation of contacts.[1543] In 2009, the German embassy was not active in the Southern regions but planned small-scale projects for 2010.[1544] The German embassy had asked the FES for its advisory skills to help with these activities. Moreover, the FES also monitored its activities and information was fed back into the FES's headquarters. Furthermore, the networking resources of the FES were enormous. As already outlined, various communication channels were established horizontally and vertically within Thai society. The FES's contacts depended in part on partners establishing contacts with other actors or securing the audience of the seminars. Political players and members of the executive were brought together with civil society actors. Similar groups were connected with the intention to bridge ethical and religious divides. Some interview partners assumed that the political foundations were better networked than the German embassy.[1545] However, in the context of the activities in the Southern provinces, the FES did not connect German actors with Thai counterparts. The FES did not bring other actors, such as journalists or academics (German or foreign), to the Southern regions. As explained by the interview partner, the people in the South were often sceptical towards foreigners. It was hard to win their trust and they often feared being politically exploited.[1546] Even some of the foundations' representatives had never been to the Southern regions.[1547] Apart from the networking resources, the FES's moral authority resources were perceived as very strong. In 2009, the FES received support from the Thai government for their conflict management activities in the South. In the time that followed, even Thai public authorities like the Thai foreign ministry had asked the FES for training in the new dialogue methods of communication. Training took place with the Southern Border Province Administrative Centre (SBPAC) in Krabi, for example. The interview partner also felt that the FES benefited from the long-standing and firm relations between Thailand and Germany. The *Stiftungen* could generally organise activities and address ideas which other organisations were not allowed to do. Germany was considered neutral in

1543 Interview 7.
1544 Interview 7.
1545 Interviews 4, 6.
1546 Interview a.
1547 Interview 4.

contrast to the USA and the EU. Along with those of the Nordic countries, Germany's basic model was in demand in Thailand due to its culture of political education and the welfare state. Although participants of the programmes in Southern Thailand were not very much interested in Germany, for them it was important that the FES was a German organisation. The USA, in contrast, was viewed with deep distrust from the Muslim side.[1548] More radical and fundamentalist Muslims often connected the activities of American organisations with the CIA and the "war on terror". The FES's credibility also profited from the long tradition of its activities in the Southern regions. The interview partner had experienced that in the interchange with the *Stiftungen*, members of the Thai political level often felt freer than in official communication since it had fewer formal consequences.[1549]

The network environment in which the FES operated was partly characterised by shared values and policy interests. This was not surprising as the FES mainly connected conflicting parties in the context of the studied activities. The FES generally chose its activities and focal points against the background of social democratic values but also considered the situation in the specific country. Social democracy highlights the political participation of socially weaker population. The political background of the Thai partners in terms of social democracy did not play a role for the FES, as political parties were not significant. Political parties were mostly oligarchic and characterised by vested interest and charismatic leaders. It was therefore not possible for the FES to define which Thai political parties could be either connected to the values supported by the SPD. Consequently, the specific political affiliation of the partner receded into the background, although the political attitude remained important. The FES felt bound to work with democratic, progressive and reform-oriented partners.[1550] Its peace activities in the Southern region as well as its security political dialogues fit largely with the German government's Asia strategy and its emphasis on peace and regional stability.[1551] In this context, the AA not only referred to the democracy assistance activities of the *Stiftungen* but also to their dialogues, consulting, and training measures in conflict prevention. The EU's security political focus in Southeast Europe was also visible in the FES's conflict management activities. The German political

1548 Interviews a, 6.
1549 Interview a.
1550 Interview a.
1551 See Ch. 9.1.3.

foundations have been mentioned as giving their constructive support as non-state actors in this context.[1552] The activities of the FES also corresponded with the SPD's pleas for strong cooperation between German foreign, security and development policy and the Asian countries as well as the overall political objective to prevent conflict and create peace in the international arena.[1553]

9.2.3.2. Types of transnational policy networks

The network in which the FES operated in the context of its conflict management activities was mixed. The observations were fairly similar to those made previously.[1554] The common issue that the activities circled around was the conflict in the Southern region, but a lack of campaigning meant that the network could not qualify as a transnational advocacy network (TAN). Thai civil servants were connected to the network, but the FES was not a ministerial staff member, and so a transnational executive network was also out of the question. Although knowledge generation played an important role in the activities of the FES, most actors were neither experts nor professionals, thereby disqualifying the network for global knowledge network (KNET) status. The network was trisectoral, including public sector officials, civil servants and civil society professionals; however, large groups of individuals, such as members of the general public, which were included in the activities of the FES are missing in the Global public policy network (GPPN) typology. As already outlined, the network members were mainly national actors and did not operate on the international level, which speaks against the GPPN. Furthermore, in 2009 the regional conflict was not a shared problem that existed across borders, making it even more difficult to speak of a GPPN.

The case largely confirmed the suggested forms of interaction between public and private actors as regards loose couplings and issue networks.[1555] The number of non-state actors in the network was relatively high and it can be expected that actors had different opinions on policy objectives. Furthermore, the permeability of the network in terms of new actors' inclusion was high as the FES generally integrated interested individuals. An

1552 *Dosch* (2004) p. 13.
1553 SPD (2007) pp. 19ff.
1554 See Ch. 8.2.3.3.
1555 See Ch. 2.3.1. and 3.1.1.

assessment of the network's integration into the policy making progress in Thailand was not possible. As outlined, the political situation in Thailand was fragile and characterised by a constant change of decision makers. We do not know if ideas from the activities of the FES were translated into the policy making process. In turn, we saw that the FES actively implemented parts of the AA's Asia strategy and of the EU's security policy. In this respect the network resembled a policy community actor.

9.2.4. Managing conflicts?

The FES's activities in the context of the conflict in Southern Thailand corresponded to all general tasks of transnational conflict management as outlined in the systematisation.[1556] They addressed trust-based communicative activities, dialogue on the security policy level, conflict analysis, knowledge generation on the conflict, and capacity building. Furthermore, several concrete conflict management instruments were visible in the FES's activities. The instruments were not clearly applied according to the conflict management cycle. This is not surprising as the smouldering conflict did not fit to the defined typical conflict phases. We could identify FES's ambitions in the field of Security Sector Reforms (SSR) when dialogues on security sector governance between the military, police forces and the political level were furthered together with the DCAF. Moreover, conflict resolution and track two were applied by the FES. Since we do not know how structured the dialogues between the decision makers in Bangkok and the community leaders from the South had been and whether the FES provided mainly logistical prerequisites for the direct talks, either mediation or good offices were applied. The commitment to several international principles was visible in FES activities. It supported local ownership by integrating local actors in the conflict to ensure the sustainability of the conflict management process. It also paid tribute to do-no-harm by being aware of the sensitivity of the activities. Finally, it furthered the principle outlined in UN resolution 1325 on the involvement of women in conflict management and their protection in conflicts. We furthermore noticed that the elements of conflict management and democracy assistance were linked in the approach of the FES. Conflict management activities in the South, for example, started under the premise of political development

1556 See Ch. 7.2.

and education and became proper, more systematic conflict management later on.

9.2.5. Impact of the FES

The impact of the FES as regards the management of conflict was difficult to estimate. Similar to the prior findings,[1557] the impact of the FES on the policy process in Thailand in terms of influence on peace furthering policies was neither found nor was it measurable. The same applies to measuring the FES's contribution to a conflict solution. According to the interview partner, it had not been the objective of the FES to resolve the conflict but rather to improve the framework conditions and further the motivation for a political solution of the conflict. In terms of success, the FES had been able to identify target groups which were working closely together with the FES and which had previously been uninvolved. Moreover, it had opened channels of communication between stakeholders that were necessary for a solution to the conflict. One concrete example of success was given by the interview partner. A delegation from the South had held talks in Bangkok with the university, the human rights commission and other institutions. It had criticised the fact that 170 young men had been released from an education camp but had not been allowed to return to their villages as they were considered a "security risk". Before the delegation went back to the Southern region, the grant permission was given for the return to the young men.[1558] However, it does not lead to results if the FES's impact is considered in terms of policy results and improvement of the conflict situation. On the other hand, we saw that the FES was involved in implementing German and European policy in Thailand. Moreover, the activities fit with the German role conception of civilian power in preferring non-military solutions to conflicts and in applying a broad notion of security.[1559] We also saw that the activities largely went beyond the broad policy formulations and that official reliance on the *Stiftungen* was already announced. German official activities through the embassy, for instance, had never been possible in the form of the FES's activities since the risk was already very high that activities would be viewed as interference.

1557 See Ch. 8.2.5.
1558 Interview a.
1559 See Ch. 7.2.

Estimating the impact of the FES in terms of communication, network operation and resources, we saw the confirmation of prior findings.[1560] The FES had a central position within the network and was mainly involved in its establishment. It often built a bridge between actors who were otherwise not connected. The target group, which included Thai public and private actors, was broad, although it did not include political party members. The desire of the German political foundations to also work with political and public levels[1561] was beneficial for the conflict management activities as it allowed the establishment of respective communication channels. We also saw that the FES adapted flexibly to a dearth of political partners by choosing members of the executive instead. It was also able to conduct activities with less political content, such as study trips for women and youth camps, if required. German politicians, members of the government, and ministerial staff members, on the contrary, were not included in the network. From the conflict management perspective concerning dialogues between *conflictive* parties, this was consistent. The FES's contribution to the relations between Thailand and Germany through the intensification of social-political links could therefore not be noted.

In 2009, at the end of the EU-funded project, the FES wanted to keep contact to the stakeholders in the South and did not want to set them adrift. Intensive work on the conflict, however, was not planned due to a lack of resources. Most of the interview partners were pessimistic about the development of the conflict.[1562] They claimed that political solutions and concepts barely existed. The conflict was completely left to the military. As long as Thailand faced inner political problems and the conflict remained limited to the Southern regions, politicians would not care for solutions.[1563] There was hardly international attention for the conflict since Thailand was "far away" and violence did not concern tourist areas.[1564] In 2015, the conflict in the Southern provinces still smouldered and had not transformed into peace, and the political situation had become more unstable. In follow-up interviews, the FES outlined that activities in the Southern region had not taken place in the last couple of years.[1565] In 2015, the FES office focused on political transformation (e.g. the facilitation of

1560 See Ch. 8.2.8.
1561 See Ch. 5.2.
1562 Interviews 1, 3, 4, 6.
1563 Interviews 1, 4.
1564 Interview 3.
1565 Interviews 15, 16.

dialogue on the political basic order), media, and political education in schools and with teachers as well as on socio-economic transformation in terms of progressive economic and social policy. Security sector related activities had been suspended due to the tense political situation. The situation in the Southern regions had neither changed nor improved. Some contacts existed to the former partners in the Southern regions and some Thai organisations were still active in the region, such as the academic institute of human rights and peace studies. In 2015, the FES did not plan to take up activities in the Southern region due to the complexity of the conflict and respective missing resources.[1566]

Conclusion

The case of the FES's activities in the context of the conflict in the Southern region of Thailand exemplified the public diplomacy ambitions of the German political foundations. It illustrated how the activities were connected to the catalytic and collaborative form of transnational conflict management. The current case substantiated the autonomy of the FES from the funder BMZ, the German embassy and the affiliated SPD in their activities on site. Presumably the funds from the EU had further enhanced its independence. The ambitions showed the primary use of dialogue instruments and the operation in a widely branched and mixed network environment which, however, mainly included relationships in Thailand. In this context, the FES operated as a gatekeeper and dialogue facilitator, encouraging different types of actors to address their ideas on the conflict solution. The absence of partners from affiliated political parties and political decision makers was overcome by the integration of ministerial staff members and those from other authorities into the network. Partners of the FES were supposed to have a progressive political background. Social democracy, though important for the FES in its decision on which objectives to pursue, did not play a role in partner selection. German actors participated only in part in the network environment. Interest of German politicians was minor, the conflict was too dangerous and the confidence environment too fragile to promote visits in the Southern regions. Still, high ideational correspondence was found with regards to German and EU policies for which the FES acted as a translator. Funding for the foundation's

1566 Interview 15.

activities in Thailand had even been kept up when development assistance declined and although there was no specific economic interest.

The activities of the FES as regards the conflict largely confirmed the general tasks of transnational conflict management and the support of the underlying international principles, such as do-no-harm, local ownership and the UN resolution 1325. Moreover, the specific tasks of SSR and conflict resolution were identified. We also observed the ability of the FES to connect its democracy assistance activities with conflict management.

The FES had several advantages compared to other international actors, such as the ability to work with actors from the social and political levels in Thailand as well as its moral authority. However, we also saw that such advantages are time-bound. They depend on a window of opportunity which had obviously been open in 2009 but was closed in 2015.

Chapter 10 – The role of the German political foundations in international relations

In this final chapter we summarise the evidence of this study regarding the transnational interaction of the German political foundations, as far as we have not yet done so in the conclusions of each chapter. We then connect these findings to the main research question on the role of the German political foundations in international relations by returning to the constructivist and rationalist assumptions on transnational actors. Finally, an explanation on the public funding of the German political foundations will be given.

The German political foundations were involved in transnational relations. We studied these relations in terms of transboundary interaction processes with the help of a public diplomacy model. While scholars generally observed increased transnational activities with the end of the Cold War, the international activities of the German political foundations date back to the 1960s. We identified the German political foundations as non-profit and public-interest-oriented transnational actors and more specifically as governmental-non-governmental-organisations (GONGOs). They were non-state actors since they were not active on behalf of the German government. They were not, as their public funding and their party-political affiliation might have originally indicated, tools of state power used to influence or manipulate foreign politics and civil society. The inability of the German government to control the foundations' international activities became particularly clear through the chapters.

In the context of these transnational interactions, the *Stiftungen* operated as public diplomats. At the same time, they targeted foreign populations, among others. *Hocking's* distinction between public diplomacy conducted by the public and public diplomacy targeting the public could therefore not be found.[1567] The *Stiftungen* neither declared public diplomacy as an objective nor did they practice it intentionally. Public diplomacy was considered more as a side effect. Furthermore, the foundations' public diplomacy was not presentational. Its main intention or objective was not to present a positive image of Germany abroad. Consequentially, we did not

1567 *Hocking* (2007), see Ch. 3.1.1.

identify public relation or national branding components in the foundations' activities. For East Asia, the German foreign office had announced that the German political foundations would actively assist the German image cultivation, but we did not find such "indirect" public diplomacy.[1568] Certainly, the foundations helped mediate German culture. However, they were not comparable to other German organisations active in German foreign and cultural policy. Although the foundations' public diplomacy approach included elements of mutual understanding in terms of two-way symmetric communication, such as cultural diplomacy and exchanges, their ambitions utilised persuasive asymmetric two-way communication practiced mainly with the help of consulting and a value-based political dialogue. The foundations' main objective was to convince the target audiences of their underlying values and norms. In the case of the KAS's RLP in Southeast Europe, this was democracy and more specifically rule of law, while in the case of the FES's program in Thailand, it concerned the creation of a peaceful situation and the sensitisation of the parties in conflict. The *Stiftungen* followed their independent agenda. Thus, their activities resembled diplomacy in its original understanding in terms of information gathering, policy advice and communication. Whether the public diplomacy of the German political foundations diminished the role of traditional diplomacy is not known. We saw that the foundations largely operated in network environments and were provided with various resources. These resources can be considered as soft power since they were not possessed by the other actors in the network who needed these resources. The German political foundations had generally more ideational and social resources than members of the German government, the parliament, personnel from the German ministries and other institutions. In comparison to foreign actors in the network, the *Stiftungen* possessed more material resources and partly more ideational and social resources. Moreover, we saw that the foundations had a high number of relationships and great centrality within the network. They had access to foreign political and civil society levels which could not be reached either by personnel from the German ministries, embassies or other institutions or by German government officials or parliamentarians. With regards to its program in Southeast Europe, the KAS established relations between foreign members of the network and those in Germany. In case of the FES, it connected actors in Thailand. The networking resources were hence employed differently by the foundations. While networking was something the foundations

1568 *Nye* (2004) p. 114.

were very aware of, they did not consider themselves as part of the network and their considerations did not include (possible) relationships with German actors. As transnational actors with a hybrid status, the *Stiftungen* were able to establish horizontal links to political actors and vertical connections to other non-state actors. In most cases, the foundations did not differentiate between collaboration with an international partner and a contact person in the network which is why we can assume that the contact was nearly as important as the partnership. In both cases it was a unique characteristic of the foundations that they could establish these connections and maintained mostly direct links to members of the network giving them a "bridging function" and a particular control of communication channels. This can be termed as communicative power or structural autonomy power.[1569] On the other hand, German public funding, i.e. material resources, made the foundations' activities possible in the first place. The environment between the political foundations and the German government was not characterised by a conflict-stereotype and public and private actors in the network generally needed each other. The network therefore embodied cooperation and absolute gains as members had mutual advantages. This derived from labour division and specific actor advantages which stemmed from the public or private characteristic of the specific actor. Although the foundations relied on public funding, their relative autonomy did not support the assumption of a states' primacy over transnational actors stated by the rationalist approaches. It instead substantiated our initial claim and the premise of constructivist thought of considering state actors and transnational actors as equally important.

In considering the network environment, we could observe that the typologies of transnational networks mostly did not fit to the foundations' undertakings. Although we found mixed networks including public and private actors in both case studies, the global issue was missing to qualify as a Global public policy network (GPPN). The subjects treated in the networks were national or regional problems. Certainly, they also appeared more broadly on the international agendas in terms of political development and peace. However, in this way almost every issue can be interpreted as a global problem. Furthermore, we did not see the involvement of international actors in the network, which goes against being described as GPPN. Although the *Stiftungen* might build such networks in global contexts, for example through the involvement of regional offices and those in industrialised countries, we have not studied these activities. Moreover, we

1569 *Jansen* (2006) p. 29.

have not analysed how the German political foundations interacted more structurally in international negotiation processes or within international organisations or institutions. Although we do not deny the foundations' participation in these environments, we observed that structured interactions neither took place regularly nor did they represent the foundations' everyday practice. Moreover, not all the *Stiftungen* were members in international organisations. Finally, the building of regimes or interaction within them could be observed neither for the KAS in Southeast Europe nor for the FES in Thailand. In contrast, multi-stakeholder diplomacy which *Hocking* considered a wise version of how governmental and non-governmental public diplomacy could be practiced,[1570] was already employed in Germany with the help of the German political foundations if we do not assume that these activities concern diplomatic negotiations only. Moreover, the activities of the *Stiftungen* did not support the assumption that "the advent of new actors has also given rise to new, unconventional modes of diplomacy".[1571] Their international practices have existed for several decades and the current public diplomacy instruments were largely those of 1973.[1572]

The German *Stiftungen* acted as democracy assistants and conflict managers. In both cases they primarily made use of dialogue public diplomacy instruments to undertake these activities and they operated in similar public diplomacy dimensions. They were therefore largely involved in collaborative and catalytic public diplomacy. The catalytic form of public diplomacy in terms of agenda-setting by transnational actors has only been touched upon.[1573] In this context, it would have been necessary to study a certain foundation's activity and its objective over a longer period of time and analyse the development of the issue on the foreign and German political agendas. We cannot therefore take a final position on these aspects. However, we saw that the foundations' transferred information and knowledge resources to German parliamentarians, to the committees of the German *Bundestag* and to the ministries on foreign and development political issues which then became part of the policy making process. More generally, we identified that the foundations' soft power resources in terms of knowledge on political situations and circumstances in foreign countries were passed on to the German political institutions and the affiliated political

1570 *Hocking* (2011), see Ch. 3.1.1.
1571 *Jönsson* (2002) p. 216.
1572 See BMZ (1973) pp. 65ff.
1573 *Hocking* (2011), see Ch. 3.1.1.

parties. This is resembled by the foundations' think tank activities and their reports to the ministries often containing information not available to the German embassies. Also, their public events in Germany on international matters were part of this called "feedback effect"[1574] which is the introduction of foreign information to Germany. We also encountered the foundations' networking resources in terms of connecting German politicians with their foreign counterparts.[1575] The foundations therefore introduced their soft power resources also into the German political process. However, some criticised that the foundations did not contribute enough of their potential and resources to the political process in Germany and that the existing capabilities of the German political foundations were not accessed enough. This was reasoned with a German disinterest in foreign policy and the tendency to take foreign political decisions primarily from a domestic political perspective which is electorally useful.[1576] Nonetheless, we noticed that the foundations were deeply involved in implementing German foreign and development policy abroad.

Social interaction, values and norms accented by constructivists became particular important for explaining how the foundations worked and what distinguished them from other actors. In their transnational interaction with foreign governments and civil society, they tried to diffuse values and acted as norm entrepreneurs towards foreign societies. Also, the building of networks by the German political foundations was norm and value driven. Moreover, in both cases, the concrete party-political background was substituted by an emphasis on a larger framework of Western political values, such as democracy and freedom. In both cases, the political foundations shared the political ideas of the German government as towards the two regions but also, more generally, as towards democracy assistance and conflict management. The implementation of German policies was the most likely reason that German politicians thought the *Stiftungen* were effective and reliable instruments of German foreign policy despite their contradicting relative autonomy. In both case studies, the foundations tried to target specific social or political disseminators that could support their cause. It caused difficulties when partners who shared these principled ideas were missing. In turn, the missing cooperation with politically affiliated partners was mostly substituted by working with members of the public administration. It was therefore not surprising that according to one in-

1574 *Bartsch* (2007) p. 287.

1575 See Ch. 5.2.4. and 5.3.2.2.

1576 Bartsch (2007) p. 287.

terview partner, the partners of the foundations in one country seemed to be interchangeable.[1577] Moreover, the involvement of the German political foundations in German policy implementation and the fact that several German ministries pursued different types of policies in the same region and towards the same subject showed the German foreign policy fragmentation. It also spoke against the unitary actor hypothesis of rationalist thought. Although this positively led to a pluralisation of policy, others criticised that the fragmented nature followed several interests to the detriment of the community.[1578] Contrary to the rationalist approaches, questions of high-level politics in terms of peace and security were handled by transnational actors, i.e. the FES in Southern Thailand. Finally, a German economic interest in the region was only stated for Southeast Europe and *Stiftungen*' activities promoting the economy could not be noted. To simply rationalise the continuous financial support of the foundations' international activities with German economic interests was therefore insufficient. Economic interests also could not explain the comprehensive network of foreign offices the foundations built up over decades. The support of these activities showed instead that the German state sought to spread Western values and peace even in areas where concrete interests were missing. In contrast to the assumptions of the rationalist approaches, we saw that in the international activities of the *Stiftungen*, "public" and "private" were not two separate spheres as the rationalist approaches assume. What *Stone* observed with regards to networks of think tanks is a rather "mythical separation" of public and private diplomacy which is maintained because it is useful to governments to make believe seemingly independent expertise and legitimacy of knowledge "outside" the state.[1579] This resembles the incorporation of NGOs by states and their "perpetuation" due to official funding.[1580] Read from a *Gramsci* perspective, the foundations' democratic assistance activities could particularly be part of the states' ambition to diffuse Western values and norms by pretending that the foundations as "civil society organisations" are norm entrepreneurs whereas they are indeed a state's extension. *Neo-Gramscian* historical materialism criticises constructivism by focussing on the usefulness or good nature of transnational actors and stresses the connectivity between the ideational and material dimension. *Wigger* outlined that behind the "allegedly independent ex-

1577 Interview 7.
1578 *Maull* (2015) p. 227.
1579 *Stone* (2011) pp. 259f.
1580 *Chandler* (2005) p. 163.

pert knowledge lurk important political questions that pertain to the distribution and concentration of power and economic wealth in society".[1581] This is connected to the question of *why* a particular set of ideas became dominant instead of asking *how* these ideas became important as constructivism does.[1582] In the current case this means looking at why the Federal Republic found it more important to spread these values with the help of the foundations instead of following material interests. We have tried to shed light on these aspects by looking in the respective chapters at the historical development of German public diplomacy, its development assistance and conflict management. The recurring focal point was the German civilian power identity which particularly emphasises values instead of hard material interests. Since military power was not an option for post-War Germany it prioritised soft power and focused from the 1960s onwards on economic and technological competence, social stability and other aspects of a "peaceful" foreign policy. It included cultural and political charisma as well as a foreign policy that is based to a large extent on civil society components and non-governmental actors.[1583] The conscious turn towards the system of Western democratic and liberal values which found its normative ground in the German Basic Law was important for Germany to win back credibility and to be able to develop politically and economically.[1584] Identity needs recognition i.e. a socially constructed category that others acknowledge as a certain kind worthy of respect[1585] and which depends on the consistency of words and actions in the process of interaction.[1586] In this context, the German political foundations have been mentioned as contributing to the socialisation of German foreign policy.[1587] The German political foundations helped Germany to maintain its civilian power identity. Through the support of the German political foundations, the characteristic of "value drivenness" was expressed to the outside and manifested the Federal Republic's focus on soft power. It reproduced the perception of being a civilian power in terms of social practice, created predictability and diminished uncertainty especially for those countries in and outside Europe carefully watching German foreign ambitions. With the continuous support of the *Stiftungen*, even when the possi-

1581 *Wigger* (2011) p. 92.
1582 *Bieler/Morton* (2008) pp. 106ff.
1583 *Staak* (2007) p. 91.
1584 *Gareis* (2006) p. 82.
1585 *Williams* (2001) p. 532.
1586 *Fierke* (2005) p. 182.
1587 *Schneider-Deters* (2005) p. 108.

bility for hard power politics became increasingly thinkable after reunification, Germany practiced the logic of appropriateness as it followed the values, norms and social role of its civilian power identity. This led to a blurred distinction between foreign and domestic policy and the projection of the domestic environment into the international environment. The assumption that the German state identity is conditioned by historical, cultural, political and social contexts[1588] is the key explanatory factor for the constant furthering of the German political foundations' international activities by the German parliament and government even in regions where material interests were absent. It also explains why Germany did not turn self-interestedly and egotistically to hard power instead. In summary, the role of the German political foundations can therefore be best described as functional providers of ideational and social resources, as transnational value and norm diffusers as well as German identity reproducers.

A point of critique toward the constructivist framework is that it does not pose the question of *cui bono*, for whom activities take place.[1589] Consequentially, we need to look at who benefited from the undertakings of the German political foundations. Chapters 6 and 7 have outlined the advantages for the German government which lie in the foundations' democracy assistance and conflict management activities. This included an extended room for manoeuvre though the foundations' work with various types of actors, their economic efficiency and their protection of international relations on a long-term basis. The historical overview on the motivation of equipping the German foundations with significant funds produced a mixed situation: While the outsourcing of activities to the *Stiftungen* had happened purposefully, the foundations were on the other hand provided with great autonomy. The activities of the foundations in recent times did not exclusively benefit the German government. However, as the network model showed, political actors, civil society organisations and individuals abroad and in Germany gained from these undertakings as well. Especially the Thailand case showed that the activities of the FES were largely designed to further the peacefulness of foreign societies while German actors were mostly not involved. The activities of the *Stiftungen* largely created a win-win situation for the foreign and German network members. The impulse of where and how to be active was taken by the foundations alone and concepts were developed independently.

1588 *Van Ham* (2008) pp. 145f.
1589 *Bieler/Morton* (2008) p. 113.

What we did not analyse in this study is whether the spreading of values and norms by the foundations was successful and whether it indeed caused social change over a longer period of time. Likewise, we cannot take a final position as regards the soft power of the German political foundations in terms of ideational persuasion power, preferences' shaping, setting the political agenda and "getting others to want what you want".[1590] As already outlined, it is difficult, to measure norm or value diffusion effects or how they impact on public attitudes and policy results.[1591] The interview partners found it particularly difficult to estimate the success of the *Stiftungen*. They either had a mixed impression on the success or outlined that they were not working towards an overall successful result. In Thailand we witnessed that the FES could not and did not want to continue its conflict management although the conflict was not resolved. Returning to *Cross's* explanation, we could try to draw the conclusion that the ideas the FES and their partners transmitted were not appealing to the audience that could react to it with respective policies (at the official levels) or to those unknown actors who were fuelling the conflict. Alternatively, the narrative used was not understood by those actors.[1592] However, we do not know whether the FES's narratives even reached both groups. In the words of *Scott-Smith*, "constructivism offers useful insights into the diffusion of ideas and helps to investigate when, why, and how ideas travel, and change occurs. Admittedly, countless other channels besides public diplomacy exist through which ideas travel".[1593] We also observed that the existence of soft power resources did not necessarily translated into actual soft power in terms of a desired result. Moreover, we should not confuse links to policy makers with influence on the political agenda. Finally, we have not systematically analysed how the network environment of transnational interaction developed over time and we cannot say whether the network became denser eventually. The Thailand case did not support the assumption. It showed instead that explanations, as constructivism highlights, were time bound[1594] and depended largely on the political circumstances.

This study is a first step to generate knowledge on the transnational interactions of the German political foundations. Still, to study profoundly every single aspect of the integrated public diplomacy model was impossi-

1590 See Ch. 2.2.2 and 3.1.1.
1591 *Risse-Kappen* (1995) p. 8.
1592 *Cross* (2013), see Ch. 3.1.1.
1593 *Scott-Smith* (2008) p. 186.
1594 *Barnett* (2011) p. 158.

ble due to its complexity of many different thoughts and ideas. Rather, the intention was to do a preliminary inventory on this neglected subject. Particularly, in-depth knowledge still needs to be produced on the moral authority resource of the *Stiftungen* as well as their perceived credibility abroad. Data from the foundations' partner organisations was not available and we had to fall back on opinions of other actors on these perceptions which obviously cannot substitute the original view. As regards the credibility of the German political foundations abroad, we could observe that the *Stiftungen* had some flexibility as to how they presented themselves towards their partners and audience. If they thought that a proximity to the German government was helpful, they put this characteristic to the fore. If they wanted to keep their distance from public bodies or even the affiliated political party, they were able to emphasise their "non-governmentalness" implied by the use of "foundation" in their name. Future research should include interviews with the partner organisations of the German political foundations abroad. For the data collection it should be considered that the foundations are partly reluctant about their contacts and access to partners is often not possible. Researchers therefore should proceed with patience and allow some time for being accepted and trusted by the foundation. Finally, we have not discussed the legitimacy of public diplomacy and whether the foundations' activities undermine political accountability or open up the political process to the public. According to *Jönsson*, representation in terms of "acting on behalf of" is "a key function of diplomacy and is recognised by most observers, regardless of theoretical background".[1595] The question remains whom the foundations represent. In their eyes they might embody the common good. However, they largely diffuse Western values and implement German foreign policy. Therefore, they are not, as some authors assume, only active in the "pre-political" sphere.[1596] Problems can occur when contacts are maintained with autocratic regimes, such as the HSS sponsoring *Gnassingbé Eyadéma* in Togo.[1597] During his military dictatorship between 1967 and 2005 several violations of human rights were committed. Future research needs to consider these representational issues.

Around the turn of the Millennium, *Mair* identified three threats for the German political foundations' international activities: Firstly, the growing competition in the field of the promotion of democracy; secondly, the re-

1595 *Jönsson* (2002) p. 213.
1596 *Pogorelskaja* (2002a) pp. 33f.
1597 *Nuscheler* (2005) p. 467.

duction of public funding; and thirdly, the new focus on conflict prevention in which the foundations were not active.[1598] At the time of writing, the situation was different. After a decrease of public funding in the 1990s, the state subsidies for the foundations had been significantly increased in the last years. As we have seen, the foundations also managed to largely integrate conflict management into their activities and to even connect it to their undertakings in democracy assistance. The competition with other actors was still visible. Both case studies showed a strong competition with U.S. government sponsored aiding organisations on site. However, we observed that the German political foundations encountered this situation with an excess of moral authority. The only current threat for the German political foundations' international activities might be the turn away from the German role conception of civilian power.

1598 *Mair* (2000) p. 145.

Bibliography[1599]

AA (Auswärtiges Amt) (1980a) '229, Aufzeichnungen des stellvertretenden SPD-Vorsitzenden Wischnewski, 9. August 1980, Helmut Schmidt-Archiv 1/HSAA 009411', printed in *Akten zur Auswärtigen Politik der Bundesrepublik Deutschland 1980*, 2011, Band 1, 1. Januar bis 30. Juni 1980 (München: Oldenbourg Verlag): 1209-15.

– (1980b) '255, Runderlass des Vortragenden Legationsrats Boll, 2. September1980, Referat 012, Bd. 115730', printed in *Akten zur Auswärtigen Politik der Bundesrepublik Deutschland 1980*, 2011, Band 1, 1. Januar bis 30. Juni 1980 (München: Oldenbourg Verlag): 1337-9.

– (2000) *Auswärtige Kulturpolitik – Konzeption 2000*, Berlin.

– (2002a) *Report on the Special Inspection of 14 German Embassies in the Countries of the European Union, Ambassador K.-Th. Paschke*, Berlin.

– (2002b) *Aufgaben der deutschen Außenpolitik, Südostasien, Australien, Neuseeland und Pazifische Inseln am Beginn des 21. Jahrhunderts*, Mai 2002, Berlin.

– (2005) *Deutsche Außenpolitik 2004/2005*, Berlin.

– (2010a) *Krisenprävention mit zivilen Mitteln, Ein Beitrag zu Frieden und Sicherheit*, Berlin.

– (2010b) *Dialog zwischen den Kulturen – Dialogue among Civilizations*, Berlin.

– (2011a) *Auswärtige Kultur- und Bildungspolitik in Zeiten der Globalisierung, Partner gewinnen, Werte vermitteln, Interessen vertreten*, Berlin.

– (2011b) *Auswärtige Kultur- und Bildungspolitik 2010/2011*, Bericht der Bundesregierung, Berlin.

– (2012a) *Abteilung Kultur und Kommunikation*, Berlin.

– (2012b) *Bericht der Bundesregierung zur Zusammenarbeit zwischen der Bundesrepublik Deutschland und den Vereinten Nationen und einzelnen, global agierenden, internationalen Organisationen und Institutionen im Rahmen des VN-Systems in den Jahren 2010 und 2011*, Berlin.

– (2014) *Auswärtige Kultur- und Bildungspolitik 2012/2013*, Bericht der Bundesregierung, Berlin.

– (2015) *Auswärtige Kultur- und Bildungspolitik 2013/2014*, Bericht der Bundesregierung, Berlin.

AAPA (Auswärtiges Amt, Political Archive) B58-IIIB1 Bd. 387 23/10/1963: 'Die Deutsche Entwicklungshilfe 1956-63', Bonn.

1599 Online resources and websites have been accessed on 24/01/2016 unless specified differently.

- B58-IIIB1 Bd. 387 26/10/1964: 'Beitrag der Abeteilung III zum Tätigkeitsbericht „Deutsche Außenpolitik 1964"', Bonn.
- B58-IIIB1 Bd. 387 20/05/1965: 'Vermerk Algerienkonferenz, Ende Juni 1965: Entwicklungspolitik ist Außenpolitik', Bonn.
- B58-IIIB1 Bd 651 15/03/1965: 'Entwicklungshilfe nicht an Hallsteindoktrin koppeln', Bonn.
- B58-IIIB2 Bd. 304 7/03/1963: 'Konstituierung des Interministeriellen Ausschusses für Bildungs- und Sozialhilfe', Bonn.
- Zwischenarchiv 118163: 'Wesentliche Auszüge aus dem zweiten Bericht über die vom Bundesministerium geförderten Arbeit der politischen Stiftungen in Entwicklungsländern dem Ausschuss für wirtschaftliche Zusammenarbeit des deutschen Bundestages vorgelegt im August 1973', Bonn.
- B58/1 Bd. 872: 'Überprüfung der Ergebnisse deutscher Entwicklungshilfe durch die deutschen Botschaften, hier: Mittel und Lateinamerika, von Asuncition bis Tegucigalpa', 1969, Bonn.

AA/BMVg/BMZ (Auswärtiges Amt/Bundesverteidigungsministerium/Bundesministerium für Zusammenarbeit und Entwicklung) (2012) *Für eine kohärente Politik der Bundesregierung gegenüber fragilen Staaten, Ressortübergreifende Leitlinien*, August 2012, Berlin.

Abirafeh, Lina (2005) *Lessons from Gender-focused International Aid in Post-Conflict Afghanistan ... Learned?*, Friedrich-Ebert-Stiftung, Bonn, Berlin.

Adam, Erfried (2012) *Vom mühsamen Geschäft der Demokratieförderung, Die internationale Entwicklungszusammenarbeit der Friedrich-Ebert-Stiftung* (Bonn: Dietz).

Adler, Emanuel (1997) 'Seizing the Middle Ground: Constructivsm in World Politics', *European Journal of International Relations*, 3(3): 319-63.

Aharoni, Sarai (2007) 'Die Herausforderung von Consciousness Raising im Kontext von Konflikten. Eine israelische Perspektive', in Klein, A./Roth, S. (eds) *NGOs im Spannungsfeld zwischen Krisenprävention und Sicherheitspolitik* (Wiesbaden: VS Verlag): 263-74.

ai (Amnesty International) (2009) *Report, Zur weltweiten Lage der Menschenrechte, Thailand* (Frankfurt am Main: S. Fischer Verlag): 454-57.

Amos, Julia (2014) 'The non-profits of peace, Conflict resolution NGOs', in Hall, R. (ed) *Reducing Armed Violence with NGO Governance* (London: Rouledge): 146-64.

Andersen, Uwe (2005) *Entwicklung und Entwicklungspolitik*, Bundeszentrale für politische Bildung (ed) Information 286 zur politischen Bildung (München: Francis' print&media).

Anholt, Simon (2005) 'Marke Rechtschaffenheit. Deutschlands „Brand Image" und seine Trümpfe für eine erfolgreiche Vermarktung', *Zeitschrift für Kulturaustausch*, 3+4: 64-67.

Arnim, Hans Herbert von (1992) 'Parteinstaat – der Staat als Beute?', in Schiller, T. (ed) *Parteien und Gesellschaft* (Stuttgart: Hirzel): 72-87.

– (1993) *Der Staat als Beute – Wie Politiker in eigener Sache Gesetze machen* (München: Droemer Knauer).

Arts, Bas (2000) 'Regimes, Non-State Actors and the State System: A "Structurational" Regime Model', *European Journal of International Relations*, 6(4): 513-42.

Askew, Marc (2007) *Conspiracy, Politics, and a Disorderly Border: The Struggle to Comprehend Insurgency in Thailand's Deep South* (Washington: East West Center).

Auga, Michèle (2007) *Crisis and Wars in Times of Globalization, How German Crisis Prevention and Peace Building could help*, Compass 2020, March 2007, FES, Berlin.

Avello, Maria (2008) *European Efforts in Transitional Justice*, Working Paper 58, June 2008, Fundación para las Relaciones Internacionales y el Diálogo Exterior (FRIDE), Madrid.

Azar, Edeward (2002) 'Protracted Social Conflicts and Second Track Diplomacy', in Davies, J./Kaufman, E. (eds) *Second Track/Citizens' Diplomacy, Concepts and Techniques for Conflict Transformation* (Lanham: Rowman & Littlefield): 15-30.

Bachrach, Peter/Baratz, Morton (1963) 'Decisions and Nondecisions: An Analytical Framework', *American Political Science Review* (September 1963): 632-42.

Baker, Gideon/Chandler, David (2005) 'Introduction, Global civil society and the future of world politics', in Chandler, D./Baker, G. (eds) *Global Civil Society* (Abingdon: Routledge): 1-14.

Bakker, Edwin (2001) 'Early Warning by NGOs in Conflict Areas', in Arts, B./Noortmann, M./Reinalda, B. (eds) *Non-State Actors in International Relations* (Ashgate: Aldershot): 263-277.

Banpasirichote, Chantana (2004) 'Civil Society Discourses and the Future of Radical Environmental Movements in Thailand', in Hock Guan, L. (ed) *Civil Society in Southeast Asia* (Singapore: ISEAS Publications): 234-64.

Barak, Oren/Cohen, Chanan (2014) 'Introduction', in Miodownik, D./Barak, O. (eds) *Nonstate Actors in Intrastate conflicts* (Philadelphia: University of Pennsylvania Press): 1-11.

Barnett, Michael (2011) 'Social constructivism', in Baylis, J./Smith, S./Owens, P. (eds) *The Globalisation of World Politics*, 5th edn (Oxford: Oxford University Press): 149-65.

Barney, Jay (1991) 'Firm Resources and Sustained Competitive Advantage', *Journal of Management*, 7(1): 99-120.

Barth, Kuno (1986) 'Die Parteistiftungen vor dem Bundesverfassungsgericht', *Betriebsberater, Zeitschrift für Recht und Wirtschaft*, 41(15): 949-53.

Bartsch, Sebastian (1998) 'Politische Stiftungen: Grenzgänger zwischen Gesellschafts- und Staatenwelt', in Kaiser, K./Eberwein, W.-D. (eds) *Deutschlands neue Außenpolitik, Band 4: Institutionen und Ressourcen* (München: Oldenbourg Verlag): 185-98.

– (2007) 'Politische Stiftungen', in Schmidt, S./Hellmann, G./Wolf, R. (eds) *Handbuch zur deutschen Außenpolitik* (Wiesbaden: VS Verlag): 280-89.

Basu, Moushumi (2011) 'Non-State Actors in the Development Aid World as seen from the South', in Reinalda, B. (ed) *The Ashgate Research Companion to Non-State Actors* (Surrey: Ashgate Publishing Limited): 405-17.

Baumann, Rainer (2007) 'Deutschland als Europas Zentralmacht', in Schmidt, S./Hellmann, G./Wolf, R. (eds) *Handbuch zur deutschen Außenpolitik* (Wiesbaden: VS Verlag): 62-72.

Beall, Jo/Goodfellow, Thomas/Putzel, James (2006) 'Introductory article: on the discourse of terrorism, security and development', *Journal of international development*, 18 (1): 51-67.

Beaugrand, Günter (2003) *Die Konrad-Adenauer-Stiftung*, Konrad-Adenauer-Stiftung e.V., Sankt Augustin.

– (2005) 'Zurück zu den Anfängen: Zur Entstehungsgeschichte der Konrad-Adenauer-Stiftung', *Die politische Meinung: Monatsschrift zu Fragen der Zeit*, 50(432): 71-9.

Becker, Howard (1998) *Tricks of the Trade: How to Think about Your Research while Doing It* (Chicago: University of Chicago Press).

Bender, Peter (2008) 'Deutsche Außenpolitik: Vernunft und Schwäche', *Aus Politik und Zeitgeschichte*, 43/2008: 3-6.

Berridge, G.R./James, Alan (2003) *A dictionary of diplomacy*, 2nd edn (London: Palgrave Macmillan).

Beswick, Danielle (2011) 'Aiding State Building and Sacrificing Peace Building? The Rwanda-UK relationship 1994-2011', *Third World Quarterly*, 32(10): 1911-30.

Betsill, Michelle M./Corell, Elisabeth (2008) *NGO diplomacy: The influence of nongovernmental organisations in international environment negotiations* (Massachusetts: Massachusetts Institute of Technology).

Bettzuege, Reinhard (2007) 'Auswärtiger Dienst', in Schmidt, S./Hellmann, G./Wolf, R. (eds) *Handbuch zur deutschen Außenpolitik* (Wiesbaden: VS Verlag): 225-45.

Betz, Joachim (1996) 'Die Demokratieexportpolitik der Bundesrepublik Deutschland', in Hanisch, R. (ed) *Demokratieexport in die Länder des Südens?* (Hamburg: Deutsches Übersee-Institut): 203-30.

Beyer, Bianca (2002) *Politische Stiftungen: Die Bedeutung der Stiftungstätigkeit für die Parteien*, Diplomarbeit, Freie Universität Berlin.

Biekart, Kees (2001) 'The impact of Private Aid Agencies on Civil Society Development', in Arts, B./Noortmann, M./Reinalda, B. (eds) *Non-State Actors in International Relations* (Aldershot: Ashgate): 247-62.

Bieler, Andreas/Morton, Adam D. (2008) 'The Deficits of Discourse in IPE: turning base metal into gold?', *International Studies Quarterly*, 52(1): 103-28.

Bloomfield, David (2006) *On Good Terms: Clarifying Reconciliation*, Bergdorf Report No. 14, October 2006, Bergdorf Research Centre for Constructive Conflict Management.

Blumer, Herbert (1954) 'What is wrong with social theory?', *American Sociological Review*, 19(1): 3-10.

BMVg (Bundesministerium der Verteidigung) (1992) *Verteidigungspolitische Richtlinien*, 29/11/1992, Bonn.

– (2006) *Weißbuch 2006, Zur Sicherheitspolitik Deutschlands und zur Zukunft der Bundeswehr*, Berlin.

– (2011) *Verteidigungspolitische Richtlinien*, 27/05/2011, Berlin.

BMZ (Bundesministerium für wirtschaftliche Zusammenarbeit und Entwicklung) (1973) *Grundsätze für die entwicklungspolitische Zusammenarbeit zwischen der Bundesregierung und den politischen Stiftungen*, Bericht an den Ausschuss für wirtschaftliche Zusammenarbeit, Bonn: 63-72.

– (1983) *Fünfter Bericht über die Entwicklungspolitik der Bundesrepublik Deutschland*, Bonn, reproduced in Kress (1985): 8f.

– (2003) *Aktionsprogramm 2015, Armut bekämpfen, gemeinsam handeln, der Beitrag der Bundesregierung zur weltweiten Halbierung extremer Armut*, 2nd edn, Bonn.

– (2004a) *Sozialstrukturförderung*, Grundsatzpapier, 1/09/2004, Bonn.

– (2004b) *Ankerländer – Partner für globale Entwicklung*, Ein Positionspapier des BMZ, 10/12/2004, Bonn.

– (2005) *Übersektorales Konzept zur Krisenprävention, Konfliktbearbeitung und Friedensförderung in der deutschen Entwicklungszusammenarbeit, Eine Strategie zur Friedensentwicklung* (Strategy for Peacebuilding), June 2005, Berlin.

– (2007) *Krisenpräventive Wirkung der entwicklungspolitischen Zusammenarbeit mit Zentralasien – Aktuelle Debatten über Instrumente und Optionen, Bericht über einen Workshop am 1. und 2. Dezember 2005*, BMZ Spezial 143, Bonn, Berlin.

– (2008) *Leitlinien für die bilaterale finanzielle und technische Zusammenarbeit mit Kooperationspartnern der deutschen Entwicklungszusmmenarbeit*, BMZ Konzepte 165, Bonn, Berlin.

– (2009) *Förderung von Good Governance in der deutschen Entwicklungszuammenarbeit*, BMZ Konzepte 172, Bonn, Berlin.

– (2010) *Die Förderung konstruktiver Staat-Gesellschafts-Beziehungen – Legitimität, Transparenz, Rechenschaft*, Bonn, Berlin.

– (2011a) *Die "Sozialstrukturförderung" in der nicht -staatlichen Entwicklungszusammenarbeit Kurzfassung der Evaluierung*, BMZ-Evaluierungsberichte 063, Bonn, Berlin.

– (2011b) *Deutsche Entwicklungspolitik in Asien, Ein strategischer Rahmen*, BMZ Strategiepapier 10/2011, BMZ: Bonn, Berlin.

– (2012) *Die Schwerpunkte der Deutschen Entwicklungspolitik*, Bonn, Berlin.

– (2013a) *Participating, engaging, making a difference, Strategy on working with civil society in German development policy*, BMZ Strategy Paper 8/2013e, Berlin.

– (2013b) *14. Entwicklungspolitischer Bericht der Bundesregierung, Weißbuch zur Entwicklungspolitik – Kurzfassung*, 2nd edn, Bonn, Berlin.

– (2013c) *Entwicklung für Frieden und Sicherheit: Entwicklungspolitisches Engagement im Kontext von Konflikt, Fragilität und Gewalt*, BMZ-Strategiepapier 3/2013, Bonn, Berlin.

Bob, Clifford (2014) 'The transnational battle over gun control, implications for NGO governance', in Hall, R. (ed) *Reducing Armed Violence with NGO Governance*, (Rouledge: London): 133-45.

Bodemer, Klaus (2002) 'Entwicklungspolitik der Bundesrepublik Deutschland', in Nohlen, D. (ed) *Lexikon Dritte Welt* (Reinbek: Rowohlt Taschenbuch): 235-40.

Böhler, Werner (1991) 'Entwicklungszusammenarbeit einer politischen Stiftung: Über Partnerorganisation und Politikdialog', in Gleich, A. von/Kohlhepp, G./ Mols, M. (eds) *Neue Konzepte in der Entwicklungszusammenarbeit mit Lateinamerika?* (Hamburg: Institut für Iberoamerika-Kunde): 128-35.

– (2005) 'Die Rolle der politischen Stiftungen in der deutschen Entwicklungspolitik', *Auslandsinformationen*, 5/07/2005, Konrad-Adenauer-Stiftung e.V., Berlin: 4-14.

Börzel, Tanja A. (1998) 'Organizing Babylon – On the different Conceptions of Policy Networks', *Public Administration*, 76 (Summer): 253-73.

Börzel, Tanja A./Risse, Thomas (2005) 'Public-Private Partnerships: Effective and Legitimate Tools of International Governance?', in Grande, E./Pauly, L. (eds) *Complex Sovereignty: On the Reconstruction of Political Authority in the 21st Century* (Toronto: University of Toronto Press): 195-216.

Bolewski, Winfried (2007) *Diplomacy and International Law in Globalized Relations* (Berlin: Springer).

Borchard, Michael (2004) 'Politische Stiftungen und Politische Beratung', in Dagger, S./Greiner, C./Leinert, K./Melìß, N./Menzel, A. (eds) *Politikberatung in Deutschland, Praxis und Perspektiven* (Wiesbaden: VS Verlag): 90-7.

Born, Manfred (2007) *Parteinahe Stiftungen: Stiftung oder Partei?* (Stuttgart: Richard Boorberg Verlag).

Borries, Bodo von (2007) 'Partnerschaft strategischer Denken? Erfahrungen mit der „Multiplikateursperspektive" in der Krisenprävention', in Klein, A./Roth, S. (eds) *NGOs im Spannungsfeld von Krisenprävention und Sicherheitspolitik* (Wiesbaden: VS Verlag): 191-204.

Bos, Ellen (2007) 'Die GUS-Staaten', in Schmidt, S./Hellmann, G./Wolf, R. (eds) *Handbuch zur deutschen Außenpolitik* (Wiesbaden: VS Verlag): 455-67.

Bourdieu, Pierre (1983) 'Ökonomisches Kapital - Kulturelles Kapital - Soziales Kapital', in Kreckel, R. (ed) *Soziale Ungleichheiten*, (Göttingen: Schwartz): 183-98.

BPB (Bundeszentrale für politische Bildung) (2014) *Vor 20 Jahren: Urteil zu Auslandseinsätzen*, Politik: Hintergrund Aktuell, 10/07/2014.

Brandenburger, Adam/Nalebuff, Barry (1996) *Co-Opetition: A Revolution Mindset That Combines Competition and Cooperation* (New York: Doubleday).

Brandt, Willy et al. (1980) *North-South: A Program for Survival, The Report of the Independent Commission on International Development Issues under the Chairmanship of Willy Brandt* (London: Pan Books).

Bredow, von Winfried (2006) 'Neue Herausforderungen', in Bundeszentrale für politische Bildung (ed), *Sicherheitspolitik im 21. Jahrhundert* (BPB: Bonn): 4-10.

Brenner, Torsten (2012) 'Responsibility to Protect', *Internationale Politik*, 2 (März/ April 2012): 62-7.

Brock, Lothar (2004) 'Der erweiterte Sicherheitsbegriff: Keine Zauberformel für die Begründung ziviler Konfliktbearbeitung', *Die Friedens-Warte*, 79(3-4): 323-44.

Brounéus, Karen (2007) *Reconciliation and Development, in: Dialogue on Globalisation*, Occasional Papers Berlin, Friedrich-Ebert-Stiftung, No 36/November 2007, Berlin.

Brown, Chris (1992) *International Relations Theory: New Normative Approaches* (Hemel Hempstead: Harvesters Wheatsheaf).

Bryden, Alan (2006) 'Towards a security governance agenda in post-conflict peacebuilding,' *Sicherheit und Frieden*, 1: 20-6.

Bryman, Alan (2016) *Social Science Methods*, 5th edn (Oxford: Oxford University Press).

BT (Deutscher Bundestag) (1973) *Unterrichtung durch die Bundesregierung, Bericht zur Entwicklungspolitik der Bundesregierung*, BT-Drs. 07/1236, 9/11/1973, Bonn.

– (1990) *Antwort der Bundesregierung auf die Kleine Anfrage des Abgeordneten Volmer und der Fraktion DIE GRÜNEN, Aktivitäten der Konrad-Adenauer-Stiftung in Nicaragua im Vorlauf der Wahlen 1990 (BT-Drs. 11/6381)*, BT-Drs. 11/636, 16/02/1990, Bonn.

– (1991) *Rede des Bundesministers der wirtschaftlichen Zusammenarbeit, Carl-Dieter Spranger, Stenographischer Bericht*, BT-Drs. 12/47, 10/10/1991, Bonn.

– (1993) *Unterrichtung durch den Bundespräsidenten, Empfehlung der Kommission unabhängiger Sachverständiger zur Parteinfinanzierung*, BT-Drs. 12/4425, 19/02/1993, Bonn.

– (1995) *Antwort der Bundesregierung auf die große Anfrage der Abgeordneten Dr. Barbara Höll, Dr. Christa Luft und die Gruppe der PDS (BT-Drs. 13835) – Finanzierung von Parteien und Parteinahen Stiftungen*, BT-Drs. 13/1895, 29/06/1995, Bonn.

– (2000) *Schriftliche Fragen mit den in der Zeit vom 14. bis 25. August 2000 eingegangenen Antworten der Bundesregierung*, BT-Drs. 14/4019, 25/08/2000, Berlin.

– (2002) *Unterrichtung durch die Bundesregierung, Bericht über den Stand der Entwicklung und Reformmaßnahmen bei der medialen Außenrepräsentanz*, BT-Drs. 14/9502, 30/05/2002, Berlin.

– (2004) *Plenarprotokoll*, BT-Drs. 15/97, 11/03/2004, Berlin.

– (2010a) *Unterrichtung der Bundesregierung, Bericht der Bundesregierung zur Zusammenarbeit zwischen der Bundesrepublik Deutschland und den Vereinten Nationen und einzelnen, global agierenden, internationalen Organisationen und Institutionen im Rahmen des VN-Systems in den Jahren 2008 und 2009*, BT-Drs. 17/2726, 5/08/2010, Berlin.

– (2010b) *Antwort der Bundesregierung auf die Kleine Anfrage der Abgeordneten Stefan Liebich, Katrin Werner, Niema Movassat, weiterer Abgeordneter und der Fraktion DIE LINKE (BT-Drs. 17/2526)*, BT-Drs. 17/2670, 23/07/2010, Berlin.

– (2011a) *Plenarprotokoll*, BT-Drs. 17/148, 14/12/2011, Berlin.

– (2011b) *Schriftliche Fragen mit denen in der Woche vom 25. Juli 2011 eingegangenen Antworten der Bundesregierung*, BT-Drs. 17/6712, 29/07/2011, Berlin.

– (2011c) *Unterrichtung durch die Bundesregierung, Bericht der Bundesregierung über die Ergebnisse ihrer Bemühungen um die Weiterentwicklung der politischen und ökonomischen Gesamtstrategie für die Balkanstaaten und ganz Südosteuropa*, BT-Drs. 17/5590, 14/04/2011, Berlin.

– (2013) *Unterrichtung der Bundesregierung, 16. Bericht der Bundesregierung zur Auswärtigen Kultur- und Bildungspolitik 2011/2012*, BT-Drs. 17/12052, 9/01/2013, Berlin.

Buchstein, Hubertus (2006) 'Demokratie,' in Göhler, G./Iser, M./Kerner, I. (eds) *Politische Theorie* (Wiesbaden: VS Verlag): 45-64.

Bundesrechnungshof (2014) *Bemerkungen 2014 zur Haushalts- und Wirtschaftsprüfung des Bundes*, Bonn.

Bundesregierung (2001) *Aktionsprogramm 2015: Armut bekämpfen, gemeinsam handeln, Der Beitrag zur Bundesregierung zur weltweiten Halbierung extremer Armut*, April 2001, Berlin.

– (2004) *Aktionsplan „Zivile Krisenprävention, Konfliktlösung und Friedenskonsolidierung"*, 12/05/2004, Berlin.

– (2006) *Sicherheit und Stabilität durch Krisenprävention gemeinsam stärken, 1. Bericht der Bundesregierung über die Umsetzung des Aktionsplans „Zivile Krisenprävention, Konfliktlösung und Friedenskonsolidierung"*, Berichtszeitraum Mai 2004 bis April 2006, Berlin.

– (2007) *Bericht der Bundesregierung über Maßnahmen zur Umsetzung von Resolution 1325 des Sicherheitsrats der Vereinten Nationen („Frauen, Frieden und Sicherheit")*, November 2007, Berlin.

– (2008) *Krisenprävention als gemeinsame Aufgabe, 2. Bericht der Bundesregierung über die Umsetzung des Aktionsplans „Zivile Krisenprävention, Konfliktlösung und Friedenskonsolidierung"*, Berichtszeitraum: Mai 2006 bis April 2008, Berlin.

– (2010) *3. Bericht der Bundesregierung über die Umsetzung des Aktionsplans „Zivile Krisenprävention, Konfliktlösung und Friedenskonsolidierung"*, Berichtszeitraum Mai 2008 bis April 2010, Berlin.

– (2012a) *Globalisierung gestalten, Partnerschaften aufbauen, Verantwortung teilen: Konzept der Bundesregierung*, Auswärtiges Amt, Berlin.

– (2012b) *Aktionsplan der Bundesregierung zur Umsetzung von Resolution 1325 des Sicherheitsrates der Vereinten Nationen für den Zeitraum 2013 bis 2016*, 19/12/2012, Berlin.

– (2014) *Vierter Bericht der Bundesregierung über Maßnahmen zur Umsetzung von Resolution 1325 des Sicherheitsrats der Vereinten Nationen zu Frauen, Frieden und Sicherheit, im Zeitraum August 2010 bis Dezember 2013*, Berlin.

Burnell, Peter (2000a) 'Democracy Assistance: The State of the Discourse,' in Burnell, P. (ed) *Democracy Assistance, International Co-operation for Democratization*, (Oxon: Frank Cass Publishers): 3-33.

– (2000b) 'Democracy Assistance: Origins and Organizations,' in Burnell, P. (ed) *Democracy Assistance, International Co-operation for Democratization*, (Oxon: Frank Cass Publishers): 34-64.

– (2006) 'Unterstützung für politische Parteien in neuen Demokratien: Parteiensysteme und Globalisierungsdenken,' *KAS/Auslandsinformation*, 9(06): 75-98.

– (2008) 'Democratization,' in Burnell, P./Randall, V. (eds) *Politics in the Developing World*, 2nd edn (Oxford: Oxford University Press): 268-90.

– (2010) 'New challenges to democratization', in Burnell, P./Youngs, R. (eds) *New challenges to democratization* (Oxon: Routledge): 1-22.

Calic, Marie-Janine (2007) 'Ex-Jugoslawien', in Schmidt, S./Hellmann, G./Wolf, R. (eds) *Handbuch zur deutschen Außenpolitik* (Wiesbaden: VS Verlag): 468-81.

Çalişkan, Selmin (2007) 'Von Bosnien nach Afghanistan – 14 Jahre Arbeit mit kriegstraumatisierten Frauen und Mädchen', in Klein, A./Roth, S. (eds) *NGOs im Spannungsfeld zwischen Krisenprävention und Sicherheitspolitik* (Wiesbaden: VS Verlag): 285-98.

Carothers, Thomas (2006) *Aiding democracy abroad, The learning curve*, 5th edn (Washington D.C: Carnegie Endowment for International Peace).

– (2009) 'Democracy Assistance: Political vs. Developmental?', *Journal of Democracy*, 20(1): 5-19.

– (2010) 'Democracy support and Development aid: the elusive synthesis', *Journal of Democracy*, 21(4):12-26.

Castells, Manuel (2008) 'The New Public Sphere: Global Civil Society, Communication Networks, and Global Governance', in Cowan, G./Cull, N. (eds) *Public Diplomacy in a Changing World* (Los Angeles: Sage): 78-93.

CDU (Christdemokratische Union) (2007) *Freiheit und Sicherheit, Grundsätze für Deutschland, Das Grundsatzprogarmm*, Beschlossen am 21. Parteitag, 3-4/12/2007, Hannover.

CDU/CSU/SPD (2013) Deutschlands Zukunft gestalten, Koalitionsvertrag zwischen CDU, CSU und SPD, 18. Legislaturperiode, Berlin.

CDU/CSU/FDP (2009) *Wachstum, Bildung, Zusammenhalt, Koalitionsvertrag zwischen CDU, CSU und FDP, 17. Legislaturperiode*, Berlin.

Chandler, David (2005) 'Constructing Global Civil Society', in Chandler, D./Baker, G. (eds) *Global Civil Society* (Abingdon: Routledge): 149-70.

CIA (Central Intelligence Agency) (2010) *World Fact Book, Thailand*, available online at: https://www.cia.gov/library/publications/the-world-factbook/geos/th.htm l#top (accessed on 16/05/2010).

Coleman, William/Perl, Anthony (1999) 'Internationalized policy environment and policy network analysis', *Political Studies*, 47(4): 691-709.

Colschen, Lars (2010) *Deutsche Außenpolitik* (Paderborn: Wilhelm Fink).

Council of the EU (European Union) (2009) *Joint Declaration of the Prague Eastern Partnership Summit*, 7/05/2009, 8435/09, Press 78, Prague.

– (2011) *Joint Declaration of the Eastern Partnership Summit*, 29-30/09/2011, 14983/11, Press 341, Warsaw.

Cowan, Geoffrey/Arsenault, Amelia (2008) 'Moving from Monologue to Dialogue to Collaboration: The Three Layers of Public Diplomacy', in Cowan, G./Cull, N. (eds) *Public Diplomacy in a Changing World* (Los Angeles: Sage): 10-30.

Cox, Robert W. (1987) *Production, Power and World Order, Social Forces in the Making of History*, Vol. 1 (New York: Columbia University Press).

Cross, Mai'a (2013) 'Conceptualizing European Public Diplomacy,' in Cross, M./ Melissen, J. (eds) *European Public Diplomacy, Soft Power at Work* (New York: Palgrave macmillan): 1-11

Cull, Nicholas J. (2008) 'Public Diplomacy: Taxonomies and Histories,' in Cowan, G./Cull, N. (eds) *Public Diplomacy in a Changing World* (Los Angeles: Sage): 31-54.

– (2011) 'WikiLeaks, public diplomacy 2.0 and the state of digital public diplomacy,' *Place Branding and Public Diplomacy*, 7: 1-8.

Cummings, Milton C. (2003) *Cultural Diplomacy and the United States Government: A survey* (Washington DC: Center for Arts and Culture).

Curbach, Janina (2009) *Die Corporate-Social-Respondability-Bewegung* (Wiesbaden: VS Verlag).

Cutler, A. Claire (2002) 'Private regimes and interfirm cooperation,' in Hall, R./ Biersteker, T. (eds) *The Emergence of Private Authority in Global Governance* (Cambridge: Cambridge University Press): 23-40.

Cutler, A. Claire/Haufler, Virginia/Porter, Tony (1999) 'Private Authority and International Affairs,' in Cutler, A./Haufler, V./Porter, T. (eds) *Private Authority and International Affairs* (Albany: State University of New York Press): 3-28.

Czempiel, Ernst-Otto (1986) *Friedensstrategien, Systemwandel durch Internationale Organisationen, Demokratisierung und Wirtschaft* (Paderborn: Schöningh).

Daase, Christopher (2010) 'Wandel des Sicherheitskultur,' *Aus Politik und Zeitgeschichte*, 50: 9-16.

Dakowska, Dorota (2002) 'Beyond Conditionality: EU Enlargement, European Party Federations and the Transnational Activity of German Political Foundations,' *Perspectives on European Politics and Society*, 3(2) (August 2002): 271-96.

– (2005a) 'German political foundations: Transnational party go-betweens in the EU enlargement process,' in Kaiser, W./Starie, P. (eds) *Transnational European Union* (London: Routledge): 150-69.

– (2005b) 'Wissengeben, Wissennehmen, Deutsche parteinahe Stiftungen in Polen,' *Osteuropa*, 55(8) (August 2005): 126-36.

– (2005c) 'Die Arbeit der Friedrich-Ebert-Stiftung in Polenzwischen 1971 und der friedlichen Revolution,' in Friedrich-Ebert-Stiftung & Institut für Sozialgeschichte e.V. Braunschweig-Bonn (eds) *Archiv für Sozialgeschichte*, (45): 325-52.

Dauderstädt, Michael (2007) 'Mittel- und Osteuropa,' in Schmidt, S./Hellmann, G./ Wolf, R. (eds) *Handbuch zur deutschen Außenpolitik* (Wiesbaden: VS Verlag): 422-35.

Davies, John/Kaufman, Edward (2002) 'Second Track/Citizens' Diplomacy: An Overview,' in Davies, J./Kaufman, E. (eds) *Second Track/Citizens' Diplomacy: Concepts and Techniques for Conflict Transformation* (Lanham: Rowman & Littlefield): 1-12.

Debiel, Tobias/Lambach, Daniel/Pech, Birgit (2007) 'Geberpolitik ohne verlässlichen Kompass?,' *Aus Politik und Zeitgeschichte*, 48: 10-16.

Delgaard-Nielson, Anja (2006) *Germany, pacifism and peace enforcement* (Manchester: Manchester University Press).

DeMars, Willian E. (2015) 'Follow the partners: agency and explanation in the color revolutions', in DeMars, W./Dijkzeul, D. (eds) *The NGO Challenge for International Relations Theory* (Oxon: Routledge): 237-61.

DeMars, Willian E./Dijkzeul, Denis (2015) 'Introduction, NGOing', in DeMars, W./ Dijkzeul, D. (eds) *The NGO Challenge for International Relations Theory* (Oxon: Routledge): 3-38.

Dennert, Jürgen (1968) *Entwicklungshilfe geplant oder verwaltet? Entstehung und Konzeption des Bundesministeriums für wirtschaftliche Zusammenarbeit, Freiburger Studien für Politik und Gesellschaft überseeischer Länder*, 2nd edn, Bielefeld.

Denzin, Norman K. (1970) *The research act in sociology* (Chicago: Aldine).

Deussen, Giso (1981) *Konrad-Adenauer-Stiftung* (Düsseldorf: Droste).

Die Grünen (1987a) *Himmel auf Erden? Kontroversen um eine grün-nahe Stiftung.*

– (1987b) *Noch mehr Himmel auf Erden? Neue Kontroversen zur grün-nahen Stiftung.*

Dijkzeul, Dennis/DeMars, William E. (2011) 'Limitations of Intergovernmental and Non-Governmental Organizations', in Reinalda, B. (ed) *The Ashgate Research Companion to Non-State Actors* (Surrey: Ashgate Publishing Limited): 209-21.

Donini, Antonio (2012) *The Goldon Fleece: Manipulation and Independence in Humanitarian Action* (Boulder: Kumuran Press).

Donnelly, Jack (2000) *Realism and International Relations* (Cambridge: Cambridge University Press).

Doornbos, Martin (2008) 'State Collapse, Civil Society and External Intervention', in P. Burnell, P./Randall, V. (eds) *Politics in the Developing World*, 2nd edn (Oxford: Oxford University Press): 249-67.

Dosch, Jörn (2004) 'Das Verhältnis der EU und der USA zur Region Südostasien', *Aus Politik und Zeitgeschichte*, B21-22: 7-14.

Doyle, Michael W./Sambanis, Nicholas (2000) 'International Peacebuilding: A Theoretical and Quantitative Analysis', *American Political Science Review*, 94(4): 779-801.

Drezner, Daniel W. (2007) *All politics is Global: Explaining International Regulatory Regimes* (Princeton: Princeton University Press).

Dückers, Daniel/Mehler, Andreas (2011) 'Deutsche Außenpolitik und Krisenprävention', in Jäger, T./Höse, A./Oppermann, K. (eds) *Deutsche Außenpolitik, Sicherheit, Wohlfahrt, Institutionen und Normen*, 2nd edn (Wiesbaden: VS Verlag): 247-72.

Dunn, Tim (2011) 'Liberalism', in Baylis, J./Smith, S./Owens, P. (eds) *The Globalisation of World Politics*, 5th edn (Oxford: Oxford University Press): 100-13.

Dunn, Tim/Kurki, Milja/Smith, Steve (2013) *International Relations Theories, Discipline and Diversity*, 3rd edn (Oxford: Oxford University Press).

Dunn, Tim/Schmidt, Brian C. (2011) 'Realism', in Baylis, J./Smith, S./Owens, P. (eds) *The Globalisation of World Politics*, 5th edn (Oxford: Oxford University Press): 84-99.

Eberwein, Wolf-Dieter (2011) 'Politics and the World of Humanitarian Aid', in Reinalda, B. (ed) *The Ashgate Research Companion to Non-State Actors* (Surrey: Ashgate Publishing): 363-75.

Eckl, Jürgen/Hofmann, Norbert von (2012) *Kooperation mit Gewerkschaften und Förderung von Wirschafts- und Sozialentwicklung, Zentrale Tätigkeitsfelder der internationalen Arbeit der Friedrich-Ebert-Stiftung seit Beginn der 1960er-Jahre* (Bonn: Dietz).

Egger, Miriam (2007) *Die Auslandsarbeit der politischen Stiftungen zwischen Entwicklungs- und Transformationskontext: Eine Untersuchung der Tätigkeit der Friedrich-Ebert-Stiftung in Lateinamerika und Osteuropa, Dissertation zu Erlangung des akademischen Grades Doktor der Politikwissenschaft*, Freien Universität Berlin.

Ehrke, Michael/Römpczyk, Elmar (2013) *Der steinige Weg nach Europa, Die Arbeit der Friedrich-Ebert-Stiftung in Serbien und den baltischen Staaten* (Bonn: Dietz).

Elster, Jon (1989) *Nuts and Bolds of the Social Sciences* (Cambridge: Cambridge University Press).

Endreß, Christian/Petersen, Nils (2012) 'Die Dimension des Sicherheitsbegriffs', in Bundeszentrale für Politische Bildung (ed) *Dossier Innere Sicherheit*, 14/06/2012.

Erdmann, Gero (1996) *Demokratie und Demokratieförderung in der Dritten Welt, Ein Literaturbericht und eine Erhebung der Konzepte und Instrumente*, Bonn.

– (2006a) 'Hesitant bedfellows: the German Stiftungen and party aid in Africa, in Burnell, P. (ed) *Globalising democracy: party politics in emerging democracies* (London: Routledge).

– (2006b) 'Probleme der internationalen Parteienförderung', *KAS/Auslandsinformation*, 11(06): 123-42.

Esty, Daniel/Geradin, Damien (2000) 'Regulatory co-opetition', *Journal of International Economic Law*, 3(2): 235-55.

European Council (1993) *Presidency conclusions, § 7) Relations with the Countries of Central and Eastern Europe, A) The Associated Countries*, Copenhagen European Council, 21-22/06/1993.

EP (European Parliament) (1994) *Entschließung zum Recht auf Intervention aus humanitären Gründen, Information*, printed in: Deutscher Bundestag, BT-Drs. 12/7513, 10/05/1994, Berlin.

Eyinla, Bolade M. (1999) 'West German Political Foundations and their Activities in Sub-Saharan Africa', *International Studies*, 36(2): 191-204.

Fahrenhorst, Brigitte (2007) 'Von der Friedensbewegung zur Friedensforderung – Reichweite zivilgesellschaftlicher Aktivitaten in Gewaltkonflikten', in Klein, A./ Roth, S. (eds) *NGOs im Spannungsfeld zwischen Krisenprävention und Sicherheitspolitik* (Wiesbaden:VS Verlag): 69-90.

Falk, Richard (2005) 'The changing role of global civil society', in Chandler, D./ Baker, G. (eds) *Global Civil Society, Contested Futures* (Abingdon: Routledge): 69-84.

Falkner, Gerda (1998) *EU Social Policy in the 1990s. Towards a Corporatist Policy Community* (London: Routledge).

Fearson, James/Wendt, Alexander (2002) 'Rationalism v. Constructivism: A Sceptical View', in Carlsnaes, W./Risse, T./Simmons, B. (eds) *Handbook of International Relations* (London: Sage): 52-72.

FES (Friedrich-Ebert-Stiftung) (2002) *Krisen vorbeugen, Konflikte lösen, Frieden sichern, Beiträge der Friedrich-Ebert-Stiftung zur zivilen Konfliktbearbeitung*, Bonn.

– (2003) 'Drahtseilakte, Demokratieförderung im Kontext von Konflikten', *FES Info*, 2/2003: 22-3.

– (2005a) *Menschenrechtspreis 2005, Anwälte der Menschenrechte – Die Wahrheitskommission in Chile und Peru*, Programm, 7. September 2005, available online at: http://www.fes.de/themen/menschenrechtspreis/common/pdf/FES_E_MRP_2005.pdf.

– (2005b) 'Demokratie braucht Frieden auf allen Ebenen, Sicherheitspolitik und zivile Konfliktbearbeitung der FES', *FES Info*, 2/2005: 2-3.

– (2005c) *Promoting Democracy, Creating Peace, Shaping Globalisation*, The international cooperation of the Friedrich-Ebert-Stiftung, Bonn, Berlin.

– (2007) *Peace and Conflict Impact Assessment, Methodical Guidelines*, Bonn, Berlin.

– (2009a) *Krisen vorbeugen, Frieden sichern, Ein Arbeitsfeld der Friedrich-Ebert-Stiftung*, Flyer, Bonn, Berlin.

– (2009b) *People in Dialogue, People in Peace, Making Steps Towards Conflict Transformation in Southern Thailand*, Bangkok.

– (2010) *Early Warning Systems in Minority Conflicts, A Framework for Development Regional Responses*, 7th Asia-Europe Roundtable Workshop, Singapore, 20-21 May 2010, Asia Europe Foundations/Friedrich-Ebert-Stiftung Office for Regional Cooperation in Asia/Singapore Institute for International Affairs (eds), Singapore.

– (2011a) 'Die Gewerkschaftsarbeit der Friedrich Ebert Stiftung in Europa', *Perspektive*, May 2011, Berlin.

– (2011b) *Evaluierungsbericht "Arbeitsbeziehungen und Sozialdialog in Ostmitteleuropa und Südosteuropa"*, Kurzfassung, June 2011, Berlin.

– (2012a) *Evaluierungsbericht, Evaluierung des Forschungsstipendiatenprojektes im Aus- und Fortbildungsprogramm der Friedrich-Ebert-Stiftung 2007 – 2011*, Kurzfassung, September 2012, Berlin.

– (2012b) *Evaluierungsbericht, Gesellschaftspolitisches Beratungskonzept Chile, Kurzfassung*, October 2012, Berlin

– (2012c) *Evaluierungsbericht, Gesellschaftspolitisches Beratungsprojekt Palästina, Kurzfassung*, November 2012, Berlin.

– (2012d) *Evaluierungsbericht, Gesellschaftspolitisches Beratungsprojekt Israel, Kurzfassung*, September 2012, Berlin.

– (2012e) *Envisioning Afghanistan Post 2014, Perspectives and Strategies for Constructive Conflict Resolution from the Neighbourhood*, Bonn, Berlin.

– (2012f) *Die Arbeit der Friedrich-Ebert-Stiftung im Bereich der Friedens- und Sicherheitspolitk, Ziele, Schwerpunkte und Arbeitsansätze*, Bonn, Berlin.

– (2013) *Afghanistan's region: 2014&beyond, Joint Declaration on regional Peace and Stability, Envisioning Afghanistan Post 2014, Perspectives and Strategies for Constructive Conflict Resolution from the Neighbourhood*, Bonn, Berlin.

FES/KAS/FNS/HSS/HBS (1998) *Gemeinsame Erklärung der Friedrich-Ebert-Stiftung, Konrad-Adenauer-Stiftung, Friedrich-Naumann-Stiftung, Hanns-Seidel-Stiftung, Heinrich-Böll-Stiftung*, Bonn/St. Augustin/Königswinter/München/Berlin of 12/12/1996 updated in 11/1998.

FES/KAS/HBS/FNS (2011) *Civil Society Forum Prior to the International Foreign Ministers' Conference on Afghanistan, Background information*, 22/09/2011.

Fierke, Katrin (2013) 'Constructivism,' in Dunn, T./Kurki, M./Smith, S. (eds) *International Relations Theories*, 3rd edn (Oxford: Oxford University Press): 187-204.

– (2005) 'Constructivism,' in Dunn, T./Kurki, M./Smith, S. (eds) *International Relations Theories*, 1st edn (Oxford: Oxford University Press): 166-84.

Finnemore, Martha (1996) *National Interest in International Society* (Ithaca: Cornwell University Press).

Finnemore, Martha/Sikkink, Katheryn (1998) 'International Norm Dynamics and Political Change,' *International Organization*, 52(4) (Autumn 1998): 887-917.

– (2001) 'Taking Stock: The Constructivist Research Program in International Relations and Comparative Politics,' *Annual Review of Political Science*, 4 (June 2001): 391-416.

Fischer, Martina (2006) *Civil Society in Conflict transformation: Ambivalence, Potentials and Challenges*, Bergdorf Research Center for Constructive Conflict Management, October 2006.

– (2011) *Evaluierung der Aktivitiäten der Heinrich-Böll-Stiftung in der Region des ehemaligen Jugoslawien „Regionalporgamm „Südosteuropa", Berichtszeitraum: 2006-2010, Kurzfassung*, 28/02/2011.

Fischer-Bollin, Peter (2006) *Parteienzusammenarbeit der KAS in Mittel-, Ost- und Südeuropa*, Konrad-Adenauer-Stiftung e.V., Sankt Augustin.

Fisher, Ali (2013) 'A Network Perspective on Public Diplomacy in Europe: EUNIC,' in Cross, M./Melissen, J. (eds) *European Public Diplomacy, Soft Power at Work* (New York: Palgrave macmillan): 137-56.

Flechtner, Stefanie (2007) *In neuer Mission, Auslandseinsätze der Bundeswehr und die deutsche Sicherheitspolitik*, Kompass 2020, Friedrich-Ebert-Stiftung, Mai 2007, Berlin.

FNS (Friedrich Naumann Stiftung) (2013a) *50 Jahre Internationale Politik - Wandel verstehen, Rechte schützen, Zukunft gestalten*, 1963-2013 Jubiläumsschrift, Potsdam.

– (2013b) 50 Jahre Internationale Politik – Für eine Welt in Freiheit, Potsdam.

Forrester, Veronica (1985) 'The German Political Foundations,' in Stevens, C./Van Themaat, J. (eds) *EEC and The Third World: Survey, Pressure Groups, Politics and Development* (London: Hodder and Stoughton): 40-60.

Frei, Daniel/Gaupp, Peter (1978) 'Das Konzept "Sicherheit" – Theoretische Aspekte,' in Schwarz, K.(ed) *Sicherheitspolitik. Analysen zur politischen und militärischen Sicherheit* (Bad-Honeff: Erpel): 3-16.

FriEnt (Arbeitsgemeinschaft Frieden und Entwickling) (2011) *Working Group on Peace and Development*, Flyer, June 2011, Berlin.

Fülle, Henning (1992) *Himmel auf Erden: Entstehung, Struktur und Arbeitsweisen der grün-nahen politischen Stiftungen,* Stiftungsverband Regenbogen e.V., Dortmund.

Gareis, Sven Bernhard (2006) *Deutschlands Außen- und Sicherheitspolitik*, 2nd edn (Opladen: UTB).

– (2011) 'Militärische Auslandseinsätze und die Transformation der Bundeswehr', in Jäger, T./Höse, A./Oppermann, K. (eds) *Deutsche Außenpolitik, Sicherheit, Wohlfahrt, Institutionen und Normen,* 2nd edn (Wiesbaden: VS Verlag): 148-70.

Grävingholt, Jörn/Hofmann, Claudia/Klingebiel, Stephan (2007) *Entwicklungszusammenarbeit im Umgang mit nichtstaatlichen Gewaltakteuren*, German Development Institute, Studies, Bonn.

Geerlings, Jörg (2003) *Verfassungs- und verwaltungsrechtliche Probleme bei der Finanzierung parteinaher Stiftungen* (Berlin: Duncker&Humblot).

Gerster, Johannes (2005) 'Friedensförderung und Dialog', *Die Politische Meinung,* 432 (November 2005): 51-8.

Gerz, Wolfgang (2005) 'Public Diplomacy als außenpolitisches Instrument nach dem 11. September', in Jäger, T./Höse, A./Oppermann, K. (eds) *Transatlantische Beziehungen, Sicherheit, Wirtschaft, Öffentlichkeit* (Wiesbaden: VS Verlag): 435-48.

Giegerich, Bastian (2012) *Die NATO* (Wiesbaden: Springer VS).

Gilboa, Eytan (2000) 'Mass communication and diplomacy: A theoretical framework', *Communication Theory*, 10(3): 275-309.

– (2001) 'Diplomacy in the media age: Three models of uses and effects', *Diplomacy and Statecraft,* 12 (2): 1-28.

– (2008) 'Searching for a Theory of Public Diplomacy', in Cowan, G./Cull, N. (eds) *Public Diplomacy in a Changing World* (Los Angeles: Sage): 55-77.

Gilpin, Robert (1971) 'The Politics of Transnational Economic Relations', in Keohane, R./Nye, J. (eds) *Transnational Relations and World Politics* (Cambridge, M.A.: Harvard University Press): 48-69.

– (1975) *US Power and the Multinational Corporation: The Political Economy of Foreign Direct Investment* (New York: Basic Books).

– (1981) *War and Change in World Politics* (Cambridge: Cambridge).

Glagow, Manfred (1990) 'Zwischen Markt und Staat: Die Nicht-Regierungsorganisationen in der Deutschen Entwicklungspolitik', in Glagow, M. (ed) *Deutsche und international Entwicklungspolitik* (Opladen: Westdeutscher Verlag): 159-79.

Glagow, Manfred/Schimank, Uwe (1983) 'Die Nicht-Regierungs-Organisationen in der deutschen Entwicklungspolitik', in Glagow, M. (ed) *Deutsche Entwicklungspolitik: Aspekte und Probleme ihrer Entscheidungsstruktur*, Beitrag in Zusammenarbeit dem Forschungsprojekt "Handlungsbedingungen und Handlungsspielräume für Entwicklungspolitik" (Saarbrücken, Fort Lauderdale: Breitenbach): 141-78.

Goldmann, Jörg (2006) 'Baustelle Entwicklungspolitik', *Blätter für deutsche und internationale Politik,* 8: 1006-13.

Goodhand, Jonathan/Walton, Oliver (2012) 'Public versus private power, Non-governmental organisations and international security', in McKercher, B. (ed) *Routledge Handbook of Diplomacy and Statecraft* (London: Routledge): 428-40.

Gordenker, Leon/Weiss, T. G. (1995) 'Pluralising Global Governance: Analytic Approaches and Dimensions', *Third World Quarterly*, 16(3): 357-87.

Gowan, Richard (2010) *Review of Political Missions 2010*, A Project of the Center on International Cooperation, New York.

Grävingholt, Jörn/Gänzle, Stefan/Ziaja, Sebastian (2009) *Policy Brief: Concepts of Peacebuilding and State Building – How Compatible Are They?*, German Development Institute (DIE), Draft, 11. March, Bonn.

Grävingholt, Jörn/Hofmann, Claudia/Klingebiel, Stephan (2007) *Entwicklungszusammenarbeit im Umgang mit nichtstaatlichen Gewaltakteuren*, German Development Institute, Studies, Bonn.

Gramsci, Antonio (1971) *Selections from the prison notebooks of Antonio Gramsci*, Hoare, Q./Nowell-Smith, G. (eds) (New York: International Publisher).

Gray, William Glenn (2003) *Germany's Cold War, The Global Campaign to Isolate East Berlin, 1949-1969* (Chapel Hill: The University of North Carolina Press).

Grimmel, Andreas/Jakobeit, Cord (2009) 'Entwicklungszusammenarbeit und aktive Krisenprävention', in Böckenförde, S./Gareis S. (eds) *Deutsche Sicherheitspolitik* (Opladen: Barbara Budrich): 209-32.

GTZ (Deutsche Gesellschaft für Technische Zusammenarbeit) (1987) *Neue Akzente der volkswirtschaftlichen Regierungsberatung, Dokumentation einer gemeinsamen Tagung von BMZ und GTZ im Dezember 1985*, Eschborn.

Günter, Uwe/Vesper, Michael (1994) 'Wie weiter mit dem Stiftungsgeld?', *Zeitschrift für Rechtspolitik*, 27(8): 289-92.

Haas, Peter M. (1989) 'Do regimes matter? Epistemic communities and Mediterranean pollution control', *International Organization*, 43(3) (Summer 1989): 377-404.

– (1992) 'Introduction: epistemic communities and international policy coordination', in Haas, P. (ed) *Knowledge, Power and International Policy Coordination* (Massachusetts: University of South Carolina Press) (= International Organization, 46[1]): 1-35.

– (1993) 'Epistemic communities and the Dynamics of International Environmental Co-Operation', in Rittberger, V. (ed) *Regime Theory and International Relations* (Oxford: Clarendon Press): 168-201.

– (2004) 'When does power listen to truth? A constructivist approach to the policy process', *Journal of European Public Policy*, 11(4): 569-92.

Hacke, Christian (1993) *Die Außenpolitik der Bundesrepublik Deutschland, Weltmacht wider Willen* (Frankfurt a.M.: Ullstein).

Hänggi, Heiner (2005) 'Sicherheitssektorreform (SSR) – Konzepte und Kontexte', *Sicherheit und Frieden*, 23(3): 119-25.

Haverland, Markus/Yanow, Dvora (2012) 'A Hitchhiker's Guide to Public Administration Research Universe: Surviving Conversations on Methodologies and Methods', *Public Administration Review*, May/June 2012: 401-8.

Hale, Thomas/Held, David (2011) 'Editors' Introduction: Mapping Changes in Transnational Governance,' in Hale, T./Held, D. (eds) *Handbook of Transnational Governance: Institutions and Innovations* (Cambridge: Polity Press): 1-36.

Halliday, Fred (1991) 'State and Society in International Relations,' in Banks, M./ Shaw, M./Shaw, M. (eds) *State and Society in International Relations* (Hemel Hempstead: Harvesters Wheatsheaf): 191-209.

– (2001) 'The Romance of Non-state Actors,' in Josselin, D./Wallace, W. (eds) *Non-state Actors in World Politics* (New York: Palgrave Publisher): 21-40.

Handley, Paul M. (2006) *The King Never Smiles, A Biography of Thailand's Bhumibol Adulyadej* (New Haven: Yale University Press).

Harnischfeger, Horst (2007) 'Auswärtige Kulturpolitk,' in Schmidt, S./Hellmann, G./Wolf, R. (eds) *Handbuch zur deutschen Außenpolitik* (Wiesbaden: VS Verlag): 713-23.

Hartmann, Jürgen (2001) *Internationale Beziehungen* (Opladen: UTB).

Hasemann, Armin/Hübner-Schmid, Katharina/Dargatz, Anja (2005) *Konfliktanalysis zur Entwicklung von Handlungsoptionen für gesellschaftspolitische Kooperationsprogramme, Erstellt im Rahmen eines Pilotprojektes der Friedrich-Ebert-Stiftung (FES) in Kooperation mit der Gesellschaft für Technische Zusammenarbeit (GTZ) und der Gruppe Friedensentwicklung (FriEnt)*, Berlin.

Hasenclever, Andreas/Mayer, Peter/Rittberger, Volker (1997) *Theories of international regimes* (Cambridge: Cambridge University Press).

Haufler, Virginia (1993) 'Crossing the Boundary between Public and Private: International Regimes and Non-State Actors,' in Rittberger, V. (ed) *Regime Theory and International Relations* (Oxford: Clarendon Press): 94-111.

Hay, Colin (2013) 'International Relations Theory in Globalization,' in Dunn, T./ Kurki, M./Smith, S. (eds) *International Relations Theories*, 3rd edn (Oxford: Oxford University Press): 287-305.

Hayden, Craig (2013) 'Logics of narrative and networks in US public diplomacy: Communication power and US strategic engagement,' *The Journal of International Communication*, 19(2): 196-218.

Hearn, Julie/Robinson, Mark (2000) 'Civil Society and Democracy Assistance in Africa,' in Burnell, P. (ed) *Democracy Assistance* (London: Frank Cass): 241-62.

Heclo, Hugh (1978) 'Issue Networks and Executive Establishment,' in King, A. (ed) *The New American Political System* (Washington DC: AEI): 87-124.

Heiduk, Felix/Möller, Kay (2004) *Southern Thailand: The origins of violence*, SWP Comments (7), May 2004, Stiftung Wissenschaft und Politik, Berlin.

Heinrich, Stephan/Lange, Hans-Jürgen (2009) 'Erweiterung des Sicherheitsbegriffs,' in Lange, H./Ohly, H./Reichertz, J. (eds) *Auf der Suche nach neuer Sicherheit. Fakten, Theorien und Folgen*, 2nd edn (Berlin: VS Verlag): 252-68.

Heisterkamp, Ulrich (2014) *Think tanks der Parteien? Eine vergleichende Analyse der deutschen politischen Stiftungen* (Wiesbaden: Springer VS).

Hellmann, Gunther (2007) 'Sicherheitspolitik,' in Schmidt, S./Hellmann, G./Wolf, R. (eds) *Handbuch zur deutschen Außenpolitik* (Wiesbaden: VS Verlag): 605-617.

– (2013) 'Reflexive Sicherheitspolitik als anti-hegemoniales Rezept: Deutschlands Sicherheit und seine gewandelte Strategie,' *Aus Politik und Zeitgeschichte*, 37: 49-54.

Hellmann, Gunther/Wagner, Wolfgang/Baumann, Rainer (2014) *Deutsche Außenpolitik*, 2nd edn (Wiesbaden: Springer VS).

Hellwig, Sabine (1998) *Politische Bildung unter besonderer Berücksichtigung parteinaher Stiftungen in Deutschland und vergleichbaren Institutionen in Österreich* (Wuppertal: Deimling).

Hellwig-Bötte, Margit (2013) *Der Internationale Strafgerichtshof als Zankapfel politischer Interessen*, SWP-Aktuell 73, December 2013, Stiftung Wissenschaft und Politik, Berlin.

Hennig, Ottried (1998) 'Aus der Vergangenheit begründet, für die Zukunft gestaltet, Perspektiven für die künftige Arbeit der Konrad-Adenauer-Stiftung,' in Rinsche, G./Friedrich, I. (eds) *Weichenstellung für das 21. Jahrhundert* (Köln: Böhlau Verlag): 395-401.

Hensgen, Leonie (2013) *Korruptionsbekämpfung in der Donauregion: eine Untersuchung regionaler Best Practices*, Max Planck Gesellschaft für Internationalen Frieden und Rechtsstaatlichkeit, Heidelberg.

Hentschel, Gitti (2010) 'Friedens- und Sicherheitspolitik braucht Geschlechteranalysen,' *Aus Politik und Zeitgeschichte*, 50: 43-6.

Herzog, Roman (1995) 'Ansprache anlässlich des 70. Jahrestages der Gründung der Friedrich-Ebert-Stiftung in Bonn,' in *Reden und Interviews*, Band 1/1 (Presse- und Informationsamt der Bundesregierung: Bonn): 322-27.

Hilhorst, Dorothea (2008) 'The Art of NGO-ing: everyday practices as key to understanding development NGOs,' in Opoku-Mensah, P./Lewis, D./Tvedt, T. (eds) *Reconceptualising NGOS and their Roles in Development: NGOs, Civil Society and the International Aid System* (Aalborg: Aalborg University Press): 297-325.

Hillebrand, Ernst and Optenhögel, Uwe (2001) 'Mediatoren in einer entgrenzten Welt, Zur außenpolitischen Rolle der politischen Stiftungen,' *Internationale Politik und Gesellschaft*, 2: 165-72.

Hippler, Jochen (2004) *Nation-Building, ein Schlüsselkonzept für friedliche Konfliktbearbeitung?* (Bonn: Dietz).

Hocking, Brain (2004) 'Diplomacy,' in Carlsnaes, W./Sjursen, H./White, B. (eds) *Contemporary European Foreign Policy* (London: Sage): 91-109.

– (2007) 'Rethinking the "new" public diplomacy,' in Melissen, J. (ed) *The new public diplomacy: soft power in international relations* (New York: Palgrave Macmillan): 28-43.

– (2011) 'Non-state Actors and the Transformation of Diplomacy,' in Reinalda, B. (ed) *The Ashgate Research Companion to Non-State Actors* (Surrey: Ashgate Publishing): 225-36.

Hoffmann, Stanley (1966) 'Obstinate or Obsolete? The Fate of the Nation-State and the Case of Western Europe,' *Daedalus*, 95(3): 862-915.

Hofmann, Norbert von/Vinnai, Volker/Benzing, Hermann (2011) *Die Arbeit der Friedrich-Ebert-Stiftung in Indonesien, Tansania und Zentralamerika seit den 1960er Jahren* (Bonn: Dietz).

Holzner, Burkhart/Marx, John H. (1979) *Knowledge Application: The Knowledge System in Society* (Boston: Allyn&Bacon): 107-11.

Hopf, Ted (1998) 'The Promise of Constructivism in International Relations Theory,' *International Security*, 23(1): 171-200.

Hopkins, Raymond F. (1992) 'Reform in the international food aid regime: the role of consensual knowledge,' in Haas, P. (ed) *Knowledge, Power and International Policy Coordination* (Columbia: University of South Carolina): 225-64.

HRW (Human Rights Watch) (2009) *Country summary: Thailand*, January 2009, New York.

– (2010), Word Report 2010, Events of 2009, New York.

HSS (Hanns-Seidel-Stiftung) (2014a) *Portrait – Struktur – Zahlen: Information zur Hanns-Seidel-Stiftung*, Munich.

– (2014b) *Development Cooperation*, Leaflet, Munich.

– (2015) *Central, East and Southeast Europe, Caucasus and Central Asia, Hanns Seidel Foundation world wide*, Leaflet, Munich.

Hunt, Todd/Grunig, James (1994) *Public Relations Techniques* (Fort Worth: Holt, Rinehart and Winston).

Hurd, Ian (2008) 'Constructivism,' in Reus-Smit, C./Duncan, S. (eds) *Oxford Handbook of International Relations* (Oxford: Oxford University Press): 298-316.

ICISS (International Commission on Intervention and State Sovereignty) (2001) *The responsibility to protect*, Report, December 2001, Ottawa.

ICTJ (International Centre for Transnational Justice) (2008) *Handbook on the special tribunal for Lebanon*, 10/04/2008, New York.

Ihne, Hartmut/Wilhelm, Jürgen (2013) 'Grundlagen der Entwicklung,' in Ihne, H./Wilhelm, J. (eds) *Einführung in die Entwicklungspolitik*, Bundeszentrale für politische Bildung (Berlin: LIT VERLAG): 5-40.

Janning, Josef (2007) Europäische Union und deutsche Europapolitik, in Schmidt, S./Hellmann, G./Wolf, R. (eds) *Handbuch zur deutschen Außenpolitik* (Wiesbaden: VS Verlag): 745-62.

Jansen, Dorothea (2006) *Einführung in die Netzwerkanalyse*, 3rd edn (Wiesbaden: VS Verlag).

Jarass, Hans D. (2000) '§ 24 GG,' in Jarass, H./Pieroth, B. (eds) *Grundgesetz der Bundesrepublik Deutschland, Kommentar*, 5th edn (München: C.H. Beck).

Jarren, Otfried/Donges, Patrick (2011) *Politische Kommunikation in der Mediengesellschaft, Eine Einführung*, 3rd edn (Wiesbaden: VS Verlag).

Jellinek, Georg (1900) *Allgemeine Staatslehre, Das Recht des modernen Staates*, Band 1 (Berlin: Häring).

Jepperson, Ronald L./Wendt, Alexander/Katzenstein, Peter J. (1996) Norms, Identity, and Culture in National Security, in Katzenstein, P. (ed) *The Culture of National Security: Norms and Identity in World Politics* (New York: Columbia University Press): 33-75.

Jönsson, Christer (2002) 'Diplomacy, Bargaining and Negotiation,' in Carlsnaes, W./ Risse, T./Simmons, B. (eds) *Handbook of International Relations* (London: Sage): 212-34.

Kahane, Benjamin (1998) 'MUT-Gesprächmit Johannes Gerste", *Zeitschrift MUT*, 374 (October 1998): 64-9.

Kaiser, Karl (1969) 'Transnationale Politik,' *Die anachronistischen Souveränität, Politische Vierteljahresschrift* (Sonderband 1969): 80-109.

Kaiser, Karl/Mildenberger, Markus (1998) 'Gesellschaftliche Mittlerorganisationen,' in Ebenwein, W./Kaiser, K. (eds) *Deutschlands neue Außenpolitik*, Bd. 4: Institutionen und Ressourcen (München: R. Oldenbourg Verlag): 199-214.

Kaldor, Mary (2003a) 'The idea of global civil society,' *International Affairs*, 79(3): 583-93.

– (2003b) *Global Civil Society: An Answer to War* (Cambridge: Polity).

Katz, Hagai (2006) 'Gramsci, Hegemony, and Global Civil Society Networks,' *Voluntas*, 17: 333-48.

Karten, Inga (2008) 'Staatliche Imagearbeit: Die Public Diplomacy das Auswärtigen Amtes,' in Jäger, T./Viehrig, H. (eds) *Die amerikanische Regierung gegen die Weltöffentlichkeit? Theoretische und empirische Analysen der Public Diplomacy zum Irakkrieg* (Wiesbaden: VS Verlag): 163-90.

KAS (Konrad-Adenauer-Stiftung e.V.) (2005) *Media and Democracy, The KAF Democracy Report 2005* (Bonn: Bouvier).

– (2006) *Rule of Law, The KAF Democracy Report 2006* (Bonn: Bouvier).

– (2007a) 'Politischer und Sicherheitsdialogue,' *KAS International*, 3: 13.

– (2007b) *Globale Ordnungspolitik, Thesenpapier zur Globalisierung als überregionale Herausforderung, Probleme, Positionen und Perspektiven für die internationale Zusammenarbeit der Konrad-Adenauer-Stiftung*, Berlin.

– (2007c) *Regionale Expertenkonferenz „Lustration and Consolidation of Democracy and the Rule of Law in Central and Eastern Europe"*, 24. Mai 2007 in Zagreb (Kroatien), Bericht, Rechtsstaatsprogramm Südosteuropa der Konrad Adenauer Stiftung, Berlin.

– (2007d) *Parties and Democracy, The KAS Democracy Report 2007* (Bonn: Bouvier).

– (2008a) *Elitenkooperation und Entwicklungszusammenarbeit*, Sankt Augustin, Berlin.

– (2008b) *Weltweit für den Rechtsstaat, Das Rechtsstaatsprogramm der Konrad-Adenauer-Stiftung*, Sankt Augustin, Berlin.

– (2008c) *Die Zukunft der Demokratie sichern – Mit der Demokratie die Zukunft sichern*, Sankt Augustin, Berlin.

– (2011) *Gut informiert - verantwortungsvoll Handeln: Das weltweite Medienprogramm der Konrad-Adenauer-Stiftung*, Sankt Augustin.

– (2012) *Beratungsgespräch über rechtsstaatliche Lösungen für die Serbien-Kosovo-Verhältnisse, Rundtischgespräch in Organisation der KAS RSPSOP und KAS Belgard,* Budva, *Montenegro 25-28/11/2012,* Berlin.

– (2013a) *Speech of Thorsten Geissler, Opening of the conference "Public Procurement. An operational approach"*, Bucharest, 20/03/2013, Rule of Law Program Southeast Europe, Bucharest.

– (2013b) *Thorsten Geissler, Operning Speech, Workshop "Media and transitional justice",* Prizren, 19/07/2013, Rule of Law Program Southeast Europe, Bucharest.

– (2013c) *Jahresbericht 2012 – Einblicke 2013*, Sankt Augustin, Berlin.

– (2013d) *Supporting the rule of law worldwide*, The Konrad-Adenauer-Stiftung rule of law programm, Berlin.

– (2013e) *Muslime in Staat und Gesellschaft, Soziales Engagement in politischer Teilhabe von Afrika bis Asien und in Europa*, Sankt Augustin, Berlin.

– (2014a) *Maßnahmenplan 2015, Rechtsstaatsprogramm der Konrad-Adenauer-Stiftung in Südosteuropa*, inspected by the author on 5/08/2014.

– (2014b) *Speech of Thorsten Geissler, Round-table debate on Roma inclusion, Event organized in cooperation with the Slovak Embassy and the Delegation of the European Commission to Romania*, Bucharest, 25/04/2014, Rule of Law Program Southeast Europe, Bucharest.

– (2014c) *Kulturenvielfalt und Dialog in einer multikulturellen Stadt: „Theorie und Praxis", Studienseminar,* 1/06/2014, Program outline, Akko, Israel.

– (2015a) *Supporting the Rule of Law worldwide, The Konrad-Adenauer-Stiftung Rule of Law Programm*, Leaflet, Konrad-Adenauer-Stiftung, Berlin.

– (2015b) *Speech held by Thorsten Geissler on the occasion of the launching of the anti-corruption-strategy for Central and Eastern Europe organized by the embassy of the United States of America to Romania*, Bucharest, 30/01/2015, Rule of Law Program Southeast Europe, Bucharest.

Katzenstein, Peter J. (1996) 'Introduction: Alternative Perspectives on National Security,' in Katzenstein, P. (ed) *The Culture of National Security: Norms and Identity in World Politics* (New York: Columbia University Press): 1-32.

Kaufmann, Walther (2007) 'Die Rolle von Nichtregierungsorganisationen bei der Bearbeitung von Konflikten im Südkaukasus,' in Klein, A./Roth, S. (eds) *NGOs im Spannungsfeld zwischen Krisenprävention und Sicherheitspolitik* (Wiesbaden: VS Verlag): 299-312.

Keck, Margaret/Sikkink, Katheryn (1998) *Activists Beyond Borders, Transnational Advocacy Networks in International Relations* (Ithaca: Cornell University Press).

Kelman, Herbert C. (2002) 'Interactive Problem Solving as a Tool for Second Track Diplomacy,' in Davies, J./Kaufman, E. (eds) *Second Track/Citizens' Diplomacy, Concepts and Techniques for Conflict Transformation* (Lanham: Rowman&Littlefield): 81-105.

Keohane, Robert O. (1983) 'The Demand for International Regimes, International Organization,' in Krasner, S. (ed) *International Regimes* (Ithaca, NY: Cornell University Press): 141-71.

– (1984) *After Hegemony, Cooperation and Discord in the World Political Economy* (Princeton: Princeton University Press).

– (1988) 'International institutions: Two approaches,' *International Studies Quarterly*, 32(4): 379-96.

Keohane, Robert O./Nye, Joseph S. Jr. (1971) 'Transnational relations and World Politics: An Introduction,' *International Organization*, 25(3) (Summer 1971): 329-49.

– (1974) 'Transgovernmental Relations and International Organizations,' *World Politics*, 27(1): 39-62.

– (1989) *Power and Interdependence: World politics in Transition*, 2nd edn (Boston and Toronto: Little Brown).

Kessal-Wulf, Sybille (2014) *Die Stellung des Bundesverfassungsgerichtes im Gefüge der nationalen und internationalen Institutionen, Vortrag von Dr. Sybille Kessal-Wulf, Richterin am Bundesverfassungsgericht*, Chisinau, 6/10/2014, Konrad-Adenauer-Stiftung e.V. (ed) Rechtsstaatsprogramm Südosteuropa, Bucharest.

Klemp, Ludgera (2001) 'Entwicklungspolitik am Scheideweg – politische Randerscheinung oder globale Sturkturpolitik?,' *Aus Politik und Zeitgeschichte*, B18-19: 13-20.

Klevenhörster, Paul/Van den Boom, Dirk (2009) *Entwicklungspolitik* (Wiesbaden: VS Verlag).

Klingebiel, Stephan (2013) 'Konfliktbewältigung und Umgang mit fragilen Staaten,' *Aus Politik und Zeitgeschichte*, 37: 23-27.

Kloke-Lesch, Adolf/Poeschke, Roman (2013) 'Entwicklungszusammenarbeit und militärische Intervention,' in Ihne, H./Wilhelm, J. (eds) *Einführung in die Entwicklungspolitik*, Bundeszentrale für politische Bildung (Berlin: LIT VERLAG): 291-308.

Koch, Martin (2011) 'Non-State and State Actors in Global Governance,' in Reinalda, B. (ed) *The Ashgate Research Companion to Non-State Actors* (Surrey: Ashgate Publishing): 197-208.

Körber, Sebastian (2009) 'Image, Marke, Branding – Die veränderte Arbeit am Deuschlandbild,' in Maaß, K.-J. (ed) *Kultur und Außenpolitik*, 2dn edn (Baden-Baden: Nomos): 185-93.

Korey, William (1999) 'Human rights NGOs: The power of persuasion,' *Ethics and International Affairs*, 1999, 13(1): 151-74.

Koschel, David (2005) *Democracy promotion in Serbia, Approaches and instruments of the German political Stiftungen and the US party institutes in comparative perspective*, Masterarbeit, Freie Universität Berlin, Otto-Suhr-Institut für Politikwissenschaften, October 2005.

Krämer Frank/Lehrke, Gunter (1996) 'Medienförderung in Entwicklungsländern, Der Beitrag deutscher politischer Stiftungen,' in Meckel, M./Kriener, M. (eds) *Internationale Kommunikation: Eine Einführung* (Opladen: Westdeutscher Verlag): 105-24.

Krause Hansen, Hans/Salskov-Iversen, Dorte/Bislev, Sven (2002) 'Discoursive Globalisation: Transnational Discourse Communities and New Public Management,' in Higgott, R./Ougaard, M. (eds) *Towards a Global Polity: Future Trends and Prospects* (London: Routledge): 107-24.

Krasner, Stephen D. (1983) 'Structural Causes and regime consequences: regimes as intervening variables,' in Krasner, S. (ed) *International Regimes* (Ithaca, NY: Cornell University Press): 1-22.

– (1995) 'Power Politics, Institutions, and Transnational Relations,' in Risse-Kappen, T. (ed) *Bringing transnational relations back in: non state actors, structures and international institutions* (Cambridge: Cambridge University Press): 257-79.

Kratochwil, Friedrich/Ruggie, John Gerard (1986) 'International Organisation: A State of the Art on the Art of the State,' *International Organization*, 40(4) (September 1986): 753-75.

Krebs, Walter (2007) § 108 Verwaltungsorganisation, in Isensee, J./Kirchhoff, P. (eds) *Handbuch des Staatsrechts, Band V: Rechtsquellen, Organisation, Finanzen*, (Heidelberg: C.F. Müller): 457-520.

Kress, Roland (1985) *Die politischen Stiftungen in der Entwicklungspolitik* (Bochum: Bockmeyer).

Krieger, Silke (1983) *Partner für den demokratischen Weg, Die gesellschaftliche Arbeit der Konrad-Adenauer-Stiftung in den Entwicklungsländern* (Bonn: Verlag Hans Richarz).

Kühne, Winrich (2010) *Gratwanderung zwischen Krieg und Frieden, Wahlen in Post-Konflikt Ländern und entstehenden Demokratien, Dilemmata, Probleme und Lessons Learned*, Internationale Politikanalyse, Friedrich-Ebert-Stiftung, Berlin.

Kumar, Krishna (2000) 'International Assistiance for Post-Conflict Elections,' in Burnell, P. (ed) *Democracy Assistance, International Co-operation for Democratization* (Oxon: Frank Cass Publishers): 191-209.

Kunczik, Michael (1989) 'Public Relations für Staaten. Die Imagepflege von Nationen als Aspekt der internationalen Kommunikation: Zum Forschungsstand,' in Kaase, M./Schulz, W. (eds) *Massenkommunikation. Theorien, Methoden, Befunde* (Opladen: Westdeutscher Verlag): 165-84.

Kurki, Milja/Wight, Colin (2013) 'International Relations and Social Science,' in Dunn, T./Kurki, M./Smith, S. (eds) *International Relations Theories*, 3rd edn (Oxford: Oxford University Press): 14-35.

Lachmann, Werner (2010) *Entwicklungshilfe: Motive, Möglichkeiten und Grenzen, Problemfelder*, 2nd edn (München: Oldenbourg Wissenschaftsverlag).

Lambach, Daniel (2014) 'Fragile Staatlichkeit als Konfliktursache und Möglichkeiten der Bearbeitung,' Bundeszentrale für Politische Bildung (ed) *Dossier Innerstaatliche Konflikte*, 11/02/2014.

Lamy, Steve (2011) 'Contemporary Mainstream Approaches: Neo-Realism and Neo-Liberalism,' in Baylis, J./Smith, S./Owens, P. (eds) *The Globalisation of World Politics*, 5th edn (Oxford: Oxford University Press): 114-29.

Lange, Sebastian (2007) *Der Erfolg von Public Diplomacy. Eine theoretische Analyse am Fallbeispiel Deutschland* (Saarbrücken: VDM Verlag Dr. Müller).

Langguth, Gerd (1993) 'Politische Stiftungen und politische Bildung in Deutschland', *Aus Politik und Zeitgeschichte*, B34/93: 38-47.

Lapins, Wulf (2007) *Demokratieförderung in der Deutschen Außenpolitik*, Friedrich-Ebert-Stiftung, Berlin.

Lederach, John Paul (1995) *Preparing for Peace: Conflict transformation across cultures* (Syracuse: Syracuse University Press).

Lentner, Howard H. (2006) 'Hegemony and Power in International Politics', in Haugaard, M./Lentner, H. (eds) *Hegemony and Power, Consensus and Coercion in Contemporary Politics* (Oxford: Lexington Books): 89-108.

Leonard, Mark/Smewing, Conrad (2003) *Public Diplomacy and the Middle East* (London: The Foreign Policy Center).

Lerch, Marika (2007) *Demokratie im Aufwind? Außenpolitische Strategien der Demokratieförderung*, Friedrich-Ebert-Stiftung, Berlin.

Leusch, Patrick H. (2013) 'Medien und Entwicklungszusammenarbeit', in Ihne, H./ Wilhelm, J. (eds) *Einführung in die Entwicklungspolitik*, Bundeszentrale für politische Bildung (Berlin: LIT VERLAG): 349-80.

Leuthold, Margit (2000) *Grüne politische Bildung, Eine problemgeschichtliche Darstellung der Entwicklung in Deutschland und Österreich* (Opladen: Leske&Budrich).

LfV (Landesamt für Verfassungsschutz) Sachsen (2005) *Verfassungsschutzbericht 2005*, Dresden.

Liese, Andrea (2005) 'Mediation', in Nohlen, D./Schultze, R. (eds) *Lexikon der Politikwissenschaften*, Band 1, 3rd edn (Munich: C.H. Beck): 549f.

Little, Richard (2011) 'International Regimes', in Baylis, J./Smith, S./Owens, P. (eds) *The Globalisation of World Politics*, 5th edn (Oxford: Oxford University Press): 294-325.

LOC (Library of Congress) (2007) *Country Profile: Thailand, Federal Research Division*, July 2007, available online at: http://www.loc.gov/rr/frd/cs/profiles/Thailand.pdf (accessed on on 16/05/2010).

Luchterhandt, Otto (2013) *Evaluierung, Rechtsstaatsprogramm Südosteuropa*, Konrad-Adenauer-Stiftung, Berlin.

Maaß, Kurt-Jürgen (2009) 'Überblick: Ziele und Instrumente der Auswärtigen Kulturpolitik', in Maaß, K.-J. (ed) *Kultur und Außenpolitik*, 2dn edn (Baden-Baden: Nomos): 25-32.

– (2011) 'Aktuelle Herausforderungen der Auswärtigen Kulturpolitik', in Jäger, T./ Höse, A./Oppermann, K. (eds) *Deutsche Außenpolitik*, 2nd edn (Wiedbaden: VS Verlag): 584-602.

Mac Ginty, Roger (2008) *No War, No Peace, The Rejuvenation of Stalled Peace Processes and Peace Accords* (Houndmills: Palgrave Macmillan).

Mair, Stefan (1997) *Internationale Demokratisierungshilfe: Erfahrungen und Aufgaben*, SWP-AP 3020, Juni 1997, Stiftung Wissenschaft und Politik, Ebenhausen.

– (2000) 'Germany's Stiftungen and Democracy Assistance: Comparative Advantages, new Challenges', in Burnell, P. (ed) *Democracy Assistance* (London: Frank Cass): 128-49.

Major, Claudia/Schöndorf, Elisabeth (2011) *Umfassende Ansätze, vernetzte Sicherheit, Komplexe Krisen erfordern effektive Koordination und politische Führung*, SWP-Aktuell 22, April 2011, Stiftung Wissenschaft und Politik, Berlin.

Major, Claudia/Pietz, Tobias/Schöndorf, Elisabeth/Hummel, Wanda (2011) *Toolbox Krisenmangement, Von der zivilen Krisenprävention bis zum Peacebuilding: Prinzipen, Akteure, Instrumente*, 2nd Edition, Stiftung Wissenschaft und Politik/ Zentrum für Internationale Friedenseinsätze, Berlin.

Mallavarapu, Siddharth (2013) 'Schutzverantwortung als neues Machtinstrument?', *Aus Politik und Zeitgeschichte*, 37: 3f.

Manheim, Jarol B. (1994) *Strategic Public Diplomacy & American Foreign Policy* (New York: Oxford University Press).

March, James G./Olsen, Johan P. (1989) *Rediscovering Institutions: The Organizational Basis of Politics* (New York: Free Press).

Martens, Jens (2006) 'Die Milleniumsziele und die UN-Reform', in Heinrich-Böll-Stiftung (ed) *Die Zukunft des Völkerrechts in einer globalisierten Welt* (Baden-Baden: Nomos): 213-25.

Martens, Kerstin (2002) 'Mission Impossible? Defining Nongovernmental Organizations', *Voluntas*, 13(3) (September 2002): 271-85.

Martin, Lisa L. (2007) 'Neoliberalism', in Dunn, T./Kurki, M./Smith, S. (eds) *International Relations Theories*, 3rd edn (Oxford: Oxford University Press): 108-26.

Masala, Carlo (2008) 'Möglichkeiten einer Neuorientierung deutscher Außen- und Sicherheitspolitik', *Aus Politik und Zeitgeschichte*, 43: 22-7.

Maxwell, Simon/Stone, Diane (2005) 'Global knowledge networks and international development', in Stone, D./Maxwell, S. (eds) *Global Knowledge Networks and International Development* (Oxon, New York: Routledge): 1-17.

Mayer, Peter/Rittberger, Volker/Zürn, Michael (1993) 'Regime Theory, State of the Art and Perspectives', in Rittberger, V. (ed) *Regime Theory and International Relations* (Oxford: Clarendon Press): 391-430.

Maull, Hanns W. (1990/91) 'Germany and Japan: The New Civilian Powers', *Foreign Affairs*, 69(5): 91-106.

– (2007) 'Deutschland als Zivilmacht', in Schmidt, S./Hellmann, G./Wolf, R. (eds) *Handbuch zur deutschen Außenpolitik* (Wiesbaden: VS Verlag): 73-84.

– (2015) 'Deutsche Außenpolitik – Verantwortung und Macht', *Zeitschrift für Außen- und Sicherheitspolitk*, 8: 213-37.

Mbabatu, Pamela K./MacLean Sandra J./Shaw, Timothy M. (2005) 'Research on reconstruction in Africa, Challenges for policy communities and coalitions', in Stone, D./Maxwell. S. (eds) *Global Knowledge Networks and International Development* (Oxon: Routledge): 156-67.

McClellan, Michale (2004) *Public Diplomacy in the Context of Traditional Diplomacy*, available online at http://www.publicdiplomacy.org/45.htm#head01.

McDonald, John W. (2002) 'The need for Multi-Track Diplomacy', in Davies, J./ Kaufman, E. (eds) *Second Track/Citizens' Diplomacy: Concepts and Techniques for Conflict Transformation* (Lanham: Rowman&Littlefield Publishers): 49-60.

Mead, Walter Russell (2004) 'America's Sticky Power,' *Foreign Policy*, 83(2): 46–53.

Mearsheimer, John J. (1994) 'The false promise of international institutions,' *International Security*, 19(3): 5-49.

– (2001) *The Tragedy of Great Power Politics* (New York: W.W. Norton).

– (2011) 'Structural Realism,' in Dunn, T./Kurki, M./Smith, S. (eds) *International Relations Theories*, 3rd edn (Oxford: Oxford University Press): 77-93.

Meertens, Christoph/Wolf, Frieder (1996) 'Gesellschaftspolitischer Auftrag und Staatliche Finanzierung politischer Stiftungen,' *Zeitschrift für Rechtspolitik*, 1996: 440-7.

Mehler, Andreas (1996) 'Chancen der Demokratisierungshilfe in Westafrika: Eindrücke und Überlegungen zum Beitrag der deutschen politischen Stiftungen,' *Afrika Spectrum*, 31(1): 27-36.

Meier-Walser, Reinhard (2004) 'Aufgaben profilpolitischer Stiftungen im erweiterten Europa, in Zeiten des Umbruchs und der Globalisierung: Politische-Studien-Zeitgespräch mit Hans Zehetmair,' *Politische Studien*, 55(395): 9-14.

Melissen, Jan (2007a) 'Introduction,' in Melissen, J. (ed) *The new public diplomacy: soft power in international relations* (New York: Palgrave macmillan): xvii-xxii.

– (2007b) 'The new public diplomacy: between theory and practice,' in Melissen, J. (ed) *The new public diplomacy: soft power in international relations* (New York: Palgrave macmillan): 3-27.

– (2013) 'Public Diplomacy,' in Cooper, A./Heine, J./Thakur, R. (ed) *The Oxford Handbook of Modern Diplomacy* (Oxford: Oxford University Press): 463-52.

Merten, Heike (1997) 'Die Genehmigung einer sog. Parteinahen Stiftung,' *Nordrhein-westfälische Verwaltungsblätter*, 2: 44-50.

– (1999) *Parteinahe Stiftungen im Parteienrecht* (Baden-Baden: Nomos).

Merz, Karolina (2006) *Deutsche Demokratieförderung in den Palästinensischen Gebieten, Inwieweit fördern Projekte der deutschen politischen Stiftungen das Demokratieverständnis der palästinensischen Jugend?*, Diplomarbeit, Freie Universität Berlin, Otto-Suhr-Institut für Politikwissenschaften, August 2006.

Milo, Paskal (2008) 'Zwanzig Jahre albanisch-deutsche Beziehungen (1987-2007),' *Südosteuropa Mitteilungen*, 1: 60-73.

Möller, Till Maximilian (2011) 'Insurgence in Southern Thailand: A Quest for Identity,' *Sicherheit und Frieden*, 1: 7-13.

Mohr, Alexander (2010) *The German Political Foundations as Actors in Democracy Assistance* (Boca Raton: Dissertation.com).

Mohr, Sabine/Weßels, Bernhard/Beyers, Jan/Kerremans, Bart (2005) *Zugang und Legitimität in der EU, Vorläufige Ergebnisse der Befragungen deutscher Interessenverbände, politischer Parteien, Ministerien und politischer Stiftungen zur Außenhandelspolitik in der EU*, Discussionpaper, WZB, Berlin.

Montville, Joseph V. (1990) 'The Arrow and the Olive Branch: A Case for Track Two Diplomacy,' in Volkan, V./Montville, J./Julius, D. (eds) *The psychodynamics of international relationships* (Lexington: MA: Lexington Books): 161-75.

Mühlen, Partrick von zur (2007) *Die Internationale Arbeit der Friedrich-Ebert-Stiftung, Von den Anfängen bis zum Ende des Ost-West-Konflikts* (Bonn: Dietz).

Mueller, Sherry (2009) 'The nexus of US public diplomacy and citizen diplomacy', in Snow, N./Taylor, P. (eds) *Routledge Handbook of Public Diplomacy* (New York: Routledge): 101-09.

Münkler, Herfried (2015) *Macht in der Mitte: Die neuen Aufgaben Deutschlands in Europa* (Hamburg: Edition Körber Stiftung).

Muñoz Sánchez, Antonio (2013) *Von der Franco-Diktatur zur Demokratie, Die Tätigkeit der Friedrich-Ebert-Stiftung in Spanien* (Bonn: Dietz).

Nachtwei, Winfried (2008) *Viel beschworen, wenig bekannt: Zivile Krisenprävention, Konfliktlösung und Friedenskonsolidierung*, March 2008, available online at: http://nachtwei.de/downloads/bericht/zkb_nachtwei.pdf.

Naím, Moisés (2007) 'What is a GONGO? How government-sponsored groups masquerade as civil society', *Foreign Policy*, 160 (May/June): 95.

Nan, Susan Allen/Druckman, Daniel/El Horr, Jana (2009) 'Unofficial International Conflict Resolution: Is There a Track 11/2? Are There Best Practices?', *Conflict Resolution Quarterly*, 27(1): 65-82.

NATO (North Atlentic Treaty Organisation) (2006) *Comprehensive Political Guidance, Endorsed by NATO Heads of State and Government on 29 November 2006*, available online at: http://www.nato.int/cps/en/natolive/official_texts_56425.htm.

– (2010) *Active Engagement, Modern Defence, Strategic Concept for the Defence and Security of the Members of the North Atlantic Treaty Organization*, available online at: http://www.nato.int/cps/en/natohq/topics_82705.htm.

Naumann, Klaus (2001) 'Krisenreaktion', in Bundesakademie für Sicherheitspolitik (ed) *Sicherheitspolitik in neuen Dimensionen, Kompendium zum erweiterten Sicherheitsbegriff* (Berlin: E. S. Mittler): 851-66.

– (2009) 'Wie strategiefähig ist die deutsche Sicherheitspolitik', *Aus Politik und Zeitgeschichte*, 48: 10-7.

Nechev, Zoran/Mesarek, Gordana Vidovic/Saranovich, Nikola B./Nikolov, Aleksandar (2013) *Embedding rule of law in the enlargement process, A case for EU political conditionality in the accession of the Western Balkan countries, Association for Development Initiatives*, Zenith, Skopje.

Nölke, Andreas (2010) 'Transnationale Akteure', in Masala, C./Sauer, F./Wilhem, A. (eds) *Handbuch der Internationalen Politik* (Wiesbaden: VS Verlag): 395-402.

Nohlen, Dieter (2005) 'NGO', in Nohlen, D./Schultze, R. (eds) *Lexikon der Politikwissenschaften*, Band 2, 3rd edn (Munich: C.H. Beck): 614-16.

Noortmann, Math/Arts, Bas/Reinalda, Bob (2001) 'The Quest for Unity in Empirical and Conceptual Complexity', in Arts, B./Noortmann, M./Reinalda, B. (eds) *Non-State Actors in International Relations* (Aldershot: Ashgate): 299-307.

Nuscheler, Franz (1993) 'Denkfabriken und diplomatische Hilfstruppen, die Politischen Stiftungen der Parteien und ihre Auslandsarbeit', in Weirich, D. (ed) *Auftrag Deutschland, Nach der Einheit: Unser Land der Welt vermitteln* (Mainz: V. Hase und Köhler): 223-40.

– (2005) *Entwicklungspolitik, Lern- und Arbeitsbuch*, 6th edn (Bonn: Dietz).

– (2006) *Entwicklungspolitik*, 6th edn (Bonn: Dietz).

– (2007) 'Entwicklungspolitik', in Schmidt, S./Hellmann, G./Wolf, R. (eds) *Handbuch zur deutschen Außenpolitik* (Wiesbaden: VS Verlag): 672-83.

Nye, Joseph S. (1990) *Bound to Lead: The Changing Nature of American Power* (New York: Basic Books).

– (2004) *Soft Power: The Means of Success in World Politics* (New York: Public Affairs).

– (2008) 'Public diplomacy and soft power', in Cowan, G./Cull, N. (eds) *Public Diplomacy in a Changing World* (Los Angeles: Sage): 94-109.

OECD (Organisation for Economic Co-operation and Development) (1995) *Participatory Development and Good Governance*, Development Co-operation Guidelines Series, Paris.

– (2005) *DAC-Prüfbericht über die Entwicklungszusammenarbeit*, Deutschland, Paris.

– (2006) *Whole of Government Approaches to Fragile States*, Paris.

– (2008) *The Paris Declaration on Aid Effectiveness and the Accra Agenda for Action*, (Paris: OECD Publishing).

– (2010) *Deutschland*, Entwicklungsausschuss (DAC), Peer Review, Paris.

– (2014) *OECD Factbook 2014: Economic, environmental and social statistics* (Paris: OECD Publishing).

Ohmstedt, Holger (1993) *Von der Propaganda zur Public Diplomacy, Die Selbstdarstellung der Vereinigten Staaten von Amerika im Ausland im Ersten Weltkrieg und bis zum Ende des Kalten Krieges* (München: Universität München).

Olins, Wally (2007) 'Making a National Brand', in Melissen, J. (ed) *The new public diplomacy: soft power in international relations* (New York: Palgrave macmillan): 169-79.

Onuf, Nicholas (1989) *World of Our Making* (South Carolina: University of South Carolina Press).

Optenhögel, Uwe (2002) 'Die politischen Stiftungen', in Bertram, C./Däuble, F. (eds) *Wem dient der Auswärtige Dienst? Erfahrungen von Politik, Wirschaft und Gesellschaft* (Opladen: Leske+Budrich): 125-40.

Ostrowski, Daniel (2010) *Die Public Diplomacy der deutschen Auslandsvertretungen weltweit* (Wiesbaden: VS Verlag).

Page Fortna, Virginia (2004) 'Does Peacekeeping Keep Peace? International Intervention and the Duration of Peace after Civil War', *International Studies Quarterly*, 48: 269-92.

Pamment, James (2013) 'West European Public Diplomacy', in Cross, M./Melissen, J. (eds) *European Public Diplomacy, Soft Power at Work* (New York: Palgrave macmillan): 13-38.

Panke, Diane/Risse, Thomas (2007) 'Liberalism', in Dunn, T./Kurki, M./Smith, S. (eds) *International Relations Theories* (Oxford: Oxford University Press): 89-108.

Papst, Siegfried (1982) *Friedrich-Naumann-Stiftung* (Düsseldorf: Droste).

Parmar, Inderjeet (2004) 'Insitutes of international affairs: their roles in foreign-policy making, opinion mobilization and unofficial diplomacy,' in Stone, D./ Denham, A. (eds) *Think Tank Traditions, Policy research and the politics of ideas* (Manchester: Manchester University Press): 19-33.

Parsons, Talcott (1991) *The Social Sytem*, 2nd edn (London: Routledge).

Pascher, Ute (2002) *Die parteinahen politischen Stiftungen – Hybride Organisation in der Globalisierung* (Berlin: Logos Verlag).

Paschke, Karl-Theodor (2000) *Report on the Special Inspection of 14 German Embassies in the Countries of the European Union*, available online at: http://grberridge.diplomacy.edu/paschke-report/.

Paul, Michael (2008) *CIMIC am Beispiel des ISAF-Einsatzes, Konzeption, Umsetzung und Weiterentwicklung zivil-militärischer Interaktion im Auslandseinsatz*, SWP-Studie, Stiftung Wissenschaft und Politik, Berlin.

Pfaffenholz, Thania (2005) *Third generation PCIA: Introducing the Aid for Peace Approach*, April 2005, Bergdorf Research Center for Constructive Conflict Management.

Philipps, Ann L. (1999) 'Exporting Democracy: German Political Foundations in Central-East Europe,' *Democratization*, 6(2): 70-98.

Pinto-Duschinsky, Michael (1991a) 'Foreign Political Aid: the German Political Foundations and their US Counterparts,' *International Affairs*, 67: 33-63.

– (1991b) 'The Party Foundations and Political Finance in Germany,' in Seidle, F. L. (ed) *Comparative issues in party and election finance* (Toronto: Dundurn Press): 179-250.

– (2002) 'International Political Finance: The Konrad Adenauer Foundation and Latin America,' in Whitehead, L. (ed) *The International Dimension of Democratization* (Oxford: Oxford University Press): 227-55.

Pogorelskaja, Swetlana W. (1997) *Die politischen Stiftungen in der deutschen Außenpolitik, Überlegungen am Beispiel der Konrad Adenauer-Stiftungen und der Hanns-Seidel-Stiftung in der Gemeinschaft der Unabhängigen Staaten und in den baltischen Staaten* (Bonn: Holos Verlag).

– (2002a) 'Deutsche parteinahen Stiftungen als Akteure und Instrumente der deutschen Außenpolitik,' *Aus Politik und Zeitgeschichte*, B6-7: 29-38.

– (2002b) 'Die parteinahen politischen Stiftungen und die Deutschlandpolitik,' *Deutschland Archiv, Zeitschrift für das vereinigte Deutschland*, 35(3): 401-12.

– (2006) *Die Bedeutung der deutschen politischen Stiftungen für die EU-Politik gegenüber den MOE- und GUS-Staaten*, Discussion Paper C163, Center for European Integration Studies, Reihnische Friedrich-Wilhelms-University Bonn, Bonn.

– (2009a) *Frei von den Zwängen der Tagespolitik, Die deutschen politischen Stiftungen im Ausland* (Frankfurt am Main: Peter Lang).

– (2009b) 'Im Ausland einmalig – Die politischen Stiftungen,' in Maaß, K.-J. (ed) *Kultur und Außenpolitik*, 2nd edn (Baden-Baden: Nomos): 293-304.

Pratkanis, Anthony (2009) 'Public Diplomacy in International Conflicts,' Snow, N./ Taylor, P. (eds) *Routledge Handbook of Public Diplomacy* (New York: Routledge): 111-53.

Pratsch-Hucko, Kristina (2004) 'Deutsche politische Stiftungen in Ostmitteleuropa, Arbeit in der Transformationsländern', *Dokumente, Zeitschrift für den deutsch-französischen Dialog*, 60(3): 17-21.

Prechtl, Christof (1996) *Innere Einheit Deutschlands, Gegenstand der schulischen und außerschulischen politischen Bildungsarbeit* (Schwalbach: Wochenschauverlag).

Preuß, Hans-Joachim (2013) 'Fragile Staatlichkeit in Afrika. Was kann Entwicklungszusammenarbeit leisten?', *Zeitschrift für Außen- und Sicherheitspolitik*, 6: 308-18.

Price, Richard/Reus-Smit, Christian (1998) 'Dangerous Liaisons? Critical International Theory and Constructivism', *European Journal of International Relations*, 4(3): 259–94.

Randall, Vicky (2008) 'Analytical Approaches to the Study of Politics in the Developing World', in Burnell, P./Randall, V. (eds) *Politics in the Developing World*, 2nd edn (Oxford: Oxford University Press): 15-34.

Rattinger, Hans (2007) 'Öffentliche Meinung', in Schmidt, S./Hellmann, G./Wolf, R. (eds) *Handbuch zur deutschen Außenpolitik* (Wiesbaden: VS Verlag): 313-25.

Rausch, Ulrike (2005a) 'Transnationale Politik', in Nohlen, D./Schultze, R. (eds) *Lexikon der Politikwissenschaften*, Band 2, 3rd edn (Munich: C.H. Beck): 1040f.

– (2005b) 'Sicherheit', in Nohlen, D./Schultze, R. (eds) *Lexikon der Politikwissenschaften*, Band 1, 3rd edn (Munich: C.H. Beck): 886f.

Raustiala, Kai (1997) 'States, NGOs and International Environmental Institutions', *International Studies Quarterly*, 41: 719-40.

Rawert, Peter (2011) 'Allgemeiner Teil, §§ 80-89', in Staudinger, J. von (ed) *Staudinger Kommentar zum Bürgerlichen Gesetzbuch, Buch 1, Allgemeiner Teil* (Berlin: Sellier-de Gruyter).

Reimann, Cordula (2007) 'Doing good? Herausforderungen für die NGOs in der Friedensförderung', in Klein, A./Roth, S. (eds) *NGOs im Spannungsfeld zwischen Krisenprävention und Sicherheitspolitik* (Wiesbaden: VS Verlag): 91-111.

Reinalda, Bob (2001) 'Private in Form, Public in Purpose: NGOs in International Relations Theory', in Arts, B./Noortmann, M./Reinalda, B. (eds) *Non-State Actors in International Relations* (Aldershot: Ashgate): 11-40.

Reinicke, Wolfgang H. (1998) *Global Public Policy: Governing without Government?* (Washington DC: Brookings).

– (1999) 'The Other World Wide Web: Global Public Policy Networks', *Foreign Policy*, 117 (Winter 1999-2000): 44-57.

Reinicke, Wolfgang H./Deng, Francis et al. (2000) *Critical Choices: The Unites Nations, Networks and the Future of Global Governance* (Ottawa: International Development Research Center).

Renvert, Nicole (2005) *Mission Possible? Die Rolle der deutschen parteinahen Stiftungen in den USA*, DAAD/AICGS Working Paper (Washington D.C.: American Institut for Contemporary German Studies).

– (2011) 'Von Soft Power zu Smart Power: Zur Rolle der Mittler in den transnationalen Beziehungen', *Aus Politik und Zeitgeschichte*, 51-52: 30-35.

– (2012) 'Vermittler in Bedrängnis, Politische Stiftungen und Demokratieförderung in der arabischen Welt', *Internationale Politik*, 4 (Juli/August): 46-9.

– (2014) *Machtmakler in schwierigen Zeiten? Die Rolle der deutschen politischen Stiftungen in den transatlantischen Beziehungen* (Trier: VWT).

Richter, Solveig (2009) *Zur Effektivität externer Demokratiesierung: Die OSZE in Südosteuropa als Partner, Mahner, Besserwisser?* (Baden-Baden: Nomos).

Riordan, Shaun (2007) 'Dialogue-based Diplomacy: a New Foreign Policy Paradigm?', in Melissen, J. (ed) *The new public diplomacy: soft power in international relations* (New York: Palgrave macmillan): 180-95.

Risse, Thomas (2000) '"Let's Argue!": Communicative Action in World Politics', *International Organization*, 54(1) (Winter, 2000): 1-39.

– (2002) 'Transnational Actors in World Politics', in Carlsnaes, W./Risse, T./ Simmons, B. (eds) *Handbook of International Relations* (London: Sage): 255-76.

– (2007a) 'Social Constructivism Meets Globalization', in Held, D./McGrew, A. (eds) *Globalization Theory: Approaches and Controversies* (Cambridge: Polity Press): 126-147.

– (2007b) 'Deutsche Identität und Außenpolitik', in Schmidt, S./Hellmann, G./ Wolf, R. (eds) *Handbuch zur deutschen Außenpolitik* (Wiesbaden: VS Verlag): 49-61.

Risse, Thomas/Ropp, Stephen C. (1999) 'International Human Rights Norms and Domestic Change: Conclusion', in Risse, T./Ropp, S.C./Sikkink, K (eds) *The Persistent Power of Human Rights: From Commitment to Complience* (Cambridge: Cambridge University Press): 275-295.

Risse, Thomas/Sikkink, Katheryn (1999) 'The Socialization of International Human Rights Norms into Domestic Practices: Introduction', in Risse, T./Ropp, S.C./Sikkink, K. (eds) *The Power of Human Rights: International Norms and Domestic Change* (Cambridge: Cambridge University Press):3-25.

Risse-Kappen, Thomas (1995a) 'Bringing transnational relations back in: introduction', in Risse-Kappen, T. (ed) *Bringing transnational relations back in: non state actors, structures and international institutions* (Cambridge: Cambridge University Press): 3-33.

– (1995b) 'Structures of governance and transnational relations: what have we learned?', in Risse-Kappen, T. (ed) *Bringing transnational relations back in: non state actors, structures and international institutions* (Cambridge: Cambridge University Press): 280-313.

Rittberger, Volker (1993) 'Research on International Regimes in Germany, The Adaptive Internalization of an American Social Science Concept', in Rittberger, V. (ed) *Regime Theory and International Relations* (Oxford: Clarendon Press): 3-22.

Rittberger, Volker/Zürn, Michael (1990) 'Towards Regulated Anarchy in East-West Relations: Causes and Consequences of East-West Regimes', in Rittberger, V. (ed) *International Regimes in East-West Politics* (London: Pinter): 9-63.

Ritter-Weil, Astrid/Treydte, Klaus-Peter (2013) *Genderpolitik und Medienförderung, Wege zur Stärkung von Demokratie und Entwicklung in der internationalen Arbeit der FES* (Bonn: Dietz).

RLS (Rosa-Luxemburg-Stiftung) (2011) *Die Rosa Luxemburg Stiftung in Osteuropa*, Leaflet, Berlin.

Rodon, Juan/Serrano, Josep F. Maria/Giménez, Cristina (2012) 'Managing cultural conflicts for effective humanitarian aid', *International Journal of Production Economics*, 139: 366-76.

Ronge, Volker/Pascher, Ute (1999) 'Die "Entwicklungszusammenarbeit" der politischen Stiftungen als Beitrag zum Frieden', in Bergem, W./Ronge, V./Weißeno, G. (eds) *Friedenspolitik in und für Europa, Festschrift für Gerda Zellentin zum 65. Geburtstag* (Opladen: Leske+Budrich): 185-98.

Roth, Silke/Klein, Ansgar (2007) 'Humanitäre NGOs im Spannungsfeld zwischen Krisenprävention und Sicherheitspolitik', in Klein, A./Roth, S. (eds) *NGOs im Spannungsfeld zwischen Krisenprävention und Sicherheitspolitik* (Wiesbaden: VS Verlag): 9-26.

Rucht, Dieter (1996) 'Multinationale Bewegungsorganisationen', *Forschungsjournal Neue Soziale Bewegung*, 9(2): 30-41.

Rudizio, Wolfgang (2006) *Das politische System der Bundesrepublik Deutschland*, 7th edn (Wiesbaden: VS Verlag).

Rudolf, Peter (2005) 'Kollektive Sicherheit', in Nohlen, D./Schultze, R. (eds) *Lexikon der Politikwissenschaften*, Band 1, 3rd edn (Munich: C.H. Beck): 443.

– (2013) 'Schutzverantwortung und humanitäre Intervention', *Aus Politik und Zeitgeschichte*, 37:12-7.

Rühle, Michael (2008) 'Der steinige Weg ins globale Zeitalter', *Internationale Politik*, 3(63) (March 2008): 6-15.

Rüland, Jürgen (2007) 'Südostasien', in Schmidt, S./Hellmann, G./Wolf, R. (eds) *Handbuch zur deutschen Außenpolitik* (Wiesbaden: VS Verlag): 559-79.

– (2009) 'Good Governance statt Demokratie? Zur Lokalisierung eines universalen Konzepts in Thailand', in Weiland, H./Wehr, I./Seifert, M. (eds) *Good Governance in der Sackgasse?* (Baden-Baden: Nomos): 107-20.

Rüland, Jürgen/Werz, Nikolaus (2002) 'Germany's Hesitant Role in Promoting Democracy', in Schraeder, P. (ed) *Exporting Democracy. Rethoric versus Reality* (Boulder: Lynne Rienner): 73-88.

Ruggie, John Gerard (1983) 'International regimes, transactions, and change: embedded liberalism in the postwar economic order', in Krasner, S. (ed) *International Regimes* (Ithaca: Cornell University Press): 195-232.

– (1998) *Constructing the World Polity, Essays on international instiutionalization* (London: Routledge).

Russett, Bruce (1993) *Grasping the Democratic Peace, Principles for a Post-Cold War World* (Princeton: Princeton University Press).

Schaller, Christian/Schneckener, Ulrich (2009) *Das Peacebuilding-System der Vereinten Nationen*, SWP-Studie, März 2009, Stiftung Wissenschaft und Politik, Berlin.

Schimmelfennig, Frank (2010) *Internationale Politik*, 2nd edn (Paderborn: Verlag Ferdinand Schöningh).

Schluckebier, Wilhelm (2013) *Buchübergabe „Ausgewählte Entscheidungen des Bundesverfassungsgerichts" im Rahmen des KAS-Rechtsstaatsprogramms Südosteuropa (RSP SOE) beim rumänischen Verfassungsgericht am 26. September in Bukarest (Rumänien), Die Stellung des deutschen Bundesverfassungsgerichts im Gefüge der Institutionen*, Rede, 26/09/2013, Konrad-Adenauer-Stiftung, Bucharest, available online at: http://www.kas.de/wf/doc/kas_36325-1522-1-30.pdf?131210123102.

Schmid, Annette (2002) 'Positivmaßnahmen', in Nohlen, D. (ed) *Lexikon Dritte Welt* (Reinbek: Rowohlt Taschenbuch): 681.

Schmidt, Siegmar (2007) 'Afrika südlich der Sahara', in Schmidt, S./Hellmann, G./ Wolf, R. (eds) *Handbuch zur deutschen Außenpolitik* (Wiesbaden: VS Verlag): 532-58.

– (2013a) 'Menschenrechte und Demokratie', in Ihne, H./Wilhelm, J. (eds) *Einführung in die Entwicklungspolitik*, Bundeszentrale für politische Bildung (Berlin: LIT VERLAG): 277-83.

– (2013b) 'Good Governance als Entwicklungsvoraussetzung', in Ihne, H./Wilhelm, J. (eds) *Einführung in die Entwicklungspolitik*, Bundeszentrale für politische Bildung (Berlin: LIT VERLAG): 284-90.

Schneckener, Ulrich (2006) 'Fragile Statehood, Armed Non-State Actors and Security Governance', in Bryden, A./Caparini, M. (eds) *Private Actors and Security Governance* (Berlin: LIT VERLAG): 23-40.

– (2007) *Internationales Statebuilding, Dilemmata, Strategien und Anforderungen an die deutsche Außenpolitik*, SWP-Studie, May 2007, Stiftung für Wissenschaft und Politk, Berlin.

Schneckener, Ulrich/Weinlich, Silke (2006) 'Die Peacebuilding-Kommission der Vereinten Nationen', *Sicherheit und Frieden*, 1: 17-21.

Schneider, Cynthia P. (2007) 'Culture Communicates: US Diplomacy that works', in Melissen, J. (ed) *The new public diplomacy: soft power in international relations* (New York: Palgrave macmillan): 147-68.

Schneider-Deters, Winfried (2005) 'Civil Diplomacy, Politische Stiftungen in Ost- und Ostmitteleuropa', *Osteuropa*, 55(8) (August 2005): 107-26.

Schreiner, Patrick (2008) *Auswärtige Kulturarbeit zwischen Konzeption und Umsetzung, Steuerungsprobleme in einem schwierigen Politikfeld*, SWP-Studie, April 2008, Stiftung Wissenschaft und Politik, Berlin.

Schubert, Klaus (2005) 'Quago/Quango', in Nohlen, D./Schultze, R. (eds) *Lexikon der Politikwissenschaften*, Band 2 (Munich: Verlag C.H. Beck): 802.

Schürmann, Maximilian (1989) *Zwischen Partnerschaft und politischem Auftrag, Fallstudie zur Entwicklungspolitischen Tätigkeit der Konrad-Adenauer-Stiftung* (Saarbrücken: Breitbach).

Schumacher, Hans (2012) *Wechselhafter Halbmond, Die Arbeit der Friedrich-Ebert-Stiftung in der Türkei* (Bonn: Dietz).

Schwarz, Hans-Peter (1994) *Die Zentralmacht Europas, Deutschlands Rückkehr auf die Weltbühne* (Berlin: Siedler).

Scott-Smith, Giles (2008) 'Mapping the Undefineable: Some Thoughts on the Relevance of Exchange Progams within International Relations Theory', in Cowan, G./Cull, N. (eds) *Public Diplomacy in a Changing World* (Los Angeles: Sage): 173-95.

Seifart, Werner (1987) *Handbuch des Stiftungsrechts* (München: C.H. Beck).

Seifert, Matthias (2009) 'Good Governance in der Sackgasse? Ein Problemaufriss', in Weiland, H./Wehr, I./Seifert, M. (eds) *Good Governance in der Sackgasse?* (Baden-Baden: Nomos): 9-27.

Sharp, Paul (2007) 'Revolutionary states, outlaw regimes and the technique of public diplomacy', in Melissen, J. (ed) *The new public diplomacy: soft power in international relations* (New York: Palgrave macmillan): 106-23.

Signitzer, Benno (1995) 'Public Relation und Public Diplomacy', in Mahle, W. (ed) *Deutschland in der internationalen Kommunikation* (München: Ölschläger): 73-81.

Sikora, Michael (1997) *Politische Stiftungen – Vita activa der Parteipolitik oder vita contemplativa der politischen Erkenntnis?* (Bochum: Bockmeyer).

Silverman, David (2005) *Doing Qualitative Research*, 2nd edn (London: Sage).

Simon, Sheldon W. (2002) 'Evaluating Track II approaches to security diplomacy in the Asia-Pacific: the CSCAP experience', *The Pacific Review*, 15(2): 167-200.

Singer, Otto (2003) *Auswärtige Kulturpolititk in der Bundesrepublik Deutschland. Konzeptionelle Grundlagen und institutionelle Entwicklung seit 1945*, Wissenschaftliche Dienste des Deutschen Bundestages, WF X – 095/03, Deutscher Bundestag, Berlin.

Slaughter, Anne-Marie (2004) *A New World Order* (Princeton and Oxford: Princeton University Press).

Smith, Brian H. (1990) *More than Altruism: The Politics of Private Foreign Aid* (Princeton: Princeton University Press).

– (2008) 'State-Building', in Burnell, P./Randall, V. (eds) *Politics in the Developing World*, 2nd edn (Oxford: Oxford University Press): 230-48.

Smith, Julie (2001) 'Political Parties in a Global Age', in Josselin, D./Wallace, W. (eds) *Non-state Actors in World Politics* (New York: Palgrave Publisher): 59-75.

Sœrensen, Georg (2008) *Democracy and Democratization, Processes and Prospects in a Changing World*, 3rd edn (Colorado: Westview Press).

Spanger, Hans-Joachim/Reddies, Bernd (2011) *Die Arbeit der Friedrich-Ebert-Stiftung in der UDSSR/Russland und der Volksrepublik China* (Bonn: Dietz).

SPD (Sozialdemokratische Partei Deutschlands) (2007) *Hamburger Programm, Grundsatzprogramm der SPD*, Berlin.

Staack, Michael (2007) 'Deutschland als Wirtschaftsmacht', in Schmidt, S./Hellmann, G./Wolf, R. (eds) *Handbuch zur deutschen Außenpolitik* (Wiesbaden: VS Verlag): 85-97.

Stake, Robert (2000) 'Case studies', in Denzin, N./Lincoln, Y. (eds) *Handbook of Qualitative Research*, 2nd edn (Thousand Oaks: Sage): 435-54.

Stein, Arthur A. (1983) 'Coordination and collaboration: regimes in an anarchic world', in Krasner, S. (ed) *International Regimes* (Ithaca, NY: Cornell University Press):115-140.

Steinbach, Udo (2007) 'Naher und Mittlerer Osten', in Schmidt, S./Hellmann, G./ Wolf, R. (eds) *Handbuch zur deutschen Außenpolitik* (Wiesbaden: VS Verlag): 494-505.

Steiner, Christian/Ademović, Nedim (2010) *Constitution of Bosnia and Herzegovina Commentary*, Konrad-Adenauer-Stiftung Rule of Law Program South East Europe (ed), Sankt Augustin, Germany.

Stephenson, Carolyn M. (2011) 'Non-state actors in the global security world', in Reinalda, B. (ed) *The Ashgate Research Companion to Non-State Actors* (Surrey: Ashgate Publishing): 391-403.

Stoffers, Andreas (2014) *Thailand und Deutschland: Wirtschaft, Politik, Kultur* (Berlin: Springer Gabler).

Stone, Diane (2004) 'Introduction: think tanks, policy advice and governance', in Stone, D./Denham (eds) *Think Tank Traditions, Policy research and the politics of ideas* (Manchester: Manchester University Press): 1-16.

– (2005) 'Knowledge networks and global policy', in Stone, D./Maxwell. S. (eds) *Global Knowledge Networks and International Development* (Oxon: Routledge): 89-105.

– (2008) 'Global Public Policy, Transnational Policy Communities, and Their Networks', *The Policy Studies Journal*, 36(1): 19-38.

– (2011) 'The ASEAN-ISIS network: interpretive communities, informal diplomacy and discourses of region', *Minerva*, 49(2): 241–62.

Strange, Susan (1983) 'Cave! hic dragones: a critique of regime analysis', in Krasner, S. (ed) *International Regimes* (Ithaca, NY: Cornell University Press): 337-54.

Stütz, Julia (2008) *"State-Building" aus theoretischer und praktischer Perspektive* (Baden-Baden: Nomos).

SWP (Stiftung Wisschaft und Politik)/GMF (German Marshall Fund of the United States) (2013) *Neue Macht Neue Verantwortung, Elemente einer deutschen Außen- und Sicherheitspolitik für eine Welt im Umbruch*, Berlin.

Tannenwald, Nina (2005) 'Ideas and Explanation: Advancing the Theoretical Agenda', *Journal of Cold War Studies*, 7(2): 13-42.

Take, Ingo (2001) 'Allianzbildungen zwischen Staat, Zivilgesellschaft und internationalen Organisationen im Nord-Süd-Verhältnis', in Brunnengräber, A./Klein, A./Walk, H. (eds) *NGOs als Legitimationsressource, Zivilgesellschaftliche Partizipationsformen im Globalisierungsprozess* (Opladen: Leske Budrich): 239-57.

Taylor, Paul/Curtis, Devon (2005) 'The United Nations', in Baylis, J./Smith, S. (eds) *The Globalisation of World Politics*, 3rd edn (Oxford: Oxford University Press): 405-24.

Tayyar, Negar (2013) 'Capacity Development als Schlüssel zur Erreichung internationaler Entwicklungsziele', in Ihne, H./Wilhelm, J. (eds) *Einführung in die Entwicklungspolitik*, Bundeszentrale für politische Bildung (Berlin: LIT VERLAG): 211-226.

Tewes, Henning (1997) 'The emergence of a civilian power: German and central Europe,' *German Politics*, 6(2): 95-116.

Thesing, Josef (1987) *Developments in Central America and the Activities of the Konrad Adenauer Foundation*, Konrad-Adenauer-Stiftung e.V., Occasional Paper Series, 7(87), Sankt Augustin.

Thesing, Josef (1997) 'Politische Stiftungen in der Entwicklungszusammenarbeit am Beispiel der Konrad-Adenauer-Stiftung,' *Die Friedens-Warte, Blätter für internationale Verständigung und zwischenstaatliche Organisation*, 72(2): 173-88.

Thunert, Martin (2003) 'Think Tanks in Deutschland – Berater der Politik?,' *Aus Politik und Zeitgeschichte*, B51/2003: 30-8.

– (2004) 'Think Tanks in Germany,' in Stone, D./Denham, A. (eds) *Think Tank Traditions, Policy research and the politics of ideas* (Manchester: Manchester University Press): 71-88.

– (2007) 'Politikberatung,' in Schmidt, S./Hellmann, G./Wolf, R. (eds) *Handbuch zur deutschen Außenpolitik* (Wiesbaden: VS Verlag): 336-350.

Tuch, Hans N. (1990) *Communicating with the World. U.S. Public Diplomacy Overseas* (New York: St. Martin's Press).

UIA (Union of International Associations) (1986) *Yearbook of International Organizations, 1986-87: Global Networks: Classified Directory* (Munich: K.G. Sauer Verlag).

UN (United Nations) (1996) *Consultative relationship between the United Nations and non-governmental organizations*, UN Economic and Social Council, Resolution E/1996/31, 25/07/1996, New York.

– (2000a) *United Nations Millennium Declaration*, Resolution adopted by the UN General Assembly, A/RES/55/2, 18/09/2000, New York.

– (2000b) *Resolution 1325*, Resolution adopted by the UN Security Council, S/Res/1325, 31/10/2000, New York.

– (2005) *2005 World Summit*, Outcome adopted by the UN General Assembly, A/60/L.1, 15/09/2005, New York.

– (2006) *Importance of preventing conflict through development, democracy stressed*, Resolution 1674 adopted by the UN Security Council, SC/810, 28/04/2006, New York.

– (2009a) *What is Good Governance?*, UN Economic and Social Commission for Asia and the Pacific (UNESCAP).

– (2009b) *Implementing the responsibility to protect*, Report of the Secretary General, A63/6/77, 12/01/2009, New York.

– (2014) *Economic and Social Council, List of non-governmental organizations in consultative status with the Economic and Social Council as of 1 September 2014*, E/2014/INF/5, 3/12/2014, New York.

UNDP (United Nations Development Program) (2008) *Post-Conflict Economic Recovery, Enabling Local Ingenuity, Crisis Prevention and Recovery Report 2008*, New York.

UN (United Nations) Secretary General (2011) *Remarks to the Security Council thematic debate on "Interlinkages between Peace, Security and Development"*, 11/02/2011, New York.

USAid (U.S. Agency for International Development) (2012) *Audit of USAid/Regional development mission for Asia's Sapan program in Thailand*, Auditreportno. 549312004P, 27/02/2012, Manila.

Vaïsse, Justin (2007) *Transformational Diplomacy*, EU Institute for Security Studies: Paris.

Van Ham, Peter (2008) 'Place Branding: The State of the Art,' in Cowan, G/Cull, N. (eds) *Public Diplomacy in a Changing World* (Los Angeles: Sage): 126-49.

– (2001) 'The Rise of the Brand State: The Postmodern Politics of Image and Reputation,' *Foreign Affairs*, 80(5): 2-6.

Varwick, Johannes (2002) 'Kriegsverhinderung und Friedenswahrung,' *Internationale Politik*, 12/12/2002: 1-10.

Veit, Winfried (2013) *Außenpolitik als international Gesellschaftspolitik, Die Arbeit der Friedrich-Ebert-Stiftung in der nördlichen Hemisphäre nach der Zeitenwende 1989/91* (Bonn: Dietz).

Vieregge, Henning von (1977a) *Parteistiftungen* (Baden-Baden: Nomos).

– (1977b) 'Globalzuschüsse für parteinahe Stiftungen: Parteienfinanzierung auf Umwegen?,' *Zeitschrift für Parlamentsfragen*, 1: 51-8.

– (1977c) 'Zur politischen Bildungsarbeit der parteinahen Stiftungen,' *Aus Politik und Zeitgeschichte*, B7: 28-54.

– (1980) *Gesellschaftspolitische Stiftungen in der Bundesrepublik* (Köln: Deutscher Instituts-Verlag).

– (1990) 'Die Parteistiftungen: Ihre Rolle im politischen System,' in Wewer, G. (ed) *Parteienfinanzierung und politischer Wettbewerb* (Opladen: Westdeutscher Verlag): 164-94.

Vinnai, Volker (2007) *Demokratieförderung in Afrika, Die Zusammenarbeit der Friedrich-Ebert-Stiftung mit politischen Parteien und Befreiungsbewegungen in Afrika*, Schriftenreihe der Friedrich-Ebert-Stiftung (LIT Verlag: Berlin).

Wæver, Ole (1996) 'The Rise and Fall of the Interparadigm Debate,' in Smith, S./ Booth, K./Zalewski, M. (eds) *International Theory: Positivism and Beyond* (Cambridge University Press): 149-85.

Waever, R. Kent (1989) 'The Changing World of Think Tanks,' *PS: Political Science and Politics*, (September): 563-78.

Wagner, Christoph (1994) 'Die offiziöse Außen- und Entwicklungspolitik der deutschen politischen Stiftungen in Lateinamerika,' in Mols, M./Wagner, C. (eds) *Deutschland – Lateinamerika, Geschichte, Gegenwart und Perspektiven* (Frankfurt am Main: Vervuert Verlag).

Wagner, Jost (2007) *Südthailand, Studien zur länderbezogenen Konfliktanalyse*, Friedrich-Ebert-Stiftung, Berlin.

Wahlers, Gerhard (2005) '"Weltinnenpolitik" im Blick, Die internationale Arbeit der Konrad-Adenauer-Stiftung,' *Die Politische Meinung*, 432 (November 2005): 43-50.

Wallace, William (2004) 'Afterword: soft power, global agendas,' in Stone, D./ Denham, A. (eds) *Think Tank Traditions, Policy research and the politics of ideas* (Manchester: Manchester University Press): 281-9.

Walt, Stephen M. (1998), 'International Relations: One World, Many Theories,' *Foreign Policy*, 110 (Spring): 29-46.

Waltz, Kenneth N. (1979) *Theory of International Politics* (Reading, Mass: Addison-Wesley).

Wapner, Paul (1995) 'Politics Beyond the State: Environmental Activism and World Civic Politics,' *World Politics*, 47: 311-40.

Watson, Alan (1976) *Die Politischen Stiftungen in West Deutschland*, London.

Weber, Max (1947) *The Theory of Social and Economic Organisations*, translated. A.M Henderson and T. Persons (New York: Free Press).

Weenink, Anton (2001) 'The Relevance of Being Important or the Importance of Being Relevant? State and Non-State Actors in International Relations Theory,' in Arts, B./Noortmann, M./Reinalda, B. (eds) *Non-State Actors in International Relations*, (Aldershot: Ashgate): 79-92.

Weilemann, Peter (2000) 'Experience of a Multidimensional Think Tank: The Konrad-Adenauer-Stiftung,' in McGann, J./Weaver, R. (eds) *Think Tanks and Civil Society* (New Brundwick: Transaction Publishers): 169-186.

Weller, Christoph (2007) 'Bundesministerien,' in Schmidt, S./Hellmann, G./Wolf, R. (eds) *Handbuch zur deutschen Außenpolitik* (Wiesbaden: VS Verlag): 210-24.

Wendt, Alexander (1992) 'Anarchy is what States make of it: The Social Construction of Power Politics,' *International Organization*, 46(2): 391-425.

– (1994) 'Collective Identity Formation and the International State,' *The American Political Science Review*, 88(2) (June): 384-396.

– (1999) *Social Theory of International Politics* (Cambridge: Cambridge University Press).

Werner, Carsten (1982) *Der Auslandsbereich der Parteistiftungen der Bundesrepublik Deutschland*, Occasional Papers, Freie Universität Berlin.

Wersch, Jos van/Zeeuw, Jeroen de (2005) *Mapping European Democracy Assistance, Tracing the Activities and Financial Flows of Political Foundations*, Working Paper 36, November 2005, Netherlands Institute of International Relations 'Clingendael.'

Werz, Nikolaus/Hofmann, Norbert von/Bussiek, Hendrik (2014) *Demokratieförderung unter schwierigen Bedingungen, Die Tätigkeit der Friedrich-Ebert-Stiftung in Venezuela, Vietnam und Simbabwe* (Bonn: Dietz).

Wesel, Reinhard (2012) *Internationale Regime und Organisationen* (Konstanz: UVK Verlagsgesellschaft).

Wewer, Gottrik (1987) 'Die "Stiftungen" der Parteien: Weltweite Aktivität, aber geringe Transparenz', in Haungs, P./Jesse, E. (eds) *Parteien in der in- und ausländischen Krise* (Köln: Verlag Wissenschaft und Politik): 215-220.

Wigger, Angela (2011) 'Unravelling the Political Role of Experts and Expertise in the Professional Service Industry', in Reinalda, B. (ed) *The Ashgate Research Companion to Non-State Actors* (Surrey: Ashgate Publishing Limited): 89-100.

Wille, Andreas/Treydte, Klaus-Peter/Vinnai, Volker (2010) *Die Arbeit der Friedrich-Ebert-Stiftung in wichtigen Schwellenländern, Chile, Indien und Südafrika* (Bonn: Dietz).

Willetts, Peter (1982) 'The Impact of Promotional Pressure Groups on Global Politics', in Willetts, P. (ed) *Pressure Groups in the Global System: Transnational Relations of Issue-Oriented Non-Governmental Organisations* (London: Pinter): 179-200.

– (2011a) *Non-Governmental Organizations in Wold Politics: the construction of global governance* (Oxon: Routledge).

– (2011b) 'Transnational actors and international organisations in global politics, in Baylis, J./Smith, S./Owens, P. (eds) *The Globalisation of World Politics*, 5th edn (Oxford: Oxford University Press): 425-47.

Williams, Douglas (1990) *The Specialized Agencies and The United Nations, The System in Crisis* (London: Hurst&Company).

Williams, Michael (2001) 'The discipline of democratic peace: Kant, liberalism and the social construction of security communities', *European Journal of International Relations*, 7(4): 525-53.

Witte, Barthold C. (1993) 'Politik, Kultur und Mittler, Die deutsche auswärtige Kulturpolitik und ihre Träger', in Weirich, D. (ed) *Auftrag Deutschland, Nach der Einheit: Unser Land der Welt vermitteln* (Mainz: V. Hase und Köhler): 197-221.

Woods, Ngaire (2011) 'International political economy in age of globalization', in Baylis, J./Smith, S./Owens, P. (eds) *The Globalisation of World Politics*, 5th edn (Oxford: Oxford University Press): 246-61.

Wolff, Jonas (2013) 'Democracy Promotion and Civilian Power: The Example of Germany's "Value-Oriented" Foreign Policy', *German Politics*, 22(4): 477-93.

World Bank (1992) *Governance and Development*, Washington D.C.

– (1998) *Post-Conflict Reconstruction: The Role of the World Bank*, Washington DC.

– (2015) *Harmonized List of Fragile Situations for Y15*, Washington D.C.

Woyke, Wichard (2011) *Handwörterbuch Internationale Politik*, 12th edn (Opladen: Verlag Barbara Budrich).

Yost, Deborah S. (2007) *NATO and International Organizations*, Forum Paper No. 3, NATO Defense College, Rom.

Zaharna, R.S. (2009) 'Mapping out a Spectrum of Public Diplomacy Initiatives', in Snow, N./Taylor, P. (eds) *Routledge Handbook of Public Diplomacy* (New York: Routledge): 86-100.

Zöllner, Oliver (2009) 'German Public Diplomacy, The Dialogues of Cultures', in Snow, N./Taylor, P. (eds) *Routledge Handbook of Public Diplomacy* (New York: Routledge): 262-269.

– (2006) 'A quest for dialogue in international broadcasting: Germany's public diplomacy targeting Arab audiences', *Global Media and Communication*, 2(2): 160-82.

Zupan, Natascha/Servaes, Sylvia (2007) *Transitional justice and dealing with the past*, Guidance Paper, Working Group on Development and Peace (FriEnt), Bonn.

Press releases

BBC, 'Profile: Thailand's reds and yellows', 13/07/2012, available online at: http://news.bbc.co.uk/2/hi/asia-pacific/8004306.stm.

Bittner, Jochen/Geis, Matthias/Lau, Jörg/Ulrich, Bernd/Wurmb-Seibel, Ronja, 'Wir tun doch nix...wir wollen nur profitieren. Deutschland ist strikt gegen Interventionen, aber für Waffenexporte, es kritisiert nicht gern Diktaturen und lässt seine afghanischen Helfer im Stich. Über die Verlogenheit der neuen deutschen Außenpolitik', Die ZEIT, 2013/13, 01/04/2013, available online at: http://www.zeit.de/2013/13/Deutschland-Aussenpolitik.

Braun, Stefan 'Die Deutschen müssen sich selbst vertrauen', Süddeutsche Zeitung Online, 25/08/2014, available online at: http://www.sueddeutsche.de/politik/direktor-des-amerikanisch-juedischen-komitees-die-deutschen-muessen-sich-selbst-vertrauen-1.2102882.

Brössler, Daniel, 'Deutsch-russische Eiszeit', Süddeutsche Zeitung, 05/04/2013, available online at: http://www.sueddeutsche.de/politik/treffen-von-putin-und-merkel-deutsch-russische-eiszeit-1.1640779.

Brössler, Daniel, 'Russische Staatsanwaltschaft ermittelt gegen deutsche Stiftungen', Süddeutsche Zeitung, 26/03/2013, available online at: http://www.sueddeutsche.de/politik/strenges-vorgehen-gegen-nichtregierungsorganisationen-russische-staatsanwaelte-ermitteln-gegen-deutsche-stiftungen-1.1633479.

Caspari, Lisa, 'EU Osterweiterung, Merkels Herz für den Balkan', ZEIT Online, 28/08/2014, available online at: http://www.zeit.de/politik/deutschland/2014-08/balkan-eu-asyl.

Der Spiegel, 'Nun siegt mal schön', 29/1994: 23-6.

Der Spiegel, 'Mehr Mut', 24/1996: 28f.

Die Welt, 'Haftstrafe für Mitarbeiter der Adenauer-Stiftung', 04/06/13, available online at: http://www.welt.de/politik/ausland/article116804322/Haftstrafe-fuer-Mitarbeiter-der-Adenauer-Stiftung.html.

Doherty, Ben, 'Thai watchdog orders dissolution of ruling party', The Guardian, 12/04/2010.

Ehrhardt, Chistroph/Hermann, Rainer, 'Kairo erhebt Anklage gegen deutsche Stiftungsvertreter', Frankfurter Allgemeine Zeitung, 06/02/2012, available online at: http://www.faz.net/aktuell/politik/ausland/adenauer-stiftung-in-aegypten-kairo-setzt-mitarbeiter-von-stiftungen-fest-11640135.html.

Frankfurter Allgemeine Zeitung, 'Deutsche Stiftungsvertreter in der Türkei freigesprochen', 04/03/2003, available online at: http://www.faz.net/aktuell/politik/spionage-prozess-deutsche-stiftungsvertreter-in-der-tuerkei-freigesprochen-193266.html.

Friedrichs, Hauke, 'Westerwelles Untätigkeit ist sein Konzept,' ZEIT Online, 15/01/2013, available online at: http://www.zeit.de/politik/deutschland/2013-01/westerwelle-mali-unterstuetzung.

Gathmann, Florian/Medick, Veit/Weiland, Severin/Wittrock, Philipp, 'Bundestagswahlkampf. Die Syrien-Falle,' SPIEGEL Online, 27/08/2013, available online at: http://www.spiegel.de/politik/deutschland/wie-ein-syrien-krieg-den-wahlkampf-beeinflussen-koennte-a-918848.html.

Handly, Paul, 'Der Letzte seiner Art,' Die Zeit, 16/04/2009.

Hausding, Götz, 'Lob für den Krisendiplomaten, Auswärtiges: Steinmeiers Etat legt zu und erhält mehr Mittel für Konfliktprävention,' Das Parlament Nr. 27, 30/06/2014: 8.

Head, Jonathan, 'Why Thailand's king is so revered,' BBC, 5/12/2007.

Heute im Bundestag (HIP), 'Arbeit der deutschen politischen Stiftungen in der Türkei bedroht,' 13/11/2002.

Joffe, Josef, 'Ein bisschen Krieg,' Die Zeit, 30/01/2014.

Köckritz, Angela, 'Blues in Bangkok,' Die Zeit, 15/04/2010.

Maiello, Lia Petridis, 'Friedrich-Ebert-Stiftung (FES) Presents Joint Declaration for Afghanistan,'Huffington Post, 14/02/2013, available online at: http://www.huffingtonpost.com/lia-petridis/friedrichebertstiftung-fe_b_4774767.html.

Mittelstaedt, Juliane von/Neukirch, Ralf/Steinvorth, Daniel/Windfuhr, Volkhard, 'Ungeliebte Gäste,' Der Spiegel, 06/02/2012: 32.

Nolke, Caroline, 'Die Steuermillionen für politische Stiftungen, Parteinfinanzierung,' Deutschlandfunk, 29/03/2015.

Palokaj, Augustin, 'No control mechanism for Croatia after EU entry,' euobserver, 16/11/2010, available online at: https://euobserver.com/news/31275.

Pöttering, Hans-Gert, 'Äußere Einmischung ist erlaubt - und notwendig,' Financial Times Deutschland, 11/06/2012: 24.

Schmidt, Friedrich, 'Einmischung ohne Einmischung,' Frankfurter Allgemeine Zeitung, 23/03/2011: 3.

Süddeutsche Zeitung, 'Berlin bestellt ägyptischen Botschafter ein,' 30/12/2011, available online at: http://www.sueddeutsche.de/politik/razzia-in-kairo-aegyptische-polizei-durchsucht-buero-der-adenauer-stiftung-1.1246752.

Taz Online, 'Steuergelder für Neonazis, NPD erschleeßt neue Einnahmequellen,' 1/09/2009, available online at: http://www.taz.de/!5157038/.